INSATIABLE CITY

Insatiable City

FOOD AND RACE IN NEW ORLEANS

THERESA McCULLA

THE UNIVERSITY OF CHICAGO PRESS

CHICAGO AND LONDON

The University of Chicago Press, Chicago 60637
The University of Chicago Press, Ltd., London
© 2024 by The University of Chicago
Published 2024
Printed in the United States of America

33 32 31 30 29 28 27 26 25 24   1 2 3 4 5

ISBN-13: 978-0-226-83380-4 (cloth)
ISBN-13: 978-0-226-83382-8 (paper)
ISBN-13: 978-0-226-83381-1 (e-book)
DOI: https://doi.org/10.7208/chicago/9780226833811.001
.0001

Library of Congress Cataloging-in-Publication Data

Names: McCulla, Theresa, author.
Title: Insatiable city : food and race in New Orleans / Theresa
   McCulla.
Other titles: Food and race in New Orleans
Description: Chicago : London : The University of Chicago
   Press, 2024. | Includes bibliographical references and index.
Identifiers: LCCN 2023045917 | ISBN 9780226833804 (cloth) |
   ISBN 9780226833828 (paper) | ISBN 9780226833811 (ebook)
Subjects: LCSH: Food industry and trade—Louisiana—New
   Orleans—History. | Food—Social aspects—Louisiana—
   New Orleans. | Food habits—Louisiana—New Orleans—
   History. | New Orleans (La.)—History. | New Orleans
   (La.)—Social life and customs. | New Orleans (La.)—Race
   relations.
Classification: LCC F379.N55 M38 2024 | DDC 976.3/35—dc23/
   eng/20231004
LC record available at https://lccn.loc.gov/2023045917

♾ This paper meets the requirements of
ANSI/NISO Z39.48-1992 (Permanence of Paper).

To Brian and Nina

The stomach has its influence we find,
And sometimes its dominion o'er the mind.
And, hence, we trav'lling gentlemen who dine
With Cuban planters, judge them by their wine;
And if they're civil, courteous, and give feasts,
We think their slaves are treated like their guests.

R. R. Madden, "The Sugar Estate," in *Poems by a Slave in the Island of Cuba, Recently Liberated*, 1840

CONTENTS

INTRODUCTION

IN LATE AUGUST 1718, the *Aurore* made landfall on the western coast of Africa. The previous month, Captain Herpin and his crew had set sail from Saint-Malo, France, on behalf of the Compagnie d'Occident. In Cape Lahou and Whydah, in present-day Côte d'Ivoire and Benin, Compagnie represen- tatives purchased 201 people as slaves. On November 30, 1718, the vessel de- parted, directed west across the Atlantic Ocean, bound for the French ter- ritory of Basse-Louisiane. During the more-than-six-month voyage, the bondspeople lay shackled on their sides inside the ship's hold. Eleven crew members and one enslaved person died on the journey. When the *Aurore* dropped anchor in June 1719, it was the first ship bearing enslaved people to arrive in Louisiana from Africa. Also among its cargo: rice. African bonds- people and one of the signature foods that would fuel their labors and adorn the tables of their enslavers arrived together on Louisiana soil.[1] The ship's name, *Aurore*, signaled the dawn of a dark day. Streams of human, edible, and inedible commodities would flow through Louisiana from that point forward, generating a consumer's paradise for some and agony for so many others.[2]

Insatiable appetites—for mastery over waterways, land, people, cotton, sugar, and the prolific wealth they generated—would stimulate the explo- sive development of New Orleans and the surrounding region. Chitimacha, Houma, Ishak, and Natchez nations traded pelts, food, weapons, and tools with the European soldiers and explorers who first arrived there in the early sixteenth century.[3] These French, Spanish, British, and Canadian invaders brought disease, land theft, and intergroup conflict to the region. They also

1

brought slavery. Europeans' first enslaved people on the soil of what would be called Louisiana were Native women, children, and men.[4] In 1699, France founded the colony of Louisiana and, in 1718, the town of New Orleans, on a crescent of Chitimacha land embraced by the Mississippi River.[5] The settlement lodged in the twisted neck of an hourglass that would funnel North America's agricultural riches downward and out, via the Gulf of Mexico to the world, and draw food, goods, and people upward into the American interior.

By the turn of the nineteenth century, New Orleans's location made the city integral to the economic and political futures that American leaders imagined for the young United States. "There is on the globe one single spot, the possessor of which is our natural and habitual enemy. It is New Orleans," proclaimed President Thomas Jefferson in 1802, almost a year to the date before the United States signed the Louisiana Purchase, shifting New Orleans to American rule.[6] A generation later, the English-born architect Benjamin Henry Latrobe offered a more deflated take. "It is a pity . . . that this is a floating city," he confided to his diary, "floating below the surface of the water on a bed of mud."[7] Even so, New Orleans rose. Architects like Latrobe, politicians like Jefferson, and planters, slave traders, and the far-flung consumers they served pitched the city on precarious foundations: shifting delta soil and an economy dependent on enslaved humans and the things they made.[8]

Often, food defines the character of a place. Nowhere is this truer than in New Orleans. Gumbo, pralines, *café au lait*, and Sazerac cocktails—together with the people who made and served such delights—created the Crescent City's enduring reputation as a place to eat, drink, and play. "Long before I'd ever tasted an oyster," wrote journalist and New Orleanian Myles Poydras in the *New York Times* in 2021, "I'd seen Black men shuck them behind bars in New Orleans. . . . The tourists (usually white) would laugh throughout the night, enjoying the service as much as what was on their plate," he observed. "To be in New Orleans was to be charmed by its locals, especially those who fit into neat caricatures . . . the confectioner, the oyster shucker (all most likely Black)."[9] Poydras watched the interaction as a native of the area and a Black man himself. The scene he witnessed, of visitors enjoying the combination of food and people in New Orleans—feeling entertained, sated, at ease even at an unfamiliar table—was far from new.

This book explores the manifold powers of food and drink in relation to race. It begins in the era of chattel slavery in Louisiana, catalyzed by the arrival of the *Aurore* with its cargo of kidnapped humans and rice, and concludes in the mid-twentieth century, when tourists and civil rights activists sat at the New Orleans table. Throughout this sweep of time, many locals and visitors enjoyed the city's singular cuisine as a realm of leisure and gratification, seemingly incapable of having harmful effects. This study reveals a different history. It argues that the sensory pleasures of eating and drinking in New Orleans were rooted in—and reveled in—social, cultural, economic, and political systems of great violence. Furthermore, the easy charms of these experiences worked to soften and obscure that violence, empowering its persistence. At antebellum New Orleans slave auctions, for example, planters and their wives sipped cups of sugared punch while bidding on enslaved men bound for sugarcane fields. Enslaved women whose skin tones onlookers compared to chocolate stood for sale near dining tables set with sweet puddings and cakes. If the enslaved people and their pain required to produce a teaspoon of sugar were abstract shadows at tea tables in Boston or New York, these entities were made plain and collapsed into one experience—one transaction—in New Orleans. Such conflation of food, drink, and people occurred throughout settings of consumption and commodification in New Orleans. Exploitative relationships and attitudes that grew out of fleeting pleasures enabled the generation and elaboration of a violent racial order that broadened beyond individual meals.

When English writer Frances Milton Trollope visited New Orleans in the winter of 1827, Louisiana's subtropical riches—"oranges, green peas, and red pepper, growing in the open air at Christmas"—seemed to offer themselves to her eyes and nose as treasures to discover. While on a walk, Trollope and her children entered a house's kitchen garden and found "a fine crop of red pepper ripening in the sun. A young Negress was employed on the steps of the house; that she was a slave made her an object of interest to us. She was the first slave we had ever spoken to." Trollope's fascination centered on the novelty of a two-part exotic find: a December harvest coupled with the travelers' "first" enslaved woman. The woman "seemed amused at our fancying there was something unusual in red pepper pods," Trollope recalled, and "she gave us several of them." Trollope feared punishment for the young woman but accepted the gift anyway.[10]

From this brief encounter, Trollope drew perilous conclusions for her readers. In Trollope's description of the exchange, the woman in her Edenic garden offered fruit to the visitors, teaching them the rules governing this New World. A scene that had appeared at first to the European travelers as upside down—the fruits and vegetables blossomed in mid-winter; the woman was enslaved, not free—proved in the end to be exactly in order, Trollope insisted. Reflecting on the incident later, she scorned the "little romance of misery" that she had imagined for enslaved people in the United States prior to her journey there. Her American tour had convinced her that slavery was not as monstrous as she had imagined.[11] Trollope's writings ran in the same track cut by others before her. They deepened the groove for those who came after her. Visitors recorded first impressions and memories of New Orleans that centered on food and people in a manner that objectified both, together. Trollope's memoir showed how political, social, and existential meanings—whether or not slavery was correct, or cruel—could grow out of even momentary encounters with food and people at their heart.

Much happened in the decades that elapsed between Trollope's visit to a New Orleans kitchen garden, where a Black hand stretched out to offer a sun-ripened pepper, and Poydras's visit to an oyster bar, where another Black hand stretched out to offer a shucked oyster. New Orleanians lived through civil war, segregation, world wars, epidemics and pandemics, hurricanes, urban change, political fracture, and currents of people, land, and water on the move. Why then, in the course of two hundred years, did the dynamics surrounding the union of food, people, and race in the Crescent City remain so remarkably consistent?

From the nineteenth century through the twentieth, New Orleans enjoyed or suffered from a persistent reputation of exceptionalism, more than a little of it self-proclaimed.[12] The city's people and cuisine, in particular, set the city apart from others. In 1835, self-described "Yankee" traveler Joseph Holt Ingraham described New Orleans as a "city of anomalies."[13] Undeniably, it stood apart from other American cities for its shameful predominance in the slave trade, hosting the nation's largest market in enslaved people. The city also functioned as one of the country's largest hubs of domestic and international trade, a major immigration port of entry, a magnet for businessmen and bohemians, and a tourist playground.[14] At the same time, New Orleans filled a singular niche in white American and European imaginations as an alluring destination that promised distinctly sensory forms of escape, often at the table and bar. "Eating was, to judge from the frequency of its recurrence, the favourite amusement of the ladies, at New Orleans," wrote one Englishwoman who visited in 1843. "They breakfasted at nine, then a luncheon was spread at eleven, dinner at four, tea at six, and supper at nine o'clock." Where there was enticing food, there were also the people who made and served it. More often than not, they were Black. Enslaved and free servants filled the tables in antebellum New Orleans's grandest hotel with banquets of fish, fruit, preserves, cakes, Philadelphia hams, buffalo tongues, and hot, buttered buckwheat cakes—all for breakfast.[15] Such meals encouraged gluttonous appetites. Diners in New Orleans and far beyond it hungered for the gastronomic and intellectual fruits of Black labor that produced such feasts—the sauces, confections, recipes, and culinary techniques they perfected.

During antebellum decades, bondspeople and free people of color in Louisiana worked to feed the hunger and quench the thirst of those in power—most often, white Europeans and Americans. Men, women, and children labored on rural plantations and steamboats and in urban markets, streets, gardens, hotels, dining rooms, and kitchens. Following emancipation, Black Louisianians were briefly extended citizenship rights, then robbed of them again. As they continued to grow, harvest, cook, and serve twentieth-century eaters, whether on upriver sugarcane plantations or in Uptown private kitchens, Black Louisianians endured and resisted violent oppression and federally mandated segregation. By the mid-twentieth century, French Quarter restaurateurs sold "Creole" dishes that New Orleanians of color cooked behind closed kitchen doors. Tourism promoters hawked romanticized and whitewashed stories about the region's past as they beckoned visitors south.[16]

In a variety of settings and across time, then, Black New Orleanians found themselves bound to assist in building a culture and economy that relied on their labor as it simultaneously repudiated their physical presence and sought to appropriate their knowledge. Eating, drinking, buying, and selling—consuming acts, all—melded the worlds of food and people in New Orleans. This fusion took place in a variety of settings, from the nakedly monstrous (the antebellum barroom auction block) to the diminutive and seemingly benign (the French Quarter restaurant menu). The system's subtlety gave its violence ever more purchase, enabling it to cut deep inequalities into the cultural fabric of the city.[17] Nevertheless, if food and food work were wielded as means of subjugation, Black New Orleanians of every era used the same tools to build autonomy, belonging, and pleasure for themselves, their families, and their communities.

Scholars have explored the long histories of New Orleans, its people, and its cuisine, yet a rigorous focus on the intersection of these subjects is scant.[18] Hungry historians of the Crescent City have generated articles or edited collections, many organized by dish or drink, or included the city's food industry as one stop along the way in wide-ranging studies.[19] An emphasis on discrete ingredients, establishments, or individuals, though, can make it difficult to see trajectories of change or persistence over time. In the past twenty years, researchers in a variety of disciplines have explored more faithfully the interplay among foodways, ethnicity, race, class, and gender within the broader frames of the American South, the Atlantic world, and beyond.[20] Journalist John Egerton suggested a potential explanation for historians' historic inattention to Southern food: "Perhaps it is simply too hard to be serious about so joyful a subject as good food—and too hard to be joyful about a subject so fraught with blood, sweat, and ambiguity."[21] In the space between those inclinations, the subject slips away, escaping unquestioned and unexamined.

Nevertheless, histories of New Orleans would be well served to include a critical, sustained consideration of food. Looking to the table helps reveal a longer history of New Orleans's appeal to travelers. The tourism industry serves as a critical revenue source for the contemporary city and one of its largest employers.[22] Historical and sociological studies of tourism have located the industry's foundational eras in the interwar and postwar periods of the twentieth century.[23] Yet the eager hunger felt by Europeans and Americans for New Orleans had strong antebellum roots. "There are few places where human life can be enjoyed with more pleasure, or employed to more pecuniary profit," than New Orleans, declared the author of the 1822 city directory.[24] Prior to the Civil War, a constellation of coffeehouses, restaurants, fine hotels, and bowling and billiard houses catered to the thousands of businessmen (and some of their wives) who traveled from European and northeastern American cities to New Orleans. Importantly, this study finds that many of these early visitors blended their appetites for the city's food and drink with their fascination with the city's slave markets. These were twinned entertainments, experienced together. Such settings taught travelers to enjoy New Orleans as a place where everything was for sale: a cup of punch, a person, a plot of land. An attendee at a slave auction in a hotel barroom could drink, eat, and smoke while bidding on a human being. In the Ladies' Ordinary upstairs, his wife dined and drank, too, her glass filled by enslaved servants. Their consumptive experiences anchored the Crescent City in the fantasies of pleasure seekers and capitalists alike. New Orleans's early notoriety also pointed to the successes of writers and print media in circulating ideas and images among an international audience, even amid sectional political divisions and long before the era of mass communications.

Looking to food, too, renders nebulous social processes and human relationships more tangible, giving them specific names, places, aromas, and tastes. Food and drink were embroiled in the conflicted workings of intimacy, violence, trust, and distrust that flourished in the perverse world of slavery and its segregated aftermath in New Orleans, as elsewhere. Slaveholders compelled enslaved women to labor as wet nurses, feeding their children with their breast milk, yet they barred the same women from sharing a table with them and feared that they might poison the meals they cooked.[25] Even with the passage of time, little changed. "My mother worked [in Tremé] . . . for middle-class whites. . . . They really loved my mother," remembered New Orleanian

Olga Jackson, interviewed for an oral history project in 1977. When Jackson was eleven or twelve, she decided to help her mother with her domestic work. At the employer's home, Jackson discovered, "My mother's dishes were kept in a little corner of the cupboard. . . . She was not allowed to wash her dishes with the family's dishes. But the dog had a special place at the table and his dishes was washed along with the rest of the family's dishes."[26] Jackson resolved to help her mother leave the job and to never do domestic work herself. Whether in the nineteenth century or the twentieth, experiences of inclusion and exclusion and notions of hygiene, pleasure, desire, and disgust all revolved around food. Food allows an entrance into intimate histories of people and place like no other medium.[27]

The bind between food and people in New Orleans—entities that figured among the most prominent imports and exports in the city's antebellum economy—expands, too, the study of commodities, people, and material things under the regime of chattel slavery and in its wake.[28] In early 1835, a New Englander traveled by steamboat from New Orleans to the Red River region of northeast Texas, where he intended to engage in land speculation. He recorded in his diary the words of a fellow traveler, who informed him that Southern planters "care[d] for nothing but 'to buy Negroes to raise cotton & raise cotton to buy Negroes.'" Enslaved people, cotton, sugar, and other raw and finished goods formed a continuous cycle of commodification. One fed the appetite of the other, which in turn reawakened the hunger of the first. Similarly, a reporter observed the extent to which Louisiana's cotton and sugar production had become inextricably entwined by the close of the nineteenth century. "It is interesting to find that one staple of the South . . . depends upon the other, for cotton seed meal is extensively used to enrich the sugar lands," he wrote. "At the same time that cotton thus helps sugar, it is in another way benefited, in turn, by sugar. The sugar is put up in sacks and bags made of cotton cloth."[29] King Cotton and Queen Sugar ruled from the same throne, siphoning their power and riches from each other and from the enslaved people who made them.[30]

In Louisiana and beyond, these interlaced appetites for food, drink, and forced labor—and the satisfaction of those hungers—rendered the commodification of people into uniquely explicit forms. Rape was one physical manifestation of the lustful violence of objectification and power by enslavers over enslaved.[31] Rapacious eating and drinking, too, enabled those in power to consume the labor and lives of those they subjugated, in conjunction with the foods they made.[32] This consumption was metaphorical, but in some cases it was more than so. In 1764, French customs officer M. Chambon wrote of a practice he observed among Portuguese, English, and Dutch slave traders in Guinea. When considering humans to purchase, "[slave traders] are not ashamed to lower themselves to the point of licking their skin to find out from the taste of their sweat if they were free of illness," he wrote. An illustration accompanying Chambon's account showed a European leaning into the face of a Guinean man.[33] The embrace initiated an abduction into enslavement and possible death. Nearly two centuries later, such appetites persisted. "My damn old missis was mean as hell," Henrietta Butler told a Works Progress Administration interviewer in 1940, about her former enslaver, Emily Haidee. Butler had been born into slavery in Lafourche Parish, Louisiana, southwest of New Orleans, in a region where the waters of the Gulf of Mexico gnawed away at the southernmost bounds of the state's dry land. "You see dis finger here?" Butler demanded of her interviewer. "Dere is where she bit it de day us was set free. Never will forget how she said, 'Come here, you little black bitch, you!' and grabbed my finger [and] almost bit it off." Haidee had forced Butler and her mother to bear children that Haidee sold or kept, according to their sex, in order to profit her or beget more enslaved children themselves. When Butler's own baby died, Haidee ordered Butler to nurse Haidee's child in the lost baby's place. Haidee's greed had been all-consuming, swallowing up Butler's kin, womb, milk—Butler's labors in all their forms. At the news of emancipation, Haidee's fury exploded through her teeth, in a bite.[34]

The attitude that people's bodies could be devoured took varied forms in realms of food production and consumption in New Orleans, during and after slavery. Planters and traders treated people of color as agricultural and industrial tools. Slaveholders graded, priced, bought, and sold men, women, and children as they did hogsheads of molasses and sugar. Tourists described food workers' bodies, especially the color of their skin, in terms of the sugar and coffee they made or sold. In 1896, decades after slavery's abolition, a New Orleans guidebook directed tourists to view the "labor department" of the Poydras Market, one of the city's public food markets. There, "numbers of negro women may be found waiting for employment, standing in long rows. Here one can hire a scrubbing woman, a washerwoman, a cook, or a housemaid, at the regular market price."[35] At the time, remnants of the city's antebellum slave auctions had become decaying tourist attractions or had vanished in fire and smoke. Nevertheless, as this guidebook informed tourists, people for a price could still be found in New Orleans markets. Such objectification would take new forms in the twentieth century. On the shelves of French Quarter souvenir shops, cookbooks and trinkets proliferated with visual stereotypes of Black women cooking and selling food—stereotyped "mammies"—even as many whites clung to segregation.[36] And in 1959, five years after the US

Supreme Court outlawed segregation, a New Orleans resident submitted a letter to the editor of the *Times-Picayune* declaring, "Africa needs educated Negroes. American Negroes would have better opportunities there, as they are fairly well educated, familiar with mass production, farming, assembly lines, entertainment and the professions. They would be welcome there."[37] Whether in the nineteenth century or the twentieth, then, many white diners wanted the labor of Black New Orleanians, the food they made, and the idea of Black New Orleanians in the kitchen, but they did not want the people.[38]

The people who populated this long history were always more than simply Black or white. They were Choctaw, Chickasaw, Senegambian, Spanish, Congolese, Jewish, Cuban, Sicilian, Irish, and much more.[39] Nevertheless, within the time span of this study, "white" and "Black" racial categorizations—and their associated political, social, and economic advantages and disadvantages—crystallized and descended on New Orleans society, as on the United States writ large. This process was neither organic nor inevitable. Europeans and Americans in seventeenth- and eighteenth-century Louisiana developed a racist racial calculus to classify people of African, Native, European, and American descents, for the purposes of including, excluding, and regulating them. In 1724, five years after French forces brought enslaved West Africans to Louisiana, the French monarchy announced the *Code Noir*, or Black Code, which enumerated the rules governing enslaved people in Louisiana. Among other measures—such as calling for the expulsion of Jews from the territory—the *Code Noir* forbade marriage or cohabitation between "white" French colonists and enslaved or free "Blacks."[40] Issued thousands of miles and an ocean away from Louisiana, from the palace of Versailles, this decree failed to define the daily experiences of colonial Louisianians and their conceptions of their own and others' identities.[41]

Nevertheless, attempts at categorization and control persisted under different regimes, with new designs. In 1808, authorities in newly American New Orleans required men and women of African descent who had been born free or manumitted from slavery to be identified as people "of color." Bureaucrats appended these official identifiers—*homme de couleur libre* (*h.d.c.l.*), free man of color, and *femme de couleur libre* (*f.d.c.l.*), free woman of color (and their English abbreviations: fmc, fwc)—to names in municipal, notarial, and judicial records, as well as in city directories. For decades, these lettered brands latched themselves onto the names of free people, so that any degree of African heritage—not even skin color, necessarily—might be visible to authorities. With such surveillance in place, antebellum Louisiana society sorted into three primary channels—whites, free people of color (or Creoles of color), and slaves—with constant intermingling, consensual and forced, among them.[42]

Following the Civil War, however, the abolition of slavery, coupled with recent, massive infusions of Irish and German immigrants to New Orleans, compelled the three streams to narrow into two. In July 1873, the French-language New Orleans newspaper *Le Carillon* announced to its readers, "The time has come . . . one must be either WHITE or BLACK, that each person must decide for himself. There are two races here: one superior, the other inferior. . . . Their separation is *absolutely* necessary." Such an imperative conveyed the novelty and artificiality of imposing two identifiers on a society that had long relied on more nuanced language.[43] In coming decades, cementing the bounds of whiteness and Blackness would have enormous political, economic, and legal implications. White Louisianians rushed to eliminate their Black neighbors from voting booths and from positions of commercial and political power. Quotidian violence—from the myriad, often invisible barbs of Jim Crow oppression and segregation to the blunt horrors of public lynchings—instilled intense, ambient threat into the lives of Black Louisianians. Being white or Black in Louisiana, as in many other American places, could be a matter of life or death. At the same time, the stark racial divide rippled through the realm of culture, too.[44]

The narrowing of vocabularies and imaginations to Black and white, the relationship of those processes to conceptions of a Louisiana Creole identity, and the relevance of those terms—Black, white, Creole—to cuisine and tourism in New Orleans are an essential thread in the second half of this book, in particular. In Louisiana and other settings colonized by Europeans, "creole," from the Portuguese word *crioulo*, was initially a geographic identifier, distinguishing those born in a colonized place. In disparate locales, including Louisiana, people, food, languages, religions, economies, and worldviews clashed and mixed, forming new, distinct creole languages, creole people, creole cuisines, and more.[45] Accordingly, the Creoles of early Louisiana were people of European and African descent who had been born in Louisiana.

Soon, though, New Orleanians imbued the term with different meanings, tied to nation, class, and, eventually, race. Following the transfer of Louisiana to the United States in 1803, many New Orleanians identified as Creoles to distinguish themselves from the Americans flooding the nation's newest, southwestern frontier. The New Orleans Creoles were of European, African, Afro-Caribbean, and mixed lineages. They were also French-speaking and Roman Catholic, distinct from the white, English-speaking, Protestant Americans. In ensuing decades, as antebellum New Orleans boomed, many "Creoles of color" formed an educated, successful class of free New Orleanians of mixed African, Afro-Caribbean, European, and American descents. They were entrepreneurs and artisans, some were slaveholders themselves, and many had roots in Saint-Domingue and Cuba. Their social and economic positions were different from those of the enslaved people brought to New Orleans auction blocks via the domestic slave trade.[46]

Coincident with *Le Carillon*'s 1873 declaration to its readers that "The time has come . . . one must be either WHITE or BLACK," white New Orleanians transformed the city's longstanding Creole identity into a battleground. Racial identity carried starkly new consequences in realms of politics, economics, and even bodily safety. Accordingly, the Creole identity could no longer belong to both worlds. So said white New Orleanians, who feared acquiring any purported taint of Blackness if they continued to call themselves Creole. Accordingly, as white New Orleanians devised an elaborate system of segregation, white guidebook authors, local historians, and tourism boosters asserted that the word "Creole" meant, and had always meant, "purely" white. The term indicated a familial lineage that could be traced to a romanticized, aristocratic French and Spanish past, they claimed. Conveniently, and not coincidentally, such a mythology could be costumed, performed, advertised, sold—and tasted, even—in an economy that was turning toward tourism. If being Creole meant belonging in and to New Orleans, its history, and its culture, then white New Orleanians set out to claim that territory solely for themselves and shut Black New Orleanians outside the castle walls.[47]

To many outsiders, the Creole culture of New Orleans that was advertised to them at the turn of the twentieth century was alluring but confusing. Some suspected that it was no more than a marketing ploy. In 1902, a journalist poked fun at the city's pride in its Creole cuisine. "Creole names attached to dishes are supposed to be a guarantee of their quality and one is amused to note the different uses to which the word has been put," he wrote. "In the French market one sees . . . Creole chickens, though it would be a little difficult to have the exact meaning of this explained. Possibly the chickens on this side of Canal street aspire to French or Spanish ancestry and are more aristocratic than the ordinary Louisiana born hen."[48] As this writer shrewdly detected, white New Orleanians' new obsession with the color of Creole identity—voiced frantically, and frequently—pointed to their insecurity and fear at its association with Blackness. All the while, many New Orleanians of color continued to identify proudly and continuously as Creoles, averring their long histories in the city. In 1943, a reporter for the Black-owned *Chicago Defender* traveled to New Orleans and concluded, "Today a creole . . . is a creole largely because he calls himself one."[49]

Black, white, and Creole—these linked identities moved forward, in tension, and often at the table, farther into the twentieth century. In November 1978, a *Washington Post* reporter attended "Creole Feast," a food festival held in New Orleans's Rivergate exhibition center that showcased thirty of the city's Black chefs. "Everybody eats their food, but few people ever get to see the chefs who prepare it," the festival organizer told the reporter. "So we decided to give the people in the city a chance to have direct contact with the chefs." Ten thousand people attended Creole Feast and other events that weekend, the reporter estimated, including the Bayou Classic football game, which matched two historically Black universities. Such large crowds notwithstanding, Creole Feast organizers decided to open their doors one hour later than planned on the morning of November 26. "A few yards" outside the exhibition center, the Knights of the Ku Klux Klan were concluding a march through the French Quarter, led by grand wizard David Duke. "Although Klan leaders denied that the march was timed to coincide with the festival, many blacks felt otherwise," the reporter observed. Chefs inside the exhibition hall were not intimidated. Artichokes Dunbar, barbecued shrimp, okra gumbo, crawfish bisque, pralines, mile-high pie—they prepared and served these and more. "Cooking food is my roots," said Samuel Pearson, an executive chef at a suburban restaurant, with a career of more than thirty-five years in the kitchen under his belt. "You can always put yourself into it—a piece of your own spirit and thought," agreed pastry chef Annie Laura Squalls, about cooking. Ignoring the ugliness outside the hall, Pearson, Squalls, and those at their sides cooked on—Creole chefs setting the table with a Creole Feast.[50]

To investigate this history, this book moves through time and place, through the varied settings associated with food, drink, tourism, and consumption in nineteenth- and twentieth-century New Orleans. The book is organized spatially and thematically, rather than strictly chronologically. Each chapter moves the book forward in time, though some double back along the way, considering the past—the origins of sugar cultivation in Louisiana, or the history of public marketing in New Orleans, for example—before advancing. Chapter 1, "Block and Table," looks to the early city's food industry, focusing on the antebellum auction block and the table, two distinct but associated settings. Already, Americans and Europeans were learning to love New Orleans as a place of indulgence and escape. If New Orleans's slave pens and auction blocks flaunted an overt commodification of human lives during this era, drinking and eating were becoming pastimes of subtler cruelty. The city's acquisition by the United States at the turn of the nineteenth century and the establishment of Louisiana's sugar industry were the catalysts for this story.

In contrast to the travelers, businessmen, and their wives who salivated at the prospect of winter sojourns in the Crescent City, enslaved people feared New Orleans as a gateway to family separation, abuse, and death. Still, some free and enslaved workers used jobs in the food industry to carve paths of mobility or stability and achieve degrees of autonomy. Chapter 2, "Apples and Oranges, Food and Freedom," presents focused histories of several enslaved and free New Orleanians of color who worked with food: street vendors, a coffeehouse proprietor, a grocer, and a woman who sold apples and oranges on a steamboat to purchase her freedom. Their paths straddled continents and oceans, languages, and legal states of slavery and freedom. Their histories show the complexities of working in an industry in which a food purveyor's financial success often meant profiting from the patronage of those tied to the city's slave trade.

Chapter 3, "Field and Levee, through the Lens," looks to the New Orleans sugar levees and Louisiana's sugarcane plantations in the decades after the Civil War. Louisiana sugar, one of the state's most profitable exports, fed the world's appetites and addictions. Perversely, sugar production was work of unparalleled brutality. Nevertheless, at the turn of the twentieth century, white photographers trained their lenses on the places and people of Louisiana's sugar industry. The postcards and stereographs they produced fueled nostalgia for an antebellum past and promoted tourism to the modernizing city. These media did other work, too, during an era marred by lynching, disfranchisement, and a new visual language of violent stereotypes. In vivid, photographic form, they presented well-worn tropes of Black workers toiling at manual labor or idle and indolent. These objects attempted to trap Black sugar workers within the visual and conceptual frames of slavery, posing them as unfit to be free, wage-working citizens. Black activists and photographers, in contrast, used the medium for very different ends.

Steps away from New Orleans's riverfront sugar levees was the French Market, the city's central food market. Choctaws first named this setting Bulbancha, the "place of many tongues."[51] Throughout the nineteenth century, European and American travelers called the French Market "Babel." In the early twentieth century, white housewives and city officials folded the French Market into Progressive and New Deal modernization campaigns. Chapter 4, "Mother Market," considers how and why these processes unfurled, excluding people of color from the renovation and its results. Published writing that lauded the French Market as "eternal" obscured the longstanding prominence of Natives and Black New Orleanians there and attempted to deny them a stake in its past, present, and future.

Finally, chapter 5, "The Creole Table and 'The Black Hand in the Pot,'" moves to the mid-twentieth century to explore how white and Black New Orleanians understood New Orleans's Creole identity in relation to its cuisine. During years when the social and political privileges associated with whiteness were eroding, white restaurateurs offered menus to diners that featured illustrations of French chefs. Guidebooks defined Creole cuisine as the legacy of the European colonial elite, even if many of the chefs and cooks in city kitchens were Black. At the same time, Black New Orleanians proudly claimed Creole cuisine as their creation and legacy. Professional chefs and activists used food, cookbooks, and restaurants as vehicles for professional advancement, political resistance, and pleasure.

The histories of these people, places, and meals are textual, oral, visual, and gustatory. Accordingly, this book relies on a heterogeneous array of sources. These include archival collections; municipal, federal, notarial, judicial, and census records stretching over 150 years, in English and French; published autobiographies and interviews of formerly enslaved people; newspapers and city directories; cookbooks; and menus. Primary sources typically associated with tourism and agriculture—such as travel guides and travel narratives, souvenir booklets, postcards, and stereographs of rural fields and urban industry—can be read for the light they shed on the region's food and labor histories, too. Material culture and visual objects—tarnished silverware handled by enslaved servants, maps, photographs, architectural plans, and editorial cartoons—hold equal if not superior importance to official archives when researching the lives of those less able to document their own histories.[52] Methodologies of history, American Studies, Black Studies, material and visual culture, and food studies enable the interpretation of these diverse fragments of the past.

This work is inspired by scholars who read both "against the grain" and "*along the bias grain*" in search of people whose experiences emerge from between the lines or in the margins of archival sources, or in other places entirely.[53] For example, when investigating the path of a young Black woman named Mattie who traveled from Virginia to New York City at the turn of the twentieth century, Saidiya V. Hartman approached the woman and her history not as archival gaps, silences, and deficiencies—not as chasms that needed filling. Rather, Hartman turned the tables, declaring, "It is a story that exceeds the archive."[54] The movements and possibilities of Mattie's life, and those of many others, were bigger, richer, and braver than the scant details accorded to them in official and institutional records. In New Orleans, histories of sugarcane grown, gumbo cooked and served, peppers harvested, and oysters shucked often exceeded the archive, too.

Looking at the long history of food in New Orleans can produce ugly histories of a place that many people flocked to specifically for its sensory comforts. Such ugliness emerges in any setting where American chattel slavery made its mark. In mid-nineteenth-century South Carolina, an enslaved woman named Rose gave a cotton sack to her nine-year-old daughter, Ashley, when Ashley was sold away from her. The little girl never saw her mother again. Inside were, as Ashley's granddaughter later embroidered on the sack, "a tattered dress 3 handfulls of pecans a braid of Roses hair." Also, "It be filled with my Love always." Historian Tiya Miles sought the history of this slip of cotton, now stained with age, which bore the weight of enormous love and sorrow within its fragile weave. Miles noted that, among other insights, the object's history pointed to "the ugliness of lovely places."[55] The goldenrod and sweetgrass of the South Carolina Lowcountry are lovely; so are the jasmine and bougainvillea that bloom in New Orleans's gardens. Within the enticing aromas and flavors of the finest dishes that touched Crescent City tables, there were rot and canker, too—families separated, children enslaved, and humans and their dignity abused, all to fill someone else's stomach. Leisure and labor, and pleasure and pain, created the ephemeral experiences of dining in New Orleans. Strands of culture, politics, economy, and society braided together, not to be disentangled. This history matters because it is our present, too. Inequities, prejudices, appropriations, stereotypes—even sugarcoated and rich on the tongue—are slavery's heritage.[56]

1

BLOCK AND TABLE

Buying and Selling People and Food
in Antebellum New Orleans

ON JANUARY 11, 1855, a Wisconsin newspaper reporter took part in a popular tourist pastime in New Orleans. "Being a looker-on in New Orleans," he wrote, "I attended a slave auction." He described his surroundings in one of the city's most luxurious settings. "The sale was held in the rotunda of the St. Louis Hotel, a circular area of something like a hundred feet diameter, over which rises a dome as lofty as a church spire," he described. The columns surrounding him and the "marble mosaic" floor beneath his feet recalled a church. So, too, did a mother named Mary, holding a baby and flanked by two small children, all elevated on a five-foot pedestal above those congregated below (fig. 1.1). Allusions to a conventional house of worship ended there, though. The woman on the block "wipes tears from her eyes; the hammer comes down." An unnamed buyer purchased the enslaved Mary, advertised as "a good French Cook, washer and ironer," and her children—nine-year-old Lionce, four-year-old Oscar, and the infant—for $2,375.[1] The group attracted the highest price within a lot of twenty-nine enslaved sugar-plantation hands sold that day. The family's value resided in the labor promised by still small, if not yet unborn, hands, shoulders, and wombs. They counted as four among approximately three hundred thousand enslaved people in Louisiana in 1855, within a larger population of about three and a half million enslaved people in the United States.[2]

Thirst and hunger—far from the spiritual kind, despite the St. Louis Hotel's ostensibly church-like features—fueled the transactions in this room and others like it in antebellum New Orleans. In surveying the rotunda, the Wiscon-

FIGURE 1.1. In January 1855, Mary and her children Lionce, Oscar, and their infant sibling stood on an auction block such as this one in New Orleans's luxurious St. Louis Hotel. They faced the crowd of bidders and the hotel bar. Detroit Publishing Co., *New Orleans, La., Old Slave Block in St. Louis Hotel*, between 1900 and 1910, dry plate negative, glass, 8 x 10". Detroit Publishing Company photograph collection, Library of Congress, Prints & Photographs Division, Washington, DC, LC-DIG-det-4a17913, https://www.loc.gov/item/2016795470/.

sin reporter noted that the hotel's bar occupied a full half of its circumference, forming a crescent that faced the room's auction blocks. Barkeepers dispensed liquors and wines to crowds that bid on people, land, furniture, animals, and agricultural equipment. A cacophony of noises reverberated in the domed chamber that smelled of cigar smoke, sweat, and alcohol. Refreshments lent an offensively easeful air to transactions that separated families and sent children, women, and men to unknown fates—for some, death—with new enslavers.

Sometime after the sale of Mary and her children, a forty-five-year-old woman named Harriet ascended the block at the St. Louis Hotel. Offers lingered around $1,450. Then, the reporter recalled, "Some one says that she is a very good cook." This changed things. "$1500 is bid, $1525—1550—1575—1600 . . . all other bids have dropped off, and the contest is between two men, both of whom . . . appear to be fond of good living. They bid lively. Each wants a cook, and each wants a triumph." Harriet's reputation in the kitchen tipped her price of sale to $1,920, the second highest of the lot, higher than the amounts paid for nine young field hands and even twenty-four-year-old George, a "good plantation engineer, coachman, and generally useful" bondsman. Harriet's price of sale also significantly exceeded the mean value—around $1,200—paid for enslaved women domestic laborers in New Orleans auctions at the time.[3] Motivated by hunger for Harriet's food and the confidence instilled by whatever may have been in their glasses, the men bid, one triumphed, and Harriet's life changed. "The sale proceeds," the reporter wrote, and "the *cattle* change hands."[4] Descriptions of past meals at Mary and Harriet's hands predicted future kitchen labor. The bidders drank as they imagined forthcoming gastronomic pleasures and fought to buy the women who could create them.

Before the Civil War, New Orleans distinguished itself on the auction block and at the table—two distinct but intimately related settings. The city hosted the nation's largest market of enslaved people as well as a roaring leisure scene that revolved around food and drink. These industries fed off each other. Slave yards, auction houses and exchanges, coffeehouses, billiard saloons, ten-pin alleys, oyster stands, and grand hotels like the St. Louis and the St. Charles proliferated to sustain the men and women who bought and sold enslaved people.[5] Food and drink played a special role in these transactions, forging a singular bond between realms of cuisine and slavery during New Orleans's earliest years as an American city. Within the blended business-and-leisure world of antebellum New Orleans, bondspeople, food, and drink were conjoined commodities—things presented for sale, often in the same place, at the same time. Knots that tethered the buying and selling of people, food, and drink in the Crescent City were tighter and deeper than coincidence or convenience, however. "New Orleans is a city of great gaiety," remarked one British writer who visited in 1839. He was struck by "the large number of strangers that visit it, chiefly for pleasure."[6] Much of this pleasure began at the table, the bar, and the block.

Building Blocks: Populating Antebellum New Orleans

Colonial governments of France, Spain, and France again dragged settlers and enslaved laborers in New Orleans through an eighteenth century of privation and disease. In April 1803, France sold the Louisiana territory to the United States. At more than eight hundred thousand square miles, the tract nearly doubled the nation's size. Americans looked to the Lower Mississippi Valley with hungry eyes. "The land yields an abundance of all the necessaries of life, and almost spontaneously; very little labour being required in the cultivation of the earth," declared Thomas Jefferson's administration to the US Congress in fall 1803.[7] The report characterized Louisiana as an expanse of unmeasurable potential, with New Orleans its crown jewel. Nearly three hundred merchant vessels had docked at New Orleans ports in 1802, ready to receive exports of cotton, sugar, molasses, indigo, rice, pelts, lumber, and flour. "Population alone is wanting to multiply them to an astonishing degree," the administration promised.[8] Americans had only to migrate to this verdant land—the region's indigenous inhabitants being "thinly scattered[,] . . . it is presumable that their claim might be extinguished for a small matter," another writer asserted arrogantly—and "New Orleans [may] become the greatest MART on the continent."[9] These reports painted a picture of a cosmopolitan outpost already embedded in global networks of trade and the gustatory pleasures they facilitated. Americans salivated at the prospect of taking the helm.

After New Orleans became American, the riches promised by Jefferson bloomed. Shipping notices printed in New Orleans's newspapers in the years following its transfer mapped the city's culinary, economic, and cultural reach. In French, Spanish, and English, readers could track vessels arriving from or departing to ports as varied as Antwerp, Baltimore, Bordeaux, Charleston, Havana, Liverpool, Mobile, New York, and Vera Cruz. Announcements in the *Louisiana Gazette* in June 1807 described the goods changing hands in this humid corner of the triangle trade: almonds, nutmeg, anchovies, "elegant fancy chairs," Madeira, silk chambray, Loaf Sugar, "Indiasoy Ketchup," and more.[10] Such notices read like fantastical shopping lists for customers of boundless means and ravenous tastes. These goods were far from the only commodities for sale, however.

Early New Orleans newspapers also taught readers to understand humans as things that could be purchased akin to, if not in the same instances as, foodstuffs like Madeira and almonds. The same June 1807 issue of the *Gazette* informed readers of the availability of "24 Young Negroes of the Congo Nation . . . boys from 16 to 18 years of age," on board the ship *Euphemis*, recently arrived from Charleston. The teens would be sold at the Exchange Coffee House on Conti Street, one block from the riverfront levee, which had been in business for less than one year. At this venue—which served as an auction house, tavern, and coffee-serving café alike—prospective buyers could also soon bid on a downriver plantation with forty acres of rice planted in the ground, to be transferred to the buyer with the "18 Negroes" living there. Humans and rice for sale in the same lot echoed the contents of the vessel *Aurore* almost a century earlier. Also for sale at the Exchange in summer 1807: "four Negro families from a cotton Plantation" totaling twenty-four people, plus a single man and a single woman, "the whole to be disposed of on reasonable terms, and a liberal credit." The *Gazette* filled its pages with things that could be acquired: plantations, businesses, buildings, humans, horses, stockings, coffee, and anchovies. The titles of adjacent announcements repeated the theme across the page: "Sheriff's Sale," "For Sale," "A Plantation for Sale," and "Negroes for Sale."[11]

The mundane appearance of humans amidst a wide variety of objects to covet or purchase confirmed the already-routine nature of their commodification in New Orleans society. Indeed, when this issue of the *Gazette* was published, Europeans in Louisiana and their North American-born descendants, Creoles, had been enslaving men, women, and children of Native, African, and Creole origins for more than a century.[12] Between 1718 and 1810— the period of European colonial rule plus the first several years of American governance—the number of enslaved people in Orleans Territory grew from about two thousand to nearly thirty-five thousand, or 45 percent of the total population.[13] The percentage of enslaved people in the Parish of Orleans, home to New Orleans, paralleled that of the larger territory in 1810, with 44 percent of residents enslaved.[14] Thus, a New Orleans reader skimming this 1807 issue of the *Gazette* would have felt no surprise when reading of a boy, a chair, and loaf sugar as belonging to the same litany of available things.

This collection was a violently assembled one, to be sure, as evidenced by bondspeople's escapes and other resistance against enslavers. Among the *Gazette*'s notices of items for sale in 1807, A. J. Thomas, a Levee Street merchant who sold goods as well as people, offered a reward for the return of eighteen-year-old Harry.[15] Five feet six inches in height, Harry was "easily known by an apparent difficulty in his walk in consequence of burns received when a boy," Thomas described. Despite his injuries, Harry had escaped successfully more than two weeks earlier. The United States had recently followed the lead of the United Kingdom in banning the importation of bondspeople into the country, but individuals like Harry could expect no recourse. The ban would not go into effect until the following year, 1808, and it would be followed by an enormous growth in the domestic trade in bondspeople. Harry could not have known, but he had fled from his enslaver in a city poised to become the nation's most powerful clearinghouse for commodities like hogsheads of sugar and molasses, bales of cotton, and enslaved humans.

In the decades following Harry's 1807 flight, a ruthless reimagining of the landscape and economy of the American Lower South and Southwest—land that stretched from Texas to Florida and Louisiana to Tennessee—would demand the forced labor of generations.[16] Louisiana sugarcane plantations, their boundaries drawn long and slender to enable Mississippi River frontage, unrolled like piano keys along the curling length of the river above New Orleans (fig. 1.2). Cotton plantations blossomed on the map farther north.[17] The number of planters living in the Territory of Orleans exploded, from ninety in 1810 to nearly 6,500 in 1850. So, too, the population of enslaved Louisianians, who counted 34,660 in the 1810 US census and nearly 245,000 in 1850. They toiled to produce sweets, intoxicants, and staples.[18] Between 1810 and 1850, Louisiana's production of cane sugar grew from less than ten thousand hogsheads to almost 230,000, and from about 3,600 hogsheads of molasses to more than 109,300. In 1850, Louisiana's enslaved laborers produced more than 90 percent of the nation's sugarcane and 86 percent of the nation's molasses. The US government valued these sweet commodities at $15.5 million.[19] In the course of just a couple of generations, enslaved workers converted the region surrounding New Orleans into agricultural factories of wealth that fed the world's appetites and addictions.

To grow, tend, harvest, and process this bounty, slave traders drove nearly one million women and men from Upper South origins to Lower South markets, where they were sold to rural and urban enslavers.[20] Jacob Stroyer, born in 1849 and enslaved in South Carolina, recalled the day when traders forced a large group of women and children, including his sisters Violet and Priscilla, to leave for Louisiana to be sold: "Louisiana was considered by the slaves as a place of slaughter, so those who were going did not expect to see their friends again. . . . [W]hen the [train] cars began to start . . . the colored people cried out with one voice as though the heavens and earth were coming together. . . . and from that time to the present I have neither seen nor heard from my two sisters."[21]

Violet, Priscilla, and their companions vanished from the lives of their families and friends as they descended into New Orleans. One estimate placed the total number of enslaved people sold there at 135,000, equivalent to the entire city's population in the mid-1850s, when Mary and her children and Harriet climbed onto the block at the St. Louis Hotel.[22] When Harry escaped from his enslaver several decades earlier, in 1807, an enormous tide of newspaper

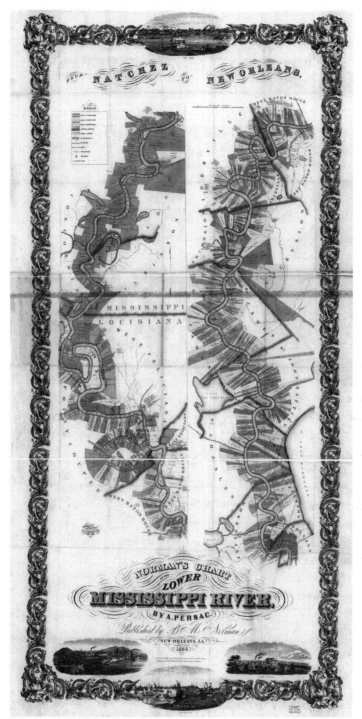

FIGURE 1.2. On each shaded sliver of land on this map, enslaved men, women, and children cultivated sugar. They also bore children, tended gardens, escaped, and buried their dead. Marie Adrien Persac, Benjamin Moore Norman, and J. H. Colton & Co., *Norman's Chart of the Lower Mississippi River* (New Orleans: B. M. Norman, 1858), colored map, 160 x 75 cm. Library of Congress, Geography and Map Division, Washington, DC, https://www.loc.gov /item/78692178/.

notices offering bondspeople for sale and seeking the recapture of fugitives followed in his wake.[23]

Even if enslaved people sought to flee New Orleans or resist a journey there, hundreds of thousands of others flocked *to* the city in the decades before the Civil War, drawn by commercial opportunities, the city's position on migration and trade routes, and its ties to European and Caribbean cultures and languages. When the United States took possession of New Orleans in 1803, the city or its surroundings were already home to Chitimacha, Houma, and Choctaw nations; free and enslaved people of African descent; French; Acadians, Germans, Spanish and Portuguese Christians and Jews; and Isleños, from the Canary Islands.[24] Beginning with a trickle in the 1790s and bursting into a flood in 1809, approximately ten thousand people fleeing the Haitian Revolution came to New Orleans via Cuba. Divided relatively evenly among whites, free people of color, and recently re-enslaved people, they redrew the region's demographics and economy. Some founded plantations, bringing sophisticated knowledge of sugarcane cultivation and processing. Others settled in New Orleans. The histories they brought with them rooted Louisiana's economy even more firmly in slavery while simultaneously inspiring hope and fear of a similar revolt on American shores.[25]

In the first decades of the nineteenth century, newly arrived Americans extended New Orleans's blocks upriver into the Faubourg Sainte Marie. Francophone, Creole New Orleanians remained entrenched in the city's colonial center, the French Quarter, and the neighboring, downriver Faubourg Marigny.[26] Dalmatian, or "Slavonian," maritime workers arrived in the city in the 1820s, joining Italians, Irish, and Jewish and Christian Germans who immigrated to the city and its surroundings throughout the first half of the century. Earlier generations of German immigrants had established farms in upriver rural districts, forming the eponymous German Coast. Later generations founded breweries, law practices, and other businesses in New Orleans. Poorer Irish immigrants clustered in the fanned streets of the working-class neighborhood that would come to be known as the Irish Channel. In the 1830s and 1840s, American and European speculators bound for northern Louisiana and Texas passed through New Orleans to acquire supplies. So, too, in the mid-1840s, did American soldiers preparing to fight Mexican forces in Texas during the Mexican-American War.[27] Thus, throughout the first half of the nineteenth century, for diverse streams of people, New Orleans served as a point of entry, a refuge, a springboard to wealth, or a portal to death by overwork, abuse, yellow fever, or the battlefield.

In these ways, antebellum New Orleans was cosmopolitan by choice and force—thousands came seeking work, fortune, or ease; others arrived in chains or fleeing poverty and war. Often, this polyglot mix met at the table. In the 1832 city directory, the proprietor of the Hotel of the Marine and of the Colonies specified that his establishment's public table—which offered daily breakfast, dinner, and "Broth, Coffee, Chocolate, and all kind of Liquors" to locals and visitors alike—was stewarded by "servants speaking French, English, German and Spanish."[28] By the eve of the Civil War, in 1860, nearly 43 percent of free New Orleanians had been born outside the United States.[29] In terms of linguistic and ethnic diversity, New Orleans was more akin to metropolises of the American Northeast and Midwest than other urban centers in the antebellum South. The Crescent City had grown fat off steamboat holds heavy with sugar, molasses, and cotton and the profits from auction blocks that had felt the feet of tens of thousands of bodies. As New Orleans worked to satisfy the world's hungers, it styled itself into a capital of eating, drinking, and consuming.

Dining, Devouring, Starving: Eating in Antebellum New Orleans

"It was a custom . . . among the southern people generally, to make much of eating—it was one of their hobbies," recalled Louis Hughes, who was enslaved on a cotton plantation in Mississippi in the 1840s and in a Tennessee mansion a decade later.[30] If dining was a hobby of many antebellum Southerners, New Orleanians elevated eating and drinking to an avocation, or an art. One visitor likened food and drink to "Gog and Magog . . . whose court, as held in New Orleans, is not to be despised or treated lightly."[31] Travelogues, memoirs, city directories, and newspapers charted the multiplication of establishments throughout New Orleans that catered to gourmets and gluttons alike. "Longer time is spent at table by the Americans, at New Orleans, than in other parts of the Union," agreed another traveler, "and greater attention is paid to the details of the *cuisine*."[32] Writings such as these installed food and drink as a cornerstone of New Orleans's cultural identity and placed eating and drinking at the center of American and European imaginations of the growing city.

Creating these leisure experiences—the cultural scaffolding of a nascent tourist destination—was often the labor of New Orleanians of African descent, enslaved and free. They worked in a wide variety of jobs to feed and serve the city, as street peddlers, market sellers, cooks and pastry cooks, domestics, waiters, bartenders, and steamboat stewards. In September 1807, New Orleans pastry cook Jean Gaston advertised in the French-language newspaper *Le Moniteur* for "one or two Negro apprentices" to assist him in creating "all sorts of pastries, sweets for desserts of all kinds," gelatins, and sugary creations to decorate the dining table.[33] Gaston's apprentices would sculpt sugar that had been grown and harvested by enslaved people to decorate tables filled by enslaved cooks and stewarded by enslaved servants.

Their customers would come from the ranks of planters, public auctioneers, cigar makers, and the managers of cotton presses and sugar refineries who appeared in New Orleans's first comprehensive directory of businesses and residents, published in 1811.[34] Hungry and thirsty residents could call on thirty-six grocers, twenty-nine bakers, twenty-two butchers, thirteen taverns, eight confectioners, six coffeehouses, three distillers, one chocolate maker, assorted liquor and wine merchants, and one *traiteur*, a caterer. Four pastry cooks, including Gaston, clustered in the blocks surrounding the St. Louis Cathedral. In coming years, the count of businesses that quelled hunger, quenched thirst, and entertained would only grow. The Exchange Coffee House—host to auctions of land, people, animals, and sugar-refining tools— rooted itself at the corner of St. Louis and Chartres Streets, future home to the St. Louis Hotel.[35] At the Café del Aguila, at the intersection of St. Ann and Chartres Streets, "coffee, chocolate or tea, steaming hot, were served on small tables to customers immersed in the mysteries of dominoes," recalled one local.[36] Newspapers tracked the opening, closing, and changing hands of such businesses, always amidst announcements of auctions and fugitives from slavery.[37]

Writers, tourists, and professionals narrated scenes of dazzled discovery when they arrived in early nineteenth-century New Orleans. Often, their amazement revolved around the food and people they found in a manner that bound the two together as subjects of their awestruck gazes. "Along the levee, as far as the eye could reach . . . were ranged two rows of market people," wrote the English-born architect Benjamin Henry Latrobe in 1819. "I cannot suppose that my eye took in less than 500 sellers & buyers." On scraps of canvas cloth and palmetto leaves, vendors displayed meat, fish, vegetables, fruit, sugarcane, and eggs to passersby. Latrobe was struck, too, by the "black negroes & negresses . . . mulattoes, curly & straight-haired, quarteroons of all shades, long haired & frizzled. . . . Their wares consisted of as many kinds as their faces."[38] A European traveler in the 1820s was similarly impressed, observing the "fine pine-apples, oranges, bananas, peccan-nuts, cocoa-nuts, and vegetables. . . . The black population appeared very large."[39] No perceptive distance separated these visitors' observations of the city's food and Black residents. Tropical fruits, sugarcane, nuts, people: visitors' perspectives registered foodstuffs and humans in tight configuration, in this place where people stood on auction blocks mere blocks away from New Orleans's public market.

In public and private dining rooms alike, eating and drinking were theater and enslaved workers were made to set the stage. "I used to pull the fan that hop off the flies while the white folks was eatin'," recalled Mary Harris of her duties as a girl younger than ten, enslaved on a Louisiana plantation before the Civil War. "My arms used to get tired, 'specially at dinner when they set so long at the table."[40] Weimar monarch Carl Bernhard was a guest at the kind of sumptuous meals stewarded by bondspeople like Harris when he visited New Orleans in 1826. In his memoir, he described the choreographed extravagance of dining in the home of a prominent attorney. "After the second course, large folding doors opened and we beheld another dining room, in which stood a table with the dessert," Bernhard wrote. "We withdrew from the first table, and seated ourselves at the second, in the same order in which we had partaken of the first." Doors opened like curtains on a stage to reveal a tableau of sweets. Bernhard and his fellow guests floated from dinner to dessert like actors in a play, and then on to other pleasures—singing, dancing, and drinking.[41] Great effort and expertise set this scene.

Preparing and serving New Orleans's elegant meals was the hard physical labor of enslaved people, especially women, even if they remained out of sight behind kitchen doors. "There was no cut nor granulated nor pulverized sugar," acknowledged one white writer, of the efforts required to host a dinner party at her family's childhood home in New Orleans in 1842. "There were no fruit extracts, no essences for seasoning . . . no ground spices, no seedless raisins." Whole spices had to be ground by hand and raisins seeded by hand, too. Ice cream "was whirled in the ice tub by hand—and a stout one at that—and required at least one hour, constant labor, to freeze," she remembered. An enslaved woman named Charlotte did this work in the household that the writer joined after her marriage. "Charlotte had complete charge of everything about the house," she recalled. "She made the jellies and the pickles, the ice cream, the cakes." Charlotte also understood the thankless nature of her work. "Often she remarked that no one in the house did more and had less to show for it at night than she did."[42] Abolitionist Frederick Douglass railed against the abuse that happened behind kitchen doors, inflicted by enslavers on the women and girls who nourished households, like Charlotte. "Every kitchen is a brothel," Douglass charged, in an 1847 address. "I ask you to consider this one feature of Slavery. Think of a million females absolutely delivered up into the hands of persons in any way they see fit."[43]

The scene was similar in rural kitchens, where bondspeople planted, harvested, prepared, and served food, creating bountiful tables for their enslavers even as many of the enslaved suffered and went hungry. Elizabeth Ross Hite remembered that three cooks fed Louisiana's Trinity Plantation, where she had been enslaved before the Civil War. "Everything was made on de plantation by plantation people," she explained to a Works Progress Administration

(WPA) interviewer many years later, whether those were meals consumed hastily by field hands or elegant repasts savored by the planter and his guests. "De cooks used to make all kinds of fancy food," Hite explained. "De master's first cousin who looked white, used to teach de cooks all de fancy dishes dat she knew about in France." With bans on teaching enslaved people to read, cooks gained expertise from knowledge passed down from a relative or work companion. They built an expertise rooted in flavors and techniques from West Africa, the Caribbean, Europe, and the Southeastern United States in order to create Creole and American cuisines.[44] As for her own family, Hite claimed that they had enough to eat—"We ate good food. Drank plenty of milk, clabber, and ate good bread,"—but she also recalled her father risking the whip to trap opossums at night, as well bondspeople tending gardens of watermelon, mushmelon, corn, and flowers, to supplement rations and earn wages.[45]

Other enslaved Louisianians described experiences of extreme hunger and punishments of sadistic violence when they stole food out of desperation. In these instances, enslavers punished starving bondspeople with food as their weapon. Israel Campbell, enslaved on a Louisiana cotton plantation as a mechanic, recalled the overseer discovering an enslaved man who was cooking a pilfered pig. The overseer forced him to eat the pork until he could not eat anymore. He whipped the man, force-fed him the soup until he vomited, and compelled him to eat everything again. "This process of vomiting and swallowing it again was continued, alternated with scourging," Campbell wrote in his autobiography, "until it seemed as if the poor fellow would die." The same overseer lashed another stolen pig to a different offender's shoulders "like a knapsack," where it rotted. "The sickening stench of the putrid meat . . . and the annoyance of the swarms of flies" created an "intolerable" torture. A different overseer recalled by Campbell bragged that he had "compelled a slave to eat the whole of a duck which he had stolen, feathers, entrails, every thing but the wings." His fellow overseers "applauded him for his skill in managing niggers."[46] Adhering a carcass to one's back and forcing others to consume bones, feathers, or vomit compelled the offenders into a perverse fusion of human and food. Such theatrical punishments were not far removed from the sadism that placed auction blocks in New Orleans barrooms, a configuration that rendered human lives and the fruits of their labor on an equal plane of public consumption.[47]

The sights, smells, sounds, and tastes of food, then, appeared on the pages of much writing about antebellum Louisiana. For powerful New Orleanians and travelers, the city's cuisine was a delight. For hungry bondspeople, it was the medium of their labor and even their torture. In all settings, food stood for more than the ephemeral meals it made. Charlotte, the enslaved cook, pulverized sugar that had been cultivated, harvested, and refined by enslaved people. She created meals to be served to her enslavers on linens whose fibers had first touched the fingers of bondspeople. She managed a pantry stocked with spices, fruits, and liquors brought to New Orleans in ships entangled in a global trade of people, cotton, sugar, molasses, and rum. These ingredients bound her to global currents of commodities and to other enslaved people, too. At the hands of one New Orleans cook, the microcosm of a single slice of cake distilled a macrocosm of human and edible commodities.

Feverish Thirst: Caffeinating and "Liquoring" in Antebellum New Orleans

If lusty appetites were on full display in antebellum New Orleans, so were insatiable thirsts. "There are certainly one hundred coffee-houses in this city," marveled one visitor in 1835, "and they have, throughout the day, a constant ingress and egress of thirsty, time-killing, news-seeking visiters [sic]."[48] Sating themselves with the city's cuisine and winding up and down with coffee and alcohol, visiting expatriates built a predominantly white, male public world that blended work and play. One European tourist in the 1840s described the twinned rise of the city's business and leisure industries, such that the two had already become indistinguishable. "Business pursues [Americans] into the very heart of their enjoyments," she observed, "because, in fact, it is their enjoyment."[49] Men's work and play thrived in a ceaseless, hurried cycle. Sumptuous meals, coffee, and alcohol set the scene for debates over the prices of commodities, human and otherwise. "At the dinner-table; between the acts at opera and theatre; in the drawing-room; at the ball or soirée . . . stocks, cotton, sugar, and money are the liveliest topics," agreed another writer. "The evening is the reaction of the day; the prolonging of the money-fever."[50]

New Orleans's "money-fever" season was dictated by multiple factors: the region's climate and the associated public health threat of yellow fever, the calendars for planting and harvesting sugarcane and cotton, and the slave market to which all were tied. Between 1817 and 1905, yellow fever killed more than forty-one thousand people in the city, with especially severe outbreaks occurring in 1819, 1853, 1854, and 1855.[51] Out of fear, seasonal visitors and businessmen made New Orleans a cold-weather destination. "Strangers from every part of the union flock into the city, like birds of passage, to pass the winter and away again in the spring," explained the 1822 city directory.[52] Most visitors departed by May or June for less humid climes. On May 18, 1853, Lewis Webb, a young clerk from North Carolina, noted in his diary, "This afternoon as

I stood in the door [of my shop] crowds in carriages and on foot were hurrying to the Louisville & Cincinnati packets to take their departure. . . . Hundreds are leaving by every boat." Webb could not yet know that the 1853 outbreak would be the city's deadliest yellow-fever epidemic on record, killing nearly eight thousand people.[53] He was watching the city's seasonal visitors use their wealth to flee from the approaching scourge. While they were present in New Orleans, though, the metropolis thrived.

From the 1830s through the 1850s, the proliferation and density of coffee-houses and commercial exchanges served as one measure of New Orleans's exploding economy and the fluctuating population of white men that these businesses served. In these boisterous settings, businessmen dined and drank, read and shared news, gambled and played dominoes and billiards, boarded overnight, and bid at auctions. Coffeehouses in early modern England had served as premier sites for the auctions of books, art, and fabric, and even the display of exotic animals. In New Orleans, coffeehouse and exchange auctions sold slaves, land, animals, and agricultural equipment.[54] William Wells Brown, an enslaved man whom a speculator brought to New Orleans, recalled how "after the best of the gang was sold off [in a slave yard], the balance was taken to the Exchange coffee-house auction rooms, and sold at public auction."[55] The prevalence and popularity of these establishments evinced the casual ease with which customers thrust the fate of enslaved people into settings designed for dining, drinking, and socializing.

The volume and format of coffee consumption in antebellum New Orleans derived from the city's cultural, geographic, and economic ties. Distinct from the tea-sipping English colonists who settled in many Northeastern and Mid-Atlantic American colonies, early New Orleanians hailed from Continental European and Caribbean origins steeped in coffee.[56] Beginning in the early nineteenth century, imported green, or unroasted, coffee beans arrived at the New Orleans port in large quantities from plantations in the Caribbean and Brazil.[57] American visitors to the antebellum city found coffee brewed in strong, small servings, a legacy of similar preparations in Saint-Domingue, Cuba, Spain, and France. One American described the coffee that concluded a meal at his boardinghouse, writing in his diary in 1835, "The last round of dinner is a cup of coffee, of smallest size, but it is pure coffee, no milk."[58] Another part-year resident—an expatriate lawyer from New York—wrote to a friend back home to instruct him on the art of preparing coffee Crescent City–style. The lawyer had learned to roast his own Mocha and Java "grains" in a ratio of 1:2—"brown, not black, for in the latter case you would obtain a decoction of charcoal only"—then pour boiling water over the grounds in a biggin, a French-style coffee pot. The grounds would absorb two-thirds of the water, and the other third would filter through. "This third will be nectar," the lawyer promised, and should be mixed with boiling milk.[59]

Some of the coffeehouses in antebellum New Orleans were luxurious, indicating the elevated status of their patrons and the work they accomplished within. The centerpiece of Bank's Arcade—a complex of offices, shops, billiard rooms, "coffee rooms, and a restaurant" on bustling Magazine Street, close to the levees—was "the grand coffee room," one hundred feet long and sixty feet wide, with ceilings of thirty-five feet. Combined with the building's upper gallery, the room could purportedly host five thousand men. "A person may very well pass the whole twenty-four hours under the roof of [the Arcade]," marveled the author of the 1838 city directory, "nor desire other means, either of repose, excitement, pleasure, or food either for mind or body."[60] Some travelers seemed to do just that. A man named Luc Thevenin named a coffeehouse as his primary address in the 1842 city directory, instructing, "Enquire at coffee house corner St. Louis st. and Exchange alley."[61] Within the coffeehouse's walls, commercial transactions and social interactions went undistinguished in terms of time and space, inserting the commodification of people into the rhythms of daily life.

City directories showed how these coffeehouses—and the transactions, relationships, and refreshments they proffered—wove themselves into the commercial geography of antebellum New Orleans as the metropolis grew. The 1811, 1822, 1832, and 1842 city directories tracked a sharp increase in the number of establishments, from six coffeehouses in 1811 to nineteen in 1822, approximately fifty-seven in 1832, and nearly four hundred in 1842.[62] From an initial cluster in the French Quarter, coffeehouses expanded along New Orleans's upriver crescent. The wedge of blocks between Canal and Poydras Streets, dominated by American businessmen and home to the magnificent St. Charles Hotel beginning in 1837 as well as the city's largest concentration of slave yards, demonstrated a significant growth in coffee saloons. Elsewhere, addresses on Old Levee, New Levee, and Tchoupitoulas Streets referenced booming riverfront activity. Other coffeehouses opened at sites close to public markets and other prominent commercial establishments.[63] H. Rinne operated a coffeehouse in 1842 "near the Orleans Cotton Press." In the same year, Joseph Moreu served coffee "below the Louisiana Sugar Refinery."[64] Coffeehouses clustered in constellations around preexisting institutions and generated traffic and energy that in turn grew new businesses.

Notwithstanding New Orleanians' longtime preference for coffee, many visitors pointed out that the city's coffeehouses invariably served something stronger. "Nobody ever saw anything drunk in these 'coffee houses' except spirits," quipped one local reporter. "Though their usual denomination is 'coffee-house,' they have no . . . right to such a distinction," agreed another writer. He noted newspaper-reading customers sipping juleps and negus, a warm punch of port, sugar, and spices, and "assisting their comprehension of abstruse paragraphs by hot 'coffee,' alias warm punch and slings."[65] They had good company in their thirst. Myriad travelers and journalists documented antebellum New Orleans as awash in alcohol, at levee grog shops, coffee-houses, hotels and boardinghouses, exchanges, and street-side stands.[66] One 1836 visitor gaped at a grog shop packed with customers only to spy another "next door, and at the next corner, and at the corner above that, and below it, and between the said corners, and across the street, and in the next street . . . and so on *ad infinitum*."[67] Grog shops seemed to repeat and reflect on New Orleans blocks as in a hall of mirrors. Sailors, tourists, and wintering business-people sipped from the ever-flowing stream. "The process of *liquoring* is gone through several times before a bargain is struck," one traveler described, of a pair of businessmen on the New Orleans levee reaching a deal.[68] For those who tippled and bid at New Orleans auctions, alcohol surely inspired wagers, celebrated victories, and assuaged losses. It also led to sloppiness.

Barred from indulging in alcohol themselves, some bondspeople used the intoxication of white men to their advantage, seizing on the vulnerability caused by inebriation to take the upper hand in some dealings.[69] After escaping from his enslaver in Georgia and fleeing to New Orleans, John Brown engaged a man on the street near the St. Charles Hotel. "I . . . almost ran up against the man whom I felt I wanted most at that moment," Brown wrote later in his autobiography. Brown's calculating perspective was more expected of the buyer in a slave auction than of the item offered for sale. "He . . . walked lazily, with rather an irregular step. I observed that he looked sleepy, and that his eyes were blood-shotten and puffy." Brown appraised the man and made his choice. "I set him down in my mind for a gambler and a drunkard . . . and I concluded he might want money." Brown convinced the man to sell him to Theophilus Freeman, who ran a notorious slave yard nearby.

Brown's position could not have seemed more disadvantaged—he had run away from his enslaver and crossed state lines, entering the belly of the nation's slave-selling beast. Nevertheless, his calculated exploitation of a white man's inebriation enabled him to bend his path in the direction he desired, even if more hardship lay ahead.[70] Once inside the pen, Brown hung back when being considered by prospective buyers in part "because I did not care to speak for myself," he recalled. He stayed there three months. Brown wanted to be sold in the direction of Mississippi and, upon hearing that buyers would be arriving from there, "I determined to pick one out." That "one" would be Jepsey James, a Mississippi man in a "shabby blanket coat" who purchased

John Brown in Freeman's auction room. Ahead of Brown waited the horrors of James's cotton fields: hampers heavy with white fluff, up to 160 pounds to pick each day, and the bullwhip, "as limber and lithesome as a snake," for those who slowed, even pregnant women.[71] Brown's sale changed the course of his life. But from the viewpoint of an auction attendee, his sale was one among many others.

Transactions that destroyed families and sent people to their deaths occurred casually and constantly in antebellum New Orleans. They took place in large yards that held hundreds of people, in small showrooms, and in exchanges, coffeehouses, and hotels throughout the city. Tourists watched slave sales as a form of amusement, even before luxury venues like the St. Louis or St. Charles Hotels existed. In early 1835, New Englander Edward Russell passed through New Orleans on his way to the Red River region of northeast Texas, where he hoped to profit from land speculation. Russell noted in his diary on January 26, 1835, that he had purchased oranges and oysters and judged New Orleans to be "a wonderful place for business & dissipation." On January 31, he wrote, "This forenoon saw slaves sold at Auction at 10, 11 & 12.00 $ each"; then he got his hair cut and purchased saddlebags and a powder flask for his journey. In a pattern of thought visible in New Orleans's earliest newspapers and travelogues, this visitor affirmed the banality of auctioned humans amongst myriad other transactions within the daily routine of antebellum New Orleans.[72]

When Russell boarded a steamboat the following afternoon, bound upriver past sugarcane fields and views of enslaved workers burning cane stubble, he left in his wake a city approaching its zenith in terms of riches and population.[73] By 1840, New Orleans was the wealthiest city in the United States and the third-largest, a destination for those who dreamt of striking it rich and spending those riches on sensory luxuries.[74] The consuming ties that bound Louisiana's cane and cotton fields to auction halls, dining rooms, coffeehouses, and kitchens, near and far, had woven a web of extraordinary riches. Such plenitude grew out of the labors of people in bondage. Nowhere was this fact on more celebratory display than in the city's fine hotels, which fused eating, drinking, and the commodification of people into the linchpins of New Orleans's identity.

Champagne, Sugar, and Slaves for Sale in New Orleans's "Palace Hotels"

"I believe I had rather see this St. Charles Hotel than any other single house I ever saw," declared Eugene Davis in February 1847. Traveling from his home in Charlottesville, Virginia, to Galveston, Texas, Davis had paused in New Orleans during the city's winter business and social season. He wrote letters to his mother-in-law and wife to describe the delights that drew businessmen to the St. Charles and St. Louis Hotels, the city's grandest luxury establishments. "The spiral staircase descends from the top of the building, like a big corkscrew, right plump into the centre of the rotunda," Davis wrote of the St. Charles, in the city's American sector. The hotel struck this newcomer as a corked bottle of champagne, buzzing with the energy and appetites of the men who filled it. "Some of the meats at table are always boiled in Champaign," Davis continued. "And the molasses . . . is manufactured expressly for this table. It is the essence of the finest loaf sugar—of which there is a copious deposit at the bottom of the jar." A ten-minute walk away, the French Quarter's St. Louis Hotel offered marvels, too: a ballroom illuminated by five chandeliers, each with "100 candles with 10,000 prismatic spangles to reflect and multiply their light" onto mirrors, curtains, balconies, carpets, cushions, and revelers.[75] To this amazed visitor, New Orleans was a cup running over—a glut of food, drink, and material wonders.

American hotels of the mid-nineteenth century functioned as economic, cultural, and culinary institutions that pitted cities against each other in contests of wealth and refinement. Visiting in the 1830s, an American writer assessed the Crescent City's Bishop's Hotel in comparison to others he had experienced, writing, "The Tremont [in Boston] possesses more architectural elegance; and Barnum's, the pride of Baltimore, is a handsomer structure." New Orleans's Bishop's Hotel distinguished itself with its barroom, the writer decided, which was "universally allowed to be the most splendid in America."[76] Across the country, grand hotels mapped where Americans were beginning to travel for business and pleasure: Astor House in New York City, Planter's House Hotel in St. Louis, the Galt House Hotel in Louisville, Kentucky, and the St. Charles and St. Louis Hotels in New Orleans, among others. These institutions defined the standards of elegance for a nation whose richest residents were learning how to consume conspicuously on new public stages. As metropolitan boosters throughout the nation scrutinized population counts and average temperatures to rank cities as the largest, richest, or most healthful, luxury hotels stood as brick-and-mortar expressions of cities' success, or at least their aspirations.[77]

New Orleans's leaders spared no expense in this realm. "By far the most splendid and the most costly of the edifices in New Orleans, are not . . . the public buildings . . . but the hotels," observed one visitor in 1839.[78] Such an investment spoke to the city's reliance on travelers and locals alike, who packed hotels' barrooms and sumptuously decorated dining rooms.[79] The Verandah

Hotel's dining room was "probably one of the highest finished apartments in America," touted the city directory. There, diners supped under "three beautiful Elliptic domes for chandeliers." The Strangers' Hotel could accommodate 150 guests for breakfast and dinner, which "for excellence in viands, wines and attendance . . . is unsurpassed in the United States," raved the same writer. Two hundred gentlemen could dine at the Orleans Hotel, even if only half that number could sleep in its beds.[80] None of these institutions could compete, however, with two monumental new hotels that drew international renown for the dining, drinking, and traffic in human beings that happened under their roofs.

The St. Charles and the St. Louis Hotels, which opened in 1837 and 1838, were the two suns around which New Orleans's American and Creole universes turned. The businesses supercharged the region's economy, despite cultural and political polarization between New Orleans's francophone, Catholic, Creole old guard and American transplants, who were largely English-speaking and Protestant. Animosity between the city's Creole and American populations split New Orleans into three municipalities from 1836 to 1852, within the larger context of deepening national and sectional divisions (fig. 1.3). Each municipality housed its own government, schools, churches, public spaces, and flagship public buildings.[81] The St. Louis and St. Charles Hotels defined the cultural identities of the First and Second Municipalities, respectively, as districts where Creole and American businessmen worked and their wives and daughters played. Both hotels were palatial complexes housing bedrooms, barrooms, public baths, dining rooms, ballrooms, commercial exchanges, and private shops.

Distinct from other luxurious American hotels, the St. Charles and St. Louis Hotels hosted slave auctions as prominent public events. Inseparable from the dining and drinking in which visitors indulged at these same establishments, auctions carved a singular niche for these hotels in the region's economy and social world, and in the imaginations—or nightmares—of those far beyond it. Some businesses elsewhere in the nation, such as the London Coffee House in late eighteenth-century Philadelphia, also auctioned bondspeople, but in most places, these transactions remained inaccessible to passersby. In New Orleans, the auctions, banquets, and barroom indulgences at the St. Charles and St. Louis drew hordes of planters, traders, reporters, tourists, and horrified abolitionists like moths to a flame.[82] There, all manner of insatiable appetites were laid bare, sated, and exposed again. Each establishment exerted a gravitational pull on the people and businesses in their orbits. "I can never forget those marvelous two blocks upon St. Charles street, running from the great hotel towards Lafayette Square," reminisced one traveler of the vicin-

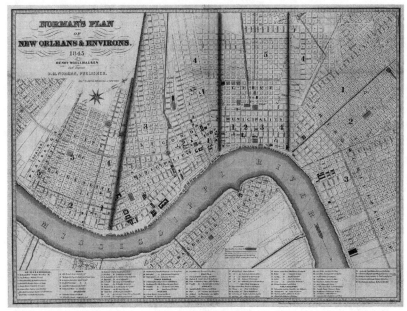

FIGURE 1.3. In mid-nineteenth-century New Orleans's First and Second Municipalities, businessmen blended work and leisure in a proliferating array of coffeehouses, exchanges, and luxurious hotels. Henry Möllhausen, engaged by Shields & Hammond, *Norman's Plan of New Orleans & Environs, 1845* (n.p.: B. M. Norman, 1845), colored map, 39 x 61 cm. Library of Congress, Geography and Map Division, Washington, DC, https://www.loc.gov/item/98687133/.

ity of the St. Charles Hotel in the 1840s. They were "redolent of oysters and lunches, juleps and punches . . . [and] filled with the echoes of falling tenpins and clicking billiard balls."[83] The sights, sounds, and tastes of New Orleans had imprinted themselves on his memories, and at their center was a grand hotel.

Occupying most of the city block bounded by St. Charles, Gravier, Carondelet, and Common Streets in the American sector, the St. Charles Hotel (also called the "Exchange Hotel," or "American Exchange") fixed itself in the impressions of many Crescent City visitors. Echoing prominent public and political buildings elsewhere in the United States and Europe, the hotel's neoclassical design proclaimed grandeur, order, and refinement for this New Orleans institution, too.[84] One English tourist called the St. Charles "the largest and handsomest hotel in the world."[85] Flaunting a symmetrical array of columns, granite, and marble, the building's façade fronted 350 guest rooms and an octagonal structure at its core. The hotel's most striking feature: a grand dome, measuring more than two hundred feet from the ground to the top of its flagstaff. The dome defined the New Orleans skyline for more than a decade—

FIGURE 1.4. With its enormous size and neoclassical design, the St. Charles Hotel towered over nearby buildings and pedestrians. Inside were women's and gentlemen's dining rooms and a lavish barroom, host to auctions of enslaved people. Lilienthal's Photographic Establishment, *St. Charles Hotel, New Orleans, La.*, ca. 1869, photographic print on stereo card. Library of Congress, Washington, DC, https://www.loc.gov/item/2005676078/.

until the hotel burned in 1851 and was rebuilt without it—and offered visitors at its summit the thrill of gazing down at the city and river with a birds-eye view.[86] Even dome-less, the second iteration of the St. Charles, which opened in 1853, awed visitors (fig. 1.4). "It is by far the most elegant hotel I ever saw," raved Lewis Webb, a young clerk from rural North Carolina. "The exterior appearance of the building is beautiful in style & archatecture [*sic*]—with the most perfect & harmonious proportions," he described in his diary, "and the interior arrangement is on a style more magnificent & elegant—than any hotel in the U.S. I spent more than an hour looking at this palace hotel."[87]

Despite its orderly façade, the St. Charles rose at great human cost on unsound foundations, presaging the nature of the transactions that would take place under its roof.[88] "The progress of the building was much retarded the first summer by the number of deaths that occurred among the workmen from sun stroke or yellow fever," wrote James Gallier, the hotel's Irish-born architect, in his memoir. "The loss of life from these causes was truly appalling." Architects and the tradespeople they employed could not avoid New Orleans in spring and summer, Gallier explained, given that most construction happened during those seasons. Dangers lurked below ground as well. "The soil of the lower part of Louisiana . . . may be literally said to be afloat," Gallier described. The foundations of his enormous hotel sank two and a half feet into the ground, a foot farther than he had projected, before coming to rest. The construction of the St. Charles took more than three years, during

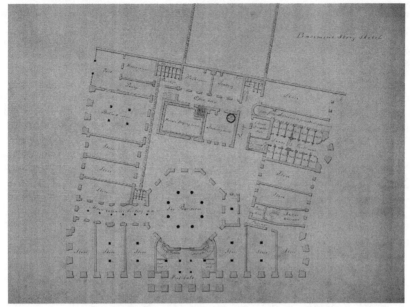

FIGURE 1.5. An octagonal barroom—site of drunken carousing and slave auctions—served as the literal and figurative foundation of New Orleans's St. Charles Hotel. George Purves, "Basement Story Sketch for the Saint Charles Hotel," 1851–1852. L. Kemper and Leila Moore Williams Founders Collection, no. 1959.26.5, The Historic New Orleans Collection.

which time Gallier contracted yellow fever and recovered. The monumental building opened finally in 1837.[89]

Encoded in the design of the St. Charles Hotel was the critical importance of drinking and dining and their proximity to—if not coincidence with—the auction of enslaved people. Architectural plans show how these activities entwined in real space (fig. 1.5). A guest on his way to bid at a St. Charles Hotel auction could pass through the structure's columned vestibule on St. Charles Street, look left to supply himself from the small cigar shop or right to the newspaper shop, pass curving flights of stairs up to the saloon, or proceed forward through doors leading to the barroom. Another guest could access the hotel's barroom from Gravier Street. The architect's plan shows a meandering line of script with an arrow instructing, "*Main entrance leading to => The Bar-room,*" past four narrow WCs positioned for the comfort of a customer imbibing. As he entered the barroom, the smells and noises of the city streets receded behind him. Before him was a temple to profit and the pleasures of its pursuit. There, one visitor observed, "Emperor Appetite and King Alcohol hold their court in a most recherché style."[90]

Embedded in the center of the St. Charles Hotel's lower level, the barroom anchored the monumental building that unfolded around and above it. Seventy feet wide with ceilings of twenty feet, the octagonal space featured "an interior circular range of Ionic columns," described the city directory, "distributed so as to support the weight of the floors and partitions of the upper stories."[91] Gallier remembered the bar that he had designed as "an extensive counter . . . constantly supplied with various kinds of eatables, furnished gratis to any one who chose to pay for one of those drinks or compounds for which American bar-rooms are celebrated."[92] Day and night, the room was populated by "hundreds of steady, conscientious lovers of lunches and liquors . . . clustering by pillar and column in social meriment [*sic*]," wrote one traveler, as well as barkeepers, auctioneers, and auctioned things and people.[93]

A *New York Daily Tribune* reporter who observed one auction of enslaved people in the St. Charles barroom in April 1861 described the discordance of a boisterous crowd of two hundred men carousing while bidding on twenty-four men, women, and children. "The marble bar, which covers the rear sides of the apartment, was doing a brisk business," the reporter wrote, with "three attendants being kept active to supply with bibulants the noisy groups before it, which sent forth a confused sound of conversation, laughter, and the clinking of glasses. The cigar stand . . . was also doing a lively trade." Auctions at the St. Charles took place several times a week, with multiple sales, some concurrent, on Saturdays. Vastly outnumbered by the hungry and thirsty crowd, which included women at a finer venue such as this one, bondspeople stood in a line waiting to be sold, their lot numbers pinned to their clothing. Attendees clutched "printed lists of the negroes" as if they were playbills and listened to the auctioneer's calls. Some bidders seemed intoxicated, the reporter noted, with "bleared eyes, significant of recent dissipation."[94]

On this day in April 1861, about a year before New Orleans would fall to Union forces, bidders at the St. Charles Hotel drank as they purchased the labor and lives of children. The reporter described the scene. Humans sold included "slight, nimble-looking" Lewis, a twelve-year-old field hand; Minerva, a "serious visaged" sixteen-year-old field hand, wearing a colorful head kerchief; fifteen-year-old Emma; and twelve-year-old Catherine, "a mere child." Betty, fifteen, held her four-month-old son, who "tossed his round head about," surely confused and frightened by the shouts and smells around him. Mary, eighteen, clutched the hand of her four-year-old "mulatto" son, who "was crying bitterly, in affright at the crowd, and nestled up to her, hiding his head in the folds of her dress." Attendees also bought Sarah, Phil, Derry, Will, Joe, Jack, and Penny and her child. So, too, for $695, an unnamed middle-aged woman house servant, bilingual in French and English. The reporter watched two men "manipulate[e] the arms, shoulders, and breasts of Clara" and laugh before an attendee purchased her for a discounted price, due to a lump—"not larger than a peccan-nut [sic]"—on her neck. Allen, a thirty-one-year-old field hand; another man named Allen, a thirty-year-old field hand and drayman; forty-one-year-old Tup; and Eldred, a thirty-one-year-old cook, stood on the block as the auctioneer called out numbers, goading the gawking crowds to reply. The four young men attracted no bids, though, and were withdrawn.[95] Throughout these transactions, bartenders mixed and served cocktails, and money changed hands. Noise, smoke, and smells hung among the columns.

If the columns of the St. Charles Hotel's barroom functioned as structural support for the building, the room played a symbolic role, too, as a generator of New Orleans's reputation for intemperance and contagious profligacy. In the eyes of pro-temperance and abolitionist critics, travelers who stepped into this place were taking a fateful step on a slippery moral slope. "Many a 'Man about town' lived nearly altogether at this, or at other bar-rooms," wrote the architect Gallier of the room that he had designed, "and frequently cut short his life by habits of intemperance, first acquired and afterwards kept up by establishments of this description."[96] Seasonal visitors first sampled New Orleans's theaters and balls, another observer recorded. Then, "From the first false step to the second, the descent is soon made. The bar-rooms of the hotels next become their haunts; smoking and drinking follows; a Quadroon mistress . . . is next taken; and habits of betting, racing, and gambling crown the whole," the writer charted. "Such is the painful history of many a young New Englander coming to New Orleans for health and pleasure; and returning home a dissipated rake."[97] In the St. Charles barroom in particular, temperance advocates found an easy target for their anxieties. "The receipts of the bar at the St. Charles Hotel . . . pay the expenses of the entire establishment," gaped Boston's *Liberator* in 1846, amounting to an average of $100 every hour or *"six to eight hundred dollars per day!"*[98]

Drinking and bidding at St. Charles Hotel auctions fueled voracious appetites for food, too. On the hotel's principal story, the Gentlemen's Ordinary and Parlor stretched nearly the entire depth of the hotel, illuminated by a row of windows overlooking Gravier Street, a major commercial spine (fig. 1.6). Newcomers marveled at the frenetic activity in the men's dining room. "The door opens. A hum of voices and a clash of knives and forks and spoons salute you stunningly. What is the occasion? A gala day? A public dinner?" one observer teased his reader. "Nothing but the gentlemen's *ordinary* of the hotel!" This crowd of hundreds "appear[ed] and disappear[ed] day by day, relentlessly eating and drinking." The writer recalled "those fresh from the gombo [sic] soup, and the ham, and the punch and julep, rushing back again, unable to be tormented by the mere looking on." Antebellum New Orleans derived

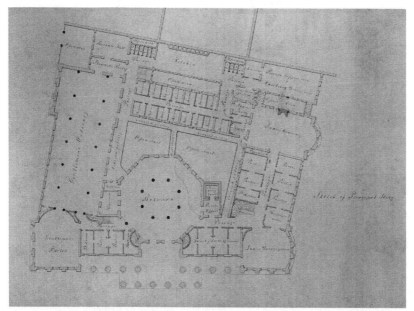

FIGURE 1.6. The large size of the Gentlemen's Ordinary at the St. Charles Hotel communicated the centrality of dining to patrons' experiences there as well as the fact that men greatly outnumbered women within the hotel's walls. George Purves, "Sketch of Principle [sic] Story for St. Charles Hotel," 1851–1852. L. Kemper and Leila Moore Williams Founders Collection, no. 1959.26.4, The Historic New Orleans Collection.

its hedonistic reputation from experiences of continuous, excessive consumption, whether in the context of a planter who cycled between buying slaves and selling sugar in order to buy more slaves, or the banquet overflowing with molasses and champagne that that same planter devoured following a sale. Reflecting on his hours at the St. Charles, the writer confessed, "I tremble to think of the juleps, and punches, and nogs, and soups, and plates of fish, and game, and beef and loaves of bread."[99] His body felt their pull long after his departure.

Menus from the Gentlemen's Ordinary of the St. Charles specified the textures, colors, aromas, and flavors of this gluttony. "The dishes . . . were almost numberless," another traveler recalled of the St. Charles's culinary offerings, "and the bill of fare . . . bore resemblance to a miniature gazette."[100] On June 14, 1848, diners in the Gentlemen's Ordinary of the St. Charles chose from dozens of dishes that drew from New Orleans's vast trade networks, Americans' fascination with French cuisine, and regional ingredients (figs. 1.7 and 1.8). Soups, boiled and roast meat and fowl, entrées, vegetables, and pastry and dessert were the order of this omnivorous feast. Boiled buffalo tongue and Fulton Market beef pointed to origins west and north, whereas the shrimp of

FIGURE 1.7. This menu from the St. Charles Hotel—dating to a decade after the hotel opened, when it still sported its grand dome—offered an extensive array of dishes and libations even during the establishment's slow summer season. St. Charles Hotel, "Bill of Fare," June 14, 1848, recto. MSS 411.2, The Historic New Orleans Collection.

LIST OF WINES,
AT THE
ST. CHARLES HOTEL.

MADEIRA.

London Dock	$1 00	Yellow Seal Monteiro	$3 00
Williams' Madeira	1 50	Wanderer	3 00
Do. Do. pints	75	Old E. & Lazock, blank seal, bottle	$4 00
Webster	1 50	racked	
Henry Clay	2 00	John Lilton, N. O. 1825	4 00
Howard, March & Co., 1825	2 00	Red Seal Theweliss, bottle racked, over 20 years old	4 00
Newton, Gordon & Murdock	3 00	W. India	4 00
Oliveira's Reserve	2 50	Old Brazil	4 00
May Flower	2 50	Old Virginia Mecheodes	4 00
Leal & Aurelio	2 50	Welsh's Old Reserve	4 00
Joy, 1834	4 00	Monteiro's bottled in Madeira, has been 2 1/2 years to the E. India	5 00
Madeira	2 00	
The Tasters, light simple and delicate	3 00	Wed'g	5 00
Grade, 1820	5 00	Trockerinth's	7 00
East India Brandy	3 00	Governor's, Philips' Several	10 00

SHERRY.

Williams' Pale	$1 00	Sayres' Amontillado	$2 50
Sayres O. S. Gold	1 50	Echecopar's Superior	2 50
O. S. Pale	1 50	Lacave & Echecopar's	3 00
Harmony Pale	1 50	St. Charles Imperial	4 00
Y Pale	1 50	Royal William Sherry	3 00
Manzinella	2 00	Old Ysnte, Brown, 1825	3 00
Topaz Amontillado	3 00	Old Ronaro, 1799	3 00
Gordon's Pale	2 00	Gorgon's Imperial Brown	4 00
Echecopar's Pale	2 00	Imperial Gold	4 00
Sayres Anchor Pale	2 00	Julian Johnson (of Cadiz) Imperial Pale	4 00
Faber & Co.	2 00	Jenny Lind	4 00
Ysnte, 1825	3 00	

PORT.

London Dock	$1 00	Demi John Port	$2 50
Smith & Co., (old Port)	1 50	Parker's Rh	2 50
Hunt & Co. bottled in Oporto	2 00	Roger's Imperial White, something rare	3 00
Faber & Co	2 00	Imperial Port	3 00

CHAMPAGNE.

Maltese Cross (Faber & Co.)	$2 00	Reisaur	$2 00
Do. do. pints	1 25	Heidsieck	2 00
Schreider, quarts	2 00	Do. pints	1 25
Schreider, pints	1 25	Bollinger	2 00
Star	2 00	Do. Pints	1 25
Star, pints	1 25	Clicquot	2 00

SAUTERNE.

Haut Sauterne, Y Quense, superior	$1 50	Lacrymae Christa, very superior	2 50
Do. Do. Do. Do. pints	75	Barsac	1 50

CLARETS.

St. Julian	$0 50	Rooker's Chateau Lafite	$1 50
Margeaux Medoc	1 00	Chateau Pauyps	2 00
Chateau La Rose	1 25	Chateau Lafaut, very superior	2 00
Fontes Canet	1 25	Haut Brien	2 50
pints	75	Chateaus, (very superior)	2 50
		Chateau Margeaux, 1834, very superior	3 00

BURGUNDY.

Chambertin qts., Burgundy	$2 00	Hermitage	2 00
		Volnay	2 00

HOCK.

Hockheimer, 1834	$1 50	Marvobrunner	
Geisenheimer	1 50	Sparkling Hock, Superior	$3 00
Dom Dechnei, 1836	1 50	Do. do. Johannesberger	3 00
Dom Prosseg or 1825	2 00	Hockheimer Dom Bechnei, 1834	3 00
Sparkling Hock, Hockheimer	3 00	Steinberger Cabinet, very superior	4 00
Rudesheimer	3 00	Rudesheimer Berg	4 00

French Liqueurs, 40—London Porter, 50 cents—Scotch Ale, 50 cents—Pints Porter and Ale 25 cts.
N. B. Gentlemen ordering WINE and not designating the particular kind, will be served at $2 per bottle.
N. B. Gentlemen drinking their own Wine will be charged corkage 50 cents on Claret, $1 for other Wines.

EXTRA DINNER, $1 00.
Printed at the office of the Picayune, 66 Camp street.

FIGURE 1.8. St. Charles Hotel, "Bill of Fare," June 14, 1848, verso. New Orleans Hotel collection, MSS 411.2, The Historic New Orleans Collection.

Crevettes au naturel, pecans, figs, sweet potatoes, rice, snap beans, and ocra [*sic*] surely came from local waters, orchards, and soils. *Escalopes de Veau sautés aux champignons*, scalloped veal sautéed with mushrooms, and *Poitrine de Mouton à la jardinière*, mutton breast with garden vegetables, conveyed a Continental sophistication to diners who read culinary French. The oranges, pineapples, and bananas featured as dessert trumpeted the kitchen's proximity to the port. So too did the varieties of Madeira, sherry, port, and Hock that filled a full-page wine menu and stocked the Wine Room, for diners whose thirsts matched their appetites. A note at the bottom of the menu alerted diners to the closing times of the Eastern, Coast, and Lake mails. This note, plus the appearance of *beignet*[*s*] *soufflés*, a fried treat popularized by African-born street vendors, tagged this bill of fare as distinctly of New Orleans.[101]

Implicit in many travelers' descriptions of antebellum hotel ordinaries and barrooms was the detail that most of these institutions focused on a narrow set of customers: white men. A male visitor in the 1840s described how so many men thronged the St. Charles that "it takes one a long time to find [acquaintances] . . . in the crowd at the hotel."[102] A white woman raised in New Orleans agreed on the gender imbalance in the public life of the antebellum city. "There were no restaurants, no lunch counters, no tea rooms, and . . . no woman's exchange, no place in the whole city where a lady could drop in," she recalled. "No doubt there were myriads of cabarets and eating places for men on pleasure or business bent." If unaccompanied, wealthy white women visitors shopped for clothes, walked and rode for pleasure, attended church services, and otherwise stayed largely within the bounds of private homes.[103]

New Orleans's grandest hotels offered exceptions to this standard, hosting settings where white women could socialize in public, though often separately from men. Gallier's plan of the basement story of the St. Charles included an entrance for ladies on Common Street as well as a door leading to hot and cold baths for women and men. Upstairs, on the hotel's principal story, a Ladies Drawingroom offered space to sit. A woman guest was more likely to be found in the Ladies Ordinary, though—positioned on the opposite side of the building from the Gentlemen's Ordinary and measuring less than one-third its size. The strike of a gong summoned women out of their rooms to each meal, remembered a visiting Englishwoman. Women's devotion to eating and drinking derived from boredom and inattention, the visitor speculated. "The ladies here see but little of their husbands. . . . All day the husband is absent attending to his everlasting business."[104]

Businessmen rushed to eat, drink, and cut deals in New Orleans because they understood their season there to be short. Similarly, the constricted time frame of a winter stay inspired visiting white women to revel in the city as a place of escape and social release. "In home circles in large cities, a kind of conventional barrier is erected around a fashionable woman," explained one American, following her visit to New Orleans in the late 1850s. "But where everybody comes and goes in a month, and memory will not stoop to record the flirtings and coquettings of the hour, there is no time to build up these artificial fences." Not just businessmen, then, but their wives and daughters, too, experienced antebellum New Orleans as a time and place apart from typical social norms—a sensation that travelers craved, then and in years to come. Describing the effervescent energy of vacationing women at the St. Charles, the 1850s visitor reached for a familiar comparison. "The drawingrooms and the broad halls of the hotel become an unobstructed area for the display of every whim or caprice born in a pretty woman's brain," she wrote, "like bubbles in the bright champagne."[105]

Similar scenes of breakfasting, flirting, and coquetting—or terror, depending on whether one reclined at table or stood on the auction block—played out in the St. Louis Hotel, the French Quarter peer of the St. Charles. Designed by French-born architect J. N. B. de Pouilly and completed in 1838, the St. Louis Hotel served as the culturally French and Creole competitor to the American-dominated St. Charles Hotel. Businessmen and revelers who stumbled down the narrow passageway of Exchange Alley found themselves spit out onto the St. Louis Hotel's doorstep on St. Louis Street. Climbing a short flight of stairs, they passed through a rectangular vestibule forested with neoclassical columns to the hotel's main entrance (fig. 1.9). Inside, luxuries awaited: a two-hundred-person hotel, a bank, the French (or "City") Exchange, shops, dining rooms, baths, and ballrooms. On the second story, men ate in a dining room with a commanding view of Royal Street.[106]

Historic architectural plans offer an omniscient perspective on these buildings that no longer stand, elevating one's viewpoint to a remove far above the ballrooms, dining rooms, and passageways where guests danced and ate and servants worked. What might the tangible, on-the-ground experiences of moving through these spaces have been like, though, for enslavers and enslaved? Similar to the way in which a menu from the St. Charles Hotel spelled out the aromas and flavors associated with cooking, serving, and dining there, the faint longhand of a notary's inventory enumerated the lustrous textures, shapes, and shine of the St. Louis Hotel's material world. An 1843 inventory of the St. Louis Hotel's contents—created in the aftermath of an 1840 fire and speedy reconstruction—catalogued the luxuries of this institution, where many labored so that some could play. With this inventory, the material contents of the St. Louis Hotel became better documented than the identities of the establishment's free and enslaved workers.

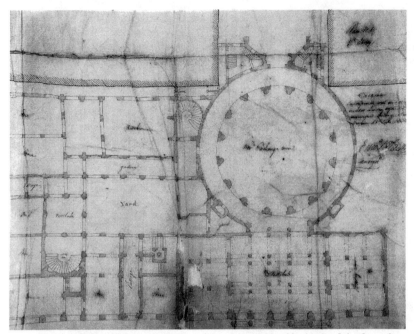

FIGURE 1.9. This plan of the principal story of the St. Louis Hotel highlighted the discordant experiences this building offered to those entering its doors. Enslaved people were held in the Yard before being led through back passages to the Exchange, to be auctioned beneath the cavernous dome. Guests, in contrast, passed through the columned grandeur of the St. Louis Street vestibule into the rotunda. Improvement Company of New Orleans with Edward W. Sewell, "Plan No. 1, 1ˢᵗ Story," St. Louis Hotel plan, F. Grima, 7: 504, September 28, 1835. Courtesy Hon. Chelsey Richard Napoleon, Clerk of Civil District Court, Parish of Orleans, New Orleans Notarial Archives.

Specifying the nature and dimensions of the St. Louis Hotel's opulence exposes the scale of riches produced by New Orleans's trades in sugar, cotton, and slaves and details the environment in which their sales were transacted and celebrated. Within the St. Louis Hotel's drawing rooms, ballroom, and dining rooms in 1843, a notary counted more than 140 wool and cotton rugs and ten sets of "beautiful and fine" drapes, which softened the footsteps and flirtations of guests. Before and after a meal, lodgers had many places to rest: 176 cane chairs, ten mahogany sofas and two rosewood sofas, horsehair and mahogany chairs, and velour and rosewood seats. "While the men are enjoying the delights of this luxurious bar-room, the women employ themselves in dressing elaborately several times a day, and sitting in the gorgeous and extensive drawing-rooms," described one woman traveler of the St. Louis. Patrons rested their feet on seven rosewood ottomans as they listened to a musician play on the rosewood piano or as they glanced at one of the two mahogany-framed clocks. When they tired, they could retire to their bedrooms and sleep on mattresses cushioned with bolsters and pillows, under red or blue wool blankets, protected by muslin mosquito nets. All these things created experiences and textures of ease and comfort.[107]

Especially impressive was the vast equipage required at table and in the barroom of the St. Louis Hotel: the crystal and glass forms of insatiable thirsts. These items signaled the establishment's focus on single male travelers and their dedication to drinking and dining.[108] The notary tabulated a portion of the hotel's glassware in October 1843 as follows:

Glassware, etc.
50 dark green crystal Hock glasses
11 light green crystal Hock glasses
16 4/12 dozen glass drinking glasses
28 crystal champagne glasses
23 crystal beer glasses
14 3/12 dozen crystal wine glasses
3 3/12 dozen crystal liqueur glasses
26 8/12 dozen small crystal wine glasses
44 blue crystal finger bowls . . .
43 plain glasses for the bedrooms
3 crystal wine carafes
4 colored crystal Hock carafes
21 crystal liqueur carafes
17 carafes belonging to the Bar Room . . .[109]

Enslaved and free servants filled and refilled these glasses and carafes. They cleaned and dried them to be free of water spots and lint. They stored them and swept up their shards after intoxicated guests knocked them to the floor. These workers also polished the hotel's German silver and fine silver: dozens of spoons (for soup, dessert, salt, sauce, mustard, cheese), sugar tongs, eight nutcrackers plated with fine silver, and one silver wine syphon (fig. 1.10). These were the material remains of ephemeral meals—the greasy, soiled things that littered the tables after fish, fruit, and puddings had disappeared into bellies.

The notary's inventory hints, too, at the very different objects that laborers touched and used when they were not working. The nature and numbers of these items point to the gulf between guests and servants in New Orleans's hotels—between onstage pleasures and offstage life. In contrast to 170 *"toile à Russie"* bedsheets for guests, the hotel stocked thirty-eight cotton bedsheets for servants. The hotel's seven "commonplace" drapes may have shaded their

FIGURE 1.10. Enslaved servants used these silver-alloy serving spoons to fill diners' plates in the St. Louis Hotel. F. Curtis and Co., St. Louis Hotel spoon set, 1848–1854. L. Kemper and Leila Moore Williams Founders Collection, no. 1957.89.1-7, The Historic New Orleans Collection.

rooms from the Louisiana sun. Places where workers could sit were scarce and simple. The notary counted only three benches, four folding seats, and four tables for servants, all of locally available cypress wood.[110] Such a short, simple list reflected the reality that laborers were nearly always on their feet at the St. Louis Hotel, serving those who rested in the mahogany, cane, horsehair, velour, and rosewood seats and sofas.

The material contents of the St. Louis and St. Charles Hotels, then, when situated within the specific architecture of the two establishments, gave tangible form to the theatrical extravagance of consuming and consumption in New Orleans. The designs of both hotels invited patrons to pass from exterior to interior, up staircases and through doorways that revealed tableaux of objects to appraise and enjoy, if not buy. Indeed, one former slave broker remembered, "The rotunda of the old St. Louis Hotel . . . was the theatre of these sales." Photographs taken before and during the eventual demolition of

FIGURE 1.11. By fall 1915, abandonment and a hurricane had converted the St. Louis Hotel into a neoclassical ruin. In this photograph, taken shortly before the hotel's demolition, wrought-iron signs for the "St. Louis Hotel" are visible at bottom right. Immediately below, a poster advertises *The Birth of a Nation*, the 1915 film that glorified the Ku Klux Klan. Charles L. Franck Photographers and Nancy Ewing Miner, printmaker, *Exterior of Rotunda of St. Louis Hotel before Demolition*, 1915–1916. Charles L. Franck Studio Collection, no. 1979.325.4462, The Historic New Orleans Collection.

the St. Louis Hotel in 1916 showed a lofty space reminiscent of a neoclassical temple (fig. 1.11). But the room's violent use—dedicated to drinking and auctions, pleasure that caused pain—was distinctly of New Orleans. "The men at the St. Louis employ their time in drinking juleps and other beverages in the grand rotunda of the hotel," observed one American traveler. "Here, over various descriptions of drinks, the principal business of the city is transacted, cotton sold, sugar bought, fortunes made and lost."[111]

Like the St. Charles Hotel barroom, the cavernous St. Louis Hotel rotunda hosted auctions of people, land, livestock, and goods, often simultaneously. Calls in French and English, the cries of humans being sold, and drinkers' noises reverberated under the dome. In 1839, a firm purchased three hundred shares of Gas Light Bank Stock at a St. Louis Hotel auction. The auctioneer made an announcement related to the sale immediately before bidding began, but the buyers alleged that the rotunda's pandemonium had made his words inaudible. They sued to recover the difference in price, in a case decided by the Supreme Court of Louisiana. "Amidst the bustle and noise generally attending auction sales at the St. Louis Coffee-house, a new condition announced by the auctioneer may not have been heard or properly understood," agreed the judge, ruling in favor of the plaintiffs. The decision set the precedent that auction buyers "are not bound by new conditions proclaimed verbally from the stand." For many onlookers, this cacophony at the St. Louis Hotel was an entertaining show. "In this establishment the *utile et dulci* are so happily blended," observed one tourist. For others, though, it was chaos.[112]

Amidst this confusion, enslaved people stood on crates and blocks, elevated above sightseers and buyers who gawked from the floor, and felt their bodies measured and lives valued. British abolitionist Ebenezer Davies described one auction that he witnessed at the St. Louis Hotel in the 1840s as transpiring amidst a "terrible din." Prior to the sale, Davies had found "about 200 gentlemen, —some drinking, some eating, some smoking, some reading, some talking," in the hotel's "vast saloon." From there, they proceeded into the adjoining rotunda, where they bid on bondspeople. Davies watched the auctioneer announce the sale of a twenty-five-year-old enslaved man named John, "an excellent French and American cook—*excellent cuisinier Français et Américain*," and begin the bidding at $600. Robert Murphy purchased John for $775; as well as Silas, a fifteen-year-old house servant, for $670; and Scipio, a twenty-four-year-old man and "excellent cook, fully warranted in every respect," for $705. The men and women on the block displayed a range of reactions to their position, Davies recalled. Twenty-seven-year-old George "kept his eyes fixed upon the dome, as if he felt above looking down on the grovelling [*sic*] creatures beneath him." Others scrutinized the clock on the opposite wall. Some fought to control tears. Others smiled appealingly.[113] Neoclassical columns on either side of the auction blocks framed these humans for sale. For observers on the floor, this architecture seemed to present John, Silas, Scipio, and so many others as living objets d'art, more inanimate treasures or tools than living humans. Those standing on the block had a different view: a clamorous mass of drinkers at their feet and opposite them, the bar.[114]

After the Civil War, the auction block of the St. Louis Hotel would become a destination of sorrowful remembrance for previously enslaved Americans and a curiosity for white tourists (figs. 1.12 and 1.13). Louis Hughes, who had been enslaved in Mississippi and Tennessee, embarked on a tour of the South in the late 1870s. Hughes found Mississippi devastated and unkempt. Then, "when I arrived at New Orleans I found the levee filled with fruit," he wrote in his autobiography. "Oranges and bananas were piled in masses like coal." Hughes saw the city's French Market, cemeteries, and churches. He also visited "some

FIGURE 1.12. The photograph on this postcard shows a woman posing on an auction block at the former St. Louis Hotel. The caption identifies the woman as having been auctioned there when she was a child. This postcard was mailed by a child traveler to his mother in Dundee, Illinois, in 1914. Aemegraph Co., *The Old Slave Block in the Old St. Louis Hotel, New Orleans, La.*, 1914, picture postcard. Gift of Alan Freedman and Patricia Mysza of the Midwest Center for Justice, Evanston, IL, no. 2015.0127.1, The Historic New Orleans Collection.

FIGURE 1.13. The illustration on this postcard, printed in England, shows a pair of well-heeled white tourists viewing one of the auction blocks in the former St. Louis Hotel, where children, women, and men were sold into forced labor, sexual violence, or death. Raphael Tuck and Sons, *Old Slave Market within St. Louis Hotel, New Orleans, LA*, message dated August 13, 1907, picture postcard. No. 1981.350.160, The Historic New Orleans Collection.

of the relics of slavery days in the shape of pens where slaves were exposed for sale. One of these was in the basement of the Hotel Royal," he described, "which would contain several hundred at once, and from which hundreds went to a bondage bitterer than death, and from which death was the only relief."[115] A little more than a decade earlier, Hughes might have found himself on the block at the St. Louis. Following the Confederacy's defeat, though, he stood on the rotunda floor, looking upward. In coming decades, the building would house the Louisiana state capitol and another hotel before the structure

FIGURE 1.14. This photograph approximated the perspective of enslaved people who stood on an auction block in the rotunda of the St. Louis Hotel. Abolitionist Ebenezer Davies wrote of a man named Ben, "He stood on the platform firm and erect, his eyes apparently fixed on the clock opposite. 'Now, gentlemen, what do you offer for Ben?' said the Frenchified salesman; 'a first-rate tailor—only twenty-one years of age.'" A buyer purchased Ben for $700. Davies, *American Scenes*, 62–63; Charles L. Franck Photographers and Nancy Ewing Miner, print-maker, *Hotel St. Louis, Interior*, 1900–1916, photograph. Charles L. Franck Studio Collection, no. 1979.325.4646, The Historic New Orleans Collection.

decayed and was abandoned. In 1915, a hurricane punched holes through the dome and the room's molding fell in chunks to the floor. The clock at which bondspeople had stared as their lives were auctioned to the highest bidder hung on the wall, still, as the hotel's final demolition approached (fig. 1.14).[116]

"Go, my kind reader, to the hotels of the South and South-west, look at the worn and dejected countenances of the slaves, and tell me if you do not read misery there," wrote an abolitionist American novelist in 1857. "Look in at the saloons of the restaurants, coffee-houses, &c., at late hours of the night; there you will see them," she predicted, "tired, worn and weary, with their aching heads bandaged up, sighing for a few moments' sleep." The novelist focused her attention on the chasm between server and served that was already invisible to those who loved New Orleans for its juleps and champagne. "There the proud, luxurious, idle whites sip their sherbets, drink wine, and crack their ever-lasting jokes, but there must stand your obsequious slave, with a smile on his face, wa[t]er in hand. . . . No matter if his tooth is aching, or his child dying, he must smile, or be flogged for gruffness," she wrote. "This 'chattel personal,' though he bear the erect form of a man, has no right to any privileges or emotions."[117]

Free and enslaved people of color created the experiences of eating and drinking in antebellum New Orleans, just as they built its hotels and wrought its famous ironwork.[118] They labored within a society that sought to render them closer and closer to the commodities that they created and served. Humans in bondage, food and drink, enjoyed in the moment or promised in the future: in New Orleans, all could be valued, priced, and purchased. Acts of consuming, consumption, and the violent power of American enslavers were manifested at the table and block in this metropolis of sugar, slaves, and cotton. These were the interlocking gears that powered the city's ever-turning wheels of labor and leisure. Food workers neither consented nor submitted readily to this system, however. Enslaved and free New Orleanians of color took up tools such as apples, oranges, and coffee and put the profits from their labors to their own ends. The history of insatiable appetites in the antebellum Crescent City may be told from the other side of the table, too.

2

APPLES AND ORANGES, FOOD AND FREEDOM

Food Workers in Antebellum New Orleans

IN JANUARY 1832, French philosopher Alexis de Tocqueville "disembarked hastily" from a vessel at the New Orleans levee. "There was no time to lose . . . to enjoy the pleasures, so celebrated, of New Orleans," he wrote afterward. Touring the young nation to observe its fledgling democratic government and social institutions, de Tocqueville was peeved to have a mere twenty-four hours in New Orleans, having been delayed by a shipwreck, ice, and other troubles.[1] Like so many other European and American travelers, this famous Frenchman rushed into the Crescent City anticipating meals, balls, and revelry, perhaps. For many others, though, the prospect of a trip to New Orleans held very different promises.

"Going to New Orleans was called the Nigger Hell, few ever returning who went there," wrote Harry Smith in his autobiography. Smith had been born in slavery in Kentucky in 1819. Decades later, writing his life story as a free man in Michigan, he recalled the terror that enslavers had instilled in his companions with the threat to sell them south, to "drink Mississippi water."[2] The specter of "being sent down the river"—"You know what that means, don't you?" concurred William Cooper Nell, a Black journalist. "It means, sent to sweat and starve, and die by inches, in the sugar-fields of Louisiana."[3] Enslaved Americans feared Louisiana—and the portal of New Orleans—as a gateway to family separation, brutal labor, starvation, sexual slavery, and death. Autobiographies and memoirs published by authors who had been enslaved described desperate attempts to evade and help others escape from a southbound journey. One man named Ennis, enslaved in Lexington, Kentucky, was a house carpenter doubtless skilled with the tools required to construct precise joints and sand beams until they were smooth. Hearing that his enslaver planned to sell him "down the river," recounted a writer who had also been enslaved, Ennis "took a broadaxe and cut one hand off; then contrived to lift the axe, with his arm pressing it to his body, and let it fall upon the other, cutting off the ends of his fingers." Ennis maimed his body to destroy his artisan abilities, which dictated his value in the slave market. But his horrific injury was for naught. "His master sold him for a nominal price," the writer recounted, "and down he went to Louisiana."[4]

As antebellum Louisiana's fields, presses, and refineries churned out bales of cotton and hogsheads of sugar, New Orleans's exploding economy treated the bodies of enslaved workers such as Ennis like cogs in vast machines. "They are food for the cotton-field, and the deadly sugar-mill," cried abolitionist Frederick Douglass about Americans in bondage.[5] Reading the perspectives of de Tocqueville, Smith, Nell, Douglass, and others side by side exposes the extent to which New Orleans's delights were a zero-sum game. Gratification came at the expense of many others' pain. One's horror and fear were the fodder for another's excitement and delight.

If the previous chapter traced the violent gluttony of early New Orleans's tables and auction blocks, this chapter looks to the other side of the table, to the diverse meanings that enslaved and free people of color drew from the same medium—food—and their labors related to it. Some New Orleanians used the profits from their food work to escape from slavery and reunite with family. Others secured financial autonomy. Still others built wealth. Their advances showed something different than simplistic expressions of resistance or "agency" in the face of overwhelming oppression, however.[6] The paths carved by antebellum New Orleans food entrepreneurs revealed ambivalent and hazardous realities. Those who achieved freedom found it to be a fragile, endangered state. Liberty promised neither independence nor peace. Furthermore, in this time and place, financial success—for the slave trader, the coffeehouse proprietor, the street vendor, or even a free or enslaved person of color—flowed from a single fount: the city's market in enslaved humans, the substratum of all wealth. Profits from New Orleans's commerce in bondspeople, cotton, and sugar rushed in an undivided torrent, snagging all within its current.

"Hell": Eating while Enslaved in Antebellum New Orleans

Experiences and places that privileged travelers enjoyed in New Orleans's nascent tourism industry inflicted trauma on enslaved people. White visitors who filled the pages of their travelogues with the city's banquets, operas, and overflowing market stalls also recorded their observations of casual violence against enslaved servants and panic at slave auctions.[7] Recalling such events at the St. Louis Hotel, one former trader admitted that bondspeople made "moan[s] for mercy and roars of agony" as they were led to auction, for they "believed that they were to be beheaded on the auction block" rather than sold.[8] One woman who had been enslaved in rural Louisiana as a child told a WPA interviewer, "I's seen slaves when dey just come off de auction block. Dey would be sweatin' and lookin' sick."[9] Slave auctions constituted the most overt example of sadistic pleasure extracted from another's pain, held in luxurious surroundings and feted with food and drink. But many settings associated with New Orleans's rising reputation as a leisure destination had a companion variant—a warped mirror image bent on the violent commodification of Black men, women, and children.

The city's "palace hotels," for example, compelled the proliferation of a different form of accommodation in surrounding blocks. On maps of mid-1800s New Orleans, slave pens and sites of slave sales clustered like speckles of mold around the organisms that were luxury hotels, exchanges, banks, and markets. "[I]t will never be possible for me to speak, write or by any means adequately explain the horrible condition of that slave pen," wrote William Walker, who had survived three months of 1841 in a New Orleans pen. "It was worse than any cattle yard I have ever seen north of the Ohio river."[10] Businesses that sold people massed around the St. Charles Hotel, as well as at the intersection of Esplanade Avenue at Moreau Street, just past the downriver edge of the French Quarter. In these places, enslaved people were held and shown for sale, enduring daily indignities and traumas. Those who survived the pens described settings in which traders and buyers stripped bondspeople of their clothing and examined them like livestock, tore children from mothers, and forced enslaved people to dance, to show their fitness. Solomon Northup, a free man of color from New York, was kidnapped in Washington, DC, and brought to Theophilus Freeman's slave yard in New Orleans, near the St. Charles Hotel. In the St. Charles, guests slept on plump mattresses under gauzy mosquito nets. Steps away, Northup spent his first night in Freeman's pen despairing, sleepless, and praying, in a square of dirt hemmed in by spike-tipped planks.[11] The relationship between New Orleans's hotels and slave pens was symbiotic, if perversely so.

If New Orleans's slave yards were brutal coordinates to nearby hotels, experiences of eating and drinking—New Orleans's great pleasures—were tinged with terror for enslaved people imprisoned in pens. "I am not superstitious," reflected William Walker, but he remembered feeling a mysterious "presentiment" the night before his purchaser came to the pen where he was held. "I knew the very minute he was coming by my feelings," he recalled. Specifically, Walker described his dread as a loss of the sense of taste. The morning of the day that Walker would be sold to Dick Fallon, a driver who would fulfill all of Walker's fears, Walker realized that "it would have been impossible for me to have tasted of the most delicious meal that was ever prepared for a king." Cornmeal and bacon were Walker's breakfast rations, but he understood his dread as obliterating any sense of the food's texture, salt, and smoke.[12]

Hunger was a constant torment to bondspeople in the course of their labors, but traders offered plenty to eat and drink for the time that they kept bondspeople in their pens. A twisted parallel to the excessive eating and drinking that happened around the clock at the St. Charles and St. Louis Hotels, slave traders set out their own banquets of sorts for bondspeople, with the aim of improving their appearance and health in order to optimize their sale price. This strategy was not lost on those they imprisoned. A man named John Brown, also held in Freeman's pen, remembered breakfasts of coffee, bread, and bacon, "of which a sufficiency was given to us, that we might plump up and become sleek." Dinner was the same, plus vegetables or fruit. Such abundance accomplished its purpose and then enslavers snatched it away. Brown recalled his subsequent bondage as years of unending hunger. "If we did not steal, we could scarcely live," he explained in his autobiography. "I believe every master is plundered of corn, hogs, chickens, turkeys . . . by his slaves. They are forced to do it. Hunger drives them to it."[13]

Beyond the bounds of New Orleans's slave pens, food was freighted with emotional meaning for enslaved and emancipated people alike. Louisa Picquet, born enslaved in South Carolina in 1828, was sold away from her mother on an auction block at the age of thirteen. As a young adult in New Orleans, Picquet was sexually abused by her enslaver and forced to bear four children. Picquet begged him to sell her away, but he refused, threatening to kill her if she tried to escape. Amidst this torture, Picquet thought of her mother every time she stirred sugar into a cup of tea. Picquet had received one letter from her mother, then in bondage in Texas, in which she asked her daughter to send her tea and sugar. "It grieved me so to think that she was where she could have no sugar and tea," Picquet later explained to an interviewer. "Whenever I set down to eat ever since, I always think of my mother."[14] Picquet's mother was deprived of tea and sugar and Picquet was deprived of her mother. Tea and sugar sat between them—in easy reach for Picquet, but the object of her mother's thirst—an endlessly repeating marker of the emotional tortures that enslavers had wrought in both lives. Whereas Picquet's cups of tea embodied enslavement and separation, some who survived slavery would claim food as a signifier of freedom. "The first money I ever made, I bought me a piece of salt meat and eat that with turnip greens and corn bread," Manda Cooper told a WPA interviewer. Years earlier, her enslaver had allowed her to eat meat only once a month. "They said meat was not good for you," Cooper remembered.[15] Following emancipation, she used her first wages—compensation for her work on sugarcane and rice plantations, cultivating food for others— to buy the food that had been denied her.

Other enslaved Louisianians used their labors with food and the places associated with it to create opportunities for fellowship and joy. "De slaves had balls in de sugar house," Elizabeth Ross Hite told her WPA interviewer, remembering her childhood enslavement on Louisiana's Trinity Plantation. No work was more brutal than that forced on sugar plantations, yet Hite recalled fellow bondspeople slipping out to the sugarhouse in the middle of the night, surely exhausted from their day's labors, to dance. "Dey would start late and was way out in de field where de master could not hear dem," she said. "Dey danced by candle light." Hite's enslaver sometimes made bondspeople drink to intoxication and dance for the entertainment of visitors from France and the northern United States. But on other nights, enslaved people danced for their own pleasure. "Dey got back in dere quarters 'fore daylight," Hite recalled. "You could not look too tired de next day neither."[16] Sacrificing sleep and risking the whip, they converted a place of toil into a setting to move as they chose, if only for a few hours. In disparate ways, then, food in and beyond New Orleans—forced, withdrawn, deprived, claimed—marked experiences of slavery and emancipation alike.

Moving with Food on Land and Water

Whether with a dance step on a sugarhouse floor or via a food vendor's route through urban streets, enslaved Louisianians used food work to take a deceptively simple action: to move. Mobility did not equate to freedom, however, within a society that surveilled enslaved and free people of color alike. Beginning with the French Black Code of 1724, French, Spanish, and American governments sought to dictate the terms of living in Louisiana as a person of African descent. A century later, between 1818 and 1831, the New Orleans mayor's office required passports for all residents of color who traveled in or out of the city. In 1840, the same office would require free people of color living in New Orleans to furnish proof of their freedom and register their residence in the city. Relentless scrutiny by authorities, regardless of one's status as free or enslaved, exposed the reality that free people of color never experienced an unconstrained state of freedom in New Orleans. In the eyes of a society reliant on enslaved labor, all people of color possessed a potential value.[17]

Within New Orleans and in surrounding regions, vending food on foot was the most visible means of moving with food. Often, women of color did this work. "In every street during the whole day women, chiefly black women, are met, carrying baskets upon their heads calling at the doors of houses," the architect Benjamin Henry Latrobe described of his time in the city.[18] Street vendors (*marchandes*) and shoppers circulated in and near the French Market, the city's central public market, wedged against the waterfront levee since 1791. There, they hawked their wares to locals, visitors, and sailors. The sights, sounds, and smells of their work bled into those of river traffic and social and religious activities in the nearby Place d'Armes and St. Louis Cathedral, embedding food and food workers in tableaux of civic life.[19]

In travelogues, memoirs, and newspaper reporting, tourists and well-to-do residents of New Orleans, Charleston, and other Atlantic world ports wrote often about *marchandes*, characterizing their calls as distinctive features of life in cosmopolitan locales.[20] When Eliza Ripley authored her memoir about growing up in New Orleans in the 1840s, she described the call of one such *marchande* who worked in her childhood neighborhood, selling to the wealthy white women cloistered in their homes. Vending Creole cream cheese, a tart, fresh farmer cheese, the seller's voice prompted "a rush to the door with a saucer for a . . . tiny, heart-shaped cheese, a dash of cream poured from a claret bottle. . . . How nice and refreshing it was," Ripley recalled.[21] Other *marchandes* sold coffee; fruits and vegetables; spruce, ginger, and pineapple beers; and pralines, clusters of Louisiana pecans bound with sugar—sweet treats that belied the labor required to procure and sell them.[22] Most depictions of *marchandes* were saturated with nostalgia. Many former customers, like Ripley, recounted vendors in terms of their calls, their skin colors, and occasionally a first name—things that could be observed or assumed during a momentary encounter on a doorstep.

Most often, though, observers identified New Orleans's *marchandes* by the foods they sold, collapsing both into a single unit, linguistically and conceptually. *Pralinières* were women who sold pralines. "*Calas* women" sold *calas*, sweetened rice fritters that originated in West Africa. Writing in a local newspaper in the early twentieth century, one author insisted that the city's *marchandes* and other itinerant workers, past and present, were innately suited to their labors because of their skin colors and purportedly exotic origins. "A real chimney sweep is born, not made," the writer reasoned. "He must be of a particular shade . . . of that fast, gleaming black upon which soot is not to be distinguished. . . . There never was such a thing as a 'high brown' or yellow chimney sweep." Memories of bygone *marchandes* lingered in the same writer's thoughts like cast members in an elaborate theatrical production who performed for the crowd's pleasure. The blackberry seller knocked on New Orleans doors like the "ebony goddess of spring," wearing a headdress of "Egyptian-like folds," she wrote, while the banana vendor "loll[ed] like a barbaric Senegambian chieftan [*sic*] against a mountain of golden fruit."[23] Vendors' skin colors, postures, and dress cohered with the substance of their work—chimney ash, berries, bananas—to convince the writer that New Orleans's *marchandes* were inseparable from the things they sold.

Beyond the realm of nostalgia, nineteenth-century municipal and legal records supplied some detail to the lives of *marchandes* who could not record their own histories, whether due to illiteracy, poverty, constant work, or a combination of those factors. These documentary fragments show New Orleans's nineteenth-century *marchandes* to have been enormously diverse in age, place of birth, language, and legal status. The records also characterize food vending as an occupation that could sustain a tenuous independence in the shadow of slavery. Marie Françoise Borga was one *marchande* who walked New Orleans's streets during Eliza Ripley's childhood in the 1840s. Borga was born in Congo in 1780. In New Orleans, she was enslaved to a grocer until 1817, when he manumitted her noting her "good conduct free from running away, robberies and all criminal fault," as he specified on his emancipation petition. Twenty-four years later, when Borga was around sixty years old, she lived as a free woman of color selling *calas*, a food whose preparation she may have learned from a mother or aunt decades earlier, before the transatlantic slave trade propelled her to Louisiana.[24]

A woman identified by the single name of Fatima worked as a *marchande*, too, during the same years as Borga. They were nearly the same age—Fatima was born in 1781—but their birthplaces were separated by an ocean. Born in Léogâne, Saint-Domingue, southwest of Port-au-Prince and on the coast of Canal de la Gonâve, facing Cuba, Fatima's arrival date in New Orleans is uncertain. Once in the city, notarial records and emancipation petitions chronicled Fatima's enslavement by the widow of a prominent banker and subsequently by Laurence Laclotte. Laclotte was a free woman of color who had fled from Saint-Domingue to New Orleans with her three sisters during the revolution. Laclotte manumitted Fatima in spring 1821, when Fatima was about forty-two years old, on account of good conduct and to satisfy the request of Fatima's former enslaver. Twenty years after her manumission, around the age of sixty-one, Fatima enrolled in a municipal register as a *marchande* selling fruit on city streets.[25] The far-flung paths and resourceful lives of Borga and Fatima were not visible to—or guessed at—by the likes of customers like Latrobe or Ripley during fleeting transactions that saw a picayune exchanged for a fig. Both women were born a generation before New Orleans became an American city and lived on other continents before enslavers brought them to Louisiana. Both had experienced slavery and manumission and were likely bilingual or multilingual. As older women, both supported themselves selling food.

Marchandes like Borga and Fatima counted among the most mobile figures in the antebellum South, traveling within and between rural and urban regions to procure and sell food and goods. Despite the humble social status of these peddlers—most subsisted on the margins of the city's economy—enslavers feared the power of their mobility, which threatened to penetrate the isolation that slaveholders tried to impose on bondspeople.[26] When a blackberry seller tapped at the door of a French Quarter home, she might bear news from an upriver plantation along with the fragile fruit mounded in her basket. Ideas could travel in the other direction, too. "The communication that is kept up, by means of these miserable and clandestine itinerant merchants, betwixt the slaves in the country and the slaves in town is perhaps little known," wrote one reader to a New Orleans newspaper in 1808, when the region was still newly American. "It may, however, be worthy of some consideration."[27] In some cases, such fears proved justified. Louis Hughes, who was enslaved on cotton plantations in Mississippi and Tennessee, recalled the dreams of freedom inspired by such exchanges between rural bondspeople and visiting vendors. "Sometimes when the farm hands were at work, peddlers would come along; and . . . tal[k] to the slaves in a way to excite them and set them thinking of freedom," Hughes remembered. "They would say encouragingly to them: 'Ah! You will be free some day.'"[28] In these instances, vending food enabled a figurative mobility that was social and informational. For still others who worked with food, their movements in real space—up and down the Mississippi River, across ocean waves, or through the ranks of a busy kitchen—helped them vault from slavery to freedom.

Compared to the physical range of *marchandes* and other vendors who traveled on foot, food-related jobs on river- and oceangoing vessels enabled mobility of a different magnitude. Working as a cook, steward, or waiter on a steamboat or schooner, along the Mississippi River and its tributaries or on saltwater routes, was a common first grasp at liberty or a flexible realm after achieving it. Maritime gigs, similar to kitchen and barroom jobs on shore, were often short-term and seasonal. Frequently, laborers combined food work on land or water with other jobs. This was the case for Joseph W. Prince, born free in Hackensack, New Jersey, who worked as a barkeeper in New Orleans in 1841 and "sometimes follow[ed] steamboats" to earn extra wages.[29] With their flexibility and range, jobs on the water proved powerful engines of employment and, for many, the most expeditious means of reaching freedom. Skills in the kitchen or behind the bar offered crucial access to such positions.

Steam power gave an added boost to the reach of Americans who boarded vessels to travel for pleasure or flee for their lives. For all who encountered this technology—free and enslaved, American and European—it transformed the definitions of proximity and speed. In 1838, a New Orleans grocer wrote to a Madeira wine dealer in London about the future promised by steam. "We shall soon look upon a voyage to Europe as a trip of pleasure," he wrote. "To us in N.O. [New Orleans] it will be almost as easy to go to spend our summers in London as to go to spend 3 to 4 months in New York & with almost as little expense."[30] By the late 1850s, New Orleans dominated American cities in steamboat arrivals, with more than 3,500 vessels disgorging their holds at its levees, annually.[31] Steamboats ferried passengers and goods among Cincinnati, St. Louis, Memphis, Natchez, New Orleans, Galveston, and beyond. Ocean-going vessels, too, conveyed people and things among American, Caribbean, Latin American, and European ports.[32]

Whereas businesspeople anticipated steam-powered vessels to enhance business and pleasure travel, bondspeople saw them as lifelines to escape. Narratives written by people formerly enslaved described easy communication among laborers and passengers on such vessels. Even a brief, clandestine exchange between a cook and a stowaway could seal an alliance necessary for flight. When Jacob Green, born in slavery in 1813, learned that his enslaver intended to move from Memphis to New Orleans, he escaped by hiding under cotton in the hold of a steamboat bound for New York City. "My being there was only known to two persons on board, the steward and the cook, both colored persons," Green recounted in his narrative, published after he successfully reached freedom.[33] Amolk, a cook enslaved by a New Orleans attorney, likewise attempted to escape from slavery on the water, using his skills in the kitchen. In May 1839, Amolk boarded the schooner *Molaeska* while it was docked in New Orleans. He worked as a cook onboard for just three days; he was discovered before the schooner set sail for Tampa Bay and New York and was returned to his enslaver.[34]

Some bondspeople luckier than Amolk used food-related work on steamboats to save money for their manumission—to purchase their own freedom from their enslavers. One of these individuals was a young woman named Catherine, who had been sold at auction in New Orleans and worked in Louisiana cotton and sugarcane fields, then as a house servant for the ill wife of a French-born slaveholder. Catherine was first able to earn wages by washing clothes. "So anxious was she to obtain her freedom," her father wrote in his autobiography, "that she worked nearly all her time, days and nights, and Sundays." A job as a steamboat stewardess enabled Catherine to finally wedge open the door to freedom. Beyond passenger tips and her monthly pay of $30, "she also had liberty to sell apples and oranges on board," her father explained. With each piece of fruit sold, Catherine saved. At last, she amassed $1,200: the price her enslaver had set for her freedom. After achieving her own manumission, Catherine plunged back into Louisiana to find her sister, Charlotte. The women persuaded Charlotte's enslaver to let the two of them work on a steamboat "together for the wages of one." They saved an additional $1,200 to manumit Charlotte, too. Charlotte's departure must have been sorrowful, though. She had to leave behind her four young children, unable to afford the $2,400 her enslaver demanded for them.[35]

With apples and oranges handed over to anonymous masses of passengers, Catherine and Charlotte clawed their way to freedom. Impatient, distracted, hungry, flirtatious, perhaps—the customers who held out their money to the women in front of them, receiving a piece of fruit in return, likely did not understand the transaction's significance. Food—cheap fruit, by the piece— served as the medium that enabled these two women, and others, to propel themselves into movement across hundreds of miles, from debt to solvency and enslavement to freedom.

Food Work in Hotels

Whether in publicly visible roles—as *marchandes*, steamboat stewards, bartenders, or waiters—or behind closed doors, out of sight—as cooks, pastry cooks, or bakers—workers of color marked virtually every food-centric experience in antebellum New Orleans. Many found work in hotels. In terms of the quantity, flexibility, and availability of positions that revolved around food and drink, New Orleans's hotels served as dry-land counterparts to steamboats. The size of the city's palatial lodgings, the popularity of their dining rooms, and the seasonal swings of these establishments generated a range of jobs for workers who were often in transit and seeking episodic employment. Even if these men and women were barred from sleeping in hotels' bedrooms and eating in their ordinaries, they churned the ice cream and poured the wines that made these institutions profitable and memorable. "No correct history of the American hotel business could be written with the negro waiters left out," wrote the author of a 1904 book profiling Black waiters in fine American hotels. Black waiters' flawless service of meals and mastery of dining-room etiquette set the standard of comportment for their white customers.[36]

Nevertheless, Black waiters—whom white diners assumed to be enslaved— were polarizing figures in antebellum New Orleans hotel dining rooms. Some customers drew an explicitly sadistic pleasure from the experience of being served the city's famed cuisine by enslaved people. Others disdained the same idea. At New Orleans's Bishop's Hotel in the early 1830s, "The table is burthened with every luxury which can be procured in this luxurious climate," raved one traveler from Maine. "The servants are numerous, and with but two or three exceptions, slaves. . . . In this important point, Bishop's hotel is in every way superior to the Tremont [in Boston]."[37] This diner reveled in watching his glass filled and plate cleared by a server in bondage, in a district of the city famed for its slave auctions. Another Northern visitor who also stayed at Bishop's Hotel in the 1830s recalled a very different staff there; he was pleased that "the waiters are Irish, and not negro slaves, with their attendant filth and negligence."[38] The presence of an enslaved server waiting at table in this hotel dining room provoked violent pleasure in one guest and disgusted another. Appealing to the latter class, by the late antebellum years, advertisements in New Orleans directories and newspapers announced white hotel workers as a feature that seemed intended to attract travelers.[39] Many tourists in the city were eager to bid on enslaved people at auction—or watch the process for pleasure—even if they despised the notion of having their meals stewarded by a Black waiter.

The histories of such a waiter and his colleagues who looked like him, enslaved and free, can be challenging to trace. Official records that might indicate people of color working in nineteenth-century New Orleans's food industry often yield scant returns.[40] But this is not because these individuals did not exist. Rather, it is because many of these forms of documentation did not generate accurate representations of food-industry labor—ephemeral, purportedly menial—or the people who did it. Federal censuses returned unreliable counts of enslaved and free African Americans in a variety of locales. The 1850 and 1860 censuses resulted in especially egregious undercounts of free people of color in New Orleans, when the city's political climate was aggressively hostile to them as a group. Members of this population were less likely to volunteer their names, dwelling places, and biographical details to a government official, if these workers were even in the city when these censuses were enumerated.[41] Such conditions were compounded by the social and legal statuses of the food industry's laborers. Food and drink workers and servers were often immigrants, enslaved, recently manumitted, or fugitives from slavery. Many who filled the ranks of New Orleans's kitchens, dining rooms, and barrooms were the working poor, stitching together multiple jobs, and on the move. Most were not the proprietors or owners of businesses, and they were unlikely to be named in association with recognizable establishments in city directories, newspaper ads, and census returns. In fact, Louisiana legislators worked to bar entrepreneurs of color from running businesses, parallel to their efforts to minimize the mere presence of free people of color in the state.

Accordingly, researchers must look, instead, to other sources to find the women and men who made New Orleans cuisine, laboring out of sight from diners and scholars. Such sources include municipal records, published narratives written by formerly enslaved people, court cases, and newspaper reporting.[42] Such documentation, though often fragmentary, points to free and enslaved New Orleanians of color working throughout the antebellum city's kitchens. Side by side with immigrants from France, Ireland, and Germany, Black New Orleanians prepared and served the elaborate repasts enjoyed in hotels and private homes in New Orleans. Hotel workers' mobility—a downstairs echo of the comings and goings of upstairs travelers in the same hotels— created opportunities for collaboration and conflict within employees' ranks. Details of some of these relationships, and of the prevalence of food jobs in these establishments, emerge in unexpected sources—even deathbed confessions.

Rascals

Madison Henderson, Charles Brown, Amos Warrick, and James Seward formed a ragtag band of self-described "rascals" who cavorted up and down the Mississippi River in the 1830s. Henderson was enslaved; his companions were free men of color. Varied paths led all four men to each other and to New Orleans. Their brief careers wove in and out of legal and extralegal markets in enslaved people and luxury goods, especially food, liquor, and silver. Published confessions taken from the group after they were convicted of arson, burglary, and murder in St. Louis, Missouri, in April 1841, revealed a common thread in their peripatetic paths: food and food work in New Orleans, often in hotels and on the water. Cooking, serving, and stealing, the men moved among the dining rooms and pastry kitchens of fine hotels, sugarcane fields, and the galleys of ocean vessels and steamboat cabins. Ultimately, their collaboration resulted in their executions.[43]

In the confession he gave as he faced his death, Charles Brown traced a direct link between working with food and resisting slavery in New Orleans. Soon after his initial arrival in the city in 1830, Brown found work for "one season" as a pastry cook at the Bishop's Hotel. A subsequent trip to Cincinnati and study at Oberlin College led to a job at the Ohio Anti-Slavery Society (a claim he later recanted).[44] Brown dedicated himself to abolitionist action from that point forward. He returned to New Orleans, resolving to help bondspeople escape. "My first attempt was on a bed-room servant . . . belonging to Mr. Bishop, and employed in the [Bishop's] Hotel," he recalled. Brown helped the man flee via steamboat to Tennessee, Ohio, and finally Canada. He was the first of many. Brown claimed to have helped "about eighty" enslaved people escape from New Orleans and "about sixteen" from Vicksburg, Mississippi, most of them on steamboats. Crucially, food and service jobs at New Orleans's St. Louis Hotel and a hotel on Conti Street—working "portions of the time as pastry cook and at other times as bedroom servant" and waiter—enabled Brown to put food on his table while helping bondspeople flee.[45]

The confessions of Brown's collaborators revealed a similar reliance on food and hotel jobs as the men balanced, or were dragged, between free and enslaved states—geographically and legally.[46] Amos Warrick, born free in North Carolina in 1815, joined a vessel traveling from Baltimore to New Orleans to work as a cook and steward. He was unaware that the ship on which he cooked, the *Tribune*, was owned by notorious Virginia-based slave dealers Isaac Franklin and John Armfield. "I did not know her cargo until I got on board," Warrick admitted. "She was freighted with 82 slaves." Warrick's kitchen labor helped power the ship to New Orleans.[47] James Seward's path was sustained similarly by food work in and beyond New Orleans. Seward was born a free man, too, in Oneida County, New York, in 1813. He learned how to counterfeit currency with organized groups in New York and Ohio. In 1837, Seward set out for the Caribbean but stopped in New Orleans. His pause there would lead to his downfall.

Like Brown and Warrick, Seward found that working with food in New Orleans supplied a ready source of income that permitted him to move within and beyond the city, on his own and in collusion with others. In New Orleans, Seward found work as a waiter at the Planter's Hotel, on Canal Street. "This was the first time I had been employed with slaves," Seward recounted in his confession, "and it was not long before a hostility sprung up between them and me." A hotel guest complained that his money had been stolen. Seward denied the crime but was blamed for it. The hotel steward had Seward jailed "on the suspicion of being a run-away slave. I had my papers with me," Seward described, "but they were informal in some respects, and I was compelled to send to New York to have them corrected." After being freed from prison, Seward returned to the hotel, only to find that "the servants at the Hotel or some one else took all my clothes and money." Seward suspected that his resentful enslaved coworkers had taken his possessions during his absence.

Subsequent steps led Seward to a job as a steamboat's cook and a plot with his fellow "rascals" to sell New Orleans-procured fruit, oysters, and cigars in St. Louis, reinvesting the money in eggs and butter.[48]

Eventually, the group's collaboration devolved into crimes that concluded with their executions in St. Louis. Hordes of city residents came to watch their deaths, as if the sentences' fulfillment were theater or sport. Following the men's executions, a drugstore in the city center displayed the men's severed heads in its front window. In a space that showcased things for sale—healing balms and elixirs, perhaps—shoppers saw instead a grotesque spectacle.[49] Having trafficked in things that consumers valued—cigars, champagne, brandy, silver, enslaved humans—the bodies of these four men were exhibited in a shop window like macabre commodities themselves, even beyond death.

Before they were killed, both Charles Brown and Amos Warrick had passed through the doors of New Orleans's St. Louis Hotel, though they did not yet know each other. Brown worked in the kitchen there. Warrick stood for sale in the hotel's rotunda, where a buyer purchased him for $700 to work on a sugarcane plantation.[50] Along with the *marchandes* Marie Françoise Borga and Fatima, and Catherine and Charlotte, the sisters who hawked apples and oranges on steamboats, Brown and Warrick circulated throughout the streets, waterways, and kitchens that fed the vast appetites and thirsts of antebellum New Orleans. These men and women left only faint, fragmentary traces behind them. Nevertheless, tracking the paths of food workers such as these reveal tenacious efforts to be free, stay free, and pull others out of enslavement. Women and men waged never-ending battles against the magnetic forces of New Orleans's economy and consumer world, which placed a value on their lives and tried—tirelessly—to subjugate them.

Lucette, William, Prosper: Three Food Entrepreneurs in Antebellum New Orleans

The paths of three people—a *marchande*, a coffeehouse proprietor, and a grocer—illuminate the opportunities and complexities of laboring with food as a person of color in antebellum New Orleans. These individuals used food work to unite and sustain families. One emerged from slavery. The work of another was instrumental in growing the city's slave trade. A third found himself drawn into white New Orleanians' early obsession with the color line. Here, their paths are reconstructed partially, with a variety of notarial, municipal, and federal records held in disparate institutions. Their trajectories outline the fragility of freedom in antebellum New Orleans, showing it to be a vulnerable state requiring careful documentation and constant defense. In tumultuous and hostile circumstances, all three used food to achieve degrees of autonomy and stability.

Lucette Barberousse was born around 1796 in the French colony of Saint-Domingue, three years after the abolition of slavery there. At some time and place—likely as a child brought to Cuba by French citizens fleeing the Haitian Revolution—Barberousse became enslaved and was conveyed to Louisiana.[51] Archival strands of Barberousse's story in New Orleans began in the 1830s. Via a notarial act dated August 1835, Marie Olive St. Laurent, a twenty-one-year-old free woman of color living in New Orleans, inherited from the estate of her grandmother three generations of enslaved women. St. Laurent's grandmother, Marie Agnès Latoison, had died intestate in New Orleans, and St. Laurent petitioned authorities to conduct an inventory of her grandmother's estate and to be considered her heir.[52] Commissioning this inventory enabled St. Laurent to inherit five women and girls whom Latoison had enslaved: Jasie, about seventy-two; her daughter Lucette, about thirty-nine; and Lucette's three daughters: Annette, twelve (b. 1823), Louisa, eight (b. 1827), and Etienne, also called Nounone, six (b. 1829). The estate inventory identified Lucette as "a *mulatresse* slave," laboring as a "*marchande* or Hawker," and estimated her value at $500. St. Laurent was married—to Pierre Boyer, a New Orleans–born free man of color, and a cabinet maker—but ownership of the enslaved women passed from grandmother to granddaughter, from the estate of Latoison to St. Laurent. The enslaved women did not move far; notarial records and parish estate files show the properties of Latoison (St. Philip Street between Royal and Bourbon Streets) and St. Laurent (Burgundy Street between St. Philip and Ursulines Streets) just a few blocks from each other within the French Quarter.[53]

When St. Laurent took possession of Lucette Barberousse and her family, the new household comprised free and enslaved women of color who had been born along the path of refugees' flight from the Haitian Revolution: Lucette and her mother Jasie, both born in Port-au-Prince, Saint-Domingue; St. Laurent, their enslaver, born in Santiago de Cuba; and Lucette's three children, all born in New Orleans. Lucette's trajectory would soon intersect with that of another migration stream to New Orleans, as well. In early 1838, St. Laurent sold Jasie, Lucette, and Lucette's new infant daughter, also named Lucette, "not yet baptized," to Michel Grabiel, a nineteen-year-old Italian immigrant, for $650. Grabiel had emigrated to the United States in 1830, when he was about eleven years old. St. Laurent specified that Grabiel should manumit the three as soon as possible, releasing them from slavery.[54] Lucette Barberousse's three older daughters—Annette, Louisa, and Etienne—remained enslaved to St. Laurent. Grabiel kept his promise, petitioning in June 1838 to manumit Jasie, Lucette, and baby Lucette. To the notary, Grabiel cited two primary motivations for the request. First, he identified himself as the father of baby Lucette. Second, "during a long and serious illness," the notary recorded, "[Grabiel] was cared for night and day by Jasie and Lucette Barberousse, whose care and kindness cannot be overstated, and he believes and will always believe that he owes them his recovery." Grabiel also petitioned for the women to be allowed to stay in Louisiana, "seeing that they are *créoles*." The three women were manumitted in November 1838, when Jasie was about seventy-five, Lucette about forty-two, and baby Lucette likely approaching one year old.[55] This was Lucette Barberousse's first experience of freedom on American soil, but not all of her family was free.

She would see to it that this would not remain the case for long. Just three months later, in February 1839, Lucette Barberousse returned to her former enslaver to purchase her three older daughters. For $700, Lucette bought Annette (sixteen), Louisa (twelve), and Etienne (ten), becoming for a time—at least in the eyes of authorities—their enslaver.[56] How did Barberousse assemble $700 to buy her three daughters shortly after her own manumission? Perhaps she had set aside wages during her years working as an enslaved *marchande*, or perhaps Grabiel assisted her with the purchase. Regardless, the year after reassembling her family under one roof—her roof—Lucette Barberousse appeared in the 1840 federal census as the head of a New Orleans household of nine women of color. One person in the household—certainly Lucette—was employed, engaged in commerce.[57] Her labors as a *marchande* supported the family. The same census recorded Michel Grabiel living adjacent to Barberousse, perhaps an additional indication of a relationship between the two, though their paths would soon diverge.[58]

In the early 1840s, the block of Dauphine Street in the French Quarter where Barberousse and her family lived—between Hospital and Barrack Streets—displayed to Barberousse what a free person of color might achieve in New Orleans.[59] Several of her immediate neighbors were free people of color who owned their homes. Their names appear in the chains of title for these properties, which stretch from the early 1700s for more than two hundred years. Most notably, Eulalie Mandeville, one of the wealthiest free women of color in the city, owned the property on Dauphine Street at the corner of Barrack, a stone's throw from Barberousse's home. Mandeville ran a profitable dry-goods business that relied on free and enslaved street vendors to sell cloth, clothing, and other items in the city's thoroughfares. Mandeville's freedom and business success, plus wealthy family ties, enabled her to live in a home of privacy and beauty: a one-story cottage "with high board fences inclosing the orchard and garden," as a local newspaper described, as well as "a fine kitchen; with several apartments for negroes." When Lucette Barberousse ventured out of her Dauphine Street home to pace the streets, calling out her wares, did she begin or end the day by peering through the slats of her neighbor's fence, taking in the "fine yard with several fruit trees," imagining what she, too, might build with her new freedom?[60]

Lucette Barberousse might have dreamed of fruit trees, but in her immediate sight was a clearer goal. In May 1841, she took a final step to unite her family. Two years after purchasing her daughters, Barberousse manumitted them from slavery. In the presence of a city official, Barberousse made her mark on a notarial act, freeing Annette, Louisa, and Etienne, as well as her granddaughter Marie-Agnès, one-year-old daughter of Annette.[61] Finally, this family of four generations of women—from baby Marie-Agnès to her great-grandmother Jasie—was free. In the years leading up to this moment, Barberousse had labored continuously as a *marchande*. When she was enslaved by Marie Agnès Latoison in the early 1830s, this work had helped determine Barberousse's value as woman in bondage. But in ensuing years, as Barberousse passed into the hands of Marie Olive St. Laurent and then into her own home as a free woman, her labors and the value of each article sold—each payment collected and slipped into a pocket—must have taken on new meaning. Working as a *marchande* enabled Barberousse to attain and sustain freedom and a home for herself and her family.

Still, freedom proved to be far from the end of their worries. New Orleans was not a safe or welcoming place for this family or others like them. During the waning years of Barberousse's enslavement and the waxing years of her freedom, free people of color in Louisiana balanced on legal ground that eroded under their feet. A growing, skilled, and prosperous community of free New Orleanians of color threatened the ironbound association between skin color and slavery upon which the economy of the city—indeed, the nation—relied. By the 1830s, white New Orleanians no longer grudgingly held the line against this third category of citizen who could work, profit, marry, and live freely while Black; they launched an offensive. Aiming to reduce the number of free people of color in the state, Louisiana restricted the conditions for manumission from slavery. Additional measures targeted the mere existence of individuals like Lucette Barberousse in Louisiana: acts passed by the state legislature, the rulings of state and district courts, harassment by police, disparagement by the press, and the aggressions of ordinary citizens against their neighbors.[62] With these strategies, white New Orleanians cut the city's population of free people of color in half, from 19,200 in 1840—its peak, and likely an undercount—to 9,900 in 1850. Then, in 1857, Louisiana abolished all manumissions from slavery.[63]

As one tool of heightened surveillance during this period, New Orleans authorities compelled free people of color who had been born outside Louisiana or manumitted after birth to register with the mayor's office and prove their rightful residence in the state. In four volumes chronicling the years 1840 to 1864, municipal employees collected nearly three thousand entries. Each line recorded a person's name, age, "sex and color," place of birth, profession, date of arrival in New Orleans, and "observations" that corroborated the person's free status, such as the name of a recommender or the date of manumission and former enslaver's name.[64] In August 1841, the adult women in Lucette Barberousse's family registered with the mayor's office as free people of color entitled to live in Louisiana. Lucette, forty-five, and her daughter Annette, eighteen, were working as *marchandes*—the mother was teaching the trade to her daughter. Jasie, seventy-eight, and her granddaughter Louisa, fourteen, worked as washerwomen. The four labored to support their household of nine free women.[65]

Because New Orleans authorities sought to track, count, and surveil free people of color like Lucette Barberousse and her family, recordkeepers wrote them into the historical record where they otherwise might not have existed. In other words, the desire to make this class of people disappear resulted in documentation of parts of their lives that were not recorded elsewhere. In addition to New Orleanians working as *marchandes*, the mayor's registry noted free people of color laboring as butchers, bakers, pastry chefs, barkeepers, steamboat stewards, grocers, restaurant waiters, and cooks. Some fed consumers in a more intimate manner, such as Françoise "Prieur" Rozine, a woman born in Charleston, South Carolina, who worked as a wet nurse.[66] In creating even a single-line record in this registry, a bureaucrat dropped a key that can unlock a linked chain of fragmented records: emancipation petitions, last will and testaments, records of baptisms and property ownership and transferals, city directories, court records, local and federal censuses, and other notarial and municipal documents. Together, these records supply names and brief biographies to New Orleans's culinary reputation, clarifying the wide-ranging roles and skills of the people who fed the city.[67]

Between the lines, these fragmented records spoke, too, to the persistence and resourcefulness of free New Orleanians of color who built homes and grew families in the face of enormous challenges. Before Barberousse turned forty, she had lived in French and Spanish colonies in the Caribbean and the United States and had labored in the service of at least three enslavers. Once manumitted, though illiterate, she pressed through a multistep bureaucratic process in a bilingual legal system to purchase and manumit her daughters and granddaughter, then support their free household.[68] Barberousse and her family were not wealthy Creoles of color with deep roots and resources in Louisiana. They were the working poor—a family of women whose generations straddled regimes, languages, and geographies.[69] Lucette Barberousse's labors as a *marchande* remained a constant thread in their story, though, as they moved from slavery to freedom to independence, together.

Who were Lucette Barberousse's customers, whose payments she saved to make her family whole? From where did their money come? Perhaps they were fellow free people of color who worked as bricklayers, stevedores, and seamstresses. If so, whose homes did they build, what goods did they move, and for whom did they sew beautiful dresses? Or perhaps her customers were travelers wandering the French Quarter's streets, or enslaved women shopping on behalf of their enslavers, in search of fresh fruit or cakes. Disparate degrees of separation stood between the customer standing in front of Barberousse and the levee's hogsheads of sugar and bales of cotton and people standing on hotel auction blocks. These commodities were the roots of the city's great wealth; from them, all money flowed. Living in slaveholding New Orleans compelled free people of color like Barberousse to navigate an economy in which succeeding in commerce often meant profiting from the patronage of those tied to the city's slave trade.

This complex dynamic resounded in the career of William Scott, a free man of color who lived and worked in New Orleans during the same years as Lucette Barberousse. While Barberousse walked the city's streets as a *marchande*, Scott sold food and drink from brick-and-mortar storefronts. The identity of his customers is more certain: Scott catered to businessmen who traded enslaved people in the heart of New Orleans's banking and commercial districts. Born in Virginia around 1800, Scott reported to the mayor's office that he had arrived in New Orleans as a young man, in March 1821.[70] The 1832 city directory noted William Scott, grocer, operating at the corner of Royal and Customhouse Streets in the French Quarter, one block from Canal Street and a few blocks from the riverfront, close enough to see the stacks of steamboats on the levee. Neither the St. Charles nor the St. Louis Hotel had been built yet. Three years later, the 1835 directory listed Scott—"fmc" (free man of color)—running a fruit shop at the same corner (54 Royal Street).[71]

The construction of the Merchants' Exchange in 1835 and 1836 across the street from Scott's business, as well as the erection of the St. Charles and St. Louis Hotels soon after, would transform the region's economy and enable

Scott to begin building his wealth. Filling the block between Royal Street and Exchange Place, the Merchants' Exchange set a luxurious tone that the city's fine hotels would echo. "Both fronts are of white marble, in a plain and bold style of design," described the 1842 city directory. "The grand Exchange room is extremely beautiful . . . and is of the Corinthian order, from the exquisite little monument of Lysicrates, at Athens." The project razed Scott's small store but he relocated across the street, ready to sell to the ravenous businessmen who flooded the Exchange. "The corner of Royal and Custom house streets, where the bank now stands, was tenanted by Scot [*sic*]," a writer remembered in 1845, "who now furnishes food for his hundreds a day directly opposite, and who laid the foundation of his fortune in the tenement that was removed to make room for the present beautiful edifice." The 1838 directory pointed to Scott's growing success, noting him as proprietor of a "fruit store" that had grown to fill two storefronts, at 56 and 58 Royal Street.[72] When customers entered or exited the Exchange, Scott's shop was before them. If its doors were open, sunlight fell, perhaps, on rainbow rows of oranges, bananas, and avocados—refreshments from the stresses of business or tropical treats for businessmen's wives waiting in hotel drawing rooms.

Despite Scott's increasing prominence, his skin color dictated that he, too, register with the New Orleans mayor to confirm his legal residence in Louisiana. Likely in 1840—the entry is undated—the mayor's office registered Scott as a "mulatto" man and "tavernkeeper" by trade. George Waggaman, a lawyer and sugar planter, vouched for Scott's free state.[73] Scott kept his business at or near the same intersection in the French Quarter for another decade, expanding his offerings for patrons of the Merchants' Exchange as New Orleans—and its slave markets—boomed. Directories throughout the 1840s listed Scott as running a fruit store (56 Royal Street, 1841), coffeehouse (48 Customhouse Street, 1842), fruit and soda shop (corner Exchange Place and Customhouse, 1843 and 1844), and "cake shop, fruit and soda water establishment" (Customhouse, near the corner of Royal Street, 1846).[74] As the city's economy exploded, business for Scott was good. The 1850 census valued real estate owned by Scott, an "eatinghouse keeper," at $9,000, making him more than four times as wealthy as his neighbor.[75]

In the 1850s, William Scott made a critical move that acknowledged the unparalleled profits to be had at the heart of New Orleans's slave-selling universe. After nearly twenty years across from the Merchants' Exchange, Scott transplanted his business across Canal St., moving from the French Quarter to the American sector. He was following the epicenter of New Orleans's business activity to the blocks surrounding the St. Charles Hotel. The 1852 directory showed William Scott, "fmc," selling "coffee, fruits, &c." at 82 Apollo

Street.[76] If Scott was operating in the neighborhood of the city's most prominent concentration of slave dealers, he would move closer still. By 1855, Scott
sold "coffee &c." at 161 Gravier Street. His next-door neighbors at 159 Gravier
Street were D. M. Matthews, Thomas J. Frisby, and C. M. Rutherford, slave
dealers. On July 4 of the previous year—Independence Day—this business
had advertised in a local newspaper: "NEGROES FOR SALE—We will receive
and offer for sale . . . at our well known stand, No. 159 GRAVIER STREET,
several choice and well selected lots of VIRGINIA and KENTUCKY negroes.
We cannot offer . . . low prices, but purchasers may be assured that they will
not be deceived in any Negro we sell." William Scott's neighbor a farther
door down, at 157 Gravier Street, was one James White, a slave dealer. On
Scott's other side, his neighbors at 163 Gravier Street were J. W. Boazman and
Thomas N. Davis, also slave dealers. William Scott was a free man of color
operating his food and drink business in between slave dealers. Additional
dealers worked on the same block of Gravier Street and on nearby stretches of
Baronne and Common Streets. A slave depot in the vicinity boasted to newspaper readers that it could accommodate "two to three hundred Negroes"
in its "large and fine yard."[77] With his "coffee &c.," Scott fed the hunger and
quenched the thirst of the people who bought and sold people.

Scott's stretch of Gravier Street and the blocks surrounding him presented
a microcosm of the New Orleans economy at this moment in time, with a
variety of businesses that catered to men's appetites and vanities. A census
of merchants conducted by the city's treasurer's office in 1854 enables a detailed reconstruction of the street on which Scott operated and the vicinity.
Sketched maps of each block of New Orleans's first, second, and third districts
produced an assemblage of squares, rectangles, and trapezoids in the pages of
municipal records. Neat lines of script that ordered the businesses found on
each facet of a given block revealed how much there was to see, smell, hear,
and taste in Scott's world. If a guest wintering at the St. Charles Hotel in 1854
exited the main door and turned right onto Gravier Street, in one block he arrived at the intersection with Carondelet Street. Standing on that corner, facing away from the river, he would have been greeted by a raucous tableau. On
his left, proceeding from Carondelet to Baronne, he passed the slave dealers
at 157 and 159 Gravier; a dime bar—and site of Scott's coffee shop—at 161 Gravier; slave dealers at 163 Gravier; then a barber, a merchant tailor, a boot- and
shoemaker, and another slave dealer at the intersection with Baronne.[78]

At a slow moment of the day or evening—if one existed—perhaps Scott
ventured to the doorway of his storefront to lean against the doorframe and
catch a passerby's eye, encouraging him inside for a coffee. Looking across the
street, Scott would have seen a similar scene reflected across from him on the

downriver side of the block. Sweeping his gaze from right to left, from Carondelet to Baronne, Scott would have seen a carriage repository; Falcon House, a dime coffeehouse and surely a competitor of his; the popular Placide Varieties theater; Tacony House, another dime coffeehouse; a livery stable; a tailor; a shoemaker; and a cigar store. In the middle of the block, Varieties Alley cut from Gravier to Common Street, connecting the walker to another block of businesses: a slave depot, a restaurant and dime coffeehouse, commission merchants, cotton brokers, and a ship broker.[79] In these blocks, Scott and his fellow entrepreneurs dedicated themselves to the gratification of present and future appetites. A cheap sip of coffee or whiskey, a cigar, an oyster, a show, a new pair of shoes, a person: all were things for sale. This was the same message that the city's newspapers had conveyed a half century earlier.

Beyond the mid-1850s, William Scott no longer appeared in New Orleans city directories or the federal census.[80] Did he leave the city, his home for nearly forty years, sensing the dangers ahead? Soon, state authorities would seek to destroy the autonomy and wealth that Scott and others like him had built. In 1856, Louisiana prohibited free people of color from acquiring liquor licenses. In 1859, the state banned free people of color from owning a "coffee house, billiard hall, or retail store where liquor was sold."[81] If Scott stayed in the Crescent City, he could no longer claim ownership of the business he operated and the profits it gathered. In fact, the 1858 city directory listed a different proprietor—Thomas W. Dick and Co.—operating a coffeehouse at 161 Gravier Street.[82] For decades, Scott had been a savvy entrepreneur, moving and growing his businesses to satisfy insatiable hungers and thirsts. To have positioned his fruit stores and coffeehouses in other neighborhoods would have ignored the profits to be had across from the Merchants' Exchange and on Gravier Street. Yet his success did not come without costs. William Scott's career evinced how a free person of color could build wealth sustaining people who traded in the lives of people who looked like him. With slave dealers on his right and left, Scott worked in the chafe between slavery and freedom. In the end, it may have squeezed him out.

William Scott's changing fortunes showed how living as a free person of color in antebellum New Orleans meant forever teetering on the brink—socially, economically, and legally. An entrepreneur with a decades-long career, Scott had complied with the order to prove his freedom and justify his residence in the city, only to have his right to own a business taken away. Scott's financial success surely protected him to some degree from the precarity of Crescent City life. For many others, though, especially those less well-off than Scott, the line separating freedom from enslavement and independence from subordination was more permeable. Once purchased or granted, freedom was far from a permanent state of existence. James Fertram, a twenty-four-year-old New Orleans native and free man of color, was working as a pastry cook on-board the steamboat *Oregon* when catastrophe struck on one trip. "Said boat was blown up and sunk—and he states he has lost all his papers . . . on board," wrote an acquaintance in a note attached to Fertram's registration with the mayor's office. "I know him and can recommend him for veracity." William Williams, a free man of color born in 1821 in Lebanon, Ohio, worked as a cook onboard various Mississippi steamboats. One day, he mislaid the papers that certified his freedom. The error required a white man, a steward, to vouch for Williams to the New Orleans mayor to prevent imprisonment or sale on a New Orleans auction block.[83] Events as dramatic as a steamboat explosion or as simple as lost scraps of paper threatened disaster once free people of color crossed land or water borders into Louisiana.

The rules were not the same for white New Orleanians. When a notary completed an inventory of the St. Louis Hotel's furnishings in 1843, it was to confirm the hotel's lease to a new lessee, a widowed woman named Louise Hawley. As security for the lease, Hawley "assign[ed], obligate[d], and mort-gage[d]" to the bank four enslaved people in her possession, vowing not to "sell, transfer, or mortgage . . . nor dispose of them in any way." In other words, the valued items that served as the security at the heart of the lease of the St. Louis Hotel—where so many men, women, and children were bought and sold—were the lives of four bondspeople. The notary identified them as Buck-ner, an eighteen-year-old "*créole*" and "mulatto" man; Mélanie, a thirty-year-old *créole* Black woman; Auguste, a nineteen-year-old *créole* mulatto man; and Norine, a fifty-year-old Black woman.[84] Incredibly, Louise Hawley admitted to the notary that she had "misplaced the titles" proving her ownership of sev-eral of these individuals. Hawley's purchases of Mélanie and Norine—as well as that of a woman named Nancy, Auguste's mother—had occurred via "var-ious acts of sale" in St. Martin Parish, which she had left "about twelve years ago," she explained. Hawley promised to obtain the paperwork and convey it to her creditors "immediately" at her own expense, a condition they "ac-cepted."[85] This was a stunning allowance granted to Hawley, considering the pressure that authorities placed on free people of color to corroborate their status. No such demands were imposed on Hawley. The financial and legal agreement that installed her as lessee of the St. Louis Hotel rested on nothing more tangible than her word and on the immense, invisible value imbued in four people. Buckner, Mélanie, Auguste, and Norine may have washed Haw-ley's bedsheets and polished her silver not knowing that their lives were the security for one of the nation's most luxurious slave markets.

Free people of color like William Scott, James Fertram, and William Williams could not afford the sloppiness of Louise Hawley. If free New Orleanians of color woke, worked, and slept with the terrorizing prospect of enslavement or re-enslavement, they also sustained more mundane aggressions in the form of daily harassment. High and low, these were the constant threats that free people of color battled—the undertow in the waves lapping at their feet.[86]

The path of one longtime city resident, a grocer and a contemporary of William Scott and Lucette Barberousse, put this reality into stark relief. Prosper Blair's path started very far from Louisiana: in Calcutta, India, where he was born around 1792. At some point, Blair emigrated to the new United States and married Jane Camilton, born in Philadelphia in 1808 and later identified in New Orleans records as a free "mulatto" woman. Prosper, Jane, and Jane's older sister, Margaret Camilton, arrived in New Orleans in 1822. Nine years later, in 1831, Prosper and Jane's first child was born: Mary Jane Blair. Within the decade, four more children followed: Margaretha Ann (b. 1833); Pierre Soude Prosper (b. 1835); Victor Nicolas (b. 1837), baptized in St. Louis Cathedral; and Victorine Julia (b. 1840). Louisiana birth records identified all five children as "colored (black)." On August 13, 1840, Prosper Blair, father of five children under ten, with his youngest about five weeks old, registered with the New Orleans mayor as a free person of color entitled to live in Louisiana. His name entered the same volume that documented the lives and work of Scott, Barberousse, and thousands of others.[87]

Blair's entry was unique, however. On this sweltering day in mid-August 1840, the official who filled the lines of the mayor's registry looked at the forty-eight-year-old grocer in front of him and put pen to paper. He did not describe Prosper Blair's skin color as "Black," "Mulatto," or "Griffe," (a person thought to have three grandparents of African descent and one of European descent, or someone of mixed African and Indigenous heritages).[88] Rather, the bureaucrat recorded Blair's own articulation of his identity: Blair was "Indian." The recordkeeper emphasized the singular nature of this description with an underline. He added a conspicuous, explanatory note below Blair's entry: "Prosper Blair is only registered here because he fears being bothered due to his brown color, and he wants the testimony of M. Jh. Paul Coulon in his favor to be preserved in this book."[89] Already a resident of New Orleans for almost two decades, Prosper Blair had volunteered himself for the mayor's registry, naming a prominent white businessman as his ally. Blair feared future harassment due to his skin tone, a decision surely made after enduring or witnessing previous provocations.[90]

White New Orleanians did not know how to categorize Blair and his family members; this fact was made clear by the changing adjectives that record-keepers used to describe them in various municipal, state, and federal documents over the course of decades. The 1841 New Orleans city directory identified Prosper Blair as a free man of color: "fmc, grocery, corner Jackson and Villere." Nevertheless, future directory listings of Blair and his grocery—from 1842 through 1866—never again identified him as a person of color. Still, as early as 1840, Blair understood that in the eyes of those he encountered in his daily work, he risked looking a shade of Black, which posed a danger to himself and his family. For this reason, Blair sought to record proactively in the mayor's book that he lived in New Orleans as a free man.

Working as a grocer gave Prosper Blair a secure existence—though one not free of discrimination experienced or observed—that enabled him to live in the same neighborhood of New Orleans for at least forty years and support a growing family. City directories of the 1840s, 1850s, and early 1860s showed Blair working as a grocer at several locations along Villere Street, on either side of Canal Street.[91] This area was a five-minute walk from the rambunctious stretch of Gravier Street where William Scott operated his coffeehouse during the same years, but Blair's neighborhood was more workaday city and less playboy's playground. Positioned several blocks beyond the bounds of the French Quarter in the direction of Lake Pontchartrain, landmarks included Charity Hospital, the city Gas Works, and Old Basin Canal. In his daily work, Blair would have seen mourners going to and from St. Louis Cemetery no. 2, one of New Orleans's major Catholic cemeteries, as well as traffic associated with Wood's Cotton Press. He may have smelled the vinegar manufacturer on Canal between Marais and Tremé Streets. Other businesses in Blair's immediate vicinity in the mid-1850s—oyster stands, beer and coffeehouses, shoe stores, wood yards, and an undertaker—served the neighborhood's lager-loving German and Irish immigrants and other working-class residents.[92] About forty years in the future, municipal authorities would designate Blair's block and others around it as Storyville, a bounded area in which prostitution was legal.[93] During Blair's lifetime, though, he lived and worked in a neighborhood peopled by immigrants, laborers, and shoppers who just needed their groceries—blocks that were not yet a tourist draw.

Prosper Blair and his family did the ordinary jobs that made the city run. Nevertheless, his children grew up during decades when white New Orleanians worked tirelessly to reduce, if not obliterate, the city's population of free people of color, which included the Blairs, Lucette Barberousse, and William Scott. During these tumultuous years, some of Prosper and Jane's children stayed in New Orleans and others moved beyond it, extending the Blair family's migrations and movements farther afield. In 1848, Proper and Jane's eldest child, Mary Jane, married in a Baptist church in Kentucky. Her father was present to give his consent.[94] Their next two children—Margaretha Ann and Pierre Soude Prosper—never enrolled in the mayor's registry of free people. Perhaps they moved away from New Orleans, as their older sister had, or one or both may have died.[95]

The Blairs' two youngest children—Victor Nicolas Blair and Victorine Julia Blair—did register with the mayor. In 1857, nineteen-year-old (Victor) Nicolas Prosper Blair submitted his name to the registry while working as a slater. A generation after his father had first registered, Nicholas stood before an employee of the mayor's office and had his skin color scrutinized, too. As before, the bureaucrat had a difficult time deciding on a racial classification for the young man; he registered the teenage Blair as "mulatto or griffe." Blair registered once more with the mayor four years later, on a date when Louisiana no longer identified itself as part of the United States. On February 6, 1861, Nicholas [*sic*] Prosper Blair reminded the mayor that he was entitled to live in the state as a free man. Now described as a "griffe man," Blair was working as a carriage driver.[96] Less than two weeks earlier, the state of Louisiana had seceded from the Union. Two days earlier, on February 4, delegates from Louisiana and five other states had met to establish what they would call the Confederate States of America. In the next several years, New Orleanians who were customers and neighbors of the Blair family—who shopped at Prosper's grocery and rode in Nicolas's carriage, perhaps—would fight and die to keep people of color like the Blairs surveilled, excluded, or enslaved.

White New Orleanians would not put up much of a fight for the city of New Orleans, though. In late April 1862, Confederate forces surrendered New Orleans to the Union Army. Once Union ships bypassed Confederate defenses on the Mississippi River, they took control of the South's largest city without struggle, on April 28, 1862. The same river that had determined New Orleans's location, defined its wealth, and served as the conduit for cotton, sugar, slaves, and fugitives from slavery brought the city's liberation from the Confederacy. Still, the arrival of Union forces did not mean emancipation for enslaved New Orleanians. Nor did President Lincoln's January 1, 1863, Emancipation Proclamation, which exempted the thirteen Louisiana parishes already under Union control. Slavery remained legal in New Orleans for almost two more years, until it was finally abolished by state constitution in December 1864.[97]

Life would change drastically for all Americans in the years following the Civil War, the Blair family included. By 1871, Nicolas Prosper Blair, son of Prosper Blair, appeared in the city directory of Columbus, Ohio, working as a drayman. That same year, a daughter, Dora, was born to him and his wife Elizabeth.[98] Their daughter Dora would grow up to marry Benjamin "Benny"

Bowles, a Black man born in Richmond, Virginia. Benny and Dora moved to the south side of Chicago in the 1890s. They had children, lost their eldest daughter in 1909, at the age of fifteen, and worked. Benny was a porter for the Pullman Company for more than twenty years before he passed away in 1921. On July 14, 1924, at the age of fifty-three, Dora (Blair) Bowles—daughter of (Nicolas) Prosper Blair of New Orleans and granddaughter of Prosper Blair of New Orleans and Calcutta, India—died in Chicago. At the time of her death, Dora was working as a cook in a hospital.[99]

The labors, movements, births, and deaths of Prosper Blair's family were at once ordinary and extraordinary. They reflected migration around the globe and within the United States. Members of this family survived discrimination, disease, and war. Following a path halfway around the world, Prosper Blair built a livelihood in New Orleans with food. He filled the shelves of his grocery with fruit, vegetables, coffee, and sugar. Nearly a century later, in a kitchen a thousand miles north, his granddaughter Dora worked with food, too. If food was a constant thread in their family history, so, too, was racism.

The original anxiety of the Indian immigrant Prosper Blair in 1840—the motivation to add his name to a roster of free New Orleanians of color in the hopes of keeping himself and his family safe—showed that the American color line had already been drawn. In 1881, Frederick Douglass would write about the discrimination that pervaded the United States even after slavery's abolition. Black Americans "carry in front the evidence which marks them for persecution," he wrote. "They are negroes—and that is enough, in the eye of this unreasoning prejudice, to justify indignity and violence." A generation later, with a famously terse prediction, W. E. B. Du Bois foresaw little improvement in coming decades: "The problem of the Twentieth Century is the problem of the color-line."[100] Before and long after Douglass and Du Bois wrote these words, the white American gaze insisted on white or Black. Bureaucratic recordkeepers in New Orleans, Columbus, and Chicago—from the 1840s to the 1920s—swallowed up and erased the South Asian branch of the Blair family tree, seeing only shades of Black when they looked at Prosper Blair and his children and grandchildren.[101] When Blair's granddaughter, Dora Blair Bowles, passed away in Chicago in 1924, the Illinois Deaths and Stillbirths Index classified her race as "black." She was buried in Lincoln Cemetery in Blue Island, Illinois, south of Chicago. A group of Black businessmen had procured the land in 1911 as a resting place because white-owned cemeteries in the vicinity refused to bury their Black neighbors in their dirt.[102]

On July 7, 1864, the New Orleans editors of *L'Union*, the South's first Black-owned newspaper, published a humorous anecdote for their readers, who were French-speaking Creoles of color. Titled, "A Scene in a New Orleans Café," the sketch began with an exchange between a coffeehouse proprietor and his new employee. "I warn you that under no circumstance should you serve a man of color," the proprietor instructed. "Yes, sir!" the waiter answered. Enforcing this rule would prove to be far from black and white, however:

> Immediately after this conversation a man of color enters, but *white* as snow, who goes to the bar and orders: "Jackson Punch." The waiter serves him, he drinks, and he leaves.
>
> After he leaves, the café owner says to the waiter: "Did I not tell you not to serve men of color? You have just served precisely a *negro*."
>
> – "Ah! I didn't know, *monsieur*."
>
> Two minutes later a white man enters, the color of *café au lait*, but in which the *café* prevails. With an urgent tone, the newcomer orders: "*Hé garçon*, a Whiskey punch, quick, I'm in a hurry." The waiter stares at him a moment and then says: "I can't serve negroes in this café."
>
> – "What[?]" says the establishment's owner, who knew the fellow, "You insult *Monsieur*, know that he is white and that I have known him as such since . . ."
>
> – "Eh! *Monsieur*, go to hell with your café. A white man comes in, you tell me he's a negro; a negro comes, you tell me he's a white man. . . . What do you want me to do!"[103]

The waiter received no answer; the scene concluded there. Readers likely laughed at the hapless employee, caught between his boss and his customers during his first day on the job. They could easily envision the scene, since the setting was familiar: one of the city's hundreds of cafés. Readers may have recognized themselves, too, within the tale's cast of characters.[104]

The sketch's humor lay in the supple space between skin color and racial classification that played out in this fictional New Orleans café. The scene satirized the setting as a world turned upside down, where a man of color could be white as snow and a white man appear dark. A café-colored patron sought to drink in a café that served coffee (*café*). People, place, and object blended such that the rules of engagement between server and served became muddled. The sequence of absurd interactions caused the reader to smile and the waiter to throw up his hands, yet a vexed helplessness underlay his distress. When he declared, "Go to hell with your café," he could have been cursing the business where he worked or, just as possibly, the manager's insistence that skin the color of *café* meant one thing and not another. "What do you want me to do!" he demanded, in this city that insisted on the importance of skin color as a standard of exclusion, even when the stakes were a cup of punch or coffee. A subjective tangle of perceptions, classifications, and proscriptions, measured in degrees of *café* and *café au lait*, impeded the waiter in his labors.[105]

When this scene appeared in print in July 1864, the editors and subscribers of *L'Union* wrote and read on the cusp of a new world. White New Orleanians felt this, too, and resented it.[106] Coffeehouses and similar businesses had long served as the stage for auctions of enslaved people, where only serendipity or a piece of paper—establishing if a person was white or Black, enslaved or free—distinguished the man standing on the block from the man standing behind the bar from the man sitting in the crowd. In the New Orleans of the near future, a freedman might work for wages or drink a cup of coffee as a customer in that same establishment. After slavery was abolished, however, the dangers for Black Louisianians metastasized. Local governments throughout the South rushed to construct Black Codes designed to crush the rights of newly free people. The 1865 Black Code of Louisiana's St. Landry Parish, for example, forbade people of color from renting property, traveling without a permit, congregating after sunset, speaking to a group of people of color without the permission of police, or carrying weapons. The code further specified, "Every negro is required to be in the regular service of some white person, or former owner, who shall be held responsible for the conduct of said negro."[107] Transformed modes of surveillance, exploitation, and violence darkened the horizon. At the dawn of this new day, in this city that had once been the nation's largest slave market, what would freedom, freedmen, and their labors look like? What remained and what had changed? With such questions in mind, eyes turned toward the Crescent City and fell on a place whose fruits had long sweetened the American table: "the sweetest spot on earth," the New Orleans sugar levees, and the cane fields to which they were bound.

3

FIELD AND LEVEE, THROUGH THE LENS

Looking at Louisiana Sugar after the Civil War

You cannot think, how soon the want of sleep
Breaks down their strength, 'tis well they are so cheap,
Four hours for rest—in time of crop—for five
Or six long months, and few indeed will thrive.

With twenty hours of unremitting toil,
Twelve in the field, and eight in doors, to boil
Or grind the cane—believe me few grow old,
But life is cheap, and sugar, sir,—is gold.

R. R. Madden, "The Sugar Estate," in
Poems by a Slave in the Island of Cuba, Recently Liberated, 1840

IN JUNE 1865, a New Orleans journalist reported on a promising change of direction in the breeze drifting over the city's levees, the earth embankments that held back the river and doubled as commercial wharves. "Since Peace has spread her wings over a reunited country. . . . The levee presents a more animated appearance than it has for a long time," he wrote. Little more than two months had passed since the Confederacy's surrender to Union forces in Virginia, ending the Civil War. Already, mounds of goods on the levee indicated that Louisiana fields were again bearing fruit. "Long rows of sugar hogsheads are to be seen side by side with barrels of molasses," the reporter described. Close by sat "bales of hay, barrels of pork and flour, [and] sacks of oats and corn." The presence of familiar faces likewise hinted that the city's prosperity was returning. He observed the "mirth loving negro . . . who works like a beaver one moment, [and] sleeps the next," and spied wealthier and whiter faces,

FIGURE 3.1. Photographs and stereographs of sugar hogsheads and cotton bales on New Orleans's levees showed the persistence of Louisiana's great staples, on the cusp of a new century. Strohmeyer and Wyman, *The Sweetest Spot on Earth—Sugar Levee, New Orleans, U. S. A.*, 1895, photograph. Library of Congress, Washington, DC, https://www.loc.gov/item/2018 649759/.

too. "The hotels are crowded with visitors. . . . We hope there is 'a good time a coming,'" he concluded wistfully.[1] Following years of Union occupation, the journalist looked to the levee and gauged its barrels of sugar, molasses, pork, and grain, together with the workers who moved them, as barometers of the city's postbellum fortunes.

If this reporter used words to sketch the initial outlines of New Orleans's recovery for his readers, many Americans decided to look for themselves. In the decades following the Civil War, travelers and businesspeople returned to New Orleans to stay in its great hotels, eat and drink, attend conventions and expositions, and see the sights.[2] But the sights—and the means of seeing those sights—were changing. Politically, economically, and culturally, the nation was stitching itself back together with a quick and heavy hand. These were years of industrialization, urbanization, swelling wealth for the economy's upper crust, and rebellious activism for those who labored to build that wealth. With guns and goods, the United States plunged into empire-building beyond its borders. Within the nation's bounds, rail lines crisscrossed plains and bored through mountains, moving people, grain, beef, and beer. In urban and rural settings alike, Americans marveled at the spectacle of progress in many forms.[3]

In Louisiana, awestruck gazes focused on New Orleans's levees—described as "the sweetest spot on earth," where sugar and molasses changed hands—as well as the state's sugarcane fields, long a wellspring of riches (fig. 3.1). Distinct from previous eras, advances in photographic and printing technologies enabled these places and their goods to become newly visible to the world. Guidebooks, photographic postcards, and stereographs spread views of the Louisiana sugar industry throughout the nation and abroad. To look at Louisiana sugar production in the late 1800s and early 1900s was to view rural plantations and sugarhouses, steamboats, crowded levees, wooden barrels, and urban sheds, plus the industry's laborers. Fields tall with cane and rows of hogsheads seemed to show the persistence of Louisiana's antebellum bounty.

These photographic mementos did other work, too, during years marred by the solidification of Jim Crow, mass disfranchisement, and a surge of lynchings. If postcards and stereographs of Louisiana's levees and sugarcane fields were sold as snapshots of American industry and agriculture, they were also carefully framed perspectives on one of the nation's favorite foods and the people who made it. American cakes, syrups, ice creams, puddings, and cordials: historically, much of their sugar had been bled from cane by Black Louisianians. These mementos showed Americans where their sugar came from and, in photographic form, bound Louisiana's emancipated workers to it. White photographers depicted Black laborers much the same as they might have fifty years in the past, toiling and in bondage, even as the world around them was modernizing. Such images waged an insidious assault on these new citizens' status in society, acting as silent accomplices to the bald-faced violence that pervaded the nation's political discourse, popular culture, and city streets.

With the Civil War in recent memory, Black Americans found themselves waging a new war, battling the assaults of different weapons. Surrounded by racist stereotypes on minstrel stages, in legislative chambers, and on food packaging and postcards, New Orleanians of color created their own visual culture to record their achievements and joys. They protested, unionized, shopped, dined, worked, and built communities in the Crescent City. Yet their activism and actions were not enough to avoid a bitter end to some of the era's most consequential battles for justice and equality.

Sweet Sublime

Before and after the Civil War, observers marveled at the New Orleans levee as a singular site of staggering abundance. There, steamboats vomited up sugar, molasses, and cotton for waiting warehouses and presses. Goods from the Mississippi Valley, the Caribbean, and farther afield were unloaded, organized, graded, purchased, sold, and moved again on the levee's vast plane. In 1860, on the eve of war, the port of New Orleans entered 630,000 tons of goods from foreign ports and cleared nearly 900,000 tons of goods bound for foreign destinations, making it the nation's second-busiest export port, trailing only New York City.[4] This was a place of human and mechanical motion, sound, and scale, monstrous in its power.[5] Visitors could not take their eyes away.

"Umbrellas overcoats carriages cabs baggage waggons [*sic*] & wheelbarrows were mingled together . . . with the noise of the owners, drivers, occupants & operatives with the squalling of children . . . & the blowing of the escape pipe," wrote Lewis Webb in his diary in 1853. Hailing from Rockingham, North Carolina, Webb had come to New Orleans to work as a clerk in a mercantile firm. A devout teetotaler, Webb shirked the many bars and gambling houses that lined the city's blocks. Instead, he passed his time reading newspapers in the lobby of the St. Charles Hotel, checking at the post office for letters from his family, and walking New Orleans's busy streets. One of Webb's favorite destinations was the levee. In his breathless descriptions, the levee's action flowed together into a river of objects and sounds that intruded, sometimes rudely, on his presence. "Thumped & pushed & elbowed off the gangway plank" of a steamboat on January 16, 1853, Webb finally escaped the crowd, only to return many times during the levee's peak winter and early spring season.[6]

Despite the levee's intrinsically tangible nature—as the place where American and global riches were made manifest in hogsheads, bales, and piles—the scene inspired Webb to reflect on abstract themes. The New Orleans riverfront convinced this young North Carolinian of the nation's political and geographic destinies, despite reporting on political and social discord that surely filled the newspapers he read. On January 25, 1853, Webb confided to his diary that the Crescent City's levees and its sumptuous steamboats made him reflect on "the supremacy of the Americans in this respect over all the world, of the fact that 50 years ago the stream upon which this monster now ploughs was navigated only by the solitary canoe. . . . What a mighty country is ours," he exclaimed, "and what a glorious destiny awaits her in the future."[7] To Webb, the levee distilled the nation's agricultural, industrial, and political potential into a single panorama. Its abundance and excitement convinced this visitor—and so many others—that the system by which it ran was correct and good, even if it relied on the labor of enslaved people.

Lewis Webb may have imagined a "glorious destiny" for the nation, but less than a decade in the future, New Orleans's destiny would be war, occupation, and defeat. The Civil War wreaked havoc on Louisiana's sugar and cotton industries. Activity at the New Orleans levees plummeted. Following the war's end, river traffic returned to the city, but a confluence of technological, commercial, and human factors—a shift to sugarcane and cotton grown in overseas fields; labor and racial strife; the rise of beet sugar—ensured that the future would not look like the past. Additionally, as miles of railroad track stretched across Louisiana's soggy landscape—increasing tenfold between 1860 and 1904, from 335 miles to more than 3,500—they spelled the end of steam travel on the Mississippi River. Nevertheless, New Orleans boosters beckoned businesspeople and travelers, insisting that the Crescent City would hold court in the twentieth century as it had in the nineteenth.[8]

For those who heeded this call, where to go and what to do? Earlier generations of visitors had relied on acquaintances to direct them to New Orleans's dinner parties, balls, and theaters. Tourists in the late 1800s and early 1900s, in contrast, reached for a new crop of guidebooks, "booster books," and volumes of souvenir views. Published by newspapers, businesses, and professional organizations—all figures invested in a revitalized economy—these texts voiced strong opinions on what the newcomer should see.[9] The author of *Jewell's Crescent City Illustrated*, a directory and booster book published in 1873, bragged that the Crescent City basked in an "unrivalled" geographic and economic position. Nowhere was its preeminence more visible than on the levee. There, "hundreds of immense floating castles and palaces, called steamboats," stretched for miles along the shore. "The transportation, by some three thousand drays, of cotton, sugar, tobacco . . . strikes the stranger with wonder and admiration," he promised.[10] Similarly, an 1873 guidebook dismissed New Orleans's libraries, art galleries, and public parks as "noticeably deficient," urging the tourist to instead visit the levee, for its "series of sights always attractive to strangers." More than one million tons of goods and almost 3,500 steamboats had touched its docks the previous year, the writer marveled.[11] There, the region's recovery could be witnessed and tallied.

Texts like these helped elevate Crescent City sites like the sugar and cotton levees to the same status as more typical tourist destinations like cemeteries, churches, and monuments to the Confederate dead. Increasingly, this project was a visual one. These books situated engravings and photographs of modernizing agriculture and industry—visions of the region's recovery and promises of its future—within the same gaze as more traditional sources of culture and history. A souvenir book sold by a local publisher to attendees at the 1884 World's Industrial and Cotton Centennial Exposition, held in New Orleans, showed such an approach. On one spread of pages, the breezy weekend pleasures of Lake Pontchartrain's West End were mirrored by views of "negroes cutting sugarcane" and picking cotton, a stately "planter's residence," and a sugar mill (fig. 3.2). Other spreads featured images of the busy levee, live oaks, New Orleans's Temple of Sinai, "a swamp view," and the vast Exposition buildings and grounds. Visual fragments of leisure, labor, industry, religion,

THE WEST END.

SUGAR CANE FIELD & MILL.   PLANTER'S RESIDENCE.   NEGROES CUTTING SUGAR CANE.

AQUARIUM, WEST END.   PROMENADE, WEST END.   PICKING COTTON.

FIGURE 3.2. Illustrated souvenir books such as this one, produced for attendees at the 1884 World's Industrial and Cotton Centennial Exposition, presented views of leisure and labor in Louisiana on a single spread of pages. In Louis Schwarz, *Souvenir of New Orleans and the Exposition* (New Orleans: L. Schwarz, 1885). Library of Congress, Washington, DC, https://www.loc.gov/item/01016529/.

landscape, and government: the visitor who perused this collection of views found all scenes presented as equally representative of New Orleans.[12]

When visitors followed the paths recommended by such manuals and found themselves at the levee, they entered a setting that entranced and overwhelmed. Some descriptions, especially in the context of foodstuffs, verged on the surreal. "The very dust we breathe here is rich, it is the essence of disintegrated cotton and sugar; the gutters flow with molasses and syrup, and the air is redolent of pine-apples and bananas," raved a local journalist in 1873.[13] The volume and sensory qualities of the riverfront's spoils were so intense, this writer imagined, that their matter evaporated into a fantastical aura of wealth. "The barrels of sweets overflow the sheds, crowd all the warehouses in the vicinity, overrun the levee and block the sidewalks. There is sugar everywhere," another writer described, later in the century.[14] Humans seemed to not belong here, though they demanded the levee's goods for their tables and looms.

Such experiences of amazement, alienation, and sensory thrill placed the New Orleans levee within a contemporaneous fascination with the "industrial sublime." Americans gazed with fearful enchantment at the factories,

FIGURE 3.3. With its hordes of laboring people and animals, mountains of goods, and bellowing steamboat stacks, the New Orleans levee awed visitors with an experience of the industrial sublime. Wood engraving from a sketch by Joseph Horton, "Louisiana—the Business Boom in the South—a Scene on the Levee at New Orleans," *Frank Leslie's Illustrated Newspaper*, January 8, 1881, 320. Library of Congress, Washington, DC, https://www.loc.gov/item/2002711652/.

railroads, and dams that were transforming the country's reach and potential and, in many places, replacing the human with the mechanical.[15] The Crescent City's waterfront inspired similar reactions. An illustration printed in *Frank Leslie's Illustrated Newspaper* in 1881, viewed by a nationwide readership, evoked this scene in New Orleans (fig. 3.3). Steamboat smokestacks belched black clouds, casting an apocalyptic shadow on the crazed field below. Hogsheads of sugar and bales of cotton assembled into phalanxes. Mules and men carried, rolled, and stacked these goods, appearing like tiny cogs within a larger machine. In the right foreground, a man ran toward an urgent task. In the left foreground, workers bowed under the weight of heavy loads. Elevated high above the shoreline, the artist had a bird's-eye view over this field of battle. Altogether, the image evoked a martial atmosphere that declared: this is the South's new war of machines and men. These riches extracted from Louisiana's fields will fuel the region's recovery.

To many readers, this illustration may have offered an unexpected view of a place already beloved by privileged travelers as a leisure destination. New Orleans's "people are fond of idleness yet build up and sustain a great commerce. It is an enigma," puzzled one writer in 1889.[16] Yet there should have been no enigma as to who sweated to create the Crescent City's wealth.

Labor and Leisure on the Levee

Alongside the vessels, animals, and goods that made the New Orleans levee sublime, the people who worked there also drew travelers' gazes. Journalists and tourists loved to watch levee laborers work. Onlookers marveled at the physical strength and inscrutable organization that forged riches and wrested order out of apparent chaos. This wary attraction to modernity's machines implied a specific racial perspective. Locals and tourists who wrote about the New Orleans levee as awesome and frightening were white. For the most part, they gazed but did not engage. Black and immigrant laborers, in contrast, experienced the levee as a place of grueling, frenzied work. When white observers looked at levee laborers and the commodities they moved, they reached for racist stereotypes that had originated under slavery and put them to work, again. Photographic representations amplified such perspectives, intensifying their impact.

Much of the effort to pack and move Louisiana's bounty happened before a vessel reached New Orleans's shores. Along the length of the Mississippi River, Black roustabouts moved goods on and off ships. Excluded from unions, they formed the lowliest class of levee laborer, doing a job that was excruciating and essential. Following the schedules of river and railway traffic, roustabouts worked around the clock. Compared to other river workers, they were more likely to have been enslaved or descended from bondspeople, poorly educated, and impoverished.[17] In 1893, a barber working on the steamboat *City of Providence* told a journalist that he would rather break the law than toil as a roustabout. "I'd go to stealin' fo' I'd be a rooster" the reporter quoted the barber as saying, "cause dey couldn't wuk a man no harder in de penitentshuary . . . dan dey do on dese boats." Roustabouts did "more work than a white man," the reporter acknowledged. "There were nights on the *Providence* when the landings ran close together, and the poor wretches got little or no sleep. They 'tote' all the freight . . . on their heads or shoulders, and it is crushing work."[18] Still, some of these roustabouts looked back later with deep pride in their labors. "I used to be able to handle a bale of cotton just like you'd handle a pillow slip," remembered Peter Barber, who had been born enslaved in Charlottesville, Virginia, in 1844. Barber told a WPA interviewer how he had escaped from his enslaver at twenty-two and worked for more than fifty years as a fireman and deckhand on Mississippi River steamboats. "Every place where we passed through there was people lined up to see us go by."[19]

Journalists and tourists marveled at roustabouts' strength and endurance, but their regard had a sharp edge of derision. Many onlookers described river

workers in a way that likened them to animals, including insects and liz-
ards, and bound them to the commodities they moved, which were often
food. Such perspectives differed little from the reflections of travelers nearly
a century earlier, who had written about New Orleans's people and food as
twinned attractions. "The long, zigzagging, shambling line ⌊of roustabouts⌋
was metamorphosed into . . . an unsteady line of flour-bags, each with ragged
legs beneath it," wrote one journalist in 1893, from his perch on a steamboat's
passenger deck. To his eye, roustabouts formed a humorous parade of conjoined people and goods. "Their coffee-colored necks and faces matched their
reddish-brown clothes. . . . When a huddle went off the boat empty-handed
they looked like so many big rats."[20] To readers dispersed throughout the nation, this reporter described the Mississippi's roustabouts—all wage-working
citizens, a generation removed from slavery—as flour-bags and coffee with
feet, and when separated from their burdens as nothing more than rats. Such
writings adhered to longstanding racist tropes that cast Black men as more
thing or animal than human, and mythically strong.[21]

In the face of such contempt, roustabouts and those who worked by their
sides were powering a stuttering return of the region's economy. This task
was Herculean in more ways than one. A wood hogshead packed with sugar
weighed 1,500 pounds. One hundred forty viscous gallons of molasses filled
the same container. Compressed into a ragged cube, a cotton bale weighed
five hundred pounds.[22] The cargo of the port of New Orleans, even if sweet
and soft, traveled in monstrous units. During the levee's peak fall and winter
season, ten to fifteen thousand men worked on a riverfront that stretched for
six continuous miles.[23] An arriving vessel required screwmen and longshoremen to unload its contents. Teamsters and loaders moved goods to cotton
yards, sugar sheds, or nearby rail lines. Scalemen, weighers (and re-weighers),
classers, and graders inspected and ranked the quality of Louisiana's two great
staples. Coal wheelers, longshoremen, and screwmen fueled and packed departing vessels.[24] This army of men—multilingual and diverse in terms of race,
class, and skills—sorted into segregated unions that worked in concert at times
and, at others, at violent odds.[25]

In New Orleans, as upriver, the feats of strength accomplished by roustabouts and longshoremen drew tourists to the urban levees as if the workers
were performers on a stage. "It is quite a comical sight to watch the unloading
of steamboats," wrote one fourteen-year-old boy in an 1897 handwritten essay,
describing tourist attractions in the city. "Sometimes you see a negro coming
down the gangplank on a full run, with a cotton bale on a truck, bouncing
like a rubber ball," the boy wrote. "If he should trip and fall it would be almost certain death for once they get started they cannot be stopped until they

FIGURE 3.4. The photograph on this postcard aimed to provoke a laugh, casting the New Orleans levee as a tourist playground. *Fun on the Levee in New Orleans*, message dated November 22, 1915, picture postcard. Author's collection.

hit the wharf." This scene, one of life or death for the worker but comedy for the viewer, occupied the boy for "a few hours" before he moved on. Another onlooker had a terser reaction. "One of the best sights was niggers unloading the boats," wrote a Pennsylvania leatherworker in his diary as he passed through the city in 1903, looking for jobs.[26] For tourists who could go to the New Orleans levee and stand safely to the side, gazing at the labor of others was their leisure.

Some onlookers, however, went beyond merely looking at the levee and its laborers. They intervened in the action, turning it into a place to frolic. One postcard, with the caption "Fun on the Levee in New Orleans," showed a line of white women in skirts smiling broadly at the camera, eyes squinting in the sunlight (fig. 3.4). The colorful ribbons on their hats made this lineup a gaudily cheerful parade. Although the cotton bale on each cart was enormously heavy, requiring three women to lift the handles of the cart pictured in the foreground, plus a fourth steadying it from behind, the scene was one of farcical fun. Black dockworkers appeared in the background. One sat on a stack of cotton bales, watching the women. The photograph was surely taken in jest; this postcard was sold by a Canal Street shop whose risqué wares had earned the attention of the New Orleans Police Department.[27] Even so, the image cast the levee and the city it served as a place whose workers would step aside so the visitor could play—even with the substance of their work.

The absurdity of a line of women in long skirts dragging and pushing the state's most valuable commodity, first cultivated by enslaved people and then by sharecroppers, mocked the burdens borne by those who toiled there. This card illustrated in full color and photographic detail something more than the coincidental proximity of labor to leisure on the Crescent City levee. As in nearby dining rooms and barrooms, here, too, the stuff of one's labor became that of another's pleasure.[28]

As displayed on this postcard, New Orleans's riverfront tableaux appealed to tourists, reporters, and faraway observers as uniquely entertaining. A half century earlier, travelers had flocked to the St. Charles and St. Louis Hotels to gawk at bondspeople paraded onto auction blocks. Now, white tourists on the city's wharves gaped and smiled at the sight of Black laborers at work. On the levee, onlookers watched American wealth in motion, but this view was only a partial one. Shifting the frame upriver or downriver revealed a closer look at one of Louisiana's edible treasures—sugar—at its source.

Louisiana's Brutal Sweet

Not all tourists stayed on the levee. Louisiana's sugarcane plantations—the rural satellites of urban landings and sugar sheds—attracted travelers, writers, and photographers, too. Purportedly weaned from the taint of slavery, this rural world became newly accessible and visible on an international stage in the decades following the war's end. Tourists refashioned Louisiana's postbellum sugar industry and its workers into reservoirs of racist nostalgia with human, agrarian, and sensory dimensions. Excursions to sugarcane plantations—places where bondspeople had toiled and died, and where freedmen continued to labor—delighted visitors in search of experiences and sights they imagined to be typical of Louisiana. As on the levee, some of these outsiders could not resist inserting themselves into the action they found there.

"Most bankers realize that if Jack is not to become 'a dull boy,' he must sometimes unbend, cultivate his social nature," announced a writer in the journal *Banking and Mercantile World* in 1902. To avoid such a fate, bankers and their families converged on New Orleans for the annual convention of the American Bankers' Association. On the meeting's final day, nearly three thousand people boarded a steamer for a "delightful outing on the river" and chugged southward to Braithwaite, a sugarcane plantation.[29] Venturing into a setting that had previously been an abstraction to many Americans, these Northern tourists left enchanted. At Braithwaite, the bankers viewed the plantation's residents and the equipment they operated to extract syrup from sugarcane. "Many Northern visitors thought they had seen 'darkeys,'" the

FIGURE 3.5. Attendees at the 1902 convention of the American Bankers' Association delighted in a tour of a Louisiana sugarcane plantation, where they marveled at its array of "darkeys" and rode for fun on carts used to haul sugarcane. W. Y. Barnet, "New Orleans Entertains," *Banking and Mercantile World* 4, no. 6 (November–December 1902). Louisiana Research Collection, Tulane University Special Collections, New Orleans, LA.

writer recounted, "but they changed their minds when they surveyed the animated scene which was enlivened with more varieties of negroes than they had dreamed of as existing. . . . the gamut of the black race seemed to be run complete, no possible specimen being omitted."[30] The visitors inspected and appraised the place, cataloguing men, women, and children as if they were varietals of exotic flora. These people "decidedly interested the ladies and gentlemen of the North, and many a coin was cast into the air to provoke an animated scramble." To a nationwide readership, the writer described the intriguing power of activating the plantation's tenants with a few coins tossed in the dust. The party toured the sugarhouse and paper mill, rode on horse-drawn carts used to haul sugarcane, and returned to the steamboat, "armed, almost to a man and to a woman, with a stalk of cane" (fig. 3.5).[31] Forty years earlier, Union forces had fought to liberate enslaved laborers from this site. Now, Northern visitors delighted in souvenir canes of sugar and photographs of impoverished sharecroppers. A generation's time had converted Braithwaite from a battleground to a tourist's playground.[32]

Such journeys to view the source of American cane sugar pulled back the veil on the makings of one of the nation's cherished foods. Americans had always loved sugar and Black Americans had always made it. Beginning in the early 1500s, European colonizers blanketed Brazil and Caribbean islands with sugarcane plantations and chattel slavery. Successful production in colonial Louisiana began in 1795. Thus, sugar was rooted in Louisiana soil before that soil was purchased by the United States. When English writer Frances Milton Trollope toured the United States in the late 1820s, she found Americans already "'extravagantly fond' . . . of puddings, pies, and all kinds of 'sweets,' particularly the ladies." At sumptuous dinners, Trollope observed, "To eat inconceivable quantities of cake, ice, and pickled oysters, and to show half their revenue in silks and satins, seem to be the chief object."[33] At the time, Louisiana counted nearly seven hundred sugar factories, all powered by enslaved workers. Men and women who toiled on these plantations produced 37,500 tons of sugar. Americans ate double that quantity, though, consuming an average of one pound of sugar each month per capita.[34] Future consumption would soar far higher.

As Trollope watched American diners fill their bellies with puddings and pies, Louisiana's sugar industry was exploding. During the first half of the nineteenth century, the number of sugar factories in the state boomed, vaulting from seventy-five to 1,536, the largest number on record. In the same span, annual production shot from 2,500 tons to nearly 135,000 tons.[35] The climate of southern Louisiana, the capacities of the Mississippi River and port of New Orleans, and access to the nation's largest slave market all enabled Louisiana to dominate domestic sugar production. By 1850, 125,000 bondspeople—approximately half of Louisiana's total enslaved population—were dedicated to sugar cultivation.[36] A decade later, in 1861, the year before Union troops' arrival, enslaved Louisianians produced the state's largest volume of sugar up to that date: 264,000 tons—98 percent of the nation's total output.[37] Thus, prior to the Civil War, American sugar was synonymous with Louisiana sugar. Federal counts of domestic sugar and molasses production often reported data for Louisiana and "Other Southern States."[38]

Louisiana's soaring sugar production came through excruciating effort. The equipment, tasks, and vocabulary of sugar-making alluded to the violence required to extract sweetness from brittle cane. Covering hundreds of thousands of humid acres, sugarcane grew in dense rows, with blade-like leaves, up to nine feet high. Louisiana's climate dictated a frenzied harvest season.

FIGURE 3.6. To viewers in the comfort of their homes, this stereograph showed the back-breaking labor of sugarcane harvesting. Tourists at cane plantations rode such carts for pleasure. J. F. Jarvis, *Sugar Cane Plantation—Loading Cane, Louisiana, U.S.A.*, 1900, stereograph. Miriam and Ira D. Wallach Division of Art, Prints and Photographs photography collection, New York Public Library.

From mid-October through December, day and night, overseers drove laborers wielding hook-tipped machetes to fell the cane by hand. Plantation mills ran around the clock. William O'Neal, born enslaved in 1827 and hired out by his enslaver to work as an engineer building sugarhouses, recalled the rush of the Louisiana harvest and the living hunger of the mill. "By October the tenth the sugar-house is ready for grinding; the fires blaze in the great furnaces, the wheels begin to revolve, and it has become a thing of life," he wrote in his autobiography. "The heavy two-wheeled carts roll by, laden with juicy cane. . . . Long trains of these immense vehicles are coming and going, in the vain attempt to satiate the maw of that great colossus which is continually belching forth smoke and flame" (fig. 3.6).[39] Inside the mill, workers fed the cane into metal rollers, most of them steam-powered, which crushed and shredded the stalks.

The pressured labor of sugarcane processing drew sightseers, too, like flies to syrup. "Our feet, while in the boiling house, were actually sticking to the floor, which was soaked with molasses and half made sugar," recalled an English traveler of her visit to a Louisiana plantation in the late 1840s. The woman had ventured inside the boiling house, where enslaved workers stood over a steaming "battery" of open-topped kettles, where cane juice concentrated into molten syrup.[40] Skilled workers judged the moments to add lime to clarify the sugar, "seed" the syrup with crystallized sugar, and remove it from the heat.[41] After the sugar cooled and crystallized, workers packed brown sugar slurry into hogsheads punctured with holes. In the "purgery," molasses dripped slowly out of the holes, leaving raw sugar behind. Finally, laborers packaged the molasses and sugar for transport to the New Orleans levees and Northern distilleries and refineries.[42] Altogether, between field and sugarhouse, this was work of cutting, grinding, smashing, boiling, seeding, and purging, accompanied by steam, smoke, blazing heat, mechanized noise, and odors. "The smell of the melting sugar, even at three hundred yards distance from it, is very oppressive," the tourist remembered, too.[43]

If sugarcane processing destroyed the cane plant, it similarly devastated the bodies of sugar workers. At table, where Frances Milton Trollope watched American ladies in satin eat cake, the brutal violence of sugar-making was invisible. Yet it flourished and festered in written descriptions of the industry and the memories and scars of its laborers. "At the time of making sugar and molasses, the slaves are kept up half the night," wrote Lewis Clarke, of his experiences enslaved on a Louisiana sugarcane plantation. A bell woke women and men at four o'clock. Dew in the cane field drenched workers' clothing. Mothers with newborns brought them to the fields, so the infants would not starve while they were away.[44] Emancipated people recalled infants starving anyway, though, when their mothers were worked to exhaustion and their bodies rendered incapable of feeding them. "Everybody worked, young and old," remembered Ceceil George, of his time enslaved on a Louisiana sugar plantation. "If you could only carry two or three sugar cane [stalks], you worked," George told a WPA interviewer. "No school, no church. . . . [D]ey strip you down naked, and two men hold you down and whip you till de blood come."[45] The demands of sugar production were so extreme that they skewed the demographics of enslaved residents of the state, distinguishing Louisiana's population statistics from those of other slaveholding states.[46]

Sugar was a parasite that devoured the bodies of those who made it. The inhumanity of Louisiana sugar-making—its monstrous incompatibility with human health and life—showed itself in the results when enslaved people were cohered to sugar, body to commodity. Ellen Broomfield, born enslaved, remembered being fed sugar and molasses as a child to maintain her health and strength. As soon as she was "big enough," her enslaver made the girl plow the plantation's fields, a job often done by grown men. "In [the] Spring they give us Sulphur and molasses to purify our blood," Broomfield later told a WPA interviewer, "and candy was made out of Jimson weed and sugar."[47] Jimsonweed is a toxic plant with no antidote. It can cause hallucinations, convulsions, and death.[48] Enslavers plied children with this poisoned candy as they began hard labor in the cane fields. Landscape architect Frederick Law Olmsted observed other means by which Louisiana planters propped

up their exhausted bondspeople as they worked. "During the grinding season . . . hot coffee was kept constantly in the sugar-house, and the hands on
duty were allowed to drink it almost ad libitum," Olmsted wrote. "They were
also allowed to drink freely of the hot sirop, or molasses."[49] Stimulants of sugar,
poisoned sugar, and coffee fueled the punishing pace of cane processing. Enslavers fed workers the fruits of their labor until their bodies were expended,
destroyed from within and without by sugar.

Long after their enslavement, Black writers pointed out the irony in Americans' love of sugar coupled with their disgust for the people who made it.
"The worst-looking creatures I ever saw were the slaves that make the sugar
for those sensitive ladies and gentlemen, who cannot bear the sight of a colored person, but who are compelled to use the sugar made by the filthiest
class of slaves," wrote Lewis Clarke. Clarke had been born enslaved in Kentucky in 1815. He came to understand that being sold to a Louisiana sugar
planter promised death: "a short but bitter doom."[50] William Robinson, who
grew up enslaved in Wilmington, North Carolina, in the 1850s, had a similar
memory of the discordance in Americans' desire for sweetness and repulsion
for its makers. When hogsheads of molasses from New Orleans arrived on
Wilmington's docks, "the hot sun would cause them to ferment and run out
through the chimes," Robinson described in his 1913 autobiography. This presented an opportunity for enslaved people to earn small amounts of money
to "hire [their] time" away from their enslavers: "The negro women would
catch this molasses by running their hands over the hogshead and wiping the
molasses from their hands into a pail. I am often made to wonder now when
I see people gagging at the idea of eating bread made up by black hands, when
in those days the poor whites were truly glad to buy the molasses caught in
the hands of our mothers, and like Elijah, who was fed by the ravens, they ate
it and asked no questions."[51] Much as enslavers hungered for meals that would
come from the hands of a cook forced to stand on an auction block, Americans could not have enough of the sweets made by bondspeople whom they
abused and disdained.[52]

Following the abolition of slavery, disparities between Louisiana's sugar
producers and consumers persisted, albeit in new forms. In the war's aftermath, white lawmakers tried and failed to replace Black sugar workers with
Chinese and Sicilian immigrants.[53] Free Black Louisianians continued to dominate the industry's workforce (fig. 3.7). Many became impoverished sharecroppers on the same properties where they had been enslaved. Nominally
free, they found little improvement in their stations. Annie Flowers was one
Louisianian who labored to make sugar both before and after enslavement.
"Worked in the sugar cane fields all my life," Flowers told a WPA inter-

FIGURE 3.7. Following the Civil War, workers in Louisiana's sugar cane fields continued to endure harsh physical conditions and exploitation by their employers. *Sugar Cane Plantation*, postmarked May 13, 1911, picture postcard. Author's collection.

viewer in 1940, "barefeeted and half-naked. I didn't work for a salary: It was something to eat and a few rags to wear."[54] Those who did earn pay might only receive fifty to sixty cents a day, remembered Charlotte Brooks, who had been enslaved on a sugar plantation and then witnessed sharecropping. Employers—many of them former enslavers, others, recent arrivals from the North—compelled workers seeking to feed and clothe their families to spend their inadequate pay at the "plantation store." Customer accounts ran into debt, as designed, and laborers were bound to "work on the next year and pay it," Brooks remembered.[55] Families were trapped in a system contrived to keep them in the same fields where they had been in bondage. When possible, wageworkers resisted such exploitative labor contracts that sought to control all aspects of their duties, movements, and expenditures. Some negotiated better agreements, voted in local elections, struck or threatened to strike, and moved to different properties. Nevertheless, most of the successes won by free Black sugar workers were crushed by century's end, when white Louisianians imposed Jim Crow.[56]

Thus, during years when guidebooks and postcards directed tourists' gazes toward sugarcane fields and levees, the work of sugar production remained tenaciously violent. In 1888, Frenchman Prosper Jacotot published an account of his journey through the Mississippi Valley, which included a stint harvesting sugarcane. He found workers cutting cane in fields full of insects, snakes, and rats, with bug-infested warm water to drink. When Black laborers committed a "misdeed," Jacotot recalled, "the whites gathered together, arrested the guilty ones, and hung them from the nearest tree, without further ceremony. One day, I saw five negroes swinging on the same tree." Jacotot warned his European readers from emigrating to the United States, advising them to search instead for work in France or its colonies.[57] Even if Jacotot, a white European man, decided to move on, leaving the Louisiana fields behind, many could not. For some, their continued confinement to cane fields was ordained by law. State authorities constructed penitentiaries, including Angola State Farm and Hope State Farm, on the sites of former sugar plantations. They forced inmates to cultivate and process sugarcane there, in some cases to the present day.[58]

Such sorrowful continuities pointed to twinned facts: sugarcane was perennial; so was the American sweet tooth. By 1900, Americans ate fifty-nine pounds of sugar per capita, almost one-quarter of the entire world's output. More than 75 percent of this sugar was imported; only 11 percent came from the continental United States.[59] Nevertheless, even if American sugar was less and less American, Americans still loved to gaze at the landscapes and people of Louisiana's sugar industry. The technology of stereography offered a uniquely powerful way to look.

Sugar in Stereo

"For nothing is [our age] more remarkable than for the multitude, variety, perfection and cheapness of its pictures," observed Frederick Douglass in 1861.[60] Technological advances in printing and photography in the second half of the nineteenth century powered an explosion of visual media—chromolithographed trade cards and posters, greeting cards, calendars, real photo postcards, and stereographs—that enabled more people to see more things. Most of these visual objects were inexpensive and small, tucked next to a purchase, tacked up on a tavern wall, pasted into a scrapbook, or mailed for pennies. Holding, collecting, and mailing them became commonplace experiences for many Americans. Created for purposes of advertisement, entertainment, instruction, and sociability, these visual things embedded themselves in the daily lives of Gilded Age Americans.[61]

The popularity of these media and the ways that viewers engaged with them—especially stereographs—held important implications for the messages they delivered about people and place, in Louisiana and beyond. To create the three-dimensional effect of a stereograph, photographers took two photographs in quick succession, shifting the camera slightly between shots, or used a specially formatted camera. They mounted the resultant images side by side on rectangles of glass or paperboard measuring approximately four

FIGURE 3.8. This stereograph featured an image reminiscent of Louisiana's past—"plantation negro houses," formerly slave quarters and now freedmen's residences—in the startling reality of three dimensions. S. T. Blessing, *Plantation Negro Houses*, 1850–1930, stereograph. Miriam and Ira D. Wallach Division of Art, Prints and Photographs photography collection, New York Public Library.

by seven inches. Popularized by Scottish physicist Sir David Brewster in the mid-nineteenth century, stereographic technology spread throughout England and France before achieving broad enthusiasm in the United States. In 1861, physician and intellectual Oliver Wendell Holmes invented a cheaply manufactured stereoscope, the tool used to view stereographs (also called stereoviews). The medium spread among consumers such that a stereoscope became a fixture of many American parlors.[62] "What is better adapted to enlarge the attention of a visitor whilst temporarily delayed, waiting for the appearance of the lady of the house?" asked a journalist in 1858. "What better interlude during an evening party than to fill up a pause with a glance at a fine stereoscopic view?"[63]

For consumers accustomed to two-dimensional images, such as engravings in illustrated news magazines, stereography invited novel modes of handling and interacting with visual fragments of the world. To look at the stereoview titled "Plantation Negro Houses"—part of a "Louisiana Scenery" series produced by New Orleans photographer Samuel T. Blessing around 1880—a viewer inserted the card into a stereoscope and raised the hooded viewer to her eyes (fig. 3.8). This action blocked out the light around her and focused her gaze. The photographs' subjects coalesced into three dimensions, forming a world of height, width, and depth. Rows of identical cabins, each with a chimney, angled roof, and porch, receded into the distance. Parallel lines of trees in full leaf stretched up toward the sky and away from the eyes. The view presented a scene of careful perspective and order. Even if this stereograph was devoid of humans—except for a faint, small figure on a porch in the right foreground—the framing and dimensionality of the view generated an unspoken invitation to ponder its details, enter the scene, and walk beneath the branches' shade.[64]

Americans became infatuated with this technology that seemed to bring photographs to life. From the 1870s through the 1920s, the scale and reach of stereographic production set it apart from other visual media. Leading national studios like Underwood and Underwood, founded in Kansas, and Keystone View Company, in Pennsylvania, produced millions of views and hundreds of thousands of stereoscopes each year. In 1890, the best-selling stereograph from the nation's largest producer—a scene of the White House dining room—was purchased by an estimated one out of every five to six Americans.[65] By 1900, approximately 50 percent of American households— eight million families—owned a stereoscope and a selection of stereoviews.[66] Such staggering figures indicated the arrival of shared visual experiences among Americans prior to the heyday of film and the advent of television. For the first time, stereographs exposed millions of Americans to the same perspectives on canyons, castles, and Civil War trenches.[67]

To appeal to such an enormous volume of consumers, photographers sold collections of stereoviews organized into geographic or thematic sets that promised to awe, inform, and charm. From the comfort of their living rooms, stereograph consumers gazed upon European fortresses and Western canyons, earthquake destruction, civic parades, religious scenes, and tableaux of bashful country lovers and naïve urban immigrants.[68] Stereoviews illustrated skin and lung diseases for medical students and plant life for schoolchildren.[69] One young Louisiana student related his class's enthusiasm for the stereoscope and its effects, describing, "We look at pictures of the mountains, rivers, lakes, and Porta [sic] Rican farms and schools. The people look as though they were standing in front of you."[70] The medium offered illusions of understanding and proximity to viewers confronted with unfamiliar, faraway things.

The accessibility and popularity of these diminutive objects empowered them with an extraordinary degree of social and political potential. Importantly, enthusiasm for stereography climaxed in assertions that viewing a stereograph could substitute for—if not improve upon—witnessing the subject in person. Sir David Brewster, the medium's first booster, avowed that with a collection of stereoviews, "a score of persons might, in the course of an hour, see more of Rome, and see it better than if they had visited it in person."[71]

Americans might imagine that there was no need to cross the ocean to see the Colosseum or endure New Orleans's humidity to view its levees. Experiences of witnessing these places and their people, and understanding them all, could be had far from the Eternal City or the Crescent City, and for just a few pennies.[72]

Furthermore, proponents argued that a stereograph's three-dimensional nature delivered truth in a way that a standard photograph could not. Presented with a three-dimensional perspective, "We see something with the second eye, which we did not see with the first," Oliver Wendell Holmes contended. "By means of these two different views of an object, the mind . . . *feels round it* and gets an idea of its solidity."[73] To Holmes, the amalgamation of two perspectives to form a three-dimensional result enhanced stereography's truthful nature, generating a more complete rendering of reality.[74] If such praise were to be believed, stereographs delivered fixed points of view in a medium that claimed to be a perfect rendering of reality, in an educational, entertaining, and massively prevalent manner.

Americans' excitement for stereography also cut across social classes, imbuing the medium with a democratic, family-friendly character. In 1873, the *Daily Picayune* published a list of household items to be sold at an estate auction in a Garden District mansion. The deceased man's possessions included "elegant household furniture, in rosewood, mahogany, oak and black walnut . . . a costly 300 view stereoscope," and more.[75] The same paper also ran advertisements for Levy's Great Southern Dollar, which offered an impressive variety of items for that single sum: "very fine Southern Birds Stuffed, under a glass globe . . . ladies' and gents' underwear . . . stereoscopes."[76] In 1910, New Orleans's Maison Blanche department store promised customers a free stereoscope with the purchase of a boys' wool suit.[77] Thus, stereoscopes could be "costly," one dollar, or given as *lagniappe*.[78] The wide spread in price and quality of stereoscopes and stereographs showed the medium's expansive appeal in the Crescent City, as throughout the nation.

If New Orleans served as an eager market for stereograph purveyors, the city and its surroundings proved to be a popular photographer's muse, too. The Crescent City's enduring prominence as a travel destination, coupled with Louisiana's international importance on economic and cultural fronts, ensured the production and wide distribution of stereoviews of the state's attractions. New Orleans photographers first sold stereographs in the 1850s, but the medium exploded in the city, as in the country, following the Civil War's end. Theodore Lilienthal, George François Mugnier, Samuel T. Blessing, and other Crescent City–based photographers produced stereoviews of New Orleans and Louisiana scenes for local and faraway buyers alike.[79] Photographers employed by studios across the nation—in Kansas, New York, New Hampshire, Pennsylvania, Washington, DC—journeyed south to document Louisiana sights. Among hundreds of examples of Louisiana stereoviews preserved in archival collections, photographers captured rural scenes—views of cotton fields and cotton picking, bayous, alligators, and live oaks, their branches dripping with Spanish moss—and New Orleans's landmarks, including the city's distinctive cemeteries, the St. Charles Hotel, Jackson Square, and the 1884 World Cotton Centennial.

Coherent with tourists' longstanding fascination with Louisiana sugar production, the places and people of the state's sugar industry served as one of the most common themes in turn-of-the-century Louisiana stereoviews.[80] Photographers documented each step in sugar production—from cultivation to cutting, processing, river transportation to New Orleans, and movement on the levees—together with the laborers who did this work. These visions of an agro-industrial sublime witnessed previously by reporters, travelers, and laborers now appeared in boxed stereographic sets distributed throughout the nation, far from the source. In one such set titled *The Mississippi River*, for example, fifteen of twenty-three views focused on the New Orleans levee and the Black men who worked there (other views showed interior and exterior photographs of notable steamboats).[81] Regardless of their location, then, stereograph buyers could watch Louisianians at work, making and moving American sugar and other goods.

These depictions of Black workers in connection with sugar were weighted with prejudice. The medium of stereography delivered this prejudice in new dimensions, though. Americans may have expected to see blatantly racist representations of Black Americans in other realms of popular culture—injurious depictions of Black mammies, "pickaninnies," Zip Coon, Jim Crow, and Uncle Tom ran rampant on minstrel stages, trade cards, and food packaging.[82] Three-dimensional stereographs posed a more subtle threat, masquerading as objective, true-to-life, and educational or entertaining. Furthermore, even if such stereoviews were sold as scenes of agriculture, industry, and transportation, they doubled as visions of American food, eating, and the people who put food on American tables. Photographers presented visions of Black children eating or being eaten, for example, as subjects of violent humor for white consumers. Stereographs titled *Grinding Cane—A Branch Establishment*, *Champion Sugar Mills*, and *No Stop for Seeds or Rind* depicted not Delta sugar mills but small groups of Black boys, sitting against wooden fences, in a cane field, and in a photographer's studio, chewing on segments of sugarcane stalks and watermelon slices. Even more disturbing, the stereoview *Terrors of the Aligator* [sic] *Swamp, Fla.*, produced by Littleton, New Hampshire–based

FIGURE 3.9. With its foreground a mess of felled stalks, this stereograph placed the viewer within the cane field. The overlaps and intersections of the cane generated impressions of immersion and depth. H. C. White and Co., *Cutting the Cane on a Sugar Plantation near New Orleans, Louisiana, U.S.A.*, 1900, stereograph. Miriam and Ira D. Wallach Division of Art, Prints and Photographs photography collection, New York Public Library.

B.W. Kilburn Co., presented a Black boy clinging desperately to a tree, the lower half of his body being devoured by an alligator. He stares into the jagged teeth of a second alligator, inches away, that is closing in on his face. The person who slipped these cards into a stereoscope did so with the purpose of watching Black children eat, if not be eaten, for a laugh.[83] In photographic form and three dimensions, for a much broader audience than those of other media, stereographs carried such crude stereotypes and a voyeuristic, rapacious right to look into a new age.[84]

At the broadest level, turn-of-the-century stereoviews of Louisiana's sugar industry trapped Black laborers within its fields and on its docks, toiling at slavery's work. Photographers' technical decisions facilitated this sense of capture of the men, women, and children—all free citizen wageworkers—who appeared in this genre of views. One of stereography's strengths was its ability to manifest scenes of scale and reach, showcasing natural panoramas and architectural wonders. Stereoviews of Louisiana sugarcane fields and levees, however, often exhibited claustrophobic qualities of enclosure, darkness, and a high or hidden horizon. Such was the case in "Cutting the cane on a sugar plantation near New Orleans, Louisiana, U.S.A.," a stereoview produced at the turn of the century by a Vermont publisher (fig. 3.9). In this view, the photographer embeds the workers within the cane stalks. Their feet, out of sight, are sunk in tall grass and felled cane and their clothing and skin blend into the cane's shadows. Here, the angles, light, and shadows of three work-

FIGURE 3.10. Viewed through a stereoscope, the young boy and the man overseeing his work would have appeared embedded in the darkness of the cane field. Samuel T. Blessing, *Cutting Sugar Cane*, ca. 1872–1882, stereograph. Gift of Weston J. and Mary M. Naef, J. Paul Getty Museum, Los Angeles, California.

ers' bodies meld with those of the cane they harvest. Human and plant forms are nearly indistinguishable. Such stereographs seemed to offer visual proof of a literally natural continuity in the people and places that made American sugar. The freedmen depicted here may have been harvesting cane that they had planted while enslaved. As the grass grew tall, the nation's politics may have changed, but the hands of the people cultivating this crop had not.

Similar perspectives were discernible in two stereographs titled *Cutting Sugar Cane*, produced by New Orleans photographer Samuel T. Blessing in the mid-1870s to early 1880s (figs. 3.10, 3.11.). The first view is very dark (fig. 3.10). A young boy is initially difficult to discern within a dense nest of cane. His clothes, skin, hair, and tool are all the same color, and the same as the shadow in which he is implanted. His feet are bare, exposed to the cane leaves' edges. His clothes are ragged, and his pants are rolled up his calves. The boy's gaze meets those of the photographer and the viewer. He holds his cane knife in his right hand, the tip of its blade resting on a stalk, prepared to sever it. A similar pose appears in the second stereograph (fig. 3.11), in which four young workers meet the look of the camera's lens. The young man in the right foreground stares directly at the viewer as he holds his machete in the air, poised to fall.

These depictions of laborers who were poorly clad, young, armed with machetes, and rooted in sugarcane played to a host of white American fears and

FIGURE 3.11. Even if these laborers appeared to have been interrupted in the course of their work, the photographer carefully posed them in receding planes to enhance the view's three-dimensional effect. Samuel T. Blessing, *Cutting Sugar Cane*, ca. 1900, stereograph. No. 1979.221.30, The Historic New Orleans Collection.

prejudices about Black men.[85] In both these views, the workers' poses might be construed as threatening were it not for their subordination to those overseeing their labors. Even harder to discern in the first stereograph (fig. 3.10) is a white man standing behind the boy, well-dressed in a suit, bow tie, and hat tipped at an angle. The man points at or just beyond the worker, seeming to direct his harvest. His white waistcoat and cuffs emerge from the photograph's darkness, but his body from the waist down recedes almost totally into the cane. The man is a ghostly presence, supervising and directing the young man's work. Gazing at these stereographs, the viewer peered into their dark world to see a Black boy working and a white man watching. The viewer added another set of overseeing eyes.

The medium of stereography expanded access to these points of view to consumers who would never traipse to a Louisiana cane field to see these scenes in person. Slim rectangles of cardboard enabled an untold number of viewers to put their eyes to a stereoscope and connect their gazes to those of young sugar workers in the eternal pause before their blades fell.[86] This visual conversation was not the sole domain of American Southerners. Rather, these views were often the work of photographers based in the Northern United States (such as H. C. White Co. in New York City) or born abroad (such as Swiss-born George François Mugnier). Consumers who purchased these views were dispersed widely, too. Stereograph captions printed in multiple

languages—the harshly titled *Away Down among 'de Cotton and de Coons,'
Louisiana, U.S.A.*, carried captions in English, French, German, Spanish,
Swedish, and Russian on its verso—betrayed the broad reach and appeal of
such racism. Many were destined for international audiences or newcomers
to the United States. To a broad public, then, collections of "Louisiana Scenery" in various combinations flaunted how little seemed to have changed for
Black Americans who made sugar and cotton. The four sides of a photograph
and three dimensions of a stereoview confined workers to these dirty, manual trades.

When photographers shifted their focus from rural fields to urban levees, they
drew on a different, yet no less hostile, array of stereotypes as they photographed the longshoremen and roustabouts whom tourists loved to watch. In
contrast to rural sugar workers in the midst of interminable toil, levee workers
were often photographed idle and relaxed, if not asleep. Stereograph viewers
saw Black workers sprawled on barrels of molasses and bales of cotton. The
noise and action of New Orleans's famed levees surrounded these figures, yet
photographers cast them as seemingly unable or unwilling to contribute to
modernity's work. Such views circulated during the same years that Black
Americans were targeted by a proliferation of laws criminalizing vagrancy,
amidst broadside assaults on their basic rights and safety.[87] These stereoviews
added a quiet, malicious voice to the chorus.

A stereograph titled *Caught Napping*, produced around 1885 and sold by
Philadelphia's Centennial Photographic Company, offered one example of this
theme (fig. 3.12). Seated on the edge of a cart used to move cotton bales, a man
in a cap and jacket sleeps on the New Orleans levee, his head and shoulders
bowed. He has turned away from the sun; his body casts a shadow in front of
him. The worker appears blind to the action that surrounds him as he sleeps—
illicitly, the title implies, given that the photographer "caught" him—next to
the things he should be moving. Unlike the workers harvesting sugarcane,
who gazed directly at the camera, this worker was depicted as seemingly unaware of the photographer's presence, even if the shot was surely posed. Similar to stereoviews of rural settings, many views of the urban levee, including
this one, featured a high horizon line that concentrated the viewer's gaze on
the human subject. The subject's closed eyes enabled the photographer and
his scores of viewers to imagine that they wielded a violating power over this
man as they discovered the pause he took from his work. Asleep, it seemed
that the laborer could not consent to the capture, replication, and sale of this
view, which froze his body at rest.[88]

Additional stereoviews repeated the theme of New Orleans levee work-

FIGURE 3.12. Titling this view *Caught Napping*, the photographer emphasized the purportedly illicit nature of this levee worker's rest. Edward L. Wilson, *Cotton Bales* [*sic*], 1881–1884, stereograph, Centennial Photographic Co. Rowles Stereograph Collection, Louisiana Historical Center, Louisiana State Museum, New Orleans.

ers as unproductive and inactive via their physical poses—sitting, leaning, reclining—presented for scrutiny in three dimensions.[89] "A Roustabout's Nap," produced by Crescent City photographer George François Mugnier around 1880, presented a reclining levee worker who also appeared to be asleep (fig. 3.13). The roustabout slouches against a pile of tarps, a setting reminiscent of a studio backdrop. Angled beams situated to his left secure the tarps and enhance the view's three-dimensional depth. Here, too, the laborer's head is bowed, and his hat shields his eyes from the sun. The roustabout's unseen and unseeing nature exists in contrast to the layers of seeing that surround him. In addition to the gazes of the photographer and his consumers, the advertisement on the card's verso announced that this object could be purchased from E. Claudel, "leading optician of the South." Claudel specialized in "fine spectacles, opera glasses, drawing instruments," and "a fine collection of views of characteristic scenery of New Orleans and vicinity, embracing views of streets, shipping, cemeteries . . . moss trees, sugar plantations, &c." In short, the purveyor of this stereoview sold things to see and the tools to see them. This view exposed a blind subject at the center of a visual world.[90]

Such stereoviews gave three-dimensional form to the racist disparagements voiced by white observers who claimed that Black freedmen were criminally idle or averse to answering the demands of wage labor. "After one year, two

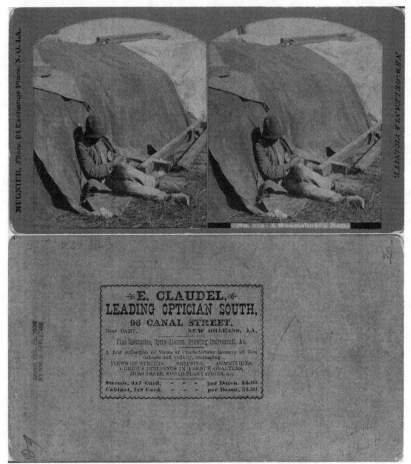

FIGURE 3.13. This stereograph of a napping roustabout played to longstanding, racist stereotypes of the idle Black worker, who seemed unable or unwilling to commit to the wage labor
required of him after emancipation. George François Mugnier, *A Roustabout's Nap*, 1880,
stereograph. Rowles Stereograph Collection, Louisiana Historical Center, Louisiana State
Museum, New Orleans.

years, three years of freedom, we know perfectly what the negroes are worth
and can do," complained an editorialist for the New Orleans *Abeille* in 1866
to his francophone readers. Reports of mountains of goods piling up on riverfront levees were driving the white public into a wrathful frenzy. "For slaves,
freedom has not been an encouragement to work but an encouragement to
indolence," the editorialist charged.[91] The *Bee* delivered the same message in
more florid prose to its English-speaking readers, announcing, "This unexam-
pled institution [of wage labor] has very much the appearance of an immense
castle of indolence."[92] Soon after the war's end, the state legislature criminal-

ized behavior that could be construed as vagrancy, ordering freedmen in rural regions to return to planters, or "employers," they had purportedly fled. New Orleanians accused of vagrancy before and after the war were incarcerated in the city's workhouse and jails and ordered to serve as a labor force for municipal projects. Stillness, rest, a purposeful pause, and even a pose designed by a photographer who knew his market—a prejudiced, suspicious point of view could construe these postures as evidence of unproductive dereliction.[93] Such prejudice was persistent. "The laboring man on the river to-day does less work than he has done on boats any time in the past forty years," grumbled a New Orleans newspaper reader in an 1890 letter to the editor. The writer objected to the younger Black men he watched on the levee. Their fathers' generation had been "honest, hard-working men" in the immediate aftermath of the Civil War, he claimed. In contrast, their sons "are of the very worst class of citizens. They are shiftless, uncomfortably clad, lazy, will not work while they have a dollar to spend, and they are profane, vulgar and dishonest."[94] Stereography lent a new plausibility to scenes of purported inaction described by writers and denounced by critical onlookers.

Reclining poses favored by white professional photographers spread to amateur photographers, too, indicating the stereotype's reach. As New Jersey–born Wilson S. Howell traveled the country inspecting electrical generating stations, photography became his hobby. In Louisiana, he took dozens of photographs of New Orleans residents, streets, steamboats, and the Ames Crevasse, an 1891 levee breach.[95] In the photograph *New Orleans Levee*, taken by Howell in March 1891, two workers sleep, their heads resting on their hands (fig. 3.14). The photograph featured props and poses that appeared in many professionally produced stereographs of the era. At least three other laborers can be seen on the edges of the frame, watching the photographer work. Unlike most stereographs of sleeping levee workers, though, Howell's photographs displayed the subjects' faces, sometimes at close range. *On the Levee*, a photograph taken one year before *New Orleans Levee*, showed a young man in full sun, asleep on hogsheads of sugar or molasses, photographed from just a few feet away. Howell's intimate distance from his subjects and the vulnerability of their exposed, sleeping faces enhanced the authority he claimed as he composed and captured his shots. From one year to the next, this visiting amateur photographer returned to the theme and poses of sleep when he went to the New Orleans riverfront and set up his camera.

Like other media, stereographs and photographs such as these communicated racial stereotypes by using visual codes that were rooted in slavery. Views of disheveled field laborers and idle levee workers adhered to conventions of pejorative pictorial representations of enslaved people, if not the

FIGURE 3.14. Amateur photographer Wilson S. Howell drew on the poses and props common in professional photography when he depicted sleeping laborers on the New Orleans levees. Wilson S. Howell, *New Orleans Levee*, March 1891. Wilson S. Howell Photograph Collection, City Archives and Special Collections, New Orleans Public Library.

farther past. Dockworkers who reclined and slept did so in forms present in sculptural classical art, which presented sleeping subjects as passive, vulnerable, and outside the bounds of rationality.[96] More recently, illustrated news magazines and abolitionist materials had exposed Americans and Europeans to a flood of depictions of enslaved people in poses of subjection and deference: kneeling, imploring, and tortured.[97] In the realm of stereography, somnolent poses served to neutralize a sense of threat that a white viewer might have imagined emanating from a Black man in particular. Eyes closed, reclining, the form evoked white memories of the imagined, submissive slave.[98] When stereographs derided the work ethic of their subjects, they contributed to racist European and American stereotypes of the indolent "other," typically encountered in tropical settings.[99] In multiple ways, then, the poses of stereographs' subjects—toiling or sleeping—propelled the viewer's mind backward, toward slavery. But the material trappings of modernity that surrounded these workers—the infrastructure of the sugar industry, edible commodities in motion—grounded the viewer in the present, if not the future. Such discordance presented Louisiana's Black sugar workers as perpetual anachronisms, rooted in slavery's cane fields or asleep in a place of ceaseless work.[100] The stereograph's three dimensions enhanced the medium's unique claim to authority.[101]

FIGURE 3.15. When Alfred Rudolph Waud sketched this scene of a photographer, his subjects, and their large audience, ogling from beyond the photograph's frame, photographs were poised to become the primary visual medium for entertaining and informing the American public. Alfred Rudolph Waud, "Itinerant Photographer May 15th, On the Levee, N. O.," illustration, *Every Saturday*, July 22, 1871, 93.

Notions of stereographic truth were an illusion, of course. Beyond the stereograph's frame lay realities unseen by the consumer who inclined toward the stereoscope in her hand. Savvy photographers posed their subjects to create photographs and stereographs that would sell to a public entertained by stereotypes' barbs (fig. 3.15). Seemingly haphazard piles of sugarcane stalks, tarps, and barrels comprised carefully arranged backdrops. Subjects who posed for photographers were working, even in postures of rest.[102] If any subjects did sleep, they did so because the work of loading and unloading steamships stretched around the clock, or because they were pausing between shifts of hard labor.[103] In multiple dimensions, then, the static views of static subjects offered by many photographs were contrived delusions. These objects tried to keep Louisiana sugar workers captive, for sale, and available for nostalgic gazes decades after emancipation. Nevertheless, many Black Americans took control of the camera and focused it on their own ends.

"Pictures and Progress"

Like most of his fellow Americans, Frederick Douglass and his family were consumers of photography. On display at Douglass's former home in Washington, DC, is the Douglass family's stereoscope and three stereographs: two are views of Niagara Falls and the third, a view of Lachine Rapids, near Montreal.[104] Douglass understood better than most Americans, though, the ways in which this technology was far more than a parlor pastime. In public lectures with titles such as "Pictures and Progress," Douglass spoke repeatedly about photography's power to enact good and evil for Black Americans, in particular. He warned of the damage that visual stereotypes could inflict and lauded the advances that could be gained with their opposites. "As to the moral and social influence of pictures," Frederick Douglass declared to a Boston crowd in 1861, "give me the making of a nation's ballads and I care not who has the making of its laws. . . . the one reaching and swaying the heart by the eye, and the other by the ear." The line of influence between realms of culture and politics was difficult to trace and quantify, Douglass acknowledged, but it was real and strong. "The mental atmosphere surrounding us is most easily moved in this or that direction. The first causes of its oscillations are often too occult for the most subtle," he observed. Nevertheless, "It is evident that the great cheapness and universality of pictures must exert a powerful, though silent, influence upon the ideas and sentiment of present and future generations."[105] Douglass understood that the impact of crude visual representations traveled far beyond a photograph's frames. Likewise, battles over Black Americans' safety, dignity, and liberty were not confined to the legislative chamber.

Accordingly, Douglass and other prominent Black activists and intellectuals of the nineteenth and early twentieth centuries used photography as a critical tool in their fight to secure rights and respect for themselves and all Black Americans. Photographed more often than any other nineteenth-century American, Douglass attended carefully to such representations of himself. Once a person's photograph was published, Douglass reflected, "The man may be considered a fixed fact. . . . His position is defined."[106] Accordingly, Douglass styled himself for photographs in refined dress, with a dignified posture and staid facial expressions. Photographs of Douglass were often head-and-shoulder portraits. Such a perspective emphasized Douglass's intellectual and oratorical prowess, distinct from the stereoviews that would offer the entire bodies of Black laborers for inspection. The body of photography of Douglass—at least 160 portraits, taken between 1841, when he was still a fugitive from slavery, and 1895, shortly after his death—communicated his stature as a thinker, self-emancipator, and political titan.[107]

As Black thinkers sat for their own photographic portraits and put the medium to work for their activism, they built visual counterarguments to the racist vitriol surrounding them.[108] Similar to Douglass's approach, the dress, pose, and serene expressions chosen by abolitionist and women's rights activist Sojourner Truth for her photographic portraits communicated her focus on her moral crusades. Truth, who escaped from slavery in New York in 1826, funded her activism by selling *cartes de visite* that displayed her portrait.

She also copyrighted her image—at a time when American enslavers still asserted their power to own people—declaring ownership of her likeness and the means of its reproduction.[109] Several decades later, sociologist W. E. B. DuBois sought to capitalize on photography's power, too. DuBois assembled nearly four hundred photographs for *Exhibit of American Negroes*, a display at the 1900 Paris Exposition. The images presented to an international audience a visual catalog of Black Americans very different from the crude stereotypes familiar to many viewers.[110] Du Bois used photography to show the world Black Americans who were educated, financially and professionally successful, and socially polished—realities often left out of the frame when a white photographer peered through the lens.

Black Americans' enthusiasm for photography was not limited to the nation's most famous and elite activists. Ordinary New Orleanians participated fully in the national fascination with the medium. Black-owned newspapers in the city printed advertisements for photography studios as well as articles about photography's technical aspects.[111] The June 15, 1889, edition of the *Weekly Pelican*, a Black-owned New Orleans newspaper, featured advertisements for [John H.] Clark[e], "Progressive and Artistic Portrait Photographer"—"the oldest and best in the city"—as well as Brandao and Gill, commercial stationers and printers. There, readers could commission printed paper items of their own design, such as pamphlets, handbills, posters, and invitations. A short article in the same issue instructed readers how to convert a room of their home into a pinhole camera by covering its windows with thick paper, poking a small hole in one sheet with a darning needle, and holding a piece of white paper to the sun ray to catch the image beamed inside. Another ad on the same page invited readers to purchase a subscription to the *Freeman*, "the great and only Illustrated Colored Newspaper." "The colored people have long needed . . . a pictorial newspaper," declared the Indianapolis-based publisher, "one which will 'paint them as they are' and not caricature them as is too often done by the white press." With these advertisements and articles, a single issue of one Black-owned newspaper showed Black New Orleanians to be immersed in the photographic culture of the day.[112] It also showed them to be fully aware of their often-disadvantaged state in this visual world.

In the immediate wake of the Civil War, Louisianians of color had achieved and enjoyed a decade of social, economic, and political advances. Black New Orleanians published newspapers, unionized, founded schools, and formed benevolent associations. Every measure of progress was hard-fought. Their organized activism—for causes such as the right to vote and the integration of public transportation—won a new state constitution in 1868. The document guaranteed equal citizenship for Louisianians of color, including public education, equal public accommodations, and the vote. Black citizens throughout the state participated in elections and served in elected office. In 1872, P. B. S. Pinchback became governor of Louisiana, and the nation's first Black governor, even if for little more than a month.[113]

Such victories would not last long, however. White Louisianians who resented each of these liberties and advances reacted with violence against their Black neighbors. Terrorist groups like the Knights of the White Camellia and the White League spread through the state. White mobs in New Orleans killed dozens in 1873 and 1874. In spring 1877, the end of Reconstruction and the withdrawal of federal forces from Louisiana and other Southern states ushered in terrors: decades of anti-Black violence, voter intimidation, and economic repression. Journalists in the June 15, 1889, edition of the *Weekly Pelican*—the same issue that taught readers how to build a pinhole camera— acknowledged the violence that had consumed the region. Since the demise of Reconstruction, "the shotgun, fraud and perjury" had been the means by which "the descendants of 20,000 slave-holders" had grabbed political power in Louisiana, one writer declared. White lawmakers had effectively erased Black citizens from the ranks of the state's voters. "In fact, they are counted for nothing except as a basis for Democratic Congressman [*sic*], for whom they are not allowed to vote, and as field hands and roustabouts."[114]

Local and regional campaigns of suppression and division were affirmed by the highest judicial authority in the land. In 1896, the US Supreme Court's *Plessy v. Ferguson* ruling confirmed race-based segregation as national law. Four years later, journalist and activist Ida B. Wells-Barnett lamented, "In no other civilized country in the world, nay, more, in no land of barbarians would it be possible to duplicate the scenes of brutality that are reported from New Orleans."[115] Between 1877 and 1950, white mobs lynched 549 Louisianians of color. Only Georgians and Mississippians murdered more Black people in this way.[116] As these events were unfolding—violence in different dimensions— white photographers sold stereographs of sharecroppers in Louisiana fields and roustabouts on the levee.

Black photographers, in contrast, looked through the lens and found other stories. They worked in a medium that one of their own had brought to the Crescent City.[117] In the early twentieth century, Black photographers focused on New Orleanians of color attending school, working at white-collar jobs, worshipping in overflowing congregations, and enjoying days at the beach— scenes never depicted in popular stereographs and postcards of the time. The city's most prominent photographer of color during this era was New Orleans–born Arthur P. Bedou. From 1900 through the 1950s, Bedou photographed wedding parties, orders of nuns, fraternity brothers, doctors, and schoolchildren. He captured graduations, ordinations, school dedications, office work, and leisure time. Bedou's career was more than one of a local photographer for hire, though. He gained national prominence photographing political leaders like Marcus Garvey and Theodore Roosevelt. Bedou also worked as the personal photographer of activist Booker T. Washington, documenting his speeches and the crowds who flocked to hear them. Institutional pillars of Black American life in and beyond New Orleans—Xavier University, Straight College, Tuskegee Institute, churches—were preserved in Bedou's work.[118]

The subjects and composition of Bedou's photographs conveyed arguments very different from the crude themes transmitted by white photographers. Large assemblages of workers, worshippers, and communicants—wholly unlike the lone or paired sugar or levee workers forced to become the sole focus of a viewer's gaze—testified to thriving communities and strong fraternal and professional organizations. Such groupings also demonstrated their members' unified, collective will to be photographed and documented together, standing, sitting, or worshipping side by side. Bedou posed his subjects with extreme precision and symmetry. All eyes meet the camera. Subjects sit or stand with straight and strong postures. Hands are folded in laps or by one's side and ankles are crossed (fig. 3.16). Members of the first graduating class from Xavier University of Louisiana, photographed in 1929, hold their diplomas at the same angle. Tassels hang straight from their mortarboards, not a strand out of place (fig. 3.17). The impeccable, black-and-white lines of waitress uniforms, tuxedoes, and commencement gowns—and the visual repetition of these elements within these photographs—announced discipline, dedication, achievement, and cohesion (figs. 3.16, 3.17, 3.18).

Not all Bedou's photographs adhered to a visual language of starched and pressed respectability, however. The smiles of two dozen swimmers pictured in *A Group of Bathers Enjoy the Inviting Waters of the Gulf* convey ease and physical pleasure (fig. 3.19). The young men and women are wearing swimsuits and swim caps. They are relaxed in their bodies and with each other, at a time when beaches and swimming pools were strictly segregated by race. Standing in nearly knee-deep water, the friends place their hands on their hips or casually around their companions' waists. A ball—proof of their play—floats on the surface of the water between them. The air is misty or foggy, the photographer seems elevated above the group, and no horizon is discernible. These elements give the scene a dreamlike quality. The crescent of friends is a vision of young Black Americans in 1920, happy. As Bedou's body of work documented, turn-of-the-century Black Americans studied, worked,

FIGURE 3.16. New Orleans photographer Arthur P. Bedou documented the Black social elite, professionals, and community gatherings—subjects often ignored by white photographers. Arthur P. Bedou, *Group of Alpha Phi Alpha, Sigma Lambda Chapter Fraternity Members*, ca. 1925. Arthur P. Bedou Photographs Collection, Archives and Special Collections, Xavier University of Louisiana, New Orleans.

worshipped, and took their leisure, too. Bedou's photography helped preserve the ordinary and extraordinary moments that were a blind spot—purposefully hewn and maintained—in the minds of so many white Americans.

Implicitly and explicitly, the photographs of Bedou and his contemporaries testified to communities fighting for stability, safety, and success in politics, education, and urban life.[119] This was also the message of *The Crescent City Pictorial*, a souvenir booklet "dedicated to the progress of the colored citizens of New Orleans, Louisiana," published in 1926 by the editor of the Black-owned newspaper *Louisiana Weekly*. Featuring the work of Villard Paddio, another local photographer of color, the twenty-eight-page book was a rejoinder to generations of illustrated guidebooks and souvenir books generated by white publishers. *Crescent City Pictorial* featured dozens of photographs of the settings where Black New Orleanians lived, worked, shopped, relaxed, and cared for each other, from their earliest days—as at Central Church's nursery school—to after their days were done, at the city's multiple Black-owned undertaking companies. Within the *Pictorial*'s pages were Flint-Goodridge Hospital, churches of many denominations, public schools,

FIGURE 3.17. The poses, gazes, gowns, and diplomas of these graduates, flanked by their instructors, displayed the dignity they had achieved through their scholarship. Arthur P. Bedou, *First Graduating Class of Xavier University of Louisiana*, 1929, photograph. Arthur P. Bedou Photographs Collection, Archives and Special Collections, Xavier University of Louisiana, New Orleans.

FIGURE 3.18. This photograph of Tuskegee Institute's dining-room waitresses, with Tuskegee president Booker T. Washington, communicated discipline, cohesion, and professionalism in their labor. Arthur P. Bedou, *Group Photo of Dining Room Waitresses and Booker T. Washington at Tuskegee Institute*, 1913, photograph. Arthur P. Bedou Photographs Collection, Archives and Special Collections, Xavier University of Louisiana, New Orleans.

FIGURE 3.19. Arthur P. Bedou showed a group of young people happy and at ease, at a time when public beaches and swimming pools were strictly segregated. Arthur P. Bedou, *A Group of Bathers Enjoy the Inviting Waters of the Gulf*, 1920, photograph. Photographs and Prints Division, Schomburg Center for Research in Black Culture, New York Public Library.

and Pythian Temple, home to the offices of Liberty Industrial Life Insurance Company (fig. 3.20). Here were the Autocrat Social and Pleasure Club, the Lions Club, the Bulls Club, and the San Jacinto Club, with two bars, a radio room, and a library, where suit-clad men sat together, reading newspapers. Empire Grocery, Broadway Mattress Works, Bertrand's photography studio, and multiple pharmacies catered to the city's consumers of color. Here was the People's Community Center, home to a Girl Scout troop and an employment bureau. Here were Straight College's football team, dining hall, and chemistry, biology, and domestic art classes. Photographs of the Astoria Hotel and Restaurant on South Rampart Street touted the venue's multiple dining rooms and barber shop. Several pages throughout the guide featured the "Homes of Colored New Orleans." Photographs of houses of all styles were arranged at familiar angles as if pasted into a scrapbook, with the names of their inhabitants printed beneath.[120]

Turning the pages of this booklet, someone who grew up in these neighborhoods in the 1920s and 1930s would have recognized names, businesses, and landmarks. The pages would have been alive with the memories of momentous events and the routines of daily life. These photographs would have

FIGURE 3.20. Published in 1926, *The Crescent City Pictorial* displayed dozens of photographs of Black New Orleans institutions, including the Pythian Temple, a grand building that housed offices, a theater, a roof garden, and the Colored Knights of Pythias, a fraternal organization. O. C. W. Taylor, *The Crescent City Pictorial* (New Orleans, LA: O. C. W. Taylor, 1926). Amistad Research Center, New Orleans, LA.

evoked the aromas of Davis' [*sic*] Sweet Shop and the music and laughter of the crowds that animated Astoria Hotel's roof garden. Even someone who had never been to these places would have seen photographic evidence of the "progress" the publisher intended to show. All these things were true, but so were the things that lay beyond the frame. Two years before this booklet's publication, the New Orleans Commission Council had ordered the segregation of residential neighborhoods in the city. Black neighborhoods were suffering from the persistent neglect of municipal authorities. School buildings attended by Black children crumbled. Community leaders and teachers had set out to photograph the decrepit buildings, hoping that such documentation would compel white authorities to see the deterioration that they saw.[121]

By the time *Crescent City Pictorial* went to print, though, many of Frederick Douglass's earlier fears about art bleeding into life had come to fruition. Despite the efforts of Black photographers, their subjects, and activists, their work competed with an avalanche of violent and crude images that darkened seemingly every facet of American life. Turn-of-the-century photographs and postcards of lynchings confronted viewers with horrifically naked brutality. Advertisements and stereographs delivered their racist messages in a more underhanded guise. Whatever the medium, popular culture that derided Black Americans was good business during this age of "visual slavery." These objects gave new dimension to contemporary prejudices, welding the link between culture and politics.[122]

Subtle "oscillations"—borne by the likes of ballads and pictures, Frederick Douglass believed—had helped push the American "mental atmosphere" into a place that devastated the rights of Black Americans. Little distance separated allegations that freedmen were not contributing to the nation's economic wellbeing from assertions that their disfranchisement was an urgent political necessity. Attendees at a New Orleans public meeting in January 1898 had argued for the "necessity for eliminating from the political life of the State a large mass of ignorance, shiftlessness, and degradation," a local newspaper reported.[123] A northern Louisiana newspaper likewise editorialized, "Born to serve. . . . [The negro] has not been, nor will he ever be, fit for politics, hence he should be removed from its uncongenial influences, and considered as an industrial factor."[124] With such reasoning, public opinion encouraged disfranchisement of Louisiana's Black citizens in the same terms used to describe the laborers that white tourists loved to watch. White Louisianans seeking to expel their Black neighbors from the voting booth bolstered their cries with allegations of servility and indolence.

Legislators confirmed Louisiana's disfranchisement of its Black citizens at a special meeting of the state's constitutional convention on March 25, 1898. Although the legislation avoided any mention of race, the "Grandfather Clause," as it would later be named, stripped Louisianians of color of the right to vote.[125] In 1890, nearly 130,000 Louisianians of color were registered to vote. Less than twenty years later, in 1908, fewer than two thousand could vote. Before and after Louisiana's move, other Southern states disfranchised their Black citizens on similar grounds, striking out the voices of an entire caste of free, wage-working citizens.[126] The prosperous, successful, community-minded New Orleanians who appeared in the pages of the *Crescent City Pictorial* and the photographs of Arthur P. Bedou lived in a time and place when most of their white neighbors rejected their citizenship rights and refused to share a dinner table or streetcar with them. In Louisiana and beyond, just as a stereograph combined two images to generate a three-dimensional whole, rampant popular stereotypes had united with malevolent public debate to produce a result all their own: anti-Black violence, disfranchisement, and generations of Jim Crow.

When tourists flocked to Louisiana's levees and sugarcane fields after the Civil War, they were gazing at a vanishing world. The state's sugar production did not top its 1861 high until 1894. Thereafter, its dominance was short-lived.[127] Louisiana sugar faced increasing competition from plantations in Cuba, Hawaii, Puerto Rico, and the Philippines. Changes to US trade policy favored overseas producers. Disease, frost, pests, and a conversion to beets—by the 1906–1907 season, American farmers produced more sugar from beets than cane—all stifled Louisiana's sugar industry.[128] Still, many continued to wax nostalgic about American cane sugar and fantasize about where and how it was made. First published in 1900, *The Picayune's Creole Cook Book*—the cookbook that would define New Orleans's cuisine to local and national readers in the twentieth century—included a simple recipe for *Eau Sucrée*, sugared water: "To one glass of fresh water allow one tablespoonful of sugar . . . stir till the sugar is dissolved." The authors explained all that this simple solution could do and the memories it could invoke. Drunk after a meal, *eau sucrée* eased digestion. It prevented insomnia for adults and could be used as a "sedative" for children. Wondrously, a glass of *eau sucrée* could also evoke a time when "there were no heartaches, no pangs, no sad thoughts" prompted by the social competition that had descended on New Orleans in the Civil War's wake. *Eau sucrée* represented "those happy innocent days," the authors insisted. "All this has passed away," they acknowledged, "but 'Eau Sucrée' remains."[129]

What also remained were the ruins of some of the places where Black Louisianians had made and processed sugarcane, which New Orleans's twentieth- and twenty-first-century tourism industry put to new uses. Tchoupitoulas Plantation Restaurant, established in the 1960s on the site of the former Cedar Grove Plantation, upriver from New Orleans, "occupie[d] the main building of one of Louisiana's most prosperous sugar plantations," announced the restaurant's menu.[130] Dining within the walls of a former planter's home constituted an attraction equal to the food and drink served there. "A visit to Tchoupitoulas Plantation is more than an experience in fine dining," gushed a 1968 *New Orleans Magazine* article, "it is an excursion into the Louisiana past, with all the trimmings." After ordering a "Jezebell" or "Southern Belle" cocktail, diners might imagine what the plantation had been like "in those days long ago," the writer suggested, when planters "laughed with their friends and dined on many-coursed meals, and argued the politics of the day. It is good to think of these things as you sit on the glassed-in porch and slowly sip your Irish coffee."[131]

Little more than a century earlier, sugar planters had bid on children in New Orleans barrooms between sips of syruped juleps. At the turn of the twentieth century, sightseers went on excursions to ride on plantation sugar carts. At home, they gazed into stereoscopes at views of cane fields and levees. In the mid-twentieth century, diners ate, drank, and relaxed in settings where enslaved people had died to make sugar. Incarcerated Louisianians—predominantly Black men—continued to make sugar in prisons built on former plantations. By the early twenty-first century, the plantation that had housed Tchoupitoulas Plantation Restaurant served as a wedding venue.[132] From the nineteenth century to the twenty-first, then, looking at Louisiana sugar exposed tangled webs—of ease and exploitation, pleasure and pain, eating and being devoured—that grew ever larger and convoluted over time. The auction block, the dining table, the cane field, and the levee were all settings in which these knots were tied and tightened. So too was one of New Orleans's most iconic institutions, intrinsic to the city's identity since its founding: the French Market.

4

MOTHER MARKET

Bulbancha, Babel, New Deal

"MANY GENERATIONS AGO ABA, the good spirit above, created many men, all Choctaw, who spoke the language of the Choctaw, and understood one another," recounted a Choctaw woman named Pisatuntema to an anthropologist on April 15, 1909. David I. Bushnell Jr. had been staying in St. Tammany Parish for the previous five months, documenting Choctaw practices such as tattooing, basketmaking, and drying wild crabapples. On the day when Pisatuntema narrated this Choctaw creation story, Bushnell was visiting her in Bayou Lacombe, across Lake Pontchartrain from New Orleans. "One day all came together and, looking upward, wondered what the clouds and the blue expanse above might be. They . . . at last determined to endeavor to reach the sky," Bushnell recounted Pisatuntema as saying. The men worked for three days, building a mound of rocks. On the fourth day, "When daylight came and they . . . began to speak to one another, all were astounded as well as alarmed—they spoke various languages and could not understand one another. . . . Finally they separated."[1] Similar to the Biblical tale of Babel, a shared language had first enabled cohesion and collaboration. Then, linguistic confusion dispersed the group.[2]

If Choctaws recalled the birth of the world as a place of many tongues, they found a similar environment in a silty crescent of soil in the Lower Mississippi Valley. There, dozens of Native nations—Acolapissa, Chitimacha, Houma, Ishak, Chawasha, Tunica, Natchez, Bayagoula, and others—exchanged corn, meat, beans, weapons, and beads with each other and European colonizers throughout the sixteenth and seventeenth centuries. Choctaws named the setting Bulbancha, "the place of many languages."[3] In 1718, French forces called it New Orleans. At the heart of this place of many languages was its role as a marketplace—a quality that European and American colonial authorities sought to formalize and control. In 1779, the Spanish colonial government announced the establishment of a regulated public food market in the settlement. Officials constructed a riverside building with stalls in 1791 that would come to be known as the French Market. The market's *Halle des boucheries*, or meat market, first rose under American governance in 1808. From the 1820s until 1870, authorities built additional structures at the French Market for the sale of vegetables, fish and game, fruit, and dry goods.[4] Concurrently, the city constructed additional public markets throughout growing neighborhoods, which, together with private competition, gave residents a growing variety of places to shop, or "make groceries."[5]

Still, the French Market exerted a unique pull. Through the close of the nineteenth century, thousands of shoppers, vendors, and tourists filled this multiplying complex of buildings. Choctaw sellers traveled by ferry from Bayou Lacombe to New Orleans, bringing corn, meat, bear oil, and persimmon bread.[6] Barred from operating within the market's brick-and-mortar stalls, Choctaw and Black vendors staked out territory on the "neutral ground," the open area in between the market's buildings, as well as on the riverfront levee (fig. 4.1).[7] Amidst thorough political, economic, and social transformations to the city and region, the Choctaw term for this place endured. An 1880 Choctaw-English dictionary translated *bulbaha* as "one that speaks in a foreign language," *bulbahah* as "to speak in a foreign language," and *Bulbancha* as, simply, "New Orleans."[8] To Louisiana Choctaws, the city and the market that fed it—Bulbancha—continued to be defined by their multiplicity of languages, people, and foods.

As white Americans solidified their political power in New Orleans in the late nineteenth and early twentieth centuries, the French Market came to rest at the heart of their conception of the city's culture and history, too. A 1932 editorial in one of the city's leading newspapers asserted that the French Market "ha[d] come to epitomize the life and color and charm of the city itself. . . . New Orleans without the old French Market would not be New Orleans at all."[9] The city's "mother" market, as another editorialist called it the following year, would indeed outlast all other public markets in the city, in form if not function, fixed in the imaginations of locals and tourists alike.[10] If Choctaws had given the place its first name, Bulbancha, many English-speaking people who came to early New Orleans and experienced the French Market reached for a similar term with very different implications to describe it. These early encounters presaged how white locals and authorities would seek to shape the

FIGURE 4.1. On Sunday mornings in the mid-nineteenth-century French Market, Choctaw and Black vendors set out their wares on the "neutral ground" between market buildings. Alfred Rudolph Waud, "Sunday in New Orleans–The French Market," illustration, *Harper's Weekly* 10, no. 503 (August 18, 1866): 517. Image courtesy of ProQuest LLC.

French Market's appearance, what its place in the city's story would be, and who would—and would not—be permitted to play a part in it.

Babel

"It is a more incessant, loud, rapid, & various gabble of tongues of all tones than was ever heard at Babel. It is more to be compared to the sounds that issue from an extensive marsh, the residence of a million or two of frogs." Arriving in New Orleans by river on a foggy day in January 1819, the architect Benjamin Henry Latrobe realized that the din he heard, which seemed more animal than human, "proceeded from the market & levee, opposite to which [they] had cast anchor." Vendors and customers packed the French Market and spilled onto the ground around it. They made a boisterous chorus. Latrobe's wife, Mary, phrased her astonished first impressions of the city in similar terms. "A jargon assailed me equal to Babel its-self," she wrote to a friend, of her experiences threading among a mass of shoppers and sellers in the French Market's orbit.[11] Traveling through the city a generation later, New Englander Edward Russell likewise characterized New Orleans in his diary as "the city of Babel," with "streets quite full of people in all customs & languages & colors and the dregs of all nations."[12] Fifteen years later, speeding to his Crescent City hotel in a horse-drawn carriage, New Yorker A. Oakey Hall passed "a brace of deserted markets, where negresses and lazy butcher boys were engaged in melodious quarrels quite anti-scriptural in their tone but yet suggestive of the tower of Babel."[13] Even after the cataclysms of the Civil War and the backlash to Reconstruction, this singular feature of the city seemed unchanged. "The various languages spoken [at the French Market]—English, French, German, Spanish . . . make it a perfect Babel," observed a writer in *Harper's Weekly* in 1881.[14] This descriptor of the nineteenth-century French Market and its city—Babel—appeared in English-language newspapers, travel guides, private journals, and letters, from the pens of local authors and newcomers alike.

Even though—or perhaps, because—the French Market appeared overwhelming and alien to the ears and eyes of many visitors, it was also irresistible. White European and American writers who labeled New Orleans and the nineteenth-century French Market "Babel" were using an outsider's word, describing a setting where they did not belong. Babel was the physical crush of people, their languages, and their foods that struck many newcomers as unintelligible. Calling this place "Babel" imparted a Biblical sense of scale, as well as a Judeo-Christian conceptualization, to a setting that predated colonization. The label also connoted a place of purported chaos in need of organization and regulation to wrestle it back into order. For most of the nineteenth century, though, the marketplace captivated visitors. If the riverfront levees were monstrous in their industrial, mechanized noise, the French Market was monstrous in its heterogeneous, human noise. Travelers may not have been able to understand all the words spoken in this Babel, yet they felt drawn to listen, look, and value.

The foods they encountered there titillated their senses and defined the city's cultural and gastronomic appeal. At the nineteenth-century New Orleans French Market, shoppers and wanderers found "Innumerable wild ducks, oysters, poultry of all kinds, fish . . . sugar cane, sweet & Irish potatoes, corn in the Ear & husked, apples, carrots & all sorts of other roots, eggs, trinkets, tin ware."[15] Caribbean and South American plantations and hillsides sent bananas and coffee beans. Oranges and lemons manifested sunlight that had fallen on Mediterranean citrus groves. Black women vendors who moved between stalls and around the market's perimeter hawked *calas*; pralines; coffee; spruce, ginger, and pineapple beers; *pain patate*, a cold sweet potato pudding; and gingerbread, called *estomacs mulâtres* ("mulatto stomachs").[16] Also at the market, recalled a late nineteenth-century writer: "Michigan apples alongside of Muscat grapes from Spain and California, with Catawbas from Ohio. . . . [P]omegranates, plantains, oranges, mandarins, limes and alligator pears from Jamaica." Crossing from one market building to the next, he beheld "great tubs of moving crabs, huge piles of shrimps and jack fish, red fish, reel trout, blue fish, red snapper, flounders, croakers and mullets."[17] Coffee stands offered cups of cocoa, *café noir*, and *café au lait*. Eating houses served quick and cheap meals to hungry vendors and visitors. In 1885, ten cents bought a repast of soup, roasted meat, fried fish, "baked beans; beet salad; cucumber salad; potato salad; [or] eggs, boiled or fried."[18] Flowers, figs, strawberries, Japanese plums, crayfish, and rabbits: all these colors, scents, and geographies could be seen, smelled, tasted, and purchased within the Crescent City's French Market.[19]

Inseparable from this riotous mix of foods, travelers found the French Market to be an intimately physical experience. The sightseer must be prepared to "elbo[w] his way through the dense crowd," warned one early guidebook author.[20] Shoppers, vendors, and sightseers congregated in the early morning hours, before the Louisiana sun rose to its powerful height. "As early as three o'clock in the morning . . . it is almost impossible to move about," observed one reporter. Nevertheless, "by nine o'clock the place is almost deserted." The group was like a noisy flock of birds that descended suddenly on the riverfront stalls and, not long afterward, fled.[21] While the crowd was present, they were a tight mass that filed down aisles and in the market's vicinity, calling out greetings, wares, offers, and counteroffers. "'Bananey–cheapee! Madamey' or 'narange (oranges) cheappey per picayuney,'" might reach a shopper's ears, another writer predicted.[22] The market was so full, recalled one New Orleans native, that "a constant ebb and flow of human streams would often obstruct locomotion, and this annoyance, increased by the interlocking of baskets, was often a source of merriment to the visitor."[23] Pressed together in the dim, predawn hours of a subtropical morning, the marketplace was a clot of people, food, noises, and smells.

Many newcomers marveled—warily—at this setting as a crucible in which seemingly discordant humans and foods mingled. There, the tourist walked amongst "one and all, rich and poor, Jew and Gentile," described one reporter in 1883. "A breast of mutton and a piece of lace hang in close proximity; small alligators and spring chickens lie down together." This writer, who called the market "Babel" elsewhere in the article, used another Biblical allegory to paint a vision of the promised land, where Jew and Gentile were neighbors and the leopard lay down with the kid.[24] A travel guide of the same era beckoned visitors to the market with a similar perspective, characterizing it as a human cabinet of wonders with fantastical mixes. "A man might here study the world," the author marveled. "Every race that the world boasts is here, and a good many races that are nowhere else. The strangest and most complicated mixture of Indian, negro and Caucasian blood, with negroes washed white, and white men that mulattoes would scorn to claim as of their own particular hybrid."[25] Visitors such as these professed a fascination with the market's diverse "types" of people, food, and languages. Many articulated their interest in the terms of a racist pseudoscience that experts were using to classify and order an expanding, diversifying American population.[26] At the same time, visitors' attitude toward the French Market's people and goods was essentially consumerist. As in nearby sugarcane fields or the urban auction blocks of a previous generation, tourists interpreted New Orleans's French Market as an emporium of food, drink, and people. The French Market was a "veritable 'curiosity-shop,'" confirmed one reporter.[27]

White male writers focused particular attention on women of color at the French Market, appraising and assessing their physical traits in conjunction with the food and drink they handled. Journalists and tourists specified the color of women sellers' skin, the texture of their hair, and their mode of speech, together with the quality and abundance of their wares. Choctaw women vendors were "strange beings, apparently half-civilized," declared the author of the 1900 *Picayune's Guide*, who infused their surroundings with the "odor of wild herbs and woodland leaves."[28] Their mien reflected, or derived from, the sassafras and woven baskets they sold, he suggested, such that the scents of their bodies and their wares pervaded their surroundings. Black women coffee sellers stimulated writers' imaginations, too. In multiple accounts, these women entrepreneurs and the dark, tropical drink they brewed coalesced to embody New Orleans's fused human and sensory charms. "Here Aglaé, stately and gracious with her turbaned head and ebony features wreathed in smiles, dispensed her steaming coffee to *mo ti moun*, as she patronizingly called her younger visitors," wrote one native New Orleanian of an 1820s seller.[29] Forty years later, another writer addressed his reader—presumed to be male, and overwhelmed by the market's Babel-like confusion—suggesting, "He finds comfort at the hands of the charming quadroon girl, who sells that most delicious of drinks, coffee . . . no one knows the secret so well as the quadroon."[30] Such descriptions cohered with contemporary stereotypes of the exoticized "quadroon," while presaging future stereotypes of the "mammy" who would appear on food packaging later in the century, ever-ready to nourish and comfort with a treat and a smile.[31] Extravagant imaginings of figures such as these—together with descriptions of piles of tropical fruit, tubs of living crabs, and hordes of noisy shoppers—tempted the fantasies and appetites of travelers, writers, and artists. Still, even as visitors stumbled and sketched their way along the arcade of the *Halle des boucheries*, the market continued to be just that—a market, whose primary function was to feed the region's inhabitants as it had for centuries. To many of these regulars, the languages, people, and practices of the French Market were perfectly intelligible.

Whereas tourists reveled in the French Market's multitudes as a novelty, many locals counted the market as a necessary component of their daily routines. The final few pages of the diary kept in 1852 by Mary Longfellow Greenleaf, sister of the poet Henry Wadsworth Longfellow, demonstrated the French Market's centrality to residents' daily needs. From 1841 to 1861, Greenleaf and her husband, James, divided their time between New England and New Orleans due to James's work in the cotton industry. In a slender journal, Greenleaf recorded her daily activities during the year she turned thirty-six. She noted the weather, the house calls she made, her dining companions, and the scripture passages featured in the day's sermon at the nearby Episcopal church. While her spare, penciled entries outlined the broad strokes of how she passed her year, the final few pages of the book added much detail. There, Greenleaf itemized her daily expenses, amassing a year's summary of her household's shopping practices.

A sample of Greenleaf's records from one week in early November 1852 spoke to the importance of daily market shopping in antebellum New Orleans:

November
1: market 1.10. soap 5 indigo 5 bread 5 linen 1.0 . . . drayage from ship 1.25
2: market 1.25 butter 25. Hops 20. Charity 1.00. lit 50
3: market 80. Bread ticket 50 . . .
4: market 2.35. fruit 20. Butter 25. Cake 30. Coffee 40.
5: market 75. Ice tickets 50. Charity 50. Yeast 5.
6: market 1.50. K. butter 25. Paid Sarah 18.50. apples 10. Drayage 1.50 . . .
    seamstress 75
8: market 1.55. apples 10 . . . saw 25.[32]

Greenleaf's first expense of the day was always the market. The repetition of this item made it the clear anchor of her routine. Still, her complete list showed that the market was not the source for everything she needed. Elsewhere, Greenleaf purchased dairy products (butter, milk), lard, and ingredients like hops, yeast, bread, cocoa, honey, salt, rice, cakes, and coffee— ingredients for brewing, baking, and cooking. These items supplemented the vegetables she grew in her kitchen garden. In spring 1852, Greenleaf sowed bush peas, carrots, parsnips, beets, and turnips. She started tomatoes and eggplants "in box" before transferring them to the garden one month later.[33] Regular payments for bread and ice tickets indicated that these, too, likely arrived at Greenleaf's door via street vendors or delivery carts. On December 2, 1852, Greenleaf purchased a cookbook, perhaps in preparation for the upcoming holiday festivities.[34] Even if market shopping was a daily necessity for Green-leaf's household, she likely did not shop herself. If she followed local conven-tion, she sent a servant or enslaved bondsperson to the market on her behalf.[35]

Travelers and writers noted that New Orleanians of color, especially Black women, dominated the French Market in the early and mid-nineteenth cen-tury. Even when acknowledging their presence and clout, though, many ob-servers could not resist conflating their bodies with the food that surrounded them. "Before every pillar [in the market], the shining face of a blackee may be seen glistening from among his vegetables," wrote the author of an 1835 travel memoir. "During the half hour I remained . . . I did not see one white person to fifty blacks. It appears that here servants do all the marketing, and that gentlemen and ladies do not, as in Boston, Philadelphia, and elsewhere, visit the market-place themselves."[36] Bondspeople bought and sold food on behalf of their enslavers. Other peddlers and neutral-ground vendors sold goods on their own time and for their own profit, in some cases working to-ward their manumission.[37] Even if many shoppers, growers, and purveyors were enslaved, their outward autonomy struck many visitors. One writer acknowledged the French Market as "the high place of the blacks—who buy and sell, and chaffer and chaff, and laugh." They filled the aisles as customers and were responsible for providing much of the food for sale. "Except for the labors of the old negroes, who bring in chickens, and artichokes, and figs, and potatoes," the writer explained, "one sees that the population must immedi-ately starve to death."[38]

Even when compelled to work at the French Market, many New Orleani-ans of color used the institution as a place to exercise commercial and financial discretion, socialize, and move with relative autonomy, albeit within the polit-ical and social limits that constrained them. When Black shoppers conducted the household's daily shopping, some learned to reserve a sliver of the budget for their own enjoyment, however brief or small. Eliza Ripley, who grew up in New Orleans in the 1840s, remembered accompanying John, an enslaved man who labored in their house, to the French Market as a child. "John, for-getting nothing that had been ordered . . . always carefully remember[ed] one most important item," Ripley recalled, "the saving of at least a picayune out of the market money for a cup of coffee at Manette's stall." The single cup of coffee and plate of beignets, which he shared with the girl, counted for a moment of rest and pleasure within the market's halls. The pause was brief, though, and "John finished the repast and 'dreened' the cup, and with the re-mark, 'We won't say anything about this,' [they] started toward home."[39] With his market coffee, John claimed a picayune's measure of independence a few blocks from French Quarter coffeehouses and exchanges where patrons bid on enslaved people at auction.

If the French Market's crowds struck many visitors as a Babel-like mayhem, market regulars demonstrated an ease that was specifically linguistic in nature. "Most of these coffee-vendors have the power of imitating all the languages spoken in the place," wrote one guidebook author, observing the multilingual fluency of workers at the French Market's coffee stands. "They make themselves understood to all their customers, and seem thoroughly posted in favorite slang phrases of the would-be fast men who come there to drink coffee."[40] A reporter for a national magazine was similarly struck by the mixed chatter that flowed around him. He sketched a crude transcription of an exchange among "that great substratum, the negro element, so exotic and interesting to the stranger":

MR. JONSING – 'Got new dog, Monser Thompsing, eh?'
BOTH – 'Waugh, waugh, waugh!'
DOG – 'Bow, wow!' snapping at Mr. Johnson's leg.
MR. THOMPSING – 'Nomporte – goin' apter he breffast, tinks you make good meat – good morn,' Mr. Jonsing.'
BOTH – 'Waugh, waugh, waugh! Waugh, waugh, waugh!' and exit.[41]

In these brief lines written like a bit of theatrical script, the writer cast the men as colorful characters and placed the noisy dog in equal rank, reporting the men's "waugh, waugh" and the dog's "bow, wow" as indecipherable noise of the same class. The men talked at the same time, which when transcribed read like little more than a jumbled babble. The observer deemed the snatches of English he could discern, inflected with accents and a measure of Creole, as meaningless small talk. The men bantered, "Mr. Thompsing" suggesting that his hungry dog judged "Mr. Jonsing" to be "good meat."[42] Even if the transcription was mocking, the accompanying illustration showed two shoppers at ease, one with a walking stick and his dog, smoking, the other carrying a market basket. They leaned eagerly toward each other, smiling and talking. The sketch displayed two figures who had found familiar faces and relaxed conversation at New Orleans's French Market, where the traveler could only see a Babel-like "substratum."

The prominence of Black New Orleanians and Choctaws at the French Market during this era was conspicuous in a full-page illustration published in *Harper's Weekly* magazine in 1882 (fig. 4.2). The accompanying article identified this place as New Orleans's "famous market . . . a perfect Babel."

FIGURE 4.2. This illustration offered a visual catalog of the people whom visitors might see at New Orleans's French Market, emphasizing the Black women who shopped there daily and Choctaw sellers, a curiosity to tourists. John W. Alexander, "In the Old French Market, New Orleans—drawn by John W. Alexander," illustration, *Harper's Weekly* 26, no. 1309 (January 21, 1882): 40. Image courtesy of ProQuest LLC.

A layered mass of vendors, goods, and shoppers lined both sides of the *Halle des boucheries*. The people pictured were engaged in myriad activities—they sat and sewed, stooped and reached into a bag, inclined to hear a quoted price, hauled a heavy basket—and their heads and bodies blended into the scrum of fruits, vegetables, flowers, and other things surrounding them. Here was the nation's subtropical Babel, a buzzing mix of humans and the things they made, bought, sold, and ate. A focused rendering of two Choctaw women, a baby, and their basket in the right foreground—even if authorities did not permit such vendors within the market's arcade—enhanced the exoticism of the scene.

Emerging up out of the chaos, the market's neoclassical colonnades imposed order and perspective on the mix and drew the viewer's eye toward the illustration's focal point: the woman shopper in the center aisle. The only figure whose form was fully articulated and who faced the viewer head-on, she trod a path that seemed magically cleared of the clutter on either side of her. Her upright posture echoed that of the columns to her right and left. The expression on her face was impassive, seemingly unaware of or disinterested in the artist's gaze. Powerful forearms and hands held stable the two baskets she carried, one already overflowing with vegetables. The other basket appeared empty, implying that she still had decisions to make and money to spend. This woman shopper seemed to claim the market as her own domain.

By the time this *Harper's* issue went to press in 1882, however, the path ahead for this customer and many of the sellers at her sides was much less clear. The limited political and social advances that Black New Orleanians had achieved in the years immediately following the Civil War were being snatched away by their white neighbors and by more powerful authorities, farther away.[43] In 1873, the US Supreme Court had ruled on the *Slaughter-House* cases, a series of suits brought by New Orleans butchers to protest the establishment of a centralized slaughterhouse in the city that prevented butchers from operating outside it. Ruling against the plaintiffs, the court eviscerated the Constitution's Fourteenth Amendment, adopted just five years earlier. The amendment affirmed the citizenship of all people born within the United States, including those formerly enslaved (but excluding Native people), and forbade any state from curtailing the "privileges or immunities" of all citizens. The court's *Slaughter-House* decision, however, drastically narrowed the realms in which the federal government guaranteed protection of citizens' rights, especially within the relationship between a state and its citizens.[44]

To Black Americans less than a decade removed from slavery, facing a battery of legal, judicial, and social assaults, the ruling was a rug pulled out from under their feet, snapping back a safeguard promised in the wake of war and emancipation. The decision's effects were not a ripple but a tidal wave. In 1896, ruling in *Plessy v. Ferguson*, a case that had also originated in New Orleans, the Supreme Court affirmed the constitutionality of a Louisiana statute that had established "separate but equal" accommodations for Black and white railway passengers.[45] "Colored" entrances to theaters; "colored" water fountains for Black children thirsty in the Louisiana heat and humidity; restaurants that employed Black cooks to stand at kitchen stoves but forbade them from sitting in dining rooms, eating the food they had prepared—these were the future for Black Americans in New Orleans and many other American places when *Harper's* published "In the Old French Market" in 1882.

As the nineteenth century came to a close, shifting winds that warned of such storms ahead were stirring among the French Market's columns. The sensory, linguistic, and human amalgamations that had thrilled visitors earlier in the century began to repel many tourists and locals by the turn of the twentieth. To eyes inspired by Progressive calls for sunlight and sanitation, New Orleans's legendary Babel now seemed a filthy wasteland. A specific group declared that they should be entrusted with cleaning it up.

Cleaning Up Babel

"It must be admitted that the French Market, if picturesque, is also dirty," acknowledged a reporter in 1890. Still, the "dingy . . . tattered awnings" that shielded market stalls from the sun "form[ed] a picturesque setting," he decided, for the people and goods beneath them.[46] The French Market's vendors, their wares, and the place where they worked created a distinctive, if dilapidated, aesthetic that continued to draw writers and artists, in particular, to this historic site (fig. 4.3). The market had become a "little city in itself," agreed a photographer, though not one laid out in orderly, gridded streets. Instead, shoppers found themselves winding their way through "queer, cramped places with narrow passages."[47] Many turn-of-the-century visitors were torn between a conviction that New Orleans's French Market remained "picturesque"—a quality they located in the market's twisting alleyways and "swarthy" vendors—and a growing disgust for what, or whom, its dark corners hid.[48]

As the French Market's cobwebs and grime accumulated, the pace, sounds, and sights of the city around it were transforming. The World's Industrial and Cotton Centennial Exposition in 1884 and 1885 drew global attention to the Crescent City. Tourists came to gaze at busy levees, cemeteries, and sugarcane

FIGURE 4.3. By the turn of the twentieth century, the French Market's crowds, dirt, and dilapidated state began to repel many visitors and prompt Progressive reformers to call for change. George François Mugnier, *French Market*, 1890, photograph. Clarence John Laughlin Archive, no. 1981.247.12.96, The Historic New Orleans Collection.

plantations and mailed postcards of the sights they saw. The city electrified. Steel and concrete buildings rose. Progressive-Era reformers campaigned to clean up water supply and sanitation systems. Wealthy and middle-class white New Orleanians moved to new, whites-only neighborhoods upriver from the Garden District and bordering Lake Pontchartrain. A Jim Crow regime of race-based segregation and disfranchisement calcified. Following an initial migration of emancipated people to New Orleans immediately after the Civil War, Black residents of the state joined Great Migration streams flowing out of the South, seeking to leave behind entrenched racism and exploitation. All the while, the sensory pleasures of cuisine, jazz, and Storyville brothels encouraged the Crescent City's international reputation as a realm for leisure and fantasy to grow larger still.

Nevertheless, New Orleans's historic dearth of manufacturing and orientation toward river versus rail dragged the city's economy behind others in the region and nation.[49] Like other public facilities, the French Market had undeniably deteriorated. Municipal authorities struggled to bring the city's infrastructure in line with modernizing national standards. In 1880, less than 20 percent of New Orleans's streets were paved.[50] A decade later, in 1890, a journalist observed that visitors were beginning to shrink from the French Market's grimy corners. "The fashionable visitors who 'do' the market on Sunday as the 'correct thing' peer curiously at the more mysterious stalls . . . and shudder a little at the dirt," he wrote.[51] From a primary attraction for travelers during the early and mid-nineteenth century, the French Market of the turn of the twentieth century had become a box to check, and a dirty one at that.

The French Market's decline as a tourist draw can be tracked in successive editions of the *Picayune's Guide to New Orleans*, the city's leading travel guide, which directed visitors to the sugar levees and the French Market alike.[52] A comparison of editions published between 1896 and 1924 reveals diminishing text and fewer photographs featuring the French Market. Similarly, enthusiasm for the market's people and goods transformed into an aloof appreciation of its architecture. According to the 1900 edition, at the French Market the tourist would find "Chinese and Hindu, Jew and Spaniard, French and Teuton, Irish and English."[53] In 1903, the diverse crowd remained, but the author now warned that their assembled impact on the visitor could be overpowering. The 1903 market was populated by the same groups, "all uniting in a ceaseless babel of tongues that is simply bewildering. . . . You turn from the market, with its singular complexity that interests while it challenges admiration, and emerge upon the levee."[54] By 1903, the tourist needed to "emerge" from the market as from a maelstrom of noise. The same mix of people that had previously intrigued now overwhelmed.

Additional edits to the *Picayune's Guide* charted this shift in narratorial perspective, from pride in the French Market in earlier editions to wariness and nostalgia in later editions. Whereas the 1903 guide still encouraged travelers to venture inside the market, despite the "Babel" inside, the 1910 edition did not. Distinct from previous versions, the guide's tenth edition focused solely—and briefly—on the French Market's architecture. From the writer's dry description of the building's brick walls, wooden roofs, and "interesting old columns," he gave the impression that he never ventured inside the structure but lingered on the perimeter.[55] By the twelfth edition, published in 1917, the author's physical distance had matured into a vague acknowledgment of the institution's decreased tourist appeal. "The French Market is greatly changed from the old days," the writer admitted.

By the *Picayune Guide*'s final edition, the difference between the French Market of 1924 and that of 1896 was literally night and day. In 1896, the author had advised an energetic morning excursion, writing, "The markets in New Orleans are well worth a visit. . . . To see them in their perfection, [the tourist] will have to arise early enough to get to the market by sunrise."[56] By 1924, the guide's author recommended that a tour of the French Quarter and the French Market begin in the late afternoon, "because at that time the soft colors of evening will fall across the battered façades of the old houses and will treat them kindly. . . . You must look with friendly eyes. If you do not, you may come away with only the ideas of dirt and squalor."[57] Fearing the bright sunlight's exposure of the market's decline, the 1924 *Times-Picayune's Guide* advised a softer lens through which to perceive the market and its surroundings. Decay and wear had aged the market's structures. The passage of time had also touched the people inside.

Writers used an additional lens through which they tracked the French Market's decline: the Choctaw vendor, long a source of objectifying intrigue for white tourists. In their explication, the dwindling presence of this class of sellers served to epitomize the market's decay. For nearly two hundred years, Choctaw vendors had sold *kombo ashish*, filé powder (dried, twice-pulverized sassafras leaves used to thicken and add sour, bitter flavors to the region's gumbo) and hand-woven baskets made from cane or palmetto stems. Displaying these wares in baskets and on leaves and mats on the ground, the sellers also brought scuppernong grapes, bay and laurel leaves, Indian turnip (boiled to treat consumption), latanier palm roots (used as brushes), and cane blow guns and arrows (fig. 4.4).[58] White tourists ogled these vendors, construing them as exotic remnants of the region's hinterlands and its past. Amplifying contemporary stereotypes, writers often described the women as silent and impassive. "Chinamen, Russians, Malays, Britons . . . stop to glance at the

FIGURE 4.4. Choctaw women vendors sold sassafras, baskets, and other goods at the French Market, where tourists gawked at their bodies, their wares, and their facial expressions. Paul Hammersmith, *French Market N.O. Feb. 91*, February 1891, photograph. Gift of Mary Louise Hammersmith, no. 1977.79.13, The Historic New Orleans Collection.

squaws," one journalist described. "Germans and Greeks, Cuban darkies and Emerald Islander[s] ask questions . . . but through it all the Indians sit motionless and scornfully contemplative."[59] The author of the *New Orleans Guide*, published in 1893, juxtaposed Black women shoppers with Choctaw women vendors to emphasize the noisiness of one and the noiselessness of the other. "Fat negresses . . . stroll along, talking gumbo French . . . exchanging sweet morsels of news or gossip," wrote the author, using culinary metaphors— gumbo, sweet morsels—to describe the women. "Amidst all this noise and confusion, the Choctaw Indians sit, silent as statues, apparently oblivious of their surroundings."[60] If turn-of-the-century tourists and writers claimed to be overwhelmed by the market's multilingual crowds, they were stymied by Choctaw vendors' quiet.[61]

Travelers who came to New Orleans during this era sought the picturesque or the sublime, but many reported themselves crestfallen by the Choctaw women they found (or missed) at the French Market. Seeking out these vendors as entertainment, white visitors arrived with distinctive expectations of what the women should look like and how they should act. "I had been told that the most curious thing about the French market was the crowd of Indians sitting around its edges begging and selling small wares," wrote a *New York Times* reporter in spring 1884. "But it was not a good day for Indians, and there were none there," he griped. Other writers had complaints of a different magnitude. "They have melted away into Mulattoes," one lamented in 1885. "The lazy, unstudied attitude of . . . these daughters of the forest is not exactly in accordance with the poetic idea one used to drink in." To nationwide readers, these writers blamed the changes they claimed to observe on Choctaw intermarriage with Black Louisianians, or so they suspected. Choctaw sellers were "the star attractions of the market in the eyes of many strangers," yet another writer agreed. Yet their "blood . . . is generally diluted with that of the negro," he continued. "There is nothing particularly noble about them, and their listless, half-sullen attitude is far from inspiring."[62] Such racist criticisms pointed to whites' own racial anxieties, during years of proliferating de jure and de facto Jim Crow measures that blocked intermarriage between Blacks and whites.

To many turn-of-the-century white marketgoers, then, the purportedly vanishing vendors of baskets and sassafras represented the ultimate dangers of the French Market's Babel and the multiracial, multiethnic metropolis it fed. Choctaws' trajectory from racial "melting" to extinction, as white observers charted it, offered evidence for why the market needed to be ordered and regulated. The vendors' evolving appearance and ultimate disappearance seemed to offer a real-time display of the repercussions of interracial sex (rather than the long-unfolding effects of European and American seizure of Native homelands, disease, and persecution).[63] In 1900, the *Picayune's Guide* declared of Choctaws, "They were crowded out of New Orleans by the superior and cultured race."[64] Just eight years later, Choctaw vendors seem to have disappeared from the market altogether. The 1908 *Picayune's Guide* described the sellers in the past tense, explaining, "Formerly the French Market was a resort for the Indians. . . . Until of their own free will the greater part of their number elected to depart."[65] What white observers characterized as the extinction of Choctaw vendors, together with the spread of cobwebs among French Market rafters, set the scene for the physical and regulatory reinvention of one of the nation's oldest public institutions.

Racial anxieties would fester at the heart of New Orleans's first major campaign to renovate the French Market, though reformers would speak primarily in terms of rats and refrigeration rather than race. Following their successful activism for slavery's abolition, American women throughout the nation had organized and become increasingly comfortable battling on public stages for a variety of causes: temperance and prohibition, women's suffrage, educational reform, and a more sanitary food industry.[66] In New Orleans, Progressive women reformers turned their attention to the city's food-provisioning system. Middle- and upper-class white housewives decried New Orleans's public markets as anti-modern and a communal health threat. They demanded technological and regulatory changes to public markets as well as an end to restrictions curtailing the development of private markets.[67] The housewives' efforts belonged to broader Progressive campaigns that were reshaping cities across the country, yet in their focus on the French Market, they targeted an institution that had never belonged to their kind. Despite the historic lack of white women shoppers at the very markets they demanded to renovate, they asserted their expertise as consumers and household managers. Their efforts would dismantle an arena in which New Orleanians of color had been able to establish economic and social footholds in a persistently prejudiced society.

The filth that inspired the complaints of New Orleans's women activists in the 1910s thrived in seemingly every public market. Inspections conducted by the Louisiana State Board of Health in 1912 confirmed a variety of problems throughout the city, ranging from "dirty refrigerators" to "defective ice boxes—unsanitary tools . . . cats and mice running over meat," and an "awful stench from [the] floor of Poydras [market]."[68] The following year, Board of Health president Dr. Oscar Dowling quantified the markets' substandard conditions when he tallied the presence or absence of screened windows, flies, running water, and covered garbage. The results were abysmal. Horses and dogs made regular appearances in the markets, Dowling observed. They trod floors encrusted with the viscera of turtles and chickens.[69] Corners that some might have called picturesque a few decades earlier now harbored mysterious grime.

The Market Committee, a white women's group that formed within the Housewives' League Division of the City Federation of Clubs, declared that they would take public market inspections into their own hands and recommend solutions. Committee member Mrs. John B. Parker inspected the Prytania Street market in May 1913 and confirmed, "Filth and dirt was [sic] all around. The only method of cleaning was to have a boy throw water once a week over the floor. . . . The flies seemed to be thoroughly enjoying themselves."[70] A chorus of women corroborated such discoveries as they aired their disgust in city newspapers. One incensed shopper wrote to the *New Orleans Item* to declare, "The public markets of New Orleans are a disgrace to civilization. . . . Why, you can smell one of these 'sanitary' markets from one to two blocks away." Open-air stalls meant "flies swarming over the meat so thick that you can not see anything but flies," she griped. "You have no way of telling how many mashed flies the butcher has wrapped up on your steak."[71]

Another shopper was careful to point out that the stakes were much greater than the unpleasant discovery of a handful of squashed bugs coating her dinner chops. In a letter to the *Times-Democrat*, Mrs. Jacob Ambrose Storck, president of the Fine Arts Club of New Orleans, explained, "No subject is more vital to the public health at large than marketing, since upon the proper nourishment of the family depends their health, happiness and efficiency." Furthermore, she reasoned, "It naturally devolves upon the woman in the home to see to it that this very essential household obligation is well discharged."[72] Productive families flourished thanks to a healthful diet, she argued, which could only be procured at clean markets. The housewife served as the vital link in this chain. Market Committee members recognized the power residing in battalions of women armed with critical eyes and noses and called on their continued watchful participation. In a 1915 report, the committee announced, "We . . . would like to have a woman from each market neighborhood to serve on the Market Committee . . . and to report to [the chairman] the sanitary condition of all markets."[73] The committee charged all women to be watchful consumers, for their observations could best dictate the markets' needs.

With the backing of an attentive press, the Market Committee formulated an official platform in 1913 that described a public market system of the future that looked very different from the markets of the past, in terms of both infrastructure and people. In place of public markets' open stalls, dim alleyways, and chaotic throngs of shoppers and vendors, the women wanted refrigerated glass cases, bright electric lighting, and ordered aisles. A newspaper editorial explained, "Food would be displayed, not in open stalls, subject to wind, dust, flies, and handling, but as in our modern restaurants, in glass counters, supplied with cold air by pipes."[74] Additionally, Market Committee members demanded "that the strictest sanitary regulations be enforced," the *Item* reported, and "that the matter of personal cleanliness of all employees in the market be rigidly enforced, and the employees be made to wear immaculate white suits." With such appeals, committee members declared their desire for grocery shopping in New Orleans to look and feel more like it did in New York City, Washington, DC, or, essentially, anywhere else.[75] "Other cities have sanitary markets, both public and private, which make us ashamed of ours," declared the head of the City Federation of Clubs, Mrs. Inez Mac-Martin Myers. "When one sees the private stores . . . in other cities, where, displayed in large, refrigerated windows, the various cuts of meat and all kinds of produce can be seen . . . the question arises why have we not the same?"[76] Whereas New Orleans's Babel-like public markets had distinguished the city as alluring in earlier eras, they now made the Crescent City look backward, critics fretted.

French Market vendors resisted the reforming efforts of the Market Committee, casting the women's complaints as a class-driven crusade, but were unable to organize effectively against them. Some market sellers scoffed at the premise of middle- and upper-class housewives claiming expertise related to marketing, since this group often sent servants in their stead. Vendor Sol Ruello scolded, "If the New Orleans housewife wants a low cost of living, why doesn't she come down to the French Market and get it? . . . She is not like her mother before her. She is too proud to go to the French Market and buy her supplies. Twenty-five years ago the housewives used to do it." Other vendors derided as frivolous the women's calls for cleanliness. French Market seller Frank Clesi declared, "It is not the poor people who are kicking [about the public markets]. . . . It is the class that rides in automobiles." An *Item* editorial agreed. "It is the club women . . . and the women at whose doors the wolf never howls who are [seeking to renovate the public markets]. The woman who trudges six or eight blocks to market every morning . . . is not spending much time thinking about modern sanitation."[77]

Even if well-to-do white housewives led the charge for market change, their historic disengagement from the labor of food shopping offered a clue to other factors at play. Local resident Judith Hyams Douglas envisioned an extra touch to suggested market renovations, eventually adopted by the Market Committee, to enhance her ideal shopping experience. Douglas wrote to the *Times-Democrat*, "My idea would be to employ girls, physically sound, who would receive an outer garment . . . of white linen."[78] These white girls clad in white linen would act as smiling guides, Douglas imagined, converting a chore conducted in a dirty and heterogeneous marketplace—a place unintelligible to tourists and many locals—into a sanitized, more legible experience. The Market Committee's white-coated guides personified Progressive ideals of cleanliness and expertise. Yet they also evinced a transparent racial perspective that idealized whiteness in the French Market's people and structures alike.[79]

As such suggestions intimated, the housewives' campaign to renovate the city's public markets stemmed from a fear that the iconic, historic marketplace of New Orleans's famous cuisine, and the rules used to govern that marketplace, were anti-modern, if not un-American. In a speech to the New Orleans Round Table Club, a whites-only men's group interested in "educational, scientific, and civic matters" that met in a mansion on St. Charles Avenue, a Market Committee member explained why New Orleans's public markets were outdated, both practically and politically.[80] "The French Market, if not physically as old as the city, was one of the European ideas brought over by the first settlers," she declared, "and it has been along European lines of government that our market system has been run." Market rules had not been modified since well before the turn of the century, she alleged, "and these in turn were based upon the old ideas that pervaded Europe before the French Revolution . . . rather than upon the more modern and more American thought that there should be no restrictions except those absolutely necessary."[81] According to her reasoning, the French Market and its smaller siblings wallowed due to an approach to marketing, business, and government that predated New Orleans's transfer to the United States. The time had come to Americanize them.

The Market Committee's characterization of the city's French Market as not quite American was nothing new; the market's mix of people had seemed alien to many visitors and locals since its start. But *who* made the market exotic had changed over time. In the nineteenth century, white shoppers had located this quality in Black women pouring coffee and Choctaw sellers vending baskets. By the 1910s, when the Market Committee set to work, the market's foreignness emanated from a different cast of characters: Sicilian immigrants, who dominated the city's trades in oranges, lemons, bananas, and oysters (fig. 4.5).

The speed and scale of Sicilian immigration to Louisiana in the decades surrounding the turn of the twentieth century transformed the state economically and socially and challenged its solidifying racial order. Steamship routes that ferried Mediterranean citrus fruits to New Orleans, as well as postbellum recruitment of Sicilians by Louisiana sugar planters, facilitated emigration directly from Sicily to the Crescent City. By 1900, US census takers calculated that one in every three foreign-born residents of Louisiana hailed from Italy. Their prominence in New Orleans's French Quarter earned the neighborhood the nickname "Little Palermo."[82] In 1884, a journalist observed that white New Orleanians had "mostly abandoned the [Vieux] Carré to the European Latins." The following year, a guidebook author conducted a voyeuristic visit to a French Quarter tenement filled with Sicilian residents and reported on "strips of maccaroni [*sic*] . . . hanging up near the ceiling to dry."[83] If writers drew on particular racist stereotypes to describe Black and Choctaw market vendors, they reached for another—Mafia references—to characterize Sicilians.[84] The poverty, illiteracy, and darker skin tones of many Sicilian immigrants contributed, too, to their positioning in a dangerous, nebulous zone between Black and white. Mobs who targeted Black Louisianians during this era assaulted Sicilians as well. Following the 1890 murder of New Orleans po-

FIGURE 4.5. By the turn of the twentieth century, Sicilian immigrants dominated New Orleans's fruit trade but suffered from racist prejudice that was often violent. George François Mugnier, *Fruit Stand, French Market*, ca. 1889, photograph. George François Mugnier Photograph Collection, Louisiana Division/City Archives and Special Collections, New Orleans Public Library.

lice chief David Hennessy, the local press proclaimed the crime to be the work of the Black Hand. On March 14, 1891, a white mob broke into the city prison and lynched eleven Sicilian men. The violence sparked national outrage.[85]

As with other groups in New Orleans, Sicilians moved through a course of social and racial classification that was rarely of their own making. A 1913 newspaper article about French Market vendors indicated that white New Orleanians had adopted a prejudiced distinction between Sicilians and peninsular Italians, writing, "Many [truck growers] are Italians of the best class which that country sends us. Many more are Sicilians, and with them most of the Italians have no dealings."[86] A poem published in the *Times-Picayune* in 1916 satirized white New Orleanians' changing perceptions of these immigrants, which could be tracked in the public's evolving, rude slang. In "Just 'Wops,'" the poet rhymed:

We first called him Italian
And brought the 'I' out strong
And praised the dark rapscallion
In romance and in song;

But soon we changed to Dago
And sang the stuff he eats,
Spaghetti and sapsago
And oil infected meats;

Yet even this name was too long
So once again we chop
And now in our Italian song
We call the Dago 'Wop.'[87]

The writer distinguished between the "we" that comprised the writer and his readers—the crowd, or the mob—and the object of their attention: "the Dago," a singular, male figure. At the time of this poem's writing, the Italian in New Orleans had been subjected to generations of pejorative nicknames according to the pleasure of the crowd, the "we." It was because the epithet "Dago" was "too long," the narrator announced, that "once again we chop"—we cleave, as a cut of meat—to give a shorter nickname more convenient for songs and poems. Even if the poem's tone was derisive—"oil infected meats" was hardly a reason to "s[i]ng" of Italians' cuisine—the verses nevertheless communicated that this group had been present in New Orleans for generations and was widely known by its foods.

During the time frame described by the poem, Italians in the United States had survived eras of distinct racial epithets as they clawed their way, slowly, to claim a white identity for themselves. Emigrants who came to Louisiana from Sicily or the Italian mainland had arrived with a stronger allegiance to their region or town than to the Italian nation, which had unified in 1871. Nevertheless, within daily social and commercial interactions and relationships, in New Orleans as in New York, Newark, and other American cities, Sicilians became Italian and Italians became white, even if federal census takers had classified them as such for decades.[88] This progression ensured that the French Market's Sicilian vendors, distinct from its Black and Choctaw sellers, would keep their stake in the market's future, not just its past.

As white writers and market visitors scrutinized the changing character and appearance of Choctaws and Sicilians at the French Market, they crafted a sharply slanted decline for Black New Orleanians. Turn-of-the-century white city residents and writers cast Black New Orleanians in the marketplace as inept, dishonest, and dirty. In doing so, they fed the racist vitriol of Jim Crow public culture. In a 1913 letter to the editor, one wealthy housewife depicted the household's servants as burdens to feed, rather than savvy shoppers themselves. She reasoned, "The servants who are, for the most part, children of a larger growth, must be well fed to keep them in a good humor and to enable them to do the really hard labor which is expected of them."[89] The woman's expectation that an input of sustenance would produce an output of "really hard labor" recalled the warped logic of slavery a century earlier. Relatedly, French Market stall keeper Frank Clesi, born in Italy, appeared to confirm suspicions that such servants could not be trusted as shoppers themselves. "Sometimes the mistress will send a negro woman to the market with a $2 bill. She will . . . spend half the money and pocket the rest and go home and tell the lady that it cost all the money she had."[90] A world apart from the authoritative shopper depicted in the 1882 *Harper's Weekly* illustration, in charge of her market baskets and the money used to fill them, such comments cast domestic workers as insatiable and deceptive, as they gobbled up the family's food and its loose change. Dishonesty was not the servants' only alleged fault, however.

Members of the Market Committee also cast New Orleans's Black population as dirty and even the cause of public markets' filth. Attendees at a June 1914 committee meeting denounced unsatisfactory market conditions such as unlidded sugar barrels and roaming animals. From there, the housewives questioned how to deal with what they described as unhygienic habits that they linked to the city's Black residents. "Conditions of a shocking nature had been unearthed in the past few weeks regarding the housing conditions among the colored people," recorded a reporter covering the committee's gathering. "The first day of May had been set by the Board of Health as a cleanup day among the colored people, and the white population was urged to have a general cleanup day . . . so that the example might make easier the work among the colored families."[91] Purportedly innate cleanliness among whites contrasted with the supposed dirtiness that marred the homes of their Black neighbors. Not considered in this meeting was municipal authorities' purposeful neglect of Black neighborhoods, which included inattention to sewage and streets and inadequate garbage collection.[92] Even if the Market Committee had met to discuss the state of the city's markets, members claimed an expanded responsibility to address the public health menace they perceived in Black communities. Their conversation echoed similar efforts in other American cities, where Progressive white women's pursuits of sanitation, light, and order often cast immigrant and Black Americans as the perpetrators of backward approaches to housekeeping, hygiene, and diet.[93]

In a 1916 speech, a Market Committee representative drew an explicit connection between Black New Orleanians' rumored dirtiness and the state of the city's public markets, intending to leave no doubt in the minds of her listeners. Reflecting on the committee's longstanding efforts to reform the markets, the speaker recalled how, several years prior, "inefficiency [had] prevailed in the cleaning of the markets. . . . Slovenly negro women prisoners . . . were assigned to clean the principal markets—but the outlying markets where a janitor was employed were far better cleaned." After four years, the situation still had not improved. She announced, "We are urging . . . the appointment of one responsible janitor . . . and to do away with . . . the gangs of sloppy negroes who are now supposed to keep [the markets] clean."[94] Black women had once been the market's proud regulars, filling its aisles as shoppers and vendors. By the early twentieth century, Black women prisoners were made to scrub the floors of public markets and disparaged for doing so. Still, the markets were not the only public place in the city that Black women were forced to service. Also in 1916, a Black journalist from Chicago decried the spectacle of Black women prisoners in New Orleans made to "clean gutters and public parks with a red neck slave driver with a Winchester rifle or automatic to shoot her down should she rebel."[95] Little distinguished these scenes from similar settings sixty years earlier, when slavery had been the law of the land.

The disgust that white writers and city residents showed for Black New Orleanians in public markets surfaced in fictionalized and commercial representations, too. *The Story of the Old French Market*, published in 1916, was an advertisement for the New Orleans Coffee Company masquerading as a souvenir booklet. In purple prose, the author recounted the market's history from colonial days to the present while hawking French Market–brand coffee. Filling her essay with blushing maidens and a gallant Andrew Jackson, champion of the Battle of New Orleans, the writer wove a taut thread of violence through her market tour. Guiding her reader down the aisles, she described "green cabbages piled high like so many decapitated heads," "the still quivering steaks" of "a large sea turtle [that] has just been cut up," and a nightmarish tangle of "pulleys, ropes, hoops and grappling tackle for handling the half of a huge beef."[96] The author reserved her most vicious descriptions for the Black vendors and shoppers there. "At one stall porky-looking chunks of meat are being eagerly bought by colored people," she described. "It is from a nice, fat alligator that, well boiled, would deceive a cannibal, it is said, so like is it to human flesh."[97]

Black New Orleanians were not only cannibalistic in the booklet's brutal narration; they were cannibalized, too. The narrator imagined a conversation with the ghost of Madame Lalaurie, a nineteenth-century New Orleans enslaver infamous for torturing bondspeople. "When [Lalaurie] stopped to order purple fillets of beef even the butcher's hand trembled as he did her bidding," the narrator confided. "'*Ma foi*,' said one, 'I should think it would remind her too much of how she cuts off them poor niggers' ears!'!'" This gory tale prompted a revolted recoil in the imagined reader as the narrator chided, "Oh! Do not shrink! It was long ago, my dear!" before describing how Lalaurie escaped punishment by fleeing to France.[98] *The Story of the Old French Market* enacted incredible violence on the Black sellers and shoppers that the narrator encountered in the French Market. Humans, vegetables, and butchered meat, some "still quivering," made for a kaleidoscope of violent death, culinary taboos, and disgust. Equally perverse, the booklet sold delusions about New Orleans history in order to sell French Market–brand coffee, a commodity that had once been a hallmark of Black women vendors in the marketplace.[99]

As this racist vitriol proliferated in multiple arenas—the private meetings of social clubs, the public meetings of municipal groups, the press, the tourism industry—the social, political, and legal tentacles of Jim Crow gripped the city ever tighter. Accordingly, defining and delimiting a white racial identity became crucial to those who sought to distance themselves from any suspicion that they descended from a mixed racial heritage. In particular, many turn-of-the-century Louisianians who identified as white began to claim exclusive ownership of the adjective "Creole." They sought to solder their lineage to European and American ancestors and verify a family tree that had been "white" for generations, or so they claimed. They did so in part because, as the Crescent City's economy inclined increasingly toward tourism at the turn of the twentieth century, "Creole"—adjective and noun—came to be synonymous with the city itself, as well as the people, cuisine, music, and history enjoyed there. *La Cuisine Creole: A Collection of Culinary Recipes from Leading Chefs and Noted Creole Housewives, Who Have Made New Orleans Famous for Its Cuisine*, compiled by Greek-born journalist Lafcadio Hearn and published anonymously by a New York publisher in 1885, defined New Orleans cuisine as "Creole" on a national stage.[100] Defining *who* and *what* were Creole had the potential to bestow cultural prestige, if not profit. Thus, whites' denial that people of African descent could be Creole was an attempt to cut them out of New Orleans's history and culture—past, present, and future—and its rewards.

Contributing to this project, white-authored travel guides that depicted Black people at the turn-of-the-century French Market were careful to define the meaning of "Creole" as a distinct racial and ethnic identifier of white New Orleanians. In his 1893 *New Orleans Guide*, local writer James Zacharie privileged an understanding of the term "Creole" as essential knowledge for newcomers to the city. "Strangers often make a great error in supposing that the Creole population is a mixed race of whites and blacks," he warned. To dissuade the reader from such a notion, Zacharie deferred to a local jurist and historian who declared, "Negroes, mulattoes, and Indians never were . . . entitled to the appellation of 'Creoles' in Louisiana." The term Creole, he insisted, "signifies only one of pure and unmixed European blood."[101]

The *Picayune's Guide* likewise fought against what seemed to be widespread confusion outside of New Orleans as to the purportedly true meaning of "Creole." The 1900 edition informed travelers, "Everything 'that is good' in New Orleans is 'Creole'" and "'Creole' in these pages means white." In response to the implied possibility that a Creole person might claim some degree of African heritage, the writer insisted, "Nothing is more erroneous. . . . There never was a nobler or more pure-blooded race than the Creoles of Louisiana."[102] This zealous defense of a strictly white perimeter around the term persisted through the guidebook's final edition, in 1924. As the narrator invited the reader on a late afternoon saunter through the French Quarter, the question seemed to casually arise as part of an imagined conversation with the reader. "What does 'Creole' mean?" the narrator repeated. "No, of course not. I don't know why tourists always say that. The Creole is not of colored blood. . . . The New Orleans Creole is our finest product."[103] Texts such as these, masquerading behind a friendly, informative tone, strove to teach readers unfamiliar with New Orleans a racist lesson about whom they should congratulate and compensate for creating the Crescent City's famous culture.

Bombarded with such exclusionary messages, New Orleanians who identified as Creole, Black, or "of color" nonetheless declared themselves intrinsic, if not preeminent, to the very definition of Creole history and culture. "A Creole is a native of Louisiana, in whose blood runs mixed strains of everything un-American, with the African strain slightly apparent," wrote New Orleans–born poet and activist Alice Moore Dunbar-Nelson in 1916.[104] Many New Orleanians of African descent had long identified as Creole and would continue to do so, despite their white neighbors' attempt to hoard the identifier only for themselves. Still, associations between the French Market's physical decline, "diluted" Choctaw vendors, and untidy or dishonest Black New Orleanians together formed a seed planted at the turn of the century that would bear fruit in the next generation. Improvements won by Market Committee housewives were partial and short-lived, and public market buildings continued to decay. The most dramatic change in the French Market's history would arrive in the 1930s, with the New Deal. City leaders would embark on a full-scale renovation, celebrating the institution as a centerpiece of the city's "Creole" history. White New Orleanians would pick up hammer, nail, and pen to definitively transform the French Market's Babel into an open book.

A New Deal for the French Market

Despite housewives' reforming efforts in the 1910s, an unrelenting tide of decay continued to emanate from the city's public markets. A new Division of Public Markets, established by municipal authorities in 1931, issued a flood of regulations that specified what could (and could not) be sold at public markets and how vendors should behave. The new rules showed that the city's public markets were no longer a setting for culinary surprise or social improvisation. Pretzels, kippered fish, chow-chow, and ice cream appeared on the two-page list of authorized foods, but vendors could sell *only* items named in the pamphlet and *only* those for which they had been approved. Furthermore, while wearing "either [a] full length white apron or coat, or white overalls and white jacket," the regulations specified, tenants were forbidden to "cry out, hawk, peddle or advertise articles about the building." Officials also proscribed "hand wagons [and] push carts," as well as cursing, tobacco use, and any behavior that could be considered "boisterous [or] . . . a nuisance or annoyance" to fellow vendors and shoppers.[105] Hushed and white-coated vendors could not prevent market buildings from continuing to fall apart over their heads, though. "The roof on the wholesale section of the French Market leaks like a crawfish net," complained a letter in the *New Orleans Item* on April 25, 1933. "In the meat section . . . are holes in the screens big enough to drive an ox through," another scolded a month later.[106] As public criticism continued to resound in newspaper coverage, shoppers began to envision or find more attractive alternatives.

Some observers critical of the French Market's state looked backward, rather than forward, when trying to imagine the institution's ideal future. The French Market of the past offered inspiration, they claimed. "People who visit [the French Market] are often disappointed to find it so dilapidated," acknowledged Dr. Oscar Dowling, past president of the Louisiana State Board of Health, in 1930. "If it were rebuilt in a way similar to its appearance twenty-five years ago . . . the city would get a showplace as well as a modern public market."[107] Dowling envisioned a renovation whose result would be simultaneously historical and modern. This yearning for the market of an earlier era, transferred to the future, surfaced among other New Orleanians as well. A short-lived suggestion to raze the French Market in 1930 prompted a city-wide flutter of nostalgia for the institution's history. "That Old French Market is probably the most romantic spot on the North American Continent," declared a local journalist in 1931. "Men know it where men know New Orleans. It lives, immortal in literature and history." The French Market was the great leveler, he insisted, as a democratic meeting place for "rich and poor, high and low."[108] Faraway observers perceived the fundamental conflict brewing between proponents of preservation and modernization. A 1931 *New York Times* article noted, "New Orleans is in need of a genius" if the city wanted to blend "the stern regulations of sanitary science and the delicate precepts of romance in such fashion as to repel germs and lure tourists." The French Market posed a unique challenge to city officials and developers, the reporter acknowledged, in both the depth of its history and breadth of its needs. "Have it sanitary if you can, but keep it colorful you must," the *Times* writer ordained.[109] Renovating New Orleans's French Market seemed akin to demanding that a chef combine oil and water.

In contrast to the languishing French Market, public markets elsewhere in the city received modernizing updates during the early 1930s. These renovations, together with the city's first private supermarket, helped paint the "mother" market as especially decrepit. When six small public markets reopened in summer 1932 after extensive improvements, a journalist gushed, "The markets had truly gone modern." In place of dim and unscreened stalls, tepid meat, and cement floors, "Mrs. Housewife" discovered "a sanitary scene of glistening white walls, rows of electric lights, tiled floors and green enameled accessories." Mahogany, marble, and electricity elevated these spaces far above the "dilapidated wooden sheds" of the French Market.[110] The disparities between this new construction and the French Market's persistent disrepair struck some as perverse. In May 1933, a disgruntled city resident lamented, "Stacks of clinking dollars are being spent building markets all over town while French Market rots. . . . It's poor progress to gild up a lot of little marts at the expense of the mother of them all."[111]

Nevertheless, enthusiasm for these modernized public showcases was strong. Journalists posited that refrigeration in particular would lure women away from the French Market. "The rehabilitated city markets . . . have not been designed to please men, but to please women, since nine out of its 10 customers are women," a reporter reasoned. At updated public markets, "the display cases . . . are equipped with lights capable of bathing the interior in a flood of light, thus displaying to the fullest advantage the 'schoolgirl complexion' of properly refrigerated meats."[112] The writer implied that shopping women found themselves reflected—in some cases quite literally—in these modern public markets, which they had demanded decades earlier.

A still greater thrill awaited New Orleans ladies elsewhere, however. In the city's first major private supermarket, opened in 1933, W. A. Green offered women a luxurious shopping experience, with amenities such as a large parking lot, a women's lounge and dressing room, and customer service for ladies who came alone. One reporter lauded the store as a "revelation" and "one of the most unusual groceries in the history of the country." The supermarket's proprietor touted his familiarity with scientific studies that would save the housekeeper from "lost motion" during her time there. He also promised a sanitary experience, explaining, "Every article in our store, even the canned goods and bottled stuff, will be kept behind glass, in plain view of every customer but protected from handling by the glass cases."[113] This market of the future incorporated the latest technology in lighting and preservation, creating extreme detachment from the food for sale. Protected by multiple barriers of aluminum, glass, and refrigerated air, the food at Green's store contrasted sharply with that fading in open-air trays at the French Market. Soon, though, the mother market would get its turn.

In 1934, a $300,000 loan from the New Deal's Public Works Administration enabled the city to finally embark on the first major physical renovation in the French Market's history. Many New Orleanians rejoiced but quickly turned protective of the appearance and history of the market. "The promise is made that the reborn structure will retain the figurative, if not all the literal, atmosphere of its historic predecessor," a *Times-Picayune* editorial had reassured readers in 1932. "So staunch are its cypress beams that there is no need to replace [them]."[114] City residents took comfort in learning that the French Market's skeleton—the early nineteenth-century beams that held up the roof, the pegs used to join them, and especially the colonnades that flanked each side like ribs—would survive the renovation process.[115]

The public placed special emphasis on the market's neoclassical columns as the site's trademark feature and evidence of the institution's solid historical foundation. "'The columnar structure is to be retained and repaired.' We quote that for [the] record," a 1936 *Tribune* editorial reported gravely. "If this promise be kept, we shall still feel at home . . . after the first strangeness of plate-glass and new paint has worn off."[116] Public conversation linked the market's physical elements with the place's ambiance, trusting that the survival of one must entail the persistence of the other. No longer was the market's appeal an ineffable quality bound up in the multilingual crowd that filled it; it was tangible, located in the brick-and-mortar components of the building's construction. The project's architect, Sam Stone Jr., took center stage as the "genius" entrusted with the market's restoration and pledged his support for maintaining these features. "The new market . . . will be in appearance and atmosphere essentially of old New Orleans," Stone promised the *Times-Picayune*, as butchers vacated their stalls on June 14, 1936, making way for Stone's crew. "The low broad columns, beloved by New Orleanians for generations, will be preserved."[117] Stone claimed to understand the two-faced need for both old and new and declared his resolve to achieve the proper mix.

Although public debate emphasized the French Market's columns, Stone's private plans for the building, coordinated with city officials, encompassed myriad details related to the project's architectural elements and the personnel who would accomplish them. While the market's foundations would remain standing, especially those of the 1813 meat market, Stone's planning documents called for "new terrazzo floors and coves . . . new dormers and cupolas . . . [and] new skylights and skylight shafts."[118] He installed electric lighting and refrigerated display cases, as well as new "weather vanes, wrought iron rail, grilles. . . . ornamental hinges, push bars, and thresholds." Stone specified that the renovated market would be crafted by hand, ordering, "No ordinary machine shop work will be accepted. . . . All work shall be forged and finished by hand."[119] Such an expert degree of work required expert workers and Stone and the city agreed on this point, too. "No alien or foreign unnaturalized labor shall be employed on the work; preference shall be given to home white labor," specified the team's "Instructions to Bidders."[120] With these words, the architect and the city shut out New Orleanians of color, noncitizens, and new or transient residents of the city from employment related to the French Market's renovation. The decision would have economic as well as cultural repercussions: all money and recognition for modernizing the historic institution would go to "home white labor."

The cast of workers, backers, shoppers, and vendors whom planners envisioned for the French Market's future was readily visible in an editorial cartoon published in the *Times-Picayune* on February 28, 1936 (fig. 4.6). "Let's Go, for a Better and Equally Picturesque Market," the title read. A triumvirate of men representing city authorities, business leaders, and workers—the latter's sleeves are rolled up, ready to swing a sledgehammer—survey the renovation plans they are about to put into action. A smiling housewife looks on, with an overflowing market basket hanging from the crook of her arm. She played a role in the lead-up to this historic occasion and now anticipates the renovated result. In the background, peering from behind one of the market's columns, is a fruit seller, identified as Italian by his black moustache and clusters of bananas. All figures in the image appear to be white. This rendering depicted the figures involved in the French Market's workings and its restoration: consumers, producers, those who planned and financed the renovation, those who would labor to build it, and the authorities who regulated the market and would continue to do so in the future. The faces in this image differed greatly from those pictured in the 1882 *Harper's Weekly* illustration,

FIGURE 4.6. This cartoon showed the parties involved in the French Market's New Deal renovation but omitted the New Orleanians of color who had dominated the market in earlier eras. Keith Temple, "Let's Go, for a Better and Equally Picturesque Market," illustration, *Times-Picayune*, February 28, 1936. Published with the permission of Capital City Press/Georges Media Group, and Baton Rouge, LA. Reproduction courtesy of City Archives and Special Collections, New Orleans Public Library.

FIGURE 4.7. Neither people nor food appeared in this photograph of the French Market's renovated fish market. Abundant light, refrigeration, white tile, and concrete generated a newly sanitary shopping experience. "What a Difference!" *The Tribune*, October 18, 1937. City Archives and Special Collections, New Orleans Public Library.

even if the colonnades remained the same. Whereas a Black woman shopper had stood as the focal point of the 1882 drawing, here, a half century later, shoppers who looked like her were nowhere to be seen. The cartoon showed who would be welcome in the renovated market and who would not.

When the French Market reopened in 1937, white shoppers and the press were enthusiastic about the renovations, which seemed to have allowed quaint customs to persist in greatly updated surroundings. The first patrons through the door of the new produce market expressed relief upon finding symbolic fragments of the old space without its previous grit. They watched produce vendors transport heavy baskets of fruits and vegetables on their heads and continue to engage in the custom of *lagniappe*, despite their stalls' fresh coat of paint.[121] Tradition persisted without the cobwebs, these initial impressions conveyed. The French Market's renovated fish market excited shoppers in a different key. "What a Difference!" trumpeted the caption of a photograph printed in a local paper (fig. 4.7). Where open trays of crawfish had sat now stood a row of professional-grade refrigerated tubs, illuminated by hanging electric lamps. "Steel and concrete are everywhere," the caption described.

"The concrete is especially treated to reduce the smells."[122] The photograph showed an empty room, devoid of shoppers, sellers, or even fish for sale. Electric and natural light filled the space, accentuating the whiteness of the walls and ceiling. These qualities, as well as the odorless nature of the materials that composed the room, formed a setting that looked sterile, if not medical. "Tourists may inspect [the new fish market], as they might view a new model refrigerator," an editorialist declared. Post-renovation, the fish market had become like a modern appliance. Many visitors expressed a preference for this updated iteration over its slippery, stinking predecessor. In this "clean, white and glistening market," the *Times-Picayune* crowed, "even an oyster might feel a thrill of gelatinous pride at the thought of being eaten alive."[123]

As the city prepared to dedicate the renovated French Market in 1938, the press and market officials extolled the changes with a flood of newspaper articles and other celebratory writings. These interpretations imposed a progressive trajectory on the market's history, from a romanticized past to a crumbling nadir to a sanitized present. Municipal authorities claimed to have achieved a seamless fusion of old and new that had retained the market's necessities and discarded the rest. "We have succeeded in meeting the demands for public health, sanitation and modern conveniences without injuring the romance and history of the old market," announced J. Richard Reuter in March 1938. Reuter was president of the French Market Corporation (FMC), an entity formed by the French Market Business Men's Association in 1932 to oversee the day-to-day running of the French Market.[124] The editorial board of a local newspaper concurred, announcing, "[The market] stands restored to all the splendors of its most glamorous days. . . . Only the dirt, rubbish, litter and odors which have characterized the market in these later years have been banished."[125]

French Market Corporation leaders published their own version of the market's journey from old to new, while simultaneously characterizing the marketplace as immemorial—an institution that had stood, and would stand, forever. "Time marches on but the French Market is eternal," the authors declared.[126] In their boosterish booklet, *Glorified French Market: Progressing with Commerce, 1813–1938*, the corporation blended advertisement, history, and the technical specifications of the latest advances in refrigeration. Also to be found among the myriad benefits of the renovated market: a new linguistic and racial balance among its sellers. The 1930s market still hosted "the sons and daughters of many nations . . . giving it a strong European atmosphere," promised the writers. "Here is the soft Spanish of Spain and Central America, German, Scandinavian, Russian, Greek, Turkish and all blending into varied patois of the American English."[127] After so many decades, the market's Babel

FIGURE 4.8. A photograph of the French Market after its New Deal update showed the extent to which the renovations had replaced natural with artificial light and accessible food with protected wares. *The Completely Modernized Meat Market*, 1938, photograph, in Emile V. Stier and James B. Keeling, *Glorified French Market: Progressing with Commerce, 1813–1938* (New Orleans, LA: French Market Corporation, 1938). City Archives and Special Collections, New Orleans Public Library.

had been tamed, FMC officials declared proudly, and melded into an accented English with a romantic hint of Europe—never West Africa or the Caribbean.

Equally praiseworthy were new technological measures that promised to prevent contamination and halt decay. "Here the foodstuffs may be viewed with only the stall operators to handle them," the authors announced, beneath a "lighting arrangement that makes the market just as bright at night as during the mid-day sun period." As in the city's new supermarkets, modernizing renovations had separated the food from shoppers and sellers (fig. 4.8). "The great foreword of 1938 throughout the United States is sanitation," affirmed the writers. "This, however, was no easy task, for the world is made up of persons who have varied ideas of sanitation, particularly in the cosmopolitan population of French Market."[128] Standing in the market's renovated central aisle, the New Orleans housewife could hear that the cosmopolitan Babel of the market's past had faded. She could no longer smell the food for sale, pungent or not. She could see her dinner's ingredients in lighted cases and verify that unsanitary hands no longer touched them.

"The story of the French Market is a spirited chapter in Creole history," a reporter had written in 1936, as the market sat on the brink of renovation. The writer looked forward to the renovated market's dedication day and predicted, "The market you will enter will be washed and cleaned and shining like a child with its face washed, its teeth cleaned and its hair brushed."[129] When that day happened, newspaper reporters recalled the French Market of previous eras as a favorite destination for Creole ladies and their "servants," and an institution first built by "white men" in the city's pre-American days.[130] When the French Market reopened in 1938, it was certainly washed clean. In most public tellings, its history received the same treatment. At the market's March 1938 dedication ceremony, city officials placed a summary of the market's history, the FMC charter, a list of the current tenants, and copies of that morning's newspapers in a concrete time capsule under a new flagpole.[131] Amidst such celebration, a local editorial evinced a sudden affection for the uglier components of the market's past, now that they had disappeared. "New Orleans was fond of the old market, forgave its sinful smells, inconveniences, and general decrepitude," the writer insisted.[132] With the market's columns freshly painted, the view backward from 1938 made the past no longer seem so grim.

Although the French Market's New Deal renovation seemed a final, triumphant solution to the site's woes, this was not to be. Baltimore's *Afro-American* newspaper panned the new look. "The New Deal, with its PWA's and WPA's, is ruining New Orleans. . . . [A]n army of busybodies, for lack of something better to do, has reconstructed the old French Market," swapping in a new "spic and span yellow frescoed sanitary building" in its stead.[133] The very next year, city authorities sued the French Market Corporation for fish-market odors that infected the French Quarter, disgusting residents and tourists. Such efforts were too little too late, however. New Orleans shoppers had turned definitively toward supermarkets. In the coming decades, the French Market's stalls would empty of food and fill with souvenirs. The long era of the public market in New Orleans had ended. "I don't deal with the public markets," a housewife declared just a few years after the renovated market had opened, "for the simple reason that I prefer the 'one stop' place. This is 1941, not 1841."[134] It seemed that the elaborate renovation of the French Market had perhaps all been for naught. Or had it? As an attempt to modernize the city's central food market, the French Market's refurbishment had failed. But as a project to overwrite the history and memory of one of the most prominent cultural landmarks of a segregated city, the renovation was a triumph.[135]

In Frances Parkinson Keyes's 1948 murder mystery novel, *Dinner at Antoine's*, Ruth Avery was a clever Washington, DC, socialite looking for a husband. Soon after she arrived in New Orleans, Russ Aldridge, a dashing archaeologist soon to be her fiancé, brought her to Café du Monde at the French Market for coffee and beignets. Ruth decided it was her favorite place in the city, but for a reason less tangible than the plate of sugar-dusted sweets in front of her. She explained: "This Café du Monde couldn't be anywhere except in

New Orleans. . . . And it isn't only unique. It's—it's *real*. . . . I like the feeling of living in day-before-yesterday and day-after-tomorrow at the same time. Nothing could be more modern than those neon signs just outside on Decatur Street. . . . But the square itself must look exactly the same tonight as it did a hundred years ago . . . I could imagine all sorts of ghosts wandering around, under the palm trees."[136] For this tourist, the French Market was *"real,"* yet populated by ghosts; it belonged to the past and the future at once. Ruth's sensations would have pleased French Market officials who insisted on its timeless, eternal magic.

The ghosts that Ruth could not see, wandering under the palm trees, may have whispered in tongues that she could not understand. In the century before she sat at Café du Monde, the history of the place around her had become a story told by a chorus of voices—travel writers, city residents, politicians, newspaper reporters—but not the voices of those who had made the marketplace Bulbancha or Babel. When white housewives and city officials modernized public markets throughout New Orleans, all within a larger political context that insisted on racial segregation, they expelled New Orleanians of color from a physical setting that had enabled certain economic and social possibilities. At the same time, these figures in the fullness of their motivations, skills, and labors were deleted from accounts of the institution's history, shunted into the realm of stereotype—memory's neutral ground. Ultimately, white New Orleanians renovated the French Market for themselves and for tourists who looked like them. Their actions in the first decades of the twentieth century set the battle lines for broader struggles in the years to come: who made Creole cuisine? Who was a New Orleans Creole? Who would enjoy the privileges and profits associated with that identity? This fight would be waged at the table, as were so many others before it.

5

THE CREOLE TABLE AND
"THE BLACK HAND IN THE POT"

AS ONE ARM OF THE NEW DEAL was busy renovating New Orleans's French Market, another was busy writing. Funded by the Public Works Administration, the renewed French Market was dedicated in 1938. That same year, the Federal Writers' Project of the Works Progress Administration published the *New Orleans City Guide*. Within its pages, the authors invited Depression-era Americans short on cash to vacation in the Crescent City. Chief among the city's charms, the writers declared, was Creole cuisine. Gumbo, jambalaya, oysters Bienville, red beans and rice, beignets, *calas*, bread pudding, *café au lait*, *café brûlot*, and Sazerac and Ramos Gin Fizz cocktails: these riches, and more, filled the Creole table. Creole cuisine was the food and drink of New Orleans, distinct from Southern and (later) Cajun cuisines, and inflected by the tastes, techniques, and ingredients of those who had passed through the Crescent City throughout its history. "To the tourist the city is first of all a place in which to eat, drink, and be merry," the *City Guide*'s authors announced. "The joys of the flesh, the traveler first remembers."[1] With suggestions for the best gumbo and absinthe drips, the *City Guide* promised to demystify the city's cooking for those unfamiliar with its pleasures.

The recommendations contained in the *New Orleans City Guide* also mapped a segregated metropolis with strict, if subtle, customs related to dining and race. Eleven hotels in the French Quarter and downtown business district offered 3,518 rooms to white visitors. In contrast, the *City Guide* noted only two hotels with a total of forty-one rooms welcoming Black travelers. Restaurants showed a similar pattern. White-tablecloth dining rooms in the

city's grand hotels and picturesque tourist areas were off-limits to Black diners. (Kitchens were another matter.) Instead, diners of color could head to a
cluster of establishments on South Rampart Street, situated on the edge of
the French Quarter and described by the *City Guide* as "the Harlem of New
Orleans."[2] Authors also recommended South Rampart Street as a drive-by attraction for white tourists as part of "Motor Tour 3," along with the Eye, Ear,
Nose, and Throat Hospital and the city's Chinatown. With its listings of New
Orleans's segregated hotels and restaurants, the *City Guide* reminded white
and Black Americans of 1938 that they belonged to different worlds. Locals
would have understood how to navigate the city. Now, the *City Guide* taught
outsiders contemplating a trip.[3]

Another book published one year after the *New Orleans City Guide*, in
1939, presented a different perspective on New Orleans's culture and cuisine.
Lena Richard's Cook Book, the first cookbook published by a Black New Orleanian, likewise promised to educate its readers. "This book is an attempt
to put the basic facts concerning the art of cooking into a form that may be
easily understood by the youngest housewife as well as the most experienced
chef," Richard wrote in the preface. As a professional cook and teacher of
public cooking classes, Richard was experienced in pleasing and educating a
variety of palates. With authority, she drew on a lengthy heritage of recipes
"used for generations in the South, the home of famous Creole cooks."[4] Her
advice was practical and sophisticated, with tips on using leftovers and creating an elegant aspic. Richard's cookbook elevated her from a popular caterer
among local high society to a national star. It also garnered her a contract with
New York–based Houghton Mifflin, the same publisher of the *New Orleans
City Guide*, which reissued Richard's cookbook for a national readership in
1940.

When the *New Orleans City Guide* and *Lena Richard's Cook Book* were
published, World War II loomed on the horizon and the Depression would
soon be in the past. Organized activism for civil rights was laying the cornerstone for the Supreme Court's *Brown v. Board* ruling in 1954, which would
outlaw the "separate but equal" spaces that had divided Americans for more
than half a century. Air and highway travel, chain supermarkets, and suburban
growth would make the Crescent City look more and more like other American cities. Amid such transformations, city boosters, restaurateurs, hoteliers,
and ordinary residents evangelized New Orleans's Creole cuisine as the city's
most valuable cultural draw. A recognizable set of dishes—chief among them,
gumbo—cohered into a singular brand that propelled the gospel of Creole
cuisine *out* of New Orleans and pulled tourists *in*. "Everybody knows some-
body who once spent a vacation in New Orleans," confirmed a *New York*

Times reporter in 1942. "Inevitably his reminiscences center about his gastronomic experiences, for Creole cookery is not easily forgotten."[5]

This tourist-focused promotion of Creole cuisine possessed a distinctive racial perspective. Menus and cookbooks leaned on antebellum imagery and stories that depicted New Orleans food as the cultural bequest of white French chefs. Private recipes, published cookbooks, and menus showed, too, how the practice of being Creole and making and eating Creole food mattered to white residents and tourists. Such sources and settings offered little, if any, acknowledgment of the longtime creativity and professionalism of people of African descent in Louisiana kitchens. Nevertheless, Black New Orleanians proclaimed that their ancestors had been the first Creoles and had produced the cuisine continuously since the city's founding. Throughout the first half of the twentieth century, they ran restaurants and managed kitchen staffs. Some planned resistance to segregation over bowls of gumbo. Others tweaked supervisors' recipes to make them their own. Activists sat at segregated lunch counters, braving verbal and physical abuse to assert that everyone had a right to a place at the table. In the mid-century Crescent City, Black New Orleanians demonstrated the many ways in which the Creole table was a political space.

Evangelizing Creole Cuisine

In June 1936, a *New York Times* advertisement invited readers to enjoy "New Orleans Creole Gumbo without traveling 1,345 miles! . . . Also genuine Sarazac [*sic*] cocktail and New Orleans gin fizz." Typically, diners consumed such pleasures on Bourbon Street in the French Quarter, yet now they needed to go no farther than 112 Greenwich Street in Manhattan.[6] People on the move were transporting New Orleans flavors throughout the country, helping the Crescent City's cuisine become more visible and accessible to national audiences than ever before. "Menu-card traveling toward Southern cookery is easily done in New York," a *Times* reporter confirmed in another piece. "Batter cakes and molasses pie have devotees who have never been south of the Mason-Dixon line except via menu card." Northern diners were eager to sample dishes that evoked a geographic escape, given that novel culinary experiences were cheaper than a vacation during these Depression days. To some, it mattered who stood at the stove. "Tuskegee Institute in Alabama is training African-American men in Southern cooking," a *Times* journalist explained, "to answer post-Prohibition demand for fine dining with a regional flair." For good Southern cooking in New York, this writer specified, "Negro cooks are the rule."[7]

Nevertheless, technological innovations were making trained chefs increasingly unnecessary for American diners hungry for Creole cooking. Thanks to advances in canning, some special foods could travel directly from New Orleans to faraway kitchens. *New York Times* ads informed shoppers that they could buy canned New Orleans gumbo straight from Louisiana, packaged in boxes that resembled cotton bales or tied together with a bandana. One such advertisement, printed in 1940, featured an illustration of a smiling Black woman erupting out of a can labeled "Creole," like a jack-in-the-box on a spring.[8] The sketch used an already well-known stereotype: the cheerful "mammy," whose face and form sold pancake mix, coffee, and oranges to Americans in the decades following the Civil War.[9] Here, the eager woman stood in for New Orleans's signature dish. She was ready to spring into kitchen pots far and wide, embodying the flavors of Louisiana cooking.

Airplanes, too, carried Southern ingredients to faraway eaters. "Once we journeyed far to enjoy . . . pompano—remembered as incomparably delicious at Havana or New Orleans," recalled a *Times* journalist in 1938. "But that was before Miami was seven hours distant by plane." Speedy planes and efficient refrigeration allowed New York City's markets to tap a worldwide larder, such that Russian caviar and French wines now seemed commonplace. "The cosmopolitan variety of [the New Yorker's] menu . . . is already an old story," the journalist reflected.[10] Diners with means now traveled via their taste buds, enjoying meals as epicurean and educational events. In January 1939, members of New York City's Gourmet Society, "a dinner club of gourmets and cosmopolites," met at New Orleans Restaurant in Midtown Manhattan. The event menu informed the group that they were about to enjoy a meal inspired by New Orleans, "a world-famous gastronomic capital." Diners feasted on Oysters Rockefeller, Shrimp and Crab Creole Gumbo, Broiled Gulf of Mexico Pompano, and New Orleans Pecan Pie, accompanied by California Chablis and *café brûlot*. "Our pompano was flown here by airplane from the Gulf," the menu noted with pride.[11] Whether traveling by market or menu, Americans with an appetite for New Orleans cuisine did not need to venture far at all.

Louisiana-based Godchaux Sugar recognized the profitable potential in making food an edible ambassador of New Orleans. The company identified grocers and housewives as the critical groups to target for sales. In a marketing booklet produced in the 1940s, Godchaux sought to win over grocery-store proprietors throughout the nation (fig. 5.1). "What city is best known for good food?" prompted the booklet's narrator, a French chef, complete with a white toque, pencil moustache, and goatee. "Right! It's New Orleans! . . . But most folks in your town can't come to New Orleans. So let's bring famous New Orleans dishes to them!" A pair of photographs showed Canal Street thronged

FIGURE 5.1. Louisiana-based Godchaux Sugar courted grocers with this marketing booklet, which depicted insatiable appetites for Louisiana sugar and Creole cuisine. "Godchaux Sugar Presents a New 'Sell-Idea' for the Grocers of America," marketing booklet, 1940s. Godchaux Sugar, Louisiana Division Vertical Files, City Archives and Special Collections, New Orleans Public Library.

with crowds celebrating Mardi Gras, the lighted Godchaux's department-store sign visible at the top center, and a dining room filled with white waiters and diners, packed elbow-to-elbow. These were insatiable masses, the reader was meant to understand—all hungry for New Orleans cuisine. "Eighty-thousand women have written in for Godchaux's cook book," the narrator claimed. "More proof women want the Creole specialties you can give them." Along with recipe cards for "Creole Pecan Pralines" and "Pain Perdu Creole," Godchaux mapped out a grocery counter display of sugar, pecans, and cinnamon that would place all the ingredients required for pralines within the shopper's easy reach.[12] Authentic New Orleans foods could be enjoyed anywhere, it seemed. All the American housewife had to do was boil sugar or reheat canned gumbo in a pot.

As antebellum days receded farther into history, New Orleans culture and cuisine crossed over even more fully into realms of fantasy and romanticization in the public eye. "Probably closer to the New Orleans of your imagination than the real city is Gay New Orleans at the Fair," wrote a *New York Times* reporter in 1940, describing the "Gay New Orleans" village at the World's Fair in New York City. "Pleasant it is to sit . . . before the pillared Southern mansion which is the New Orleans restaurant and be served such authentic Creole dishes as gumbo." This simulated, polished New Orleans at the Fair was likely better than the authentic thing, he suggested, in that it met the visitor's imagined expectations.[13] A short subway ride could reward the New Yorker with decadent pleasures: "The shrimps, large ones, are folded into a smooth sauce in which are combined onion, paprika, olive oil, vinegar, celery, pepper and mustard."[14] Diners measured their experiences against an idealized standard, the reporter understood, and the Fair's offerings mapped perfectly onto their fantasies of the antebellum South.[15]

For those who did make the trip to New Orleans, white-tablecloth restaurants were the stage on which such fantasies could be rehearsed and performed. *Dining in New Orleans*, a 1945 guide written by a local radio host, offered ample contributions to the mythology of Creole cuisine as uniquely transportive. "One moment you are bounding about on one of America's most famous cock-a-hoop streets; the next you are in the middle of the 19th century . . . being served an ambrosial meal by charming Negro girls," the author observed of Courtyard Kitchen, a restaurant close to Bourbon Street. The restaurant's allure radiated from its food, people, plants, and setting. The combination of these things enabled the customer to travel in time. "Everything here belongs to another world," the writer marveled, "the azaleas, the camellias, the banana trees . . . the flagstones as freshly scrubbed as the waitresses and the kitchen."[16] His sense of dislocation repeated at additional restaurants where he was again served by Black waitresses and waiters. At Marigold restaurant, "Negro girls serve the very excellent food. They are taught to serve with the best manners." And at Patio Royal, "The waiters are unobtrusive, efficient Pullman-like colored folks," he wrote. Proprietors of fine dining establishments used their employees and the food they served to create experiences of sensory escape for white tourists and locals alike. At Corinne Dunbar restaurant, in a mansion on St. Charles Avenue, the guide's author confirmed, "Everything is arranged to convey the impression that you are dining in the home of an aristocrat of the old south." To eat there was to enter an illusion of effortless pleasure and gratification. Following the meal, the proprietor had to "ushe[r] you into the street beyond—into a world of reality."[17] The New Orleans of 1945 was very different from the New Orleans of 1845. Yet the essential, twinned appeal of the city's food and people, locked in commercial transactions catering to the appetites of the powerful, remained much the same.

Whether in New York City or New Orleans, such flights of fancy worked. When National Restaurant Association president Andrew J. Crotty Jr. visited the Crescent City in 1950, he announced that New Orleans's savvy culinary marketing was making it the envy of restaurateurs and hoteliers in other regions. "New Orleans has done such a 'beautiful job in popularizing its Creole cuisine,'" the *Times-Picayune* reported him saying, "that other sections are trying to achieve the same national and international fame for their dishes." Hailing from Boston, Crotty announced that he planned to copy New Orleans's food-related promotional methods to excite Americans about Beantown's clam chowder and lobsters. "'What we're after with our 'Yankee cooking' . . . is the same thing you're after with Creole cooking, and that is—tourists,' he said."[18] Crotty's enthusiasm revealed the purposeful approach and profitable rewards of calling New Orleans cooking a cuisine—with the enigmatic adjective "Creole" to describe it—and proclaiming its delights to the masses.

Gumbo Wars

New Orleans home cooks were the foot soldiers in the battle to promote the city's cuisine to a broad public. In at least one case, their evangelization of Creole food was literal. When Kathryn Gould of New Orleans married Lars-Erik Hesslow of Sweden in 1949, Gould packed a copy of *The Picayune Creole Cook Book*, the city's best-known cookbook, already in its eleventh edition, for her transatlantic move. She was soon "spreading the message of her Creole cookbook like a missionary among the heathen," her husband said.[19] Gould's passion was far-flung but not atypical. As Creole cuisine became more familiar to national, if not international diners, some New Orleanians exhibited a chauvinistic defense of their food, claiming it as a unique element of their identity and heritage that must not be insulted.[20] Perceived slights or threats to Creole cooking, understood to be New Orleans's cultural cornerstone, by association called into question basic conceptions of regional and even racial identity.

A singular set of letters and recipes sheds light on the degree to which the notion of Creole cuisine mattered in the private kitchens of white New Orleanians. On August 13, 1951, Hermann B. Deutsch, a daily columnist for the *New Orleans Item*, alleged that an act of cultural and culinary blasphemy had occurred. Addressing New Jersey's Campbell Soup Company, Deutsch wrote, "Where in hell do you get 'Creole gumbo SOUP?' . . . When you call your chicken-with-vegetable soup a Creole gumbo, you're as wrong as a heart in the hole with four spades showing."[21] Two days earlier, Campbell's had run a full-page ad in the *Saturday Evening Post* for its new canned product (fig. 5.2). Under illustrations of a steamboat paddling the Mississippi by moonlight and a bowl of gumbo studded with okra, the ad's text proclaimed, "One taste . . . and you'll know why the Creole recipes of Old New Orleans are so famous."[22] The claim made Deutsch fume.

What irritated him most, however, was the image at the bottom of the page. "That picture of a Negro mammy," he wrote: "She's seated on the hearth of such a fireplace as never was in New Orleans . . . while beside her is a basket containing, as nearly as I can make out . . . two bunches of radishes . . . and a leaf of . . . tobacco. If that's what she's about to make a 'gumbo soup' out of, I'll take a New England boiled dinner, which is the ultimate low of edibilia."[23] Deutsch took offense at the new soup's mysterious ingredients and the copy the company used to advertise the product to a national audience. His outrage also seemed to emanate from a possessive knowledge of the ingredients that a "Negro mammy" would use to make gumbo and what the hearth or stove where she worked—surely in a private home—looked like. Louisianans knew these things; Campbell's of New Jersey could not. Accordingly, the company's transgressions were downright "impious," Deutsch announced. He predicted that New Orleanians stood ready to enlighten Campbell Soup Company as to the makings of an authentic Creole gumbo. He promised a prize of $5.55 to the authors of the two best gumbo recipes he received. Deutsch's readers responded. Some letters came typewritten on personal or business letterhead, others in neat cursive on lined notepaper, and still others arrived scrawled in messy script, stained with splatters of grease.[24] As the writers described how gumbo was made in their own kitchens, many declared that they shared Deutsch's outrage at what they considered to be a gross misrepresentation of a treasured dish.

Deutsch's readers bristled at Campbell's decision to can gumbo in partic-

FIGURE 5.2. New Jersey–based Campbell Soup Company infuriated *New Orleans Item* readers with this advertisement for gumbo, the city's trademark dish. "A Tradition in Old New Orleans," *Saturday Evening Post*, August 11, 1951. Author's collection, published with the permission of Campbell Soup Company.

ular, as opposed to, perhaps, tomato soup. A stew containing chicken, sausage, crabs, shrimp, or oysters, thickened with okra or filé, and served with rice, gumbo had long stood as the hallmark of New Orleans cuisine. The 1885 *Historical Sketch Book and Guide to New Orleans* proclaimed gumbo to be "the great dish of New Orleans. . . . There is no dish which at the same time so tickles the palate, satisfies the appetite . . . and costs so little as a Creole gombo."[25] *La Cuisine Creole*, also published in 1885 and one of the city's first cookbooks, contained eight variations of "gombo," made with crabs, shrimp, oyster, and chicken, thickened with okra or "filee." "Maigre Oyster Gombo," the *maigre* designating the dish as approved to eat on Catholic feast days requiring abstinence from meat, was nonetheless far from austere. The recipe began with "100 oysters with their juice" added to an onion fried in lard, then simmered with red pepper, flour, butter, and filé. Similarly, the *Picayune's Creole Cook Book*, first published by the *Picayune* newspaper in 1900 and considered by many New Orleanians to be the encyclopedia of Creole cuisine, also privileged the dish. In successive editions, the authors characterized gumbo as simultaneously original and timeless. "Indeed, the word 'evolution' fails to apply when speaking of Gumbo," the authors of the tenth edition declared, "for it is an original conception, a something sui generis in cooking, peculiar to this ancient Creole city alone."[26] Gumbo persisted as essential to New Orleans cooks and eaters through the decades for an additional reason, however.

More than any other dish, gumbo embodied New Orleans's history and population. Combining flour and fat to make a roux, a thickening and enriching base for a sauce or soup, was a French technique. Okra and rice were ingredients brought to Louisiana from West Africa. Shrimp, crabs, and oysters came from local waters. Choctaw market vendors contributed the filé that further thickened the pot. Accordingly, popular and scholarly writers reached repeatedly for "gumbo" as a locally inspired metaphor to characterize New Orleans society as similar to, yet distinct from, the American "melting pot." "The true Creole is like the famous gumbo of the state," wrote Alice Moore Dunbar-Nelson in 1916, "a little bit of everything, making a whole, delightfully flavored, quite distinctive, and wholly unique."[27] Creole gumbo represented the city's people, foods, and their history, literally and figuratively.

With this local understanding of the dish, *Item* readers rebelled at Campbell's attempt to can and sell a gumbo and call it "Creole." Twenty-one-year-old Jeanne R. Franklin, newly married and living in Uptown New Orleans, wrote to Deutsch, "I, too, have often fumed over Campbell's misuse of that sacred word Gumbo—and labeling it Creole, yet! . . . This dish is the one reason I'll never move North." She added, "P.S. In case you're sending a petition to Campbell's—please add my name—Those Yankees shouldn't be allowed to get away with this fraud."[28] In another letter, Ida Honold, fifty years old and a public elementary school teacher, concurred. "It is about time for someone to call the hand of those people who foist so-called Southern dishes upon the unsuspecting public who disgustingly cry out: 'Is this the famous GUMBO of the South!!!' No, no, it is not even a kissing cousin of our delicious Creole

Okra Gumbo," she declared. "More power to you . . . for rising on your hind legs and challenging the Campbells of New Joisey [*sic*]."[29]

In these two letters, the writers were certain that there existed such a thing as a Creole gumbo and equally certain that Campbell's had gotten it wrong. But their letters, and those that accompanied them, emphasized the degree to which there was neither a common understanding of what "Creole" meant, even in New Orleans, nor a standard recipe for Creole gumbo. Whereas Franklin and Honold equated "Creole" with "Southern"—in contrast to the "Yankees" of the North—other writers identified themselves as both Creole and Cajun in the same letter, or as Creole and French.[30] Even if Franklin voiced an ardent defense of "that sacred word Gumbo—and labeling it Creole, yet!" she was not a native Louisianian; she had been born in Kentucky.[31] Letter writers' recipes called for a wide range of ingredients, from duck, prairie hen, turkey necks, and veal stew meat to canned okra and tomatoes. Even the fat used to start the roux differed. Ham scraps, lard, bacon, Crisco, Oleo, and Snowdrift, a vegetable shortening derived from cottonseed oil, all seemed to work. Of special note, the catsup called for by Rose Bourgeois of Baton Rouge would have seemed a crime to many gumbo cooks. Furthermore, Bourgeois clarified that she never began her gumbo with a roux and in fact loved the taste of Campbell's Gumbo Soup.[32]

If anything, the only unequivocal lesson conveyed by the letters was that a marked variety of people cared enough to write to Deutsch about Campbell's apparent blunder. Their numbers crossed social and educational classes, ages, and occupations and stretched over a wide geographic spread. In all their kitchens, gumbo bubbled in pots on stoves and figured into their understandings of what it meant to live in New Orleans, or Louisiana, or to be Creole. Louisiana Guedry, who had completed one year of high school, lived with her husband, a maintenance worker for the city, in a St. Roch home adjacent to a Norfolk Southern railyard. She prepared gumbo with cured ham hock and diced beef and served it in a molded "Louisiana Rice Ring" spiced with Tabasco sauce. Another recipe came to Deutsch from fifty-seven-year-old Rose Boisseau, wife of Henry Boisseau and mother of Henry Boisseau Jr., typed neatly on Rose's own letterhead from their home near Metairie Cemetery. "Fry okra until slime disappears," Boisseau instructed Deutsch. Irma Fasnacht, forty-eight, never married, lived on Bourbon Street in the French Quarter with her sister Yvonne and two lodgers. Fasnacht's best gumbo had "celery branches with leaves," bacon, shrimp, crabs, and tomatoes and okra, "smother[ed] until real brown."[33] Letters were mailed to Deutsch from far outside New Orleans, as well—from readers in Baton Rouge, Lafayette, Houma, and Lake Charles, Louisiana, well into the region where many would identify as Cajun, and from the Mississippi Gulf Coast. While some recipes landed on Deutsch's desk with creative misspellings (several writers rendered the French "roux" as r-u-e), others were carefully precise, as in the case of Blanche Copping, who scolded Deutsch, "By the way, you omitted the accent . . . in filé."[34]

Notably, the one arena in which the letter writers appeared homogeneous was race. Among the names that could be cross-referenced in the 1950 federal census and city directories, everyone who submitted a Creole gumbo recipe to Deutsch was white.[35] This fact, however, did not mean that all the cooks behind the recipes were white. Several letters indicated that Black cooks were the authors and preparers of letter writers' prized gumbos. Hazel Smith wrote to Deutsch from the US Marine Hospital in New Orleans, where her husband was chief of the medical service. "I am entering the gumbo recipe of my cook, Mary Washington," Smith wrote. "I watched her make it and tried to get it down as she went along. . . . If this is not the prize winning recipe it is because I have not written it down correctly." Similarly, Lottie Keife Swift of Pass Christian, Mississippi, submitted the recipe of "Azalea," her cook. H. J. D'Aquin, manager of New Orleans's Paul Morphy Chess Club, wrote to Deutsch, "Our Crab & Shrimp Gumbo is very popular with the Members. We are enclosing our recipe and wish to enter it in your contest."[36] The identities of the chefs and cooks cloaked in the "our" of "our recipe" went unnamed, but they may be guessed, or suspected. D'Aquin's letter was far from the only that left names and details unsaid, between the lines.[37] Beyond debates over whether the best gumbo contained okra or filé, Deutsch's folders of letters and recipes prompted much bigger questions. Who was a Creole, exactly? What did being Creole have to do with being white or Black? And what did all of that, stirred, simmered, and melded, have to do with food?

Creole Food, Creole People

When *Item* readers sat down in August 1951 to respond to Deutsch's call, the world around them was changing. They would have understood this reality as soon as they opened their pantries. Until the early twentieth century, New Orleans had distinguished itself among American cities for its robust network of public food markets and corner stores. But the 1919 arrival of Tennessee grocery store Piggly Wiggly and the 1946 opening of Schwegmann's, the city's first supermarket, changed that system. "The atomic age is . . . the quick freeze age," a *Times-Picayune* columnist announced in October 1947. "An entire meal may be delivered to your door, frozen, cooked, ready to warm up and serve."[38] Several years later, a reporter marveled at all that was new in food provisioning, coupled with the old that still remained. The Crescent City housewife of 1953 could "visit her super market and buy ready mix cake, complete-in-one package meals and avacodos [sic] . . . or she can shop at the stalls of the French Market."[39] A nearly full-page *Item* ad for Pap's Food Store charted these changing tastes. Brands like Godchaux's sugar, French Market coffee, Borden's Creole cream cheese, Snowdrift shortening, and Purnell's Pride frozen chicken all came from regional sources. But national products such as Dulany frozen vegetables, Duncan Hines cake mixes, and Jewel salad oil could make meals in New Orleans taste like dinners anywhere else.[40] Such shifts at the table were concurrent with comprehensive transformations to the local economy and society.

In New Orleans of the 1940s and 1950s, the relationship between race and economic, political, and cultural privilege wavered in a state of greater flux than in any era since the immediate wake of the Civil War. During World War II, the city served as a major wartime manufacturing center for amphibious boats, or "Higgins boats," that proved critical in European and Pacific theaters. Bucking the national norm, Higgins Industries pledged to hire Black women into positions equal to white workers. Jobs opened to them in other industries, as well. Some found work as waitresses and elevator operators in city department stores. Black domestic workers seized the opportunity to demand higher hourly wages from employers who were scrambling to find staff to cook and clean for them. Others quit their posts. "I feel like a woman instead of a slave since I stopped working," one unnamed New Orleanian told a *Chicago Defender* reporter in 1943. "Now I don't have to run and say 'yes ma'am' everytime someone calls my name." Still, higher wages evaporated in the face of "skyrocket[ing] prices" and inadequate housing stock.[41]

Within New Orleans and beyond, Black Americans strained against segregation, exclusion, and violence. After the war's end, a second major outmigration of Black New Orleanians left the South, eager to escape from entrenched racism and segregation.[42] Among those who stayed, white and Black, their families expanded. Newspaper advertisements for laundry machines, such as the "New De Luxe Norge Triple-Action Washer," which claimed to launder "9 lbs. of clothes in only 7 minutes," pointed to booming families' spending money as well as the bulk of soiled diapers they needed to wash. Ads for lawn mowers indicated the proliferation of suburban lawns to mow. Beginning in 1951, middle- and upper-class white families moved into the new Lakefront suburban development of Gentilly Woods. The suburban dream was so good they refused to share it. In 1953, more than a thousand of these white homeowners signed a failed petition to halt the development of Pontchartrain Park, a similar, nearby development for Black New Orleanians.[43] As local newspapers reported on integration efforts across the nation—at the Young Women's Christian Association, General Motors, the armed forces—Crescent City activists accelerated their efforts to desegregate places of work, recreation, and, above all else, education.[44]

Amidst such developments, white New Orleanians' defensive and exclusionary use of the term "Creole" to describe the city's culture and cuisine had much to do with the tenuous state of white privilege. By the mid-twentieth century, consumer products like Godchaux Sugar and Campbell's gumbo had persuaded Americans to be intrigued by New Orleans's Creole culture. But bewilderment about the meaning of "Creole" food expanded to a national scale, such that white New Orleanians who declared themselves experts on the state's cuisine and segregated social world found themselves defending both at once. In an introductory glossary of terms, the author of New Orleans's 1949 *City Directory* defined "Creoles" as "the white descendants of Spanish and French colonists. There are no Negro Creoles, but there are Creole Negroes who belonged to Creole families, just as there were Creole horses, or eggs."[45] Such tired, didactic racism repeated across a variety of publications, barely paraphrased. Still, confusion persisted. In April 1951, just a few months before Campbell's advertised its new Creole gumbo, a reader wrote to a Cleveland, Ohio, newspaper to ask, "Will you please explain what a Louisiana creole is?" The columnist's response, while generous, likely offered little clarity. "Sometimes the term is applied to persons of mixed Negro and creole blood . . . and sometimes to any American Negro. . . . In many regions the term indicates a certain excellence of origin and culture."[46]

Such catholic explanations drove many white New Orleanians into a frenzy. Local writers tied themselves into knots attempting to defend the indefensible. The author of *New Orleans from A to Z*, a 1951 guidebook, insisted, in capitalized letters, "A Creole is ALL WHITE. . . . The capitalized noun, referring to a person . . . definitely and without exception refers to the descendants of those noble blooded . . . Spanish and French colonists."[47] In his frantic defense, "Creole" conveyed a strain of refinement and sophistication that was historical, proprietary, and racially white. The term signified quality and authenticity, he claimed. In short, it was a brand. The foray waged by the Campbell Soup Company into gumbo represented a novel and dangerous affront because it appropriated the Crescent City brand. Now, a Northern company, a national company, claimed to serve an authentic taste of New Orleans and advertised it with imagery that had been white New Orleanians' stock-in-trade for decades.

In the same era, a legal challenge to whites' claims to Creole identity caused additional consternation in New Orleans. In March 1953, a Mobile,

Alabama, court ruled that seven-year-old Michael Chestang Jr. could not attend a white school. Although his mother "was of proven Caucasian descent," the *Item* reported, his father possessed "a trace of Negro blood" and the family identified as Creole. The boy worshipped at white churches, played with white friends, and had been attending a white school, but his family's identification as Creole—and their community's understanding that being Creole implied having an ancestor of color—meant that Chestang was not white, the court ruled. "Much of the trial . . . centered on that word," the *Item* explained. "Despite different meanings given the word in other localities. . . . Trial witnesses testified that in Mobile [the word Creole] is applied to a mixed race in which Negro blood is present."[48]

The court's decision, which paradoxically upheld school segregation by confirming an integrated understanding of the term "Creole," distressed a New Orleans writer whose expertise extended to Creole cuisine. Stanley Arthur, the author of several travel guides, French Quarter histories, and a cookbook, *Famous New Orleans Drinks and How to Mix 'Em*, called the ruling "a big mistake. . . . It's going to make a lot more people believe that 'Creole' has something to do with mulatto." Creole tomatoes and Creole corn were the same as "'Creole' Negroes," Arthur explained in an interview. They were products that had originated in Louisiana and were enrolled in the service of, or consumed by, the European and American Creole "aristocracy."[49] Arthur's consultation in the matter by a local newspaper, plus his explanation of his reasoning in culinary terms, demonstrated the ease with which a New Orleans cultural and culinary authority could rationalize people of color as consumable things—a tomato, an ear of corn—nearly a century after slavery's abolition.[50]

The stubborn refusal by many whites to acknowledge Black New Orleanians as Creoles signified a broad-ranging effort to sever New Orleanians of color from narratives, settings, and products linked to the city's history and culture—a culture that tourism was making increasingly profitable. Invented distinctions between Creole tomatoes and "'Creole' Negroes" were white New Orleanians' attempt to convince themselves that they still belonged to an exceptional and valuable cultural legacy during the twilight years of de jure segregation. Then, the sun set. In 1954, ruling in *Brown v. Board of Education of Topeka*, the US Supreme Court ordered an end to "separate but equal" spaces. The ruling shed "a blinding flash of light and hope" for people around the world, the *San Francisco Chronicle* predicted. It was "a boost to the spirit of democracy," applauded the *Atlanta Daily World*. Many white Louisianians, in contrast, were furious. Governor Robert Kennon retorted, "We don't want anybody from a town on the Potomac River to handle our children in

Louisiana."⁵¹ The Joint Committee to Maintain Segregation, founded by the Louisiana legislature immediately after the *Brown* decision, fought with special venom to retain segregation in schools and eliminate Black Louisianians from the voting booth.⁵² Beyond these blatantly political goals of Massive Resistance, many white New Orleanians remained intent on guarding their privileges in the cultural realm, too. Creole cuisine, as they imagined it, was an arena in which they could still lay claim to a privileged heritage that divided along racial lines. In a variety of settings, they set out to write—or rewrite—this history.

Creole Culinary Literacy

White New Orleanians who claimed ownership of Creole identity and Creole food prized text as the ideal medium—and literacy as a necessary skill—to document and celebrate Creole cuisine. This perspective was evident in the letters that *Item* readers sent to Hermann Deutsch in August 1951. Lottie Keife Swift, of Pass Christian, Mississippi, explained to Deutsch, "This recipe is not written professionally as Azalea makes it from an old recipe given her by her mother. . . . Everyone who eats it (especially Yankees) always ask for a second helping."⁵³ Swift's casual characterization of the gumbo prepared by Azalea as unprofessional revealed a persistent trope in the way that whites had learned to claim authority over Creole cuisine. White journalists and cookbook authors had long portrayed Black Americans' culinary skills as magic and intuitive. Swift depicted Azalea's gumbo as bewitching everyone, "especially Yankees," into a second helping. Furthermore, Swift classified Azalea's recipe as unprofessional—it "[was] not written professionally"—because it had been transmitted orally, from one Black woman to another. Swift made this assessment even though Azalea was literally a professional, employed by Swift to cook. Linking literacy and the written word to authority and professionalism was one means by which white Americans excluded Black Americans from the kitchen and other arenas of expertise.⁵⁴ In this case, Swift dismissed Azalea from a cultural pantheon of kitchen professionals. But this was an era in which literacy had more overt political consequences, too. Until the Voting Rights Act of 1965, Louisiana insisted on literacy—proven via an array of convoluted voter-registration applications and citizenship tests—to exclude Black Louisianians from the polls.⁵⁵

When white writers depicted people of color in the kitchen as illiterate, they also characterized Black culinary knowledge as ephemeral, divorced from the textual realm of history. Such a perspective underlay the writing of the *Picayune's Creole Cook Book*, one of New Orleans's foundational culinary texts. Issued in fifteen editions beginning in 1900, the *Picayune's Creole Cook Book* enjoyed massive popularity among readers in New Orleans and far away. Authors of the first edition recognized the skill of Black women kitchen workers but acknowledged their knowledge to be oral and therefore perishable. Accordingly, they sought to "gather [New Orleans recipes] from the lips of the old Creole negro cooks . . . ere they, too, pass away."[56] This body of culinary knowledge was fleeting because elderly cooks were ageing, taking their recipes with them when they died.[57] Domestic workers were also fleeing service jobs, leaving white women to pick up kitchen spoons and wonder how their favorite gumbo recipes were made. Recording a body of Creole recipes in the *Picayune's Creole Cook Book* made the formulas public and repeatable. The action also allowed white readers to separate Black cooks and chefs from the fruits of their labor, appropriate such knowledge as their own, and define, in writing, a Creole culinary canon. Indeed, in the *Picayune* cookbook's sixth edition, published in 1922, the authors revised the emphasis on "Creole negro cooks" on the book's title page to read "Creole cooks."[58] This deletion was important, uncoupling "Creole" and "negro" and removing Black women from an emphasized, authorial role on the first page of this culinary and cultural handbook. Black cooks could cook Creole food. Creoles could cook Creole food. But Black cooks could not *be* Creole, this alteration suggested.[59]

Two cookbooks written by New Orleanian Natalie V. Scott in 1929 and 1931 added new, sharp dimensions to portrayals of Black illiteracy and Creole cuisine. *Mirations and Miracles of Mandy*, published in 1929, began with a crude transcription of the words of the protagonist's cook, named Mandy. "'My madam say she writin' mah cookin' down. Lawdy, put me front' a cookin' stove, an' I don't needs no prescription,' says Mandy." Mandy stirred, baked, and sautéed without need of a cookbook. Mandy was an invention, Scott clarified—a fantastical amalgamation of all the Black women who cooked for Scott and her friends. "Mandy, of course, is a composite," Scott divulged. "My own Mandy's name is Pearl. . . . There are the Mandys of all my friends— Mammy Lou, and Phrosine, and Tante Celeste, Venida, Felicie, Mande, Titine, Elvy, Mona, Relie."[60] Scott's writing declared a sense of ownership that she and her friends felt of the cooks working in their kitchens. The cover of Scott's cookbook featured a kaleidoscopic array of these "Mandys," all the same woman, with identical red bandanas, starched white collars, and smiles tilted at slightly different angles (fig. 5.3). Scott acknowledged these cooks as individuals by naming them, yet she blended them all into one "Mandy" for the purposes of the cookbook. They became a sequence of interchangeable, undistinguishable, cooking women, who described their recipes reluctantly for Scott's eager pen.

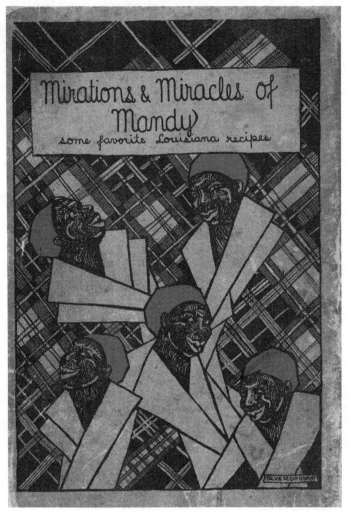

FIGURE 5.3. The kaleidoscopic array of "Mandys" on the cover of this cookbook collapsed the city's Black women cooks into a single, interchangeable source of recipes and labor. Illustration by Olive Leonhardt, in Natalie V. Scott, *Mirations and Miracles of Mandy* (New Orleans: R. H. True, 1929). Newcomb Archives and Vorhoff Collection, Newcomb Institute at Tulane University, New Orleans, LA.

Scott's cookbooks functioned as a thorough catalogue of the stereotypes that white New Orleanians created to disparage Black women in the kitchen. Mandy created "miracles" in the kitchen, Scott wrote, due not to her lifelong training or hard work but to her "sixth culinary sense." Such accidental wonders made Scott ponder whether Mandy was related to the "witch doctors of North Africa [who] have a mastery of mental telepathy."[61] In Scott's 1931 cookbook, *200 Years of New Orleans Cooking*, Mandy reappeared. There, Mandy's illiteracy was unambiguous. "The A.B.C.'s of vegetable cookery are well-known to Mandy," Scott declared, "though she is often innocent of the alphabetic ones."[62] Scott's cookbooks presented particularly egregious examples of the ways in which whites had learned to constrict the authority and deride the intelligence of Black women in the kitchen. But the hurtful tropes that appeared in Scott's recipes were hardly rare, nor were they destined for a small and local readership. Of the seven New Orleans cookbooks that the 1938 Federal Writer's Project's *New Orleans City Guide* recommended to its national readers, two were these cookbooks by Scott.[63]

New Orleans's fine dining restaurants, too, privileged a form of Creole culinary authority that was literate and literary in nature. Established in 1840 by French immigrant Antoine Alciatore, Antoine's restaurant claimed to be the nation's oldest restaurant operated continuously by the same family. Composed of a warren of private and public dining rooms that filled a French Quarter block, its kitchens could feed more than seven hundred diners.[64] Proprietors decorated the restaurant's many dining rooms with thousands of *things*: shelves of cookbooks, menus, obscure kitchen gadgets, and wine glasses touched by politicians, actresses, and sports stars. In his 1945 restaurant guide, *Dining in New Orleans*, writer and radio personality Scoop Kennedy described Antoine's as "both restaurant . . . and exposition, with its hundreds of autographed photographs, its priceless collection of cups."[65] Eating at Antoine's felt like dining in a museum of Creole cuisine. The sheer volume and array of materials on display evinced a business saturated in history and rooted in networks of European and American tastemakers and celebrities alike—a world apart from the recipes that existed only in the head of a domestic servant.

Materials produced to celebrate Antoine's centennial in 1940 demonstrated the specifically literary nature of Antoine's fame. "As a poet blends words to produce a sonnet; [proprietor Roy Alciatore] blends ingredients to produce a sauce," a *Times-Picayune* reporter proclaimed.[66] He praised Alciatore in the terms of an author, rather than a restaurant owner.[67] An illustration of author Irvin S. Cobb emphasized this theme, showing Cobb in need of a rhyming dictionary to pen his "Ode to Creole Cooking" after enjoying a meal at Antoine's (fig. 5.4). Proprietors recorded such praise in a 1940 booklet, *Centennial Souvenir du Restaurant Antoine*, which recounted the restaurant's history and listed the illustrious diners who had passed through its doors. Expert New Orleans cooking, grounded in archived history, required literacy beyond Mandy's "A.B.C.s of vegetable cookery," such materials claimed. Celebrations of New

FIGURE 5.4. Writers who celebrated the centennial of Antoine's restaurant in 1940 declared the skill of proprietor Roy Alciatore to be like those of a poet, deserving of a literary form of praise. "Irvin S. Cobb," illustration, in Roy L. Alciatore, *Centennial Souvenir du Restaurant Antoine* (New Orleans, LA: Antoine's, 1940), 2.

Orleans's finest restaurants as literary and literate spaces only exacerbated the illiteracy common to representations of Black Americans in the kitchen.

New Orleans restaurateurs also forced a sense of illiteracy among their diners in an extra bid to characterize Creole cuisine as exclusive knowledge. Antoine's printed its menu entirely in French, which resulted in trouble for one diner in 1943. Perhaps with the help of a tablemate or waiter, the guest annotated his menu with blue pen, adding clumsy English translations of Creole dishes listed in French: "Mushrooms Fresh on Toast," "Soupe Onion ~~Fried~~ Baked with Cheese," "Crabs Soft Shell Fried in Deep Fat."[68] A menu from Arnaud's, a French Quarter neighbor and competitor of Antoine's, featured a similar pride in its inscrutability. "Some of the names in this menu will probably puzzle you," the restaurant proprietors wrote in a note to diners. "They are the names of dishes belonging to what we call 'La Cuisine Classique,' as expounded by great chefs. . . . We cannot simplify, alter or change them. The waiters will gladly tell you what they constitute." La Louisiane restaurant, too, printed a "Dictionary of Delectable Dishes" to help guests struggling with French-language menu descriptions.[69] All these restaurants conveyed the message that fine New Orleans cuisine, developed by French and Creole chefs, could only be described, ordered, and served in a particular vocabulary.

John and Helen Abbot of Andover, Massachusetts, were two American tourists who vacationed in New Orleans and ordered from menus such as these. In January 1953, the Abbots fled a New England snowstorm and endured a turbulent flight to New Orleans. For the next three days, they dined at La Louisiane and Antoine's restaurants and drank Sazerac cocktails at the Absinthe House and Ramos Gin Fizzes at the Roosevelt Bar. After they returned home from their trip, Helen, most likely, assembled a scrapbook to remember their vacation. On its black paper pages, she glued a menu from Antoine's and postcards showing the French Market and banana conveyors on the levee. On the scrapbook's first page, she attached a small booklet, "Condensed History of New Orleans for the Tourist," published by Gray Line Motor Tours, Inc., likely distributed to passengers for free. "Because of the fact that there are 'Creole negroes,' that is, colored people . . . whose ancestors as slaves belonged to the Creoles, some uninformed persons have inferred that the term designates Louisianians having a 'touch of the tar brush,'" the booklet's author acknowledged. "This is entirely incorrect. . . . There never was a nobler or more pure-blooded race than the Creoles."[70] The Abbots had spent just three days in the Crescent City; this scrapbook would serve as the tangible reminder of the meals they had enjoyed and the things they had learned there.

Tourists' exposure to the consumable pleasures of New Orleans was brief. Exclusionary lessons about cultural belonging and racial identity lurked among ephemeral, seemingly inconsequential objects. Menus, cookbooks, private correspondence, newspaper reporting, and guidebooks created a textual system that cast figures like Azalea, Mandy, and others as the unlettered antitheses of elite white restaurateurs. By mid-century, the authors of these kinds of texts had perfected descriptions of Creole culture, cuisine, and history that were as enticing to outsiders as they were exclusive to those close at hand. Nevertheless, even if they omitted the skill, creativity, and history of Black Creole chefs and cooks, the authority of these New Orleanians in the kitchen marked every Creole meal.

"The Black Hand in the Pot"

The 1938 *New Orleans City Guide* had suggested one cognitive map of the city to its readers, in which whites sent Black tourists to swim on separate beaches and dine in restaurants far from the likes of Antoine's. *Lena Richard's Cook Book* laid out an altogether different perspective on New Orleans of 1939, in which a Black woman sounded as the sole voice of artistic, professional, and literate authority. Chef Lena Richard would become a multimedia kitchen star. But many more New Orleans chefs and cooks worked without recognition, underpaid and unsung. Even so, they declared a sense of ownership of the city's Creole cuisine, knowing that New Orleanians of color had created it from the start. With pride and creativity, they resisted a social and legal system that kept them out of fine dining rooms, behind closed kitchen doors.

Caterer, cookbook author, teacher, restaurateur, and television personality Lena Richard achieved national fame for her food before many chefs were nationally famous. Born in 1892 in New Roads, Louisiana, a small town in the northwestern part of the state, Richard's family moved to New Orleans when she was young. She learned to cook alongside her mother, who worked in the kitchen of a white New Orleanian, Alice Vairin.[71] Recognizing Lena Richard as a "child prodigy of the kitchen," as the New York–based food writer Clementine Paddleford reported, Vairin allowed Richard one day a week to read cookbooks and funded her enrollment in the Fannie Farmer Cooking School in Boston. There, Richard realized the extent of the expertise she already had, taught by her mother. "I found out in a hurry they can't teach me much more than I know," Richard told Paddleford. "I cooked a couple of my dishes like Creole gumbo . . . and they go crazy, almost, trying to copy down what I say. I think maybe I'm pretty good, so some day I'd write down myself." In Boston, rather than New Orleans, Richard was empowered to understand that she could translate her skills to the printed page and author her own book.

After returning south, she did so, self-publishing *Lena Richard's Cook Book* in 1939. The book included recipes for a variety of dishes, from the everyday to the embellished. Caviar Canapé, Crab Mousse, Gumbo Filé and Okra Gumbo, Calas Tous Chaud, Chicken Fried Creole Style, and much more—the table of contents detailed the delights of eating at Chef Richard's table. Richard also suggested menus for luncheons and dinners, ranging from the "plain" to the "formal." Within the copy preserved at Tulane University's Newcomb Institute, the spread of pages containing recipes for Lena's Baked Custard, Meringues, Lena's Apple Bread Pudding, and Soufflé Cream Pudding is spattered and stained, evidence of a decades-ago dessert.[72] Throughout the book, Richard claimed multiple recipes by name—Lena's Corn Bread, Lena's Lamb Chops and Pineapple, Lena's Red Sauce, Lena's Stuffed Tomatoes, Lena's Watermelon Ice Cream—adding her authorial stamp at every course. *Lena Richard's Cook Book* was "the pride of her life," Clementine Paddleford noted.[73]

Upon the cookbook's publication, Richard was eager and prepared to share her expertise with the world beyond New Orleans. She resolved to "travel with my book" to the World's Fair in New York City in 1939—the same fair where visitors could dine in front of a fictionalized antebellum mansion and romp through a "Gay New Orleans" fantasyland. Richard, though, had come to work. She brought the tools of her trade: her cookbook, a suitcase of Louisiana ingredients (dried shrimp, cane syrup, pecans, brown sugar), and specialized kitchen tools for making her most famous dishes. "I'm here and ready for showing my work," Richard announced to Paddleford. Richard confirmed that New Orleans cuisine could, indeed, travel—most authentically, with a fully provisioned, confident chef.[74] Boosted by Paddleford's support and enthusiasm from writer and gourmand James Beard, Houghton Mifflin republished Richard's cookbook in 1940 for a national audience, albeit with the new title *New Orleans Cook Book*. The publisher eliminated Richard's name from the title and removed a photographic portrait of Richard that had appeared in her self-published cookbook.[75]

Nevertheless, throughout the 1940s, Richard's fame surged, locally and nationally. She was a versatile entrepreneur, excelling in every medium. Enthusiastic crowds of white and Black women flocked to Richard's public classes—separately, in segregated New Orleans—eager to learn time-tested favorites as well as some of Richard's more spectacular techniques. Some of Richard's most renowned dishes relied on stunning aesthetics and surprise—qualities more likely to be experienced in the city's white-tablecloth restaurants. To create her "Scale Fish," for example, Richard lined a metal mold with sliced olives and pimentos, filled the mold with flaked fish set with gelatin, and unmolded the creation so it appeared to be a whole fish on a plate. The preparation was a delicious illusion, upscaling wedding cakes at receptions, Paddleford described. Richard also managed a catering business, frozen foods line, and restaurants of her own, at a time when Black-owned food businesses—much less businesses that fed Black diners—were rare. In 1941, the year when Richard opened Lena's Eatery, the *Negro Motorist Green Book* noted only two restaurants in the city that welcomed Black customers. (In contrast, the 1942 city directory listed hundreds of restaurants and lunchrooms serving whites.) By 1949, when Richard opened another restaurant, Lena Richard's Gumbo House, there were still only eleven restaurants dedicated to Black diners in the city.[76] Beyond New Orleans, Richard also cooked professionally at a small inn in New York state and in Colonial Williamsburg, Virginia, at a tavern. Her food left diners speechless with satisfaction. Kenneth Chorley, president of Colonial Williamsburg, wrote to Richard after a meal that she had cooked for him and guests in April 1943. "You are developing a state-wide reputation with your oysters," Chorley acknowledged. "And the birthday cakes were so light and fluffy and yet so tasty that I just cannot find words to describe them."[77] Following another meal, a diner visiting from New York City left more concise feedback in the tavern's guestbook: "I'd like to borrow Lena."[78]

Most exceptionally for a Black woman, much less a Black woman chef, Richard hosted a live cooking program in the early days of New Orleans tele-

FIGURE 5.5. Lena Richard filmed an innovative cooking program on Louisiana's first television station, New Orleans–based WDSU, from fall 1949 until fall 1950. *WDSU Filming Lena Richard*, ca. 1950, photograph. Lena Richard Papers, Collection NA-071, Newcomb Archives and Vorhoff Collection, Newcomb Institute at Tulane University, New Orleans, LA.

vision (fig. 5.5). Thirty minutes long, it aired two evenings each week from October 1949 until November 1950.[79] On the set, Richard and her assistant stood in front of a backdrop painted to look like a colonial American kitchen, with wood-paneled walls and a stone hearth. A photograph of a filming in progress showed Richard behind a table, with brewed coffee and a hot plate in front of her. She wears a simple, button-down blouse and white apron: the dress of a kitchen professional. Richard's assistant is holding something, ready to hand it to the chef when needed. A WDSU cameraman focuses on Richard, broadcasting the techniques she is demonstrating and explaining. A program host stands at her side with a plate in his hand, tasting what she has prepared. Everyone's attention, in the studio and at home, focuses on Lena Richard and her food.

Richard's skills were exemplary and so the discourtesy that she received from many white New Orleanians emphasized their insecurity with the fact that a Black woman was the chief expert on the city's cuisine. In 1938, a *Times-Picayune* journalist attended one of Richard's public cooking classes and reported incredulously, "That a negro woman should undertake to teach white folks about Creole cooking seems eminently sensible to Lena." Richard responded, "'That's what we been doing every [*sic*] since slavery time. . . . That's what we're good at.'" As the daughter of a professional cook, trained as a professional herself, the prospect of a Black woman as a culinary authority was apt to Richard. But such an equation confounded the reporter, who sought to rationalize a distinction between Richard's race and the Creole dishes she had perfected. "All Lena's cooking is Creole, though some of her recipes are her own invention," he wrote. Richard, as well as many of her fans outside of New Orleans, found no tension in the notion that her cooking was original *and* Creole *and* she was a woman of color. "A lot of 'quality' white women have wandered in the past into the kitchen of Lena M. Richard," the reporter continued, assuring readers that they would not suffer any loss in pride or social status if they, too, happened to "wander" into one of Richard's lessons. In contrast, when Richard first taught a cooking class to a crowd of three thousand Black housewives, she remarked, "This is the first time that I have supervised a school exclusively for Negroes and I do not know when I have had a more responsive, courteous and gracious audience."[80]

Press coverage of Richard's cooking classes—even if enthusiastic—pointed to the danger inherent in Richard sharing her knowledge in classroom and textual settings. When the *Pittsburgh Courier* printed a photograph of Richard teaching in New Orleans in May 1938, the caption described the event as "crowded with representatives of the white haute monde who wished to learn her culinary secrets."[81] Similarly, when the *Times-Picayune* book reviewer announced the Houghton Mifflin edition of Richard's cookbook, he disclosed, "In offering [her recipes] she bares all of her secrets of measuring, mixing and timing."[82] Despite assertions by mid-century white cookbook authors and restaurateurs that literacy equaled authority, the unwritten, if not illiterate, nature of Black women's culinary skills involved a power all its own. A praline seller working in Biloxi, Mississippi, in 1937 understood this well. When a *New York Times* journalist pressed her for her recipe, she responded, "Ah nevah tells mah recipe to nobody."[83] Disclosing the formula would have damaged, if not extinguished, her business. Similar to when recipes invented by the fictional Mandy or true-to-life Azalea appeared in print, when Richard published her cookbook or stood in front of an audience hungry to copy her technique, she relinquished a degree of control over her hard-earned knowledge.[84]

In fact, white employers coveted the expertise of Black women cooks because it often remained unwritten. This dynamic was clear in a letter sent to *Item* columnist Hermann Deutsch in 1951. "I'm wondering if you would know how and where one can get some good homemade mayhaw and wild crabapple jelly in this vicinity," wrote Eugénie Lavedan Maylié, proprietor of the New Orleans restaurant Maylié's Table d'Hote. "Since the death of our old Creole cook, (Thérèse Coquillion of Mandeville) we have not been able to get any of these delicious sweets." Coquillion had been the daughter of an enslaved person, Maylié explained, and a longtime cook in the restaurant kitchen.[85] Several of Coquillion's recipes appeared in the restaurant's 1941 cookbook, which acknowledged Coquillion's contributions by name and also called her Creole, unlike most culinary texts. Some of Coquillion's recipes, and even her knowledge of where to find mayhaw and crabapple jellies, never made it to paper and died with her.[86] Likewise, enthusiasm among newspaper reporters and members of the public for Lena Richard's cooking classes and recipes betrayed a certain eagerness to pilfer her knowledge. Publishing the recipe and procedure for Scale Fish let it exist on tables other than ones where Richard had crafted it for her own credit and pay.

Even though Richard's cookbook featured extravagant, classical dishes that demanded great skill—omelet soufflé, asparagus *vol-au-vent*, artichoke mousse, crab aspic—the New Orleans public lavished special praise on something else: Lena Richard's Watermelon Ice Cream. In 1939, a local reporter acknowledged Richard as "perhaps known best of all for the watermelon ice cream which has delighted many a New Orleans socialite." This fruit, long associated with Black Americans in racist postcards, stories, and poems, emerged as one of Richard's most prominent legacies in the memories of many white New Orleanians.[87] Lena Richard's Watermelon Ice Cream may have enchanted eaters because it proved doubly pleasing, as a slice of the colorful fruit, presented by a familiar source, but proving to be an elaborate surprise. Into a watermelon-shaped mold, Richard layered frozen whipped cream, tinted green and white, to make the rind. Next, strawberry sherbet and raisins stood in for the fruit's flesh and seeds. Like Richard's Scale Fish, her Watermelon Ice Cream was a beautiful, delicious illusion. Components that seemed inedible—a fish tail, sharp scales, the watermelon's tough rind and seeds—slipped down eaters' throats, prompting surprise and delight. Descriptions of Richard's Watermelon Ice Cream cast the technical skills and creativity underlaying this dish as secondary to well-worn tropes of the Black cook's innate intuition and "sixth culinary sense." Richard called the confection her "dream melon." A *Times-Picayune* journalist confirmed, "It's a 'dream melon' in more than one sense, because Lena conceived the idea in her sleep."[88] The complete dish had come to Richard without effort, the reporter related—dropped into her mind when her eyes were closed.

Despite their enthusiasm for Richard's food and expertise, white New Orleanians diluted and neglected her legacy after her sudden death in the fall of 1950. Richard's television show had been on the air for little more than one year. Her cookbook was just a decade old. The day after Richard passed away of a heart attack at her home on November 27, 1950, the *Times-Picayune* printed a brief notice that read, "Lena M. Richard, 51, Negro, caterer and author of 'New Orleans Cook Book,' died. . . ."[89] In this short obituary, Richard was a Negro first, then a caterer, and only lastly an author. She was neither a Negro author, nor just an author. The notice's syntax betrayed the way New Orleans society had understood her. In contrast, the *Cleveland Call and Post*, a Black-owned newspaper in Ohio, notified its readers of Richard's death with the announcement, "New Orleans, Louisiana's fabulous Lena Richard was buried last Friday morning. A television star and cateress, she recently published a book on Creole cuisine."[90] The *Chicago Defender*, also a Black-owned publication, likewise honored the multifaceted talent of this chef who lived very far from Chicago. "Mrs. Lena Richard, television personality, caterer and author," was the proprietor of her own restaurant and a televised chef, the obituary specified.[91] Richard had attracted devoted attention far beyond New Orleans and such obituaries that elaborated her accomplishments first, rather than her race, showed the respect she had won.

Arguably the greatest insult to Richard's legacy came not in New Orleans newspapers, though, but on television, the medium in which her presence had been most innovative. One and a half years after Richard's death, the *Times-Picayune* reported on a daily cooking program on WDSU that had become a "local favorite." "With affable Amanda Lee as culinary artist, 'New Orleans Cookbook' features the secrets of fine creole cooking," the reporter wrote. The televised cook wore a red and white checked dress and bandana, the classic costume of the Southern mammy. "Since the beginning of the program, there have been two Amanda Lees," the writer summarized. "The first was the late Lena Richard, one of the South's leading Negro cooks. . . . The current 'Mandy' dressed the part of the old-time Southern cook." Such changes offered what the reporter described as a "fresh new touch" to what had been a groundbreaking educational program, in a new medium, led by a nationally known professional. WDSU broadcast the show's second iteration while continuing to use the title of Richard's cookbook. But the producers had substituted another woman—Ruth Prevost, a school lunchroom supervisor from St. Tammany parish—to play the role of cook. Designating Prevost as the second Amanda Lee suggested that the two cooking women, Prevost and Richard, were interchangeable. Even more astonishing, WDSU nicknamed this new, "affable" cook "Mandy," which might have struck many New Orleanians as familiar, from the kaleidoscopic, composite, illiterate "Mandy" pictured on the cover of Natalie Scott's cookbooks published twenty years earlier.[92]

During Ruth Prevost's tenure as Amanda Lee, WDSU published a cookbook, though one very different from Lena Richard's cookbooks. The cover

WDSU·TV
CHANNEL 6
NEW ORLEANS

FRIED SOFT SHELL CRAB

4 soft shell crabs (cleaned)	Salt and pepper
	1½ cups flour
1 cup milk	¼ tsp. baking powder

Clean and wash crabs. Dry well. Season flour with salt and pepper and baking powder. Dip crab in flour, then in milk and back in flour. Fry at 400° F. Drain on heavy paper. Serve hot with tartar sauce and garnish with lemon.

OLD PLANTATION OKRA GUMBO

2 lbs. shrimp (cleaned)	2 bay-leaves, chopped fine
6 crabs (cleaned)	2 lbs. okra, washed and cut (not too fine)
2 No. 2 cans tomatoes	
1 cup celery, chopped fine	2½ qts. water (OYSTER water if possible)
1 cup onions, chopped fine	Salt and pepper to taste
2 cloves garlic, chopped fine	½ tsp. sugar

Clean shrimp and crabs. Make gravy by cooking cut-up okra, garlic, celery and tomatoes; cook until tender. Add to water or oyster water. Add salt and pepper to taste and sugar. Cook for about 30 minutes. Add shrimp and crabs and cook 20 minutes longer.

— 25 —

MANDY LEE'S
RECIPES
for
GOOD NEW ORLEANS
DISHES

MANDY LEE SAYS...

Always refrigerate shellfish and keep covered with wax paper to prevent absorbing or giving off of odors.

FIGURE 5.6. Following Lena Richard's sudden death in 1950, WDSU continued her cooking program but fell back on old stereotypes of a cooking mammy, employing Ruth Prevost to perform as "Mandy Lee." Ruth Prevost and Harnett T. Kane, *Mandy Lee's Recipes for Good New Orleans Dishes* (New Orleans, LA: WDSU-TV Channel 6 New Orleans, 1950). Newcomb Archives and Vorhoff Collection, Newcomb Institute at Tulane University, New Orleans, LA.

of *Mandy Lee's Recipes for Good New Orleans Dishes* featured a photograph of Prevost in Southern garb, serving herself from a large plate of fried chicken (fig. 5.6).[93] Spiral-bound, the cookbook was narrow and tall, its dimensions more like those of a shopping list than a book. As a gimmick, the cookbook doubled as a kitchen helper, with a base that folded into a triangle. "This book stands on its own feet!" the back cover announced. "Fold the cover over . . . and the book will stay upright on your work surface for easy reference." The bottom of each page featured an illustration of Mandy's face alongside a snippet of advice that began, "Mandy Lee says . . ." Under a recipe for Old Plantation Okra Gumbo, Mandy Lee advised, "Always refrigerate shellfish."

Such was New Orleans's commemoration of the fabulous Lena Richard: nostalgia for Watermelon Ice Cream, a TV show featuring a woman made to play the part of the costumed, cooking mammy, and a cookbook that stood like a woman on a counter, offering simplified advice. In the end, white audiences were unable or unwilling to commemorate Lena Richard in a realm other than that of a familiar, flattened stereotype. If Richard's time on air was tragically brief, so was Ruth Prevost's. Prevost died on March 7, 1954, of a cerebral hemorrhage, at just thirty-six. She left a seventeen-year-old daughter, Yvonne, and a husband, Robert. Recordings of Lena Richard or Ruth Prevost did not survive, but their cookbooks lived on.[94]

Distinct from Lena Richard and Ruth Prevost, the majority of Black cooks and chefs in mid-twentieth-century New Orleans worked far from television cameras and newspaper reporters. Nevertheless, they took deep pride in their work, despite the insults of segregation and low pay. Like Richard, they identified as members of a long line of Black Creole culinary professionals. The words of many of these individuals who worked in New Orleans kitchens of the 1930s through 1970s became available thanks to a singular book, published in 1978: *Creole Feast: 15 Master Chefs of New Orleans Reveal Their Secrets*. The book's co-authors were Nathaniel Burton, a longtime chef in the city's white-tablecloth restaurants, and Rudy Lombard, a lawyer and civil rights activist. Late in life, Lombard recalled a moment in his childhood in the 1940s, when he stood outside the Uptown restaurant Pascal's Manale, knowing that he was forbidden from going inside because of his skin color, even though the chef cooking inside was also Black. Early experiences such as this—ordered to stand on the outside, looking in—inspired Lombard to lead sit-ins in New Orleans in the 1960s, serve as the plaintiff in the landmark US Supreme Court case *Lombard v. Louisiana* in 1963, and co-author *Creole Feast* in 1978. With this collection of transcribed interviews and recipes, Burton and Lombard set out to correct the deep imbalance in the culinary historical record that had privileged the voices of whites and silenced those of Blacks. The book showed Black New Orleanians' essential roles in creating Creole cuisine, as well as the reverse: the significance of food to the work, pleasure, and activism of Black New Orleanians.[95]

Burton and Lombard's writing of *Creole Feast* had an urgent purpose during an era when many young New Orleanians of color preferred to call themselves Black, not Creole. In 1970s New Orleans, following national movements for civil rights and Black power, many young New Orleanians expressed greater affinity for an ideology of expansive Black solidarity. Some perceived a shameful dimension to Creole identity, believing that the word linked them to a past in which their ancestors had been the mistresses of white men or the offspring of such relationships.[96] Other New Orleanians dismissed the term as a disruptive wedge. "The issue of creolism was a divisive thing imposed upon us by the white community," said attorney Ronald Nabonne to an oral historian in 1978. "Creolism was imposed . . . by those in power and that was the white community. If we continue to emphasize this especially among blacks, it will be just useless." To Nabonne and some of his neighbors in Tremé/Seventh Ward, fretting over who was and was not a Creole, and what that meant, distracted from efforts to unify and work on behalf of all New Orleanians of color.[97]

With *Creole Feast*, Burton and Lombard offered a different take: Creole identity and Creole culture were the birthrights of Black New Orleanians, they declared, and best expressed, understood, and enjoyed through food. "It is difficult to arrive at a universally satisfying definition of Creole cuisine," they admitted in their introduction. "The one feature, however, that all previous definitions have in common is a curious effort to ascribe a secondary, lowly or nonexistent role to the Black hand in the pot, in spite of the fact that everything that is unique about New Orleans culture . . . can be traced to that city's Black presence." In the kitchen, as in other realms, Black New Orleanians should claim Creole history and identity as their unique, creative legacy, Lombard and Burton urged. "The single, lasting characteristic of Creole cuisine is the Black element," they wrote. The words of the Black chefs and cooks they interviewed bolstered the authors' claims that people of African and Afro-Caribbean descents in New Orleans were and had always been Creoles and had played the predominant role in inventing, perpetuating, and modernizing Creole cuisine.

Most importantly, *Creole Feast* allowed culinary professionals who worked behind closed doors to finally speak for themselves. When diners, critics, and tourists flocked to the city's white-tablecloth restaurants to worship at the altar of Creole cuisine, few understood that Black chefs, line cooks, and pastry cooks created their experiences. Mostly unacknowledged, these professionals circulated among the city's elite kitchens, teaching each other. "They say [Creole cuisine] is a mixture of Spanish and French, but the only people who seem to know all about it are neither Spanish nor French, they're Blacks," said Sherman Crayton, a chef interviewed for the book. "They got it from their grandparents."[98] Crayton began working as a dishwasher at the French Quarter restaurant Arnaud's in 1936 and started to cook soon thereafter, rising quickly in the ranks. During his time at Arnaud's, the restaurant's menu emphasized to diners "our own creations"—the establishment's specialties. As guests in the dining room perused the menu and contemplated their choices, Crayton stood at the stove, turning out *Filet de Truite Meunière Amandine* and dozens of other dishes.[99] His skills and repertoire kept pushing him upward. Crayton attained the rank of head chef at nearby Vieux Carré Restaurant in the 1970s.

Black chefs and cooks were the backbone of New Orleans's restaurant world, supplying the consistency and enabling the volume that distinguished the city's best restaurants. Working during the same era as Crayton, Nathaniel Burton, *Creole Feast*'s co-author, scaled similar heights in the city's culinary scene. Born in 1914 in McComb, Mississippi, Burton memorized the tomes of iconic French chef Auguste Escoffier—rebuking stereotypes of the illiterate, accidental Black cook—and became executive chef at Broussard's restaurant. Like its companion French Quarter restaurants, Broussard's venerated the city's historical ties to France. "Have your waiter ring the bell and salute the statue of Napoleon with 'Courvoissier [*sic*],' the brandy of Napoleon," the menu instructed diners.[100] Specific people, places, and tastes that evoked European, colonial, and antebellum histories suffused diners' experiences at restaurants like Broussard's, even if those restaurants' chefs came from very different backgrounds.

Charles Kirkland, too, contributed to the city's Creole fine dining scene in a humbler, though no less essential, position. When local writer Scoop Kennedy dined at Commander's Palace, a sumptuous Garden District restaurant, he marveled at the longstanding establishment's remarkable consistency, despite changes in management. "All through the years, whether the operator be Italian or Irish, the food always has been of the highest quality," he remarked. Kennedy was remiss in searching for continuity in the front of the house, however. Charles Kirkland began working in Commander's kitchen in 1942 and continued there for twenty-seven years. "An undisputed specialist in salads and dressings of all kinds," Burton and Lombard noted, Kirkland made nine hundred salads every weekend night and up to a thousand salads during the busiest shifts. At Commander's Palace, as at many other establishments, continuity came from the back of the house.[101]

With such details, the interviews and recipes that Burton and Lombard recorded for *Creole Feast* functioned as a corrective key to many mid-century restaurant menus and guides, supplying omitted names and voices and revealing hidden inequities. The labor of Black culinary professionals generated huge profits for their employers—Arnaud's earned a staggering gross revenue of more than one million dollars in 1944, Kennedy claimed in his dining guide, with eighty-two staff members serving 1,500 customers per day—and yet this money rarely trickled down to the Creole chefs and cooks who cooked the city's Creole food.[102] When Charles Kirkland worked at Court of the Two Sisters during the late 1930s and early 1940s, prior to moving to Commander's Palace, he cooked seventeen hours a day, earning thirty-eight cents an hour.[103] During that same era, the price of a "miscellaneous whiskey" at Court of the Two Sisters cost forty-seven cents.[104] Thus, Kirkland's hourly wage totaled less than the price of a shot of mediocre whiskey at the same restaurant.

The culinary skills of Black New Orleanians were enormously valuable yet not valued. Nevertheless, many of these professionals cared deeply about the dishes they created.

Some chefs showed this passion when they exhibited a resistant culinary creativity in the kitchen. Annie Laura Squalls, a self-taught baker who began cooking professionally in 1949 and entered the Pontchartrain Hotel pastry kitchen in 1960, revised recipes continually, to the frustration of managers who valued consistency and demanded that she cook the same formula. "But I still had ideas about the food I was assigned to cook," she explained. Squalls added and subtracted ingredients to and from her cakes, pies, and pastries, obsessed with refining and perfecting the recipes. She went so far as to swipe ingredients from the restaurant's pantry to improve her dishes. She admitted to Burton and Lombard:

> When I started doing apple pies at the Pontchartrain Hotel I sneaked a little vanilla and lemon juice into them while the head baker was away. It wasn't in the recipe they gave me, and I promised not to do it again, but when I had to do the orange cake, I sneaked grated orange rind into the icing. . . . The same thing happened with the mile-high ice cream pie. . . . I didn't like the way it looked. . . . There was too much white. . . . I tried to stay in good with the cooks and the pantry so I could get a little extra cream or butter . . . Frequently I'd wait until [the chef's] back was turned and pilfer it.[105]

When Squalls saw "too much white" in her sweets, she would not stop until they bore her own stamp. Similarly, Milton Prudence, the first Black executive chef at Galatoire's restaurant, devised soups and sauces according to his taste. Prudence had started at Galatoire's as a dishwasher—his mother and grandmother did the same work, in the same kitchen—and worked his way up to the pantry, the line, and then to executive chef. "Each individual chef has his own touches," he explained in a 2006 oral history. "Turtle soup, oyster artichoke soup . . . Marchand de Vin—certain other sauces, they became mine—crawfish étouffée—that became mine." Galatoire's ownership permitted creativity within strict constraints; any of Prudence's modifications required "approval" at a tasting with the owners. Even so, chefs like Prudence and Squalls cooked and baked to satisfy their own tastes—until they could look at a dish and say, "That became mine." Their artistic and professional judgments made mid-century Creole cuisine famous and profitable alike.[106]

During the same years, other Creole chefs made their restaurants explicitly political spaces. Foremost among them was Leah Chase, who fed civil rights activists, celebrity athletes, musicians, politicians, local business leaders, clergy, and neighborhood regulars, too. Chase's initial encounter with the New Orleans restaurant industry came in a setting in which she was paid to serve but not welcomed to eat alongside her customers. Having worked as a waitress at French Quarter café the Coffee Pot in the 1940s, Chase remembered, "There were no restaurants for black people to go to." By the 1950s, even if there were Black-owned restaurants, "tables weren't being set in black restaurants. When you went in they would just hand you a fork and a knife or whatever," she described.[107] In 1957, Leah and her husband, Edgar "Dooky" Chase Jr., took over his parents' restaurant, Dooky Chase. The business was located at the corner of North Miro Street and Orleans Avenue in Tremé, one mile beyond the lakeside border of the French Quarter. Less than twenty years earlier, in 1939, the Federal Home Owners Loan Corporation had stamped that intersection and surrounding blocks red on its maps, calling it a "hazardous" zone occupied by "low class common laborers" and mechanics, 90 percent of whom were Black.[108] Nevertheless, the Chases set out to give New Orleanians of color a cultural and culinary institution that they had long lacked. Leah Chase understood that Black cooks and servers had long helped produce the aesthetic and gustatory experience of the Creole meal. Chase sought to provide a place where Black diners could finally enjoy that experience themselves.[109]

With Dooky Chase, Leah Chase created the first white-tablecloth restaurant for Black New Orleanians. "I wanted mirrors on one wall and another wall with red velour," she described. Despite protests from her spendthrift mother-in-law, Chase insisted on a particular object for the renovated dining room. "I remembered a beautiful chair I had seen at a restaurant in the French Quarter called the Vieux Carré. . . . Each chair was twenty-five dollars. . . . But I won the battle."[110] In a city where Black Americans fought to sit in the same streetcar, bus, and lunch-counter seats as whites, Chase insisted on the same elegantly designed chair for her restaurant dining room that white diners enjoyed in the French Quarter. Such attention to detail struck a young Raphael Cassimere Jr., who first came to Dooky Chase while participating in the 1960 National Association for the Advancement of Colored People (NAACP) state convention. "I was very impressed, because we had little Black restaurants that were okay, they were clean, but they may have had maybe four to six tables, did not have tablecloths," he recalled in an oral history. "But this was kind of a fancy restaurant . . . similar to what I had seen on television."[111] Cassimere would return many times in ensuing years to enjoy the mouthwatering "Authentic Creole Dishes" that earned Chef Chase fame: Veal Panné, Court Bouillon, Grillades, Gumbo, Jambalaya, Shrimp Clemenceau, Fried Oysters, Stuffed Crabs, Praline Pudding, and more. On Holy Thursday, Chase prepared Gumbo Z'herbes, made with nine greens—watercress, beet tops, mustard greens, collard greens, carrot tops, lettuce, spinach, cabbage, and Swiss chard—enriched and flavored with smoked sausage, smoked ham, hot chaurice, boneless brisket, and brisket stew meat. Customers lined up outside the restaurant for this indulgence, enjoyed alongside fried chicken, anticipating Good Friday's abstinence from meat.[112]

Under Leah Chase's decades-long leadership, the restaurant became much more than a destination for a good meal in a beautiful setting. Leah Chase and others later recalled Dooky Chase as an epicenter of the local and regional civil rights movement. Chase said, "I feel like in this restaurant we changed the course of the world over bowls of gumbo. . . . That's how we always did the planning—over gumbo."[113] Newspaper articles throughout the 1950s noted lunches at Dooky Chase sponsored by the Frontiers of America and local Black men's and women's social and political clubs. In 1957, a leader of the Urban League of Greater New Orleans reassured the assembled crowd that public school integration would come soon.[114] Chase cooked for Jackie Robinson, Harry Belafonte, and, in 1959, Nerius Namaso Mbile, a Cameroonian journalist and politician. Earlier in the day, Mbile had received a key to the city and a "certificate of honorary citizenship" at City Hall, yet he could not have celebrated afterward with a meal at nearby Antoine's or Galatoire's. Instead, he traveled across the French Quarter to Tremé to eat at Dooky Chase.[115] By the early 1960s, Raphael Cassimere Jr. remembered the restaurant serving as an "unofficial base" of civil rights planners. He explained: "It was sort of a cooling off place, [after] leaving meetings" down the street at the Knights of Peter Claver, the headquarters of the New Orleans NAACP, where members planned boycotts of Canal Street businesses and other action.[116] When the Congress of Racial Equality (CORE) hosted a banquet meal to honor Freedom Riders, they held the event at Dooky Chase (fig. 5.7).

When Dooky Chase celebrated CORE activists in May 1961, some arenas of urban life were desegregating with relatively little conflict. New Orleans's libraries, buses, and streetcars had desegregated in 1955 and 1958. Integration at the table came slower. "To talk about hiring some black clerks in stores . . . was one thing," remembered New Orleans activist and lawyer Lolis Elie. "But to start talking about social change, social life, going to the same restaurants, was considered to be *really* radical."[117] Louis Lautier, a Black journalist who had attended Dillard University and was the first Black member of the White House Correspondents' Association and National Press Club, agreed. Having traveled the world, Lautier concluded in 1960, "The glamor [of New Orleans] may be there for the white visitor. He can visit the city's renowned restaurants. . . . But New Orleans is still strictly Jim Crow."[118]

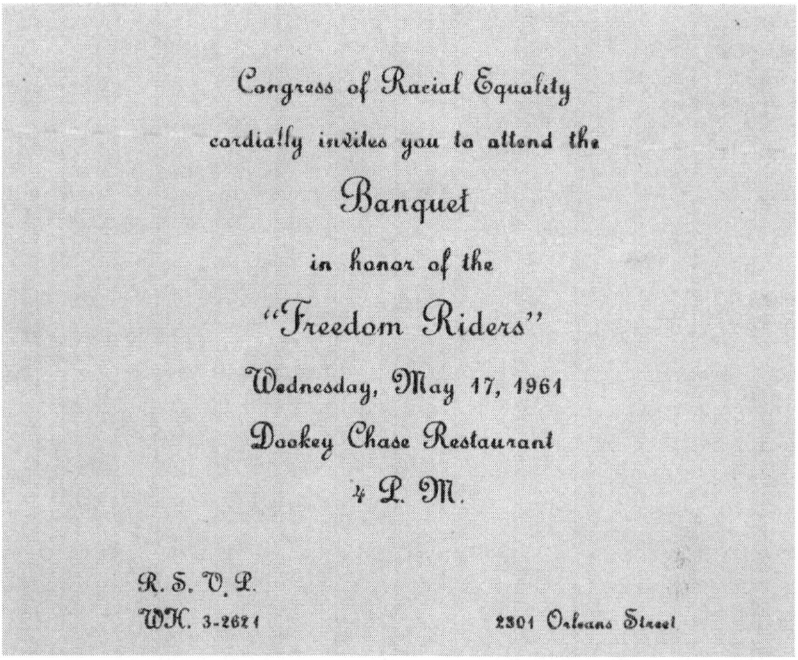

Congress of Racial Equality

cordially invites you to attend the

Banquet

in honor of the

"Freedom Riders"

Wednesday, May 17, 1961

Dooky Chase Restaurant

4 P. M.

R. S. V. P.

WH. 3-2621

2301 Orleans Street

FIGURE 5.7. Dooky Chase fed civil rights activists, celebrities, and local residents. Congress of Racial Equality banquet invitation, May 17, 1961. Connie Harse Papers, Amistad Research Center, New Orleans, LA.

Focusing on the city's segregated tables, in 1960, Black and white CORE activists led sit-ins and picketing of the lunch counters at Woolworth's and McCrory's Five and Dime, both prominent businesses on the commercial artery of Canal Street. Dorotha Smith-Simmons, a New Orleans activist, remembered the training that CORE had required as preparation for these sit-ins and other efforts. Activists read books about the nonviolent philosophy of Mahatma Gandhi, practiced extended periods without speaking or eating, and participated in "social dramas." CORE members role-played activists and aggressors, Smith-Simmons recounted in an oral history. "We were slapped, we were thrown off the chair and we were called names."[119] Such training would help them sustain physical and verbal abuse. Betty Daniels Rosemond, another local activist, decided to participate in the Woolworth's sit-in because her mother "used to like a certain sandwich" served there. "I wanted her to be able to sit at any lunch counter," Rosemond explained. She sat at the lunch counter and picketed outside. One day, two teenage boys "blocked my path, they began to harass me, they called me names, they spit in my face. . . . I don't think it could have hurt any more if they had knocked me down."[120] Another New Orleans activist recalled a lunch-counter waitress directing an electric fan toward a mound of pepper on the counter, blowing the spice into activists' faces.[121]

New Orleans lunch-counter sit-ins took on special significance in a city where eating and drinking were the centerpiece of local culture and a valuable tourist activity. Yet this activism would have momentous legal consequences of national import, too. CORE activists' September 17, 1960, sit-in at McCrory's produced a lawsuit that activists took to the US Supreme Court and won. In *Lombard v. Louisiana*, decided in May 1963, the court ruled in favor of CORE activist Rudy Lombard, who, together with three companions, had been arrested for requesting service at McCrory's lunch counter. In his opinion, Chief Justice Earl Warren affirmed that running a business "on the basis of apartheid" was "foreign to our Constitution." To those who might try to argue that a restaurant was a private, rather than public, space, the Court declared, "Access by the public [to a restaurant] is the very reason for its existence."[122] This victory was generations in the making and the result of careful training, study, and bravery. Lombard and his fellow activists had demanded a place at the New Orleans table and won on behalf of Americans of color everywhere.

In ensuing decades, Black chefs in New Orleans continued to feed and nourish the customers who walked through their doors. Leah Chase never moved her business from its original location, for reasons more philosophical than practical. "It would have been easy to relocate to what some would call a 'better' place," she acknowledged early in the first decade of the 2000s. "We are surrounded by the projects." But Chase explained that the restaurant sent a message to the neighbors next door as well as diners who came from far away.[123] Everyone deserved a beautiful place to eat. Her restaurant belonged to—and within—a community. "It wasn't very large but it was comfortable and it was cozy," remembered Raphael Cassimere Jr., who became a professor and an activist years after first setting foot in the restaurant as a young person. "It was so alive," he said. "You'd see the pillars of the Black community."[124] Carmen Morial, a lifelong New Orleanian and another patron, agreed. Within a segregated city, and even a city in segregation's wake, Dooky Chase was "a good haven for all of us who wanted to go somewhere nice," Morial recalled. "It was a good place to go, where you were safe from criticism."[125] With bowls of gumbo, white tablecloths, and a door open to all, Leah Chase upheld a Black Creole culinary heritage that had been built by the likes of Lena Richard and would be bolstered by Nathaniel Burton, Rudy Lombard, Annie Laura Squalls, Milton Prudence, and many others. On its visible corner spot in Tremé it would stay. "I go to sleep thinking about food," Leah Chase wrote in 1990, at the age of sixty-seven. "I have a stack of cookbooks by my bed. You read things or hear ideas and then your mind starts turning." For nearly three decades more, Chase continued to read, her mind continued to turn, and she continued to cook.[126]

In the midst of *Item* columnist Hermann B. Deutsch's 1951 gumbo recipe contest, he received a letter from Henry M. Stevens, the advertising manager in charge of soups at Campbell Soup Company. Stevens wrote in reference to the *Saturday Evening Post* ad that had so angered Deutsch, to address Deutsch's criticism of the illustration of a Black woman at a hearth, a basket of dubious gumbo ingredients by her side. Stevens defended the imagery in the Campbell's ad, explaining to Deutsch, "The kitchen in our advertisement was practically a replica of the frontispiece of a cook book put out by the Times Picayune Publishing Company in 1945. This publisher authenticated the drawing of the courtyard kitchen and reported that several were still in existence in . . . the French Quarter."[127] True enough, Campbell's had copied almost exactly an illustration that ran nearly continuously as a frontispiece in eight editions of the *Picayune Creole Cook Book*, from 1922 until 1987 (fig. 5.8). Curiously, however, the woman pictured at the hearth in the Picayune cookbooks tended a series of completely *empty* pots. For more than fifty years, the publisher of

FIGURE 5.8. *Item* columnist Hermann Deutsch protested as inauthentic an illustration of a woman at a hearth that Campbell's Soup Company featured in a 1951 gumbo advertisement (fig. 5.2). But Campbell's admitted that its illustration was a near-replica of this image, published as a frontispiece in eight editions of New Orleans's famed *Picayune's Creole Cook Book*. "A Creole Kitchen of Sixty Years Ago," *The Original Picayune Creole Cook Book*, 11th ed. (New Orleans, LA: Times-Picayune Publishing Co., 1947). Image courtesy of Newcomb Archives and Vorhoff Collection, Newcomb Institute at Tulane University, New Orleans, LA.

New Orleans's most famous cookbook had released new editions, updating the book's recipes, but recycled the same image of the woman at the hearth. The publisher kept her static and ahistorical—cooking, but not cooking any food. Deutsch had protested Campbell's illustration in the *Saturday Evening Post* as fully invented, a representation of a kitchen that "never was in New Orleans," he had written. But Campbell's had drawn the illustration from the Crescent City's preeminent culinary text, which surely sat on many of his readers' shelves. As Deutsch's error showed, white New Orleanians had long trafficked in an imagined history that was so artificial at times they duped themselves.

EPILOGUE

IN APRIL 2015, New Orleans Mayor Mitch Landrieu celebrated the reopening of St. Roch Market. The building had been a longtime food market on St. Claude Avenue, in a predominantly Black community off the typical tourist track. The business stood at an intersection beyond the bend where the Mississippi River flowed past the French Market, beyond Esplanade Avenue, long home to prominent Creoles of color, and farther downriver still. Municipal authorities constructed the building as a public market in 1875 in what was then a largely Sicilian and Black neighborhood. The structure's first refurbishment came in 1914, when white housewives belonging to the City Federation of Clubs' Market Committee called for improvements to the French Market and its smaller companions. Like the French Market, too, St. Roch underwent a full-scale renovation funded by the New Deal's Works Progress Administration in 1937 and 1938. The result was a Progressive-Era shopper's dream: walls, columns, and a high ceiling painted a bright white; a newly ventilated roof to freshen the air; electric lights and windows to illuminate the activity below; and rows of refrigerated cases displaying the food for sale. In 1945, Anthony Lama Sr., a St. Roch poultry vendor, took over the institution's lease and converted the building into a seafood market. His family sold fish, oysters, and shrimp there until early in the first decade of the 2000s. After damage caused by Hurricane Katrina in 2005, St. Roch lay vacant and in disrepair. Mayor Mitch Landrieu, first elected in 2010, identified the market's refurbishment as "an absolute priority." With the aid of federal hurricane-recovery funds, the city commissioned a total restoration of the market building and selected a team of local entrepreneurs to manage the lease.[1]

When the refurbished St. Roch Market opened its doors in April 2015, city officials celebrated its return in language reminiscent of the renovated French Market's reopening in 1937. Mayor Landrieu called the market "iconic" and "historic." City councilmembers, too, tagged the market as "rooted in history" and a "once-blighted gem returned to glory and to the stream of commerce." Unlike the French Market's New Deal renovation, however, the renewed St. Roch Market aimed to draw from and serve the community in its immediate vicinity, city officials claimed. Most of St. Roch's thirteen vendors hailed from the comparatively disadvantaged Seventh, Eighth, and Ninth Wards, noted one councilmember. Another insisted that the market would "provid[e] a necessary service to residents of the surrounding neighborhoods."[2] Several sellers vowed to offer wares at affordable prices. Inside, though, shoppers found a specialty food hall rather than a destination for weekly groceries. Vendors offered oysters on the half shell, raw kale salad, cold-pressed juice, and lamb chops. Food and travel writers and some city residents rejoiced in the market's selections—kimchi, "Koreole fried chicken," jollof rice—that ventured beyond the typical canon of Creole dishes.[3]

Soon after St. Roch Market opened, though, vandals smashed windows, threw paint, and painted "Fuck yuppies" on the market's exterior walls.[4] Three months into the market's run, a local reporter inquired with its owners about the products the local community was requesting. "They're asking for more rices, beans, pastas," acknowledged co-owner Will Donaldson. "We have that, but it's not in a section that the consumer can understand." The owners were confident, though, that the market would spur significant neighborhood change in the next five years. "I think the blighted commercial spaces are going to get built out," Donaldson said. "Right now, it's a little bit of a desert for commercial activity in this neighborhood, because nobody has jumped out and planted a big flag. But the city did everybody that favor with St. Roch Market."[5] Donaldson articulated his vision in terms that critics surely found to be the standard vocabulary of gentrification. The market had reopened in a longstanding neighborhood rather than a "desert," of course, where New Orleanians lived and operated businesses, even if they were not of the ilk of the "big flag" that was St. Roch Market. Divided reception of the business was just one node in a web of debates about rapid gentrification and demographic change in the city.[6]

The conditions that bred such anxieties about people, place, and culture had been brewing for decades. Throughout the second half of the twentieth century and spilling into the twenty-first, New Orleanians experienced thorough demographic, urban, and economic transformation, bookended by two devastating hurricanes, in 1965 and 2005. During the 1960s, mandated school integration tipped white flight to the suburbs into a paranoid exodus. In ensuing years, many businesses followed, including the French Market's Morning Call Coffee Stand, bringing their tax revenue with them. Urban renewal reshaped the city skyline and modified, if not obliterated, experiences of walking, driving, and living in the Crescent City. Major highways crosshatched maps of the city center and suburbs, leaving wealthy areas like the Garden District untouched but barreling through Black neighborhoods like Tremé/Seventh Ward. Containerization at the port and expansion of the oil and gas industries eliminated swaths of longstanding blue-collar jobs, like the city's longshoremen, and left behind a polarized spectrum of white-collar and service positions. Central American immigrants and Vietnamese refugees settled in suburban neighborhoods like Kenner, Metairie, and New Orleans East. Starting in the 1970s, municipal officials laid the groundwork for an economic future reliant on tourism, ordering construction of the Superdome stadium, a convention center, large hotels, and yet another renovation of the French Market.[7]

Tourism rose to the fore, indeed, when the petroleum industry's fortunes fell in the 1980s and shifted to Houston as it recovered. A century after the city hosted the World's Industrial and Cotton Centennial Exposition in 1884, New Orleans welcomed global visitors again, to the 1984 Louisiana World Exposition. In the mid-1990s and early in the first decade of the 2000s, a large casino, a World War II history museum, and other tourist-friendly attractions opened downtown. Many felt little benefit from this wave of growth, however. By 2005, more than 40 percent of city residents lived below the poverty line. Overwhelmingly Black, the poorest New Orleanians were isolated in concentrated urban neighborhoods of extreme poverty. As tourists caroused on Bourbon Street and bused out of the city to tour sugar plantations and swamps, hundreds of thousands of New Orleanians struggled to make ends meet, lacking quality housing, schools, and streets safe from violence. A different storm darkened the horizon, though.[8]

On August 29, 2005, Hurricane Katrina made landfall near New Orleans. In subsequent days, the floodwaters that breached the city's levee system inundated homes and businesses. Extreme heat and mildew amplified the effects. More than 1,800 New Orleanians died in the storm's immediate aftermath. The majority were elderly, Black, and infirm men and women.[9] Leah Chase's restaurant, Dooky Chase, flooded. So did a neighboring restaurant, Willie Mae's Scotch House, and scores more in the city's low-lying neighborhoods. At Brennan's, in the French Quarter, a walk-in refrigerator exploded and thirty thousand bottles of wine spoiled.[10] Block-by-block destruction of New Orleanians' home kitchens could be witnessed in the repetition of refrigerators dragged out to curbs, wrapped tightly to guard against the stench of rotting food inside.[11] The city's destruction, like its success and appeal in other eras, could be specified in terms of food. So, too, could its recovery.

In Hurricane Katrina's wake, food and drink nourished city residents and those who came to help. Chefs cooked on generators amidst power outages and without running water for rescue workers and electricians. Chef Linda Green, owner of the Ya-Ka-Mein Lady, fed musicians. Over time, Katrina's aftereffects amplified enthusiasm among a broad American public for the value and preservation of New Orleans's cuisine and culture. Local food writers and celebrity chefs published cookbooks proclaiming the city's resilience via recipes "lost and found." The Southern Food and Beverage Museum, dedicated to the preservation and celebration of Southern foodways, opened on the Mississippi riverfront in 2008. In 2010, the HBO television series *Treme* premiered, bringing New Orleans's people, food, and music to a national viewership. Major sports events, conventions, film projects, Mardi Gras celebrations, and festivals further boosted the city's recovery.[12]

Tourists and their money heeded the call and returned to the Crescent City. The New Orleans Convention and Visitors Bureau announced that more than 9.5 million visitors spent nearly 7 billion dollars in the city in 2014, making it the most profitable year yet for the tourism industry. In 2015, a decade after Katrina and the year that St. Roch Market reopened, the count of New Orleans's restaurants pushed above 1,400, or six hundred more than the total prior to the hurricane. "New Orleans has a proud history of attracting visitors from around the world to experience our unique music, food and culture," announced Mayor Mitch Landrieu. Indeed, national surveys conducted by popular travel and food magazines throughout the 2010s showed that Americans regularly ranked New Orleans as one of the top destinations for eating and drinking.[13]

Still, even as tourists returned to New Orleans, many New Orleanians could not, or did not. Media coverage and scholarly attention to the ten-year anniversary of the hurricane in 2015 emphasized the unequal fortunes of white and Black New Orleanians and the persistently low levels of return among Black residents who had been scattered by the storm.[14] In 2015, the city counted almost one hundred thousand fewer African American residents than it had in 2005. Black and white populations had had divergent experiences of recovery, with sluggish insurance payouts and inadequately mitigated reconstruction in poorer areas.[15] Observers and researchers agreed that severely incompetent preparation of and response to impoverished Black neighborhoods had damned their residents to higher mortality rates and far slower and incomplete rehabilitation. Such outcomes grew out of structural prejudices and inequities embedded deeply in the city's past and present.[16]

In this setting—an energetic, gentrifying, hungry, unequal New Orleans of April 2015—Nigerian-born chef Tunde Wey opened Lagos, his restaurant at the renovated St. Roch Market. Wey had come to the United States about fifteen years earlier, at the age of sixteen, to Detroit. There, he lived with family, attended school, and started cooking professionally. In early 2015, he moved to New Orleans and opened Lagos. Wey's menu featured dishes like jollof rice, pepper soup, fried plantains, and fish with pepper sauce. Their ingredients— fish, rice, beans, chili peppers—clarified how much of New Orleans's Creole cuisine had West African roots. Wey contributed "fiery . . . food" and a "voluble personality" to St. Roch, a local reporter wrote, but the business closed quickly, at a loss, after just four months. Wey was far from done with food, though.[17]

Chef Wey's most innovative work would happen off the plate yet still at the table. After his move to the United States, Wey explained to a journalist, he had needed to learn what it meant to live as a Black person there. Unfamiliar with the history, culture, and economics of the past that had borne the present, Wey read literature, sociology, and history to understand.[18] Smaller familial wealth, barriers to property and land ownership, police violence, ambient microaggressions, and other disadvantages pulled at the advances of Black Americans, Wey learned. In the dining industry, Wey saw glaring evidence of the continuing repercussions of slavery, rippling through generations, and persistent discrimination. "The time of dining as escape is over; the notion of food as art is finished; the era of dining as protest is now!" Wey declared in a 2016 essay. He believed in restaurants' power. And precisely because of that power, he argued, chefs and other food-industry members could not permit dining to revolve around the diner's comfort. "The only way to force change is to say something—however inconvenient," Wey wrote. "The truth must . . . spill onto our dinner plates."[19]

Chef Wey spilled the truth onto the plates of diners in New Orleans, Pittsburgh, Nashville, Las Vegas, and across the United States. Following the closure of Lagos, Wey hosted a series of communal dinners, "Blackness in America," as well as experiences designed to provoke conservations about American racism, over a plate of food.[20] Among these projects was Saartj, a pop-up lunch stall in Center City New Orleans that Wey ran in February 2018.[21] "THIS IS MORE THAN LUNCH / THIS IS AN EXPERIMENT," a chalked sandwich board announced next to the window where diners placed their orders. On the menu were Dodo + Ayamase, "Fried plantains with sweet peppers braised in blanched palm oil," and Jollof Rice + Frejon with Garri Eggplant Fritters, "Rice in broken tomato sauce + coconut and bean pudding with cloves. Served with cassava fried eggplants." Before a diner placed her order, Wey asked her if she understood the meaning of the racial wealth gap, and what it looked like locally and nationally. When a Black diner ordered lunch, Wey charged $12. When a white diner ordered the same meal, Wey asked, but did not require, the diner to pay $30. The price difference was not arbitrary. He calculated the divide based on disparities in median wealth and income between white and Black Americans.[22]

International media reaction was incredulous. Even if "nearly 80 percent" of white diners chose to pay $30 for their lunches, as Wey reported, other public responses on social media were profanely furious. "Racist bullshit," commented one Instagram user, replying to Wey's invitation on the platform to have lunch at Saartj. "I'm sure this is well-intended," wrote another, "but it ultimately perpetuates the focus on skin color (discrimination)." These commenters felt targeted for different treatment—a separate level of service at a restaurant, and more asked of them—simply because of the color of their skin. The terms of their outrage, together with ample scholarship on the realities and effects of racial wealth disparities, proved the conceptual basis of Wey's experiment. Feeling uncomfortable at one of Wey's meals pointed to the other side of the coin—the comfort that that diner was used to feeling at all other meals. At Dooky Chase, Leah Chase had been one of the first to invite everyone to her table. Tunde Wey invited everyone to his table, too. He placed a dollar amount on the privilege with which some had arrived, though, and asked them what they wanted to do about it.[23]

This book began with rice—the grass, together with 201 enslaved people, that a French slave ship transported from Whydah to Louisiana in 1719. This book concludes, too, with rice—prepared and sold in New Orleans in 2015 and 2018 by a West African–born chef, three centuries after the *Aurore*'s arrival.[24] This story does not end in the same place where it began, though. "White folks will consume me," Wey told a journalist. "They will consume my work." Even consumed, though, Wey was chef, and in charge. He extended the invitations to his meals; with great care and skill, he prepared the dishes his diners would eat; and he sat with his guests, initiating their conversations and listening to their ideas and questions. Having cooked, read, and lived in New Orleans, this African and African American chef had come to understand the often-ugly history of dining and drinking in the United States, as well as the conversations and actions that could transform them. "What I *want* is racial equity," Wey told the journalist. "The discomfort is just something that happens along the way."[25] Chef Wey set the table for diners' experiences of pleasure, pain, comfort, and discomfort. He extended the ugly alongside the lovely, inviting eaters to taste history and make a different future.

ACKNOWLEDGMENTS

THROUGHOUT MORE THAN A DECADE of writing and revising this book, reading the acknowledgments of fellow authors became motivation for me, enabling me to anticipate the day when I could recognize all those who helped this book come to be. I feel so fortunate that that day has come. My first thanks go to Joyce Chaplin, who let me enroll in her seminar on American food history at Harvard University while I was still an employee of Harvard University Dining Services. That course gave me my first taste of archival research and confirmed my hopes to make historical work my daily work. I thank Joyce for her sense of humor, for hashing out research ideas over lunch at Café Pamplona, and for suggesting that I purchase my first plane ticket to New Orleans. I am also so lucky to count myself a mentee of Lizabeth Cohen, a historian of enormous force on the page and in person. When I write, her voice is in my head, urging me to make arguments bolder, clearer, better. Along with Herrick Chapman, Liz has offered professional and personal advice more times than I can count. I am also grateful to Jennifer Roberts, a gifted lecturer and scholar of amazing versatility and breadth. Learning to teach with objects and art in her course "American Art and Modernity" convinced me that I wanted to write about and with material and visual culture. Nancy Cott taught the seminar on twentieth-century US history that met during my first semester of graduate school. It was a rigorous, perfect introduction to the study of American history that gave me confidence for everything that followed. While in Harvard's Program in American Studies, I also benefited from the instruction and mentorship of Glenda Carpio, Rachel St. John, Matthew Jacobson, and Lisa McGirr. Thank you all.

Intellectual, financial, and logistical aid came from many corners. I am grateful to Tim Mennel, my editor at the University of Chicago Press, for his counsel, patience, and skillful advocacy, steering this project to completion. Thank you also to UCP staff, especially Andrea Blatz, Susannah Engstrom, Jess Wilson, Anne Strother, and Elizabeth Ellingboe. Resources that enabled me to travel to conduct research and take time to write came from the Massey Fund of the Program in American Studies, the Charles Warren Center for Studies in American History, the Sarah Bradley Gamble Fund, the Center for American Political Studies, and the Graduate School of Arts and Sciences, all of Harvard University. Arthur Patton-Hock, Larissa Kennedy, and Dawn Ling kept the wheels turning smoothly at the Program in American Studies, the Warren Center, and the Radcliffe Institute, respectively. I am also grateful to the Department of History at the University of Wisconsin–Madison and the Department of American Studies at the University of New Mexico (UNM) for hosting me as a research affiliate, providing access to their libraries, and, at UNM, giving me an office in which to write. Sunny New Mexico skies and, in the right season, hot-air balloons were the backdrop as I thought and wrote about the Crescent City.

Researching New Orleans holds many pleasures beyond research, of course. For friendship and hospitality, especially over a meal or cocktail, I thank Nathalie Jordi, Brett Anderson, Andy Horowitz, Ashley Rose Young, Jessica Pearson, Jessica Dorman, Andrew Baker, Justin Nystrom, David Beriss, and Liz Williams. I am grateful to Grace Millsaps and Ryan Murphy for hosting me in their lovely Irish Channel home. From the upper-floor gallery windows at night, I could see cloudy skies made purple by downtown lights and the dark silhouettes of palm trees. That view, plus the house's two cats, helped make the home a peaceful retreat after days in the archives.

In New Orleans and beyond, my research developed thanks to the skillful assistance of many archivists and librarians. They pointed me toward unexpected collections, let me comb through vertical files, tracked down sources to scan, and showed me for the second, third, and fourth times how to load microfilm reels onto the reader. Thank you to Yvonne Loiselle, Greg Osborn, Irene Wainwright, Christina Bryant, and the staff of the City Archives and Special Collections at the New Orleans Public Library; Sean Benjamin, Kevin Williams, and Lori Shexnayder at Tulane University Special Collections; Susan Tucker and Chloe Raub at Tulane University's Newcomb Institute; Heather Green, Rebecca Smith, and Jennifer Navarre at the Historic New Orleans Collection; Siva Blake at the Notarial Archives Research Center; Irwin

Lachoff and Vinny Barraza at the Archives and Special Collections of Xavier University of Louisiana; Erin Patterson at the Louisiana State Museum; Anna LeBlanc-Mulder at Amistad Research Center; and Trina Brown, Jim Roan, and Alexia MacClain of Smithsonian Libraries and Archives. I thank Campbell's Soup Company for granting permission to publish a reproduction of a historic advertisement. Their staff noted that the company would not consider this imagery appropriate in their contemporary work. Their generous permission to reproduce the ad enabled me to interpret it within its historical context. I also thank the archivists of the Arthur and Elizabeth Schlesinger Library at the Radcliffe Institute for Advanced Study at Harvard University. It was in their sunny reading room that I first discovered the excitement that archival research can hold: the sense of anticipation when a new box is delivered to the researcher and she flips back the top, wondering what will be discovered inside.

Others have supported my scholarship in a different vein, over the course of many years. I am so grateful to my teachers and peers who have encouraged and critiqued my writing. Jane Stinchfield, my fifth grade teacher, told me that I would write a book one day and that she would look for it on bookstore shelves. Chris Tharp, Bear O'Bryan, Maxine Rodburg, and Liz Cohen taught me how writing could be funny, immersive, moving, and strong. Instructors such as these made the excitement and readiness to write a physical feeling—an eagerness to get words on the page that can be felt in my fingertips and that wakes me up in the morning, sentences already in my head. For feedback on my work and the opportunity to be involved in the writing of others, I thank the student, faculty, and affiliate members of Liz Cohen's twentieth-century US history dissertation workshop at Harvard, including Claire Dunning, Shaun Nichols, Casey Bohlen, and Andrew Pope. For long-distance writing exchanges, thank you to Brian Goodman, Heather Lee, Sam Rosenfeld, and John Bell. I am grateful to attendees of meetings of the Boston Seminar in Immigration and Urban History, American Historical Association, Louisiana Historical Association, Southern Association for Women Historians, Urban History Association, and American Studies Association. Thank you to the four anonymous readers selected by UCP. The engaged, constructive comments of Reader 3 in particular charted a path forward. At the National Museum of American History, Alana Staiti, Abeer Saha, Tony Perry, Crystal Moten, Sam Vong, Ashley Rose Young, and Josh Levy (of the Library of Congress) read and commented on portions of the manuscript. Jennifer Jordan, Johanna Winant, Lee Graves, Tiah Edmunson-Morton, Sandy Zipp, Brian Alberts, Liz Garibay, Maureen Ogle, Tara Nurin, Suzy Denison, and Mike Stein have encouraged my scholarship and writing from afar (and near). In a different realm, winning a James Beard Foundation Media Award in 2022 for a piece of writing—an essay about Patsy Young, a brewer and a fugitive from slavery in early 1800s North Carolina—was nothing short of electrifying. With all these mentors, peers, and experiences in mind, I hope to pay forward such support to others, offering generous and effective feedback that challenges, builds confidence, and inspires beautiful, impactful writing.

Yet another essential, supporting pillar of this book are the skilled child-care providers who cared for my daughter while I was writing. Thank you to the teachers and staff at CommuniKids Language Immersion Preschool, Murch Elementary School, and Capitol Language Services, all in Washington, DC. They opened their doors during the COVID-19 pandemic. With masks, social distancing, and daily temperature checks, they nonetheless created loving, fun, safe classrooms for my daughter and other children, who desperately needed to be with other kids and teachers. In this realm, thank you also to my husband, Brian Goldstein, for dividing evenly, to the hour, our childcare and work responsibilities, as we both continued to work full-time from home while also caring for our daughter from March 2020 to June 2021. Long walks with her let us slow down and watch two springs unfold in colorful, fragrant stages: first crocuses, daffodils, and snowdrops, then saucer magnolias, cherry blossoms, pear trees, tulips, azaleas, irises, roses, and dogwoods. Our respective work hours were precious and productive, at a bedroom desk with the door closed. Dividing our time was an exercise in mutual respect.

During the past ten years, we have crisscrossed the country and been so fortunate to build fantastic friendships at every stop. Christina Traugott, Christine Ajudua, Liz Maher Wright, Shweta Motiwala, Erin Perzov, Benita Liao, Alisha Fernandez Miranda, Laura Weidman Powers, Rebecca Stone, Sammy Ford, Blake and Phyllis Johnson, Sunil Sheth, Rahul Sheth, Erin Kelly, Joseph Manganiello, Mat George, and Neha Bhatnagar—all have been friends for a long time. Great friends helped me love grad school and count those among my favorite years. At Harvard, I was so fortunate to land in a cohort whose members were so collegial, creative, and sharp: Sandy Placido, Brian Goodman, Eva Payne, and Steven Brown. Within Harvard's American Studies community, I am also grateful for the friendships of Becca Scofield, John Bell, Carla Cevasco, Chris Allison, Dan Farbman, Maggie Gates, Aaron Hatley, Stephen Vider, Pete L'Official, Katie Gerbner, Holger Droessler, and others. For neighborly beers when we lived close and Google video hangouts when we moved far apart, I thank Elisa Minoff, Ramesh Nagarajan, Ross Mulcare, Erin Quinn, Sam Rosenfeld, and Erica De Bruin. Rachel Silver, Nathan Englander, Ane González Lara, Miguel Cortabarria, Nora Wendl, Kathy Kambic, Amber Dodson, Virginia Scharff, Chris Wilson, Cathleen Cahill,

Andrew Sandoval-Strausz, Margaret Lopez, and Christopher Frechette became friends during our sojourns in Madison and Albuquerque. Since 2017, I have been so fortunate to work at the Smithsonian Institution, which names a simple, elegant purpose—"the increase and diffusion of knowledge"—and where the expertise and dedication of its employees run broad and deep. At the National Museum of American History and beyond, I am grateful for the friendship, mentorship, encouragement, or some combination of the above of Paula Johnson, especially, and of Alex Harris, Ed Schupman, Nick Pyenson, Jon Grinspan, Katherine Ott, Eric Calhoun, Abeer Saha, Tony Perry, Crystal Moten, Sam Vong, Alana Staiti, Kathy Franz, Steve Velasquez, John Troutman, Amanda Moniz, Mireya Loza, Ellen Feingold, Fath Davis Ruffins, Ashley Rose Young, Shannon Perich, Eric Hintz, Kristen Frederick-Frost, Modupe Labode, Ryan Lintelman, Kelsey Wiggins, Craig Orr, Valeska Hilbig, Mike Johnson, Benjamin Filene, Anthea Hartig, and John Gray. In the final stages of completing these revisions, wonderful friends emerged among fellow parents at Murch Elementary School. They are smart, fun, and kind, and I am lucky to send my daughter to school with their kids and to count them as friends, too: Becky Alprin, Russell Flench, Nicole Bambas, Scott McGoohan, Radhika Mohan, Lionel Lynch, Eliza and Matt Ward, Amrita Ibrahim, Adil Qureshi, Marnique Heath, Kenyattah Robinson, Patty and Erwin Franz, Emily Wack, Nick Perros, Claire d'Alba, and Graham Wilson.

Any project that takes more than a decade to complete will count among its years times of challenge, upheaval, and joy alike. That has certainly been the case for this book, on global, national, and personal scales. While completing my dissertation in 2015, I was pregnant with our twin daughters, Ruth and Marian. They became constant company and felt like even closer companions when complications of twin-to-twin transfusion syndrome forced me on modified bedrest. In November 2015, the twins were born suddenly and much too early. They lived for one day and we held them as they passed away. Their deaths stunned me to my core. At the time, I had one chapter left to draft, but for a while I could not write. I strung words together because that is how sentences are made, but they did not make sense. This was a sign that something deep in my mind was unwell. After some time had passed, I found that I could begin to write again. Something tiny, somewhere, had begun to mend. Writing became a solace and completing the draft was a critically important goal. On days that felt unbearable, the love of Brian Goldstein and friends and family carried me. I am deeply grateful, always, to Mary Brennan-Hoover, Stacy Keif Dobbs, Johanna Winant, Geoff Hilsabeck, Amber Dodson, Kim Newstadt, Danny Warshawsky, Sarah King, Alex Rothenberg, Amanda Pirt Meyer, John Bell, Leah Giles, Elisa Minoff, Ramesh Nagarajan, Phyllis and Blake Johnson,

Neha Bhatnagar, Ashley Rose Young, Heather and Jamie Hannon, Lucy and Mark Wysong, and Arthur Patton-Hock. Garth McCavana, dean of Student Affairs at the Harvard Graduate School of Arts and Sciences (GSAS); Bob LaPointe, assistant director of financial aid for the Humanities at GSAS; Alison Van Volkenburgh, also of the Office of Financial Aid, and the staff of the Harvard University Student Health Plan offered immediate assistance. I will never forget their kindness and generosity. Marian and Ruth are still with me. I wear rings whose bands are engraved with their names so that they touch my skin. They are in the pages of this book, as they are in everything I do.

Thank you to my family for their love and patient interest in the lengthy process of writing a book, in which little visible progress happens, often for years at a time. I thank my mom, Ann McCulla, for teaching me how to read and asking to read what I wrote, from grade school to grad school. She will surely read this book more closely than any other reader. I thank my dad, John McCulla, for the brown paper bags of books that he gives to all of us each Christmas. Whatever our current interests, he assembles stacks of books, new and used, that go into the now-battered bags. I thank my siblings, their spouses, and their families for their love and friendship: Bridie McCulla, Francesco Da Vela, Lorenzo and Luisa Da Vela; James McCulla, Carrie Young, and Mary Abigail Huang (Bea) and Lucy Hom McCulla. Thank you, too, to my in-laws for their encouragement and love: Shelley and Steven Goldstein and Rebecca, David, Lewis, Nathan, and Audrey Silber. My large extended family of dozens of McCulla and Furey aunts, uncles, and cousins cheered this book to completion. I am so fortunate to be older than forty and still have a grandparent, much less one who lives close enough to share dinner with. James (Jim) McCulla had a long career as a writer, working as a reporter and editor for *Stars and Stripes* and the *Milwaukee Journal*, among other publications. In recent years he has asked, "When are you going to finish the book? I want to see what it's all about."

Finally, I offer my thanks and love to my little immediate family. Kitty, our shiny gray cat, now sixteen, has accompanied the writing of two dissertations, two editions of one book, this book, and yet another book in process. Occasionally she sits on keyboards, though she favors laps. She also excels as lumbar support behind lower backs. I am grateful for her gentle affection and companionship.

Nina, now almost six ("five and three-quarters," as she specifies), arrived healthy and yelling in June 2017. Since then, she has infused our days with happiness, laughter, energy, and love. She is learning how to read and will soon complete kindergarten. Nina, you are intensely creative, joyful, perceptive, empathetic, funny, and smart. You brighten the days of everyone you meet. Already and always, you have been more than I could have ever imagined or hoped a daughter could be. I cannot believe how lucky I am to be your mommy. I hope you always love yourself as much as I and others love you. I believe that you, too, will write a book someday if you want to.

Finally, my gratitude to Brian Goldstein. A talented and dedicated researcher, writer, and teacher, he is my most trusted reader. Without fail, he has encouraged this project, my writing, and my work. He is an undoer of knots, literally and figuratively. If the chain of one of my necklaces or bracelets becomes tangled, he has the patience to untangle it. Similarly, he will talk through an idea and clarify a muddled sentence. I have always loved our neighborhood walks, cooking side by side, and working at the same desk, facing each other. Together, we have moved from Cambridge to DC to Somerville to Madison to Albuquerque and back to DC. Our wedding vows came from the Book of Ruth and read, "Wherever you go, I will go, wherever you lodge, I will lodge." I thank him for always making a home with me, wherever we find ourselves, and for being my best friend.

NOTES

Introduction

1 The mortality rate of bondspeople during this trip was much lower than the average of 12 percent who perished on more than thirty-four thousand transatlantic voyages documented by the Slave Voyages Consortium ("Trans-Atlantic Slave Trade Database—*Aurore*, Voyage ID 33115," Slave Voyages Consortium, accessed August 6, 2021, https://www.slavevoyages.org/voyage/database#results); "Summary Statistics," Trans-Atlantic Slave Trade Database, accessed May 19, 2022, https://www.slavevoyages.org/voyage/database#statistics; "Untitled Image (Cross-Section of French Slave Ship *L'Aurore*)," *Slavery Images: A Visual Record of the African Slave Trade and Slave Life in the Early African Diaspora*, accessed May 19, 2022, http://www.slaveryimages.org/s/slaveryimages/item/3002. These were the first bondspeople imported directly from Africa. Several enslaved Africans were brought to Louisiana about a decade earlier, from Havana, Cuba. See Gwendolyn Midlo Hall, *Africans in Colonial Louisiana: The Development of Afro-Creole Culture in the Eighteenth Century* (Baton Rouge: Louisiana State University Press, 1992), 10, 57–63. See also Emily Clark, Ibrahima Thioub, and Cécile Vidal, eds., *New Orleans, Louisiana and Saint-Louis, Senegal: Mirror Cities in the Atlantic World, 1659–2005* (Baton Rouge: Louisiana State University Press, 2019); and Daniel H. Usner Jr., "From African Captivity to American Slavery: The Introduction of Black Laborers to Colonial Louisiana," *Louisiana History* 20, no. 1 (Winter 1979): 25–48.

2 Global movements in the name of exploration and the search for new foods became inseparable from processes of colonization, enslavement, and forced migration. "At great human cost," Hortense J. Spillers writes, "this cuisinart of the modern has blood on its hands, as the pillage and enslavement of millions are implicated in its development" (*Black, White, and in Color: Essays on American Literature and Culture* [Chicago: University of Chicago Press, 2003], 43).

3 On Native nations in the Lower Mississippi valley and interactions with European

invaders, see Elizabeth N. Ellis, *The Great Power of Small Nations: Indigenous Diplomacy in the Gulf South* (Philadelphia: University of Pennsylvania Press, 2022); Daniel H. Usner Jr., *American Indians in Early New Orleans: From Calumet to Raquette* (Baton Rouge: Louisiana State University Press, 2018); Robbie Ethridge, *From Chicaza to Chickasaw: The European Invasion and the Transformation of the Mississippian World, 1540–1715* (Chapel Hill: University of North Carolina Press, 2010); Michelene Pesantubbee, *Choctaw Women in a Chaotic World: The Clash of Cultures in the Colonial Southeast* (Albuquerque: University of New Mexico Press, 2005); and Elizabeth Ellis, "The Natchez War Revisited: Violence, Multinational Settlements, and Indigenous Diplomacy in the Lower Mississippi Valley," *William and Mary Quarterly* 77, no. 3 (July 2020): 441–72.

4   Hall, *Africans in Colonial Louisiana*, 2–3; Daniel H. Usner Jr., *Indians, Settlers, and Slaves in a Frontier Exchange Economy: The Lower Mississippi Valley before 1783* (Chapel Hill: University of North Carolina Press, 1992).

5   On French and Spanish colonial rule of Louisiana, see Cécile Vidal, *Caribbean New Orleans: Empire, Race, and the Making of a Slave Society* (Williamsburg, VA and Chapel Hill, NC: Omohundro Institute of Early American History and Culture and the University of North Carolina Press, 2019); Lawrence N. Powell, *The Accidental City: Improvising New Orleans* (Cambridge, MA: Harvard University Press, 2012); and Shannon Lee Dawdy, *Building the Devil's Empire: French Colonial New Orleans* (Chicago: University of Chicago Press, 2008).

6   Thomas Jefferson to Robert R. Livingston, April 18, 1802, *Founders Online*, National Archives and Records Administration, https://founders.archives.gov/documents /Jefferson/01-37-02-0220.

7   Benjamin Henry Boneval Latrobe, diary entry of February 27, 1819, in Latrobe, *Impressions Respecting New Orleans: Diary and Sketches 1818–1820*, ed. Samuel Wilson Jr. (New York: Columbia University, 1951), 67. Geographer Peirce F. Lewis distinguished between the city's "wretched" site and advantageous "situation" (*New Orleans: The Making of an Urban Landscape*, 2nd ed. [Santa Fe, NM: Center for American Places, 2003], 19–20).

8   On Jefferson's visions for Louisiana, see Walter Johnson, *River of Dark Dreams: Slavery and Empire in the Cotton Kingdom* (Cambridge, MA: Belknap Press, 2013), 18–45.

9   Myles Poydras, "Going Deep into Oyster Country," *New York Times*, December 3, 2021.

10   Frances Milton Trollope, *Domestic Manners of the Americans*, vol. 1, 2nd ed. (London: Printed for Whittaker, Treacher, 1832), 9–10.

11   Trollope's views on slavery became more supportive upon seeing what she described as the "real situation" in the United States (*Domestic Manners*, vol. 1, 10).

12   In 1978, historian and native New Orleanian Joseph G. Tregle Jr. wrote critically of his city's self-absorption, "New Orleans . . . is a truly narcissistic city. . . . The true New Orleanian finds it utterly incomprehensible that his own infatuation with this inamorata is not the universal response of all those who come to know her." In public and academic forums, Tregle argued tirelessly against racist voices that sought to define the "Creole" identity as "white" (Joseph G. Tregle Jr., "Foreword," in Henry C. Castellanos, *New Orleans as It Was: Episodes of Louisiana Life*, ed. George F. Reinecke [Baton Rouge: Louisiana State University Press, 1895, repr. 1978]). See also Thomas Jessen Adams and Matt Sakakeeny, eds., *Remaking New Orleans: Beyond Exceptionalism and Authenticity* (Durham, NC: Duke University

Press, 2019); and Richard Campanella, "The Seduction of Exceptionalism," *Louisiana Cultural Vistas* (Summer 2014): 24–25.

13 Joseph Holt Ingraham, *The South-West, by a Yankee*, vol. 1 (New York: Harper and Brothers, 1835), 185.

14 Essential studies of these topics include Calvin Schermerhorn, *The Business of Slavery and the Rise of American Capitalism, 1815–1860* (New Haven, CT: Yale University Press, 2015); Scott P. Marler, *The Merchants' Capital: New Orleans and the Political Economy of the Nineteenth-Century South* (Cambridge: Cambridge University Press, 2013); Richard Campanella, *Bienville's Dilemma: A Historical Geography of New Orleans* (Lafayette: Center for Louisiana Studies, University of Louisiana at Lafayette, 2008); Walter Johnson, *Soul by Soul: Life inside the Antebellum Slave Market* (Cambridge, MA: Harvard University Press, 1999); and A. Oakey Hall, *The Manhattaner in New Orleans; or, Phases of "Crescent City" Life* (New York: J. S. Redfield, Clinton Hall, 1851).

15 Mrs. [Matilda Charlotte] Houston, *Texas and the Gulf of Mexico: Or, Yachting in the New World*, vol. 1 (London: John Murray, Albemarle Street, 1844), 159–60.

16 Justin A. Nystrom, *New Orleans after the Civil War: Race, Politics, and a New Birth of Freedom* (Baltimore, MD: Johns Hopkins University Press, 2015); Rebecca J. Scott, *Degrees of Freedom: Louisiana and Cuba after Slavery* (Cambridge, MA: Belknap Press, 2008); John W. Blassingame, *Black New Orleans, 1860–1880* (Chicago: University of Chicago Press, 1973); Ida B. Wells-Barnett, *Mob Rule in New Orleans: Robert Charles and His Fight to Death, the Story of His Life, Burning Human Beings Alive, Other Lynching Statistics* (Chicago: n.p., 1900); and Kim Lacy Rogers, *Righteous Lives: Narratives of the New Orleans Civil Rights Movement* (New York: New York University Press, 1993).

17 On the deceptively subtle power of food, Hortense J. Spillers writes, "[Food] enters the port, often unseen, unobtrusively, but like the weather, the climate, the slightest shift in the wind currents, it might well alter a mood, and what we believe and who we think we are" (*Black, White, and in Color*, 64). See also Katharina Vester, *A Taste of Power: Food and American Identities* (Oakland: University of California Press, 2015), 4.

18 Excellent studies, though focused on a narrower group of people or time period, are Justin A. Nystrom, *Creole Italian: Sicilian Immigrants and the Shaping of New Orleans Food Culture* (Athens: University of Georgia Press, 2018); Zella Palmer, "Belle New Orleans: The History of Creole Cuisinières," *Africology* 11, no. 6 (April 2018): 186–91; and Rien T. Fertel, "'Everybody Seemed Willing to Help': The Picayune Creole Cook Book as Battleground, 1900–2008," in *The Larder: Food Studies Methods from the American South*, ed. John T. Edge, Elizabeth S. D. Engelhardt, and Ted Ownby (Athens: University of Georgia Press, 2013), 10–31. For explorations of the history of food and ethnicity in the orbit of New Orleans, see C. Paige Gutierrez, *Cajun Foodways* (Jackson: University Press of Mississippi, 1992); and Jean Ann Scarpaci, *Italian Immigrants in Louisiana's Sugar Parishes: Recruitment, Labor Conditions, and Community Relations, 1880–1910* (New York: Arno Press, 1980). Jessica B. Harris has inspired the study of New Orleans cuisine via her cookbooks, including *Beyond Gumbo: Creole Fusion Food from the Atlantic Rim* (New York: Simon and Schuster, 2003) and *Iron Pots and Wooden Spoons: Africa's Gifts to New World Cooking* (New York: Simon and Schuster, 1989).

19 Sue Strachan, *The Café Brûlot* (Baton Rouge: Louisiana State University Press, 2021); Tim McNally, *The Sazerac* (Baton Rouge: Louisiana State University Press,

2020); Maggie Heyn Richardson, *Hungry for Louisiana: An Omnivore's Journey* (Baton Rouge: Louisiana State University Press, 2015); Olive Leonhardt and Hilda Phelps Hammon, *Shaking Up Prohibition in New Orleans: Authentic Vintage Cocktails from A to Z*, ed. Gay Leonhardt (Baton Rouge: Louisiana State University Press, 2015); and Susan Tucker, ed., *New Orleans Cuisine: Fourteen Signature Dishes and Their Histories* (Jackson: University of Press of Mississippi, 2009). New Orleans's food businesses and workers appear within studies such as Robert F. Moss, *The Lost Southern Chefs: A History of Commercial Dining in the Nineteenth-Century South* (Athens: University of Georgia Press, 2022); David S. Shields, *The Culinarians: Lives and Careers from the First Age of American Fine Dining* (Chicago: University of Chicago Press, 2017); Paul Freedman, *Ten Restaurants That Changed America* (New York: Liveright, 2016); and David S. Shields, *Southern Provisions: The Creation and Revival of a Cuisine* (Chicago: University of Chicago Press, 2015).

20 Rafia Zafar, *Recipes for Respect: African American Meals and Meaning* (Athens: University of Georgia Press, 2019); Michael W. Twitty, *The Cooking Gene: A Journey through African American Culinary History in the Old South* (New York: Amistad, 2017); Krishnendu Ray, *The Ethnic Restaurateur* (New York: Bloomsbury, 2016); Marcie Cohen Ferris, *The Edible South: The Power of Food and the Making of an American Region* (Chapel Hill: University of North Carolina Press, 2014); Elizabeth S. D. Engelhardt, *A Mess of Greens: Southern Gender and Southern Food* (Athens: University of Georgia Press, 2011); Jessica B. Harris, *High on the Hog: A Culinary Journey from Africa to America* (New York: Bloomsbury, 2011); Frederick Douglass Opie, *Hog and Hominy: Soul Food from Africa to America* (New York: Columbia University Press, 2008); Marcie Cohen Ferris, *Matzoh Ball Gumbo: Culinary Tales of the Jewish South* (Chapel Hill: University of North Carolina Press, 2005); and Harris, *Beyond Gumbo*. Studies of food, ethnicity, race, and class beyond New Orleans that have influenced this project include Angela Jill Cooley, *To Live and Dine in Dixie: The Evolution of Urban Food Culture in the Jim Crow South* (Athens: University of Georgia, 2015); Andrew P. Haley, *Turning the Tables: Restaurants and the Rise of the American Middle Class, 1880–1920* (Chapel Hill: University of North Carolina Press, 2011); Psyche Williams-Forson, *Building Houses out of Chicken Legs: Black Women, Food, and Power* (Chapel Hill: University of North Carolina Press, 2006); Doris Witt, *Black Hunger: Soul Food and America* (Minneapolis: University of Minnesota Press, 2004); Hasia Diner, *Hungering for America: Italian, Irish, and Jewish Foodways in the Age of Migration* (Cambridge, MA: Harvard University Press, 2001); and Donna Gabaccia, *We Are What We Eat: Ethnic Food and the Making of Americans* (Cambridge, MA: Harvard University Press, 1998).

21 John Egerton, *Southern Food: At Home, on the Road, in History* (Chapel Hill: University of North Carolina Press, 1993), 4.

22 In March 2023, cruise ships that docked at the Port of New Orleans set an all-time passenger record, delivering more than 155,000 tourists to the city in that month alone. See Maria Clark, Todd A. Price, and Andrew Yawn, "How the New Orleans Tourism Industry Perpetuates Its Glaring Racial Wealth Gap," *Nashville Tennessean*, July 15, 2021, https://www.tennessean.com/in-depth/news/american-south/2021/07/15/how-new-orleans-tourism-industry-perpetuates-glaring-racial-wealth-gap/7779563002/; Richard Campanella, "New Orleans: A Timeline of Economic History," *New Orleans Business Alliance Opportunity Guide*, February 2020, https://richcampanella.com/wp-content/uploads/2020/02/article_Campanella_New-Orleans-Timeline-of-Economic-History_NOBA.pdf; and Kimberly Curth, "Port

of New Orleans Sets New Monthly Record for Cruise Passengers," press release, April 24, 2023, Port NOLA, https://portnola.com/info/news-media/press-releases /port-of-new-orleans-sets-new-monthly-record-for-cruise-passengers.

23 Kevin Fox Gotham, *Authentic New Orleans: Tourism, Culture, and Race in the Big Easy* (New York: New York University Press, 2007); Mark J. Souther, *New Orleans on Parade: Tourism and the Transformation of New Orleans* (Baton Rouge: Louisiana State University Press, 2006); and Anthony J. Stanonis, *Creating the Big Easy: New Orleans and the Emergence of Modern Tourism, 1918–1945* (Athens: University of Georgia Press, 2006). A newer study of tourism that privileges the voices of Black New Orleanians is Lynnell L. Thomas, *Desire and Disaster in New Orleans: Tourism, Race, and Historical Memory* (Durham, NC: Duke University Press, 2014). Stanonis notes travelers' enthusiasm for New Orleans cuisine in the nineteenth century but focuses on the Mardi Gras celebrations and cookbooks of later years—the late nineteenth and early twentieth centuries—as generators of culinary tourism. See Stanonis, "The Triumph of Epicure: A Global History of New Orleans Culinary Tourism," *Southern Quarterly* 46, no. 3 (Spring 2009): 145–61.

24 John Adems Paxton, *The New-Orleans Directory and Register* (New Orleans, LA: John Adems Paxton, 1822), 46.

25 Marcus Wood, *Black Milk: Imagining Slavery in the Visual Cultures of Brazil and America* (Oxford: Oxford University Press, 2013); Diana Paton, "Witchcraft, Poison, Law, and Atlantic Slavery," *William and Mary Quarterly* 69, no. 2 (April 2012): 235–64; and John Savage, "'Black Magic' and White Terror: Slave Poisoning and Colonial Society in Early 19th Century Martinique," *Journal of Social History* 40, no. 3 (Spring 2007): 635–62. In March 1860, Ann, a woman enslaved in New Orleans, was accused of poisoning a charlotte russe, an elegant dessert composed of vanilla custard cooled in a mold lined with ladyfingers, which was served at her enslaver's dinner party. Following the party, at least eighteen people present became violently ill and three died. Family friends suggested a motive: Ann was distraught that her enslavers had beat her and had taken her son to a trader, intending to sell him away. Nevertheless, Ann denied the crime, saying, "If I had wanted to do such a thing, I could have done it any time for years past" (news column, *Washington Constitution*, April 5, 1860, 3, with reporting from *New Orleans Delta*, no date).

26 Olga Jackson, interviewed in St. Mark's Community Center, *Treme/7th Ward Griots: A Video Documentary: An Oral History of New Orleans' Oldest and Most Diverse Black Community* (1977), narrated by Vyonne Clavor, videorecording (56 min.), VC-16; VHS, Media Collection, University Library, Xavier University of Louisiana, New Orleans, Louisiana. Rafia Zafar argues for the singular insult of segregation at the table, writing, "The refusal to grant the simple act of commensality . . . would be the most pointedly symbolic of racist efforts to humiliate African Americans" (*Recipes for Respect*, 1). See also Rebecca Sharpless, *Cooking in Other Women's Kitchens: Domestic Workers in the South, 1865–1960* (Chapel Hill: University of North Carolina Press, 2010), 143–44.

27 Tara McPherson describes such twinned, oppositional forces as operating according to a "lenticular logic." See McPherson, *Reconstructing Dixie: Race, Gender, and Nostalgia in the Imagined South* (Durham, NC: Duke University Press, 2003), 7. For intimate histories of food, gender, and race, see Kelley Fanto Deetz, *Bound to the Fire: How Virginia's Enslaved Cooks Helped Invent American Cuisine* (Lexington: University Press of Kentucky, 2017); Lisa Lowe, *The Intimacies of Four Continents* (Durham, NC: Duke University Press, 2015); Sharpless, *Cooking in Other Women's*

Kitchens; and Mary Titus, "The Dining Room Door Swings Both Ways: Food, Race, and Domestic Space in the Nineteenth-Century South," in *Haunted Bodies: Gender and Southern Texts*, ed. Anne Goodwyn Jones and Susan V. Donaldson (Charlottesville: University of Virginia Press, 1997), 243–56.

28 See Jeff Forret and Christine E. Sears, eds., *New Directions in Slavery Studies: Commodification, Community, and Comparison* (Baton Rouge: Louisiana State University Press, 2015); Lowe, *Intimacies of Four Continents*; and Christina Sharpe, *In the Wake: On Blackness and Being* (Durham, NC: Duke University Press, 2016). On the history of assessing value to the bodies of enslaved and emancipated Black Americans, see Aaron Carico, *Black Market: The Slave's Value in National Culture after 1865* (Chapel Hill: University of North Carolina Press, 2020) and Daina Ramey Berry, *The Price for Their Pound in Flesh: The Value of the Enslaved, from Womb to Grave, in the Building of a Nation* (Boston, MA: Beacon Press, 2017).

29 Edward Russell, travel journal and transcript, 1834–1835, MSS 424.2, Historic New Orleans Collection (hereafter THNOC), New Orleans, LA. Julian Ralph, "New Orleans, Our Southern Capital," *Harper's New Monthly Magazine* 86, no. 513 (February 1893): 383–84. See also Spillers, "Introduction," in *Black, White, and in Color*, 42–43.

30 On the antebellum power of "Queen Sugar," see Khalil Gibran Muhammad, "The Sugar That Saturates the American Diet Has a Barbaric History as the 'White Gold' That Fueled Slavery," in Nikole Hannah-Jones et al., *The 1619 Project*, an ongoing initiative by the *New York Times Magazine*, August 14, 2019, https://www.nytimes.com/interactive/2019/08/14/magazine/sugar-slave-trade-slavery.html.

31 In his study of rape perpetrated by slaveholders and slave traders, Edward Baptist argues that sexual violence was entwined with the psychology and practice of buying and selling people, such that "one act symbolized another, sliding together in a cloud of buying, selling, raping, and consuming." Baptist calls on historians to consider "other forms of desire" in addition to the sexual. "Such complexities lead one to wonder whether historians might do well to reinterpret the antebellum South . . . as a complex of inseparable fetishisms." This study investigates eating, drinking, and the commodification of people as an expression of such logic. See Edward E. Baptist, "'Cuffy,' 'Fancy Maids,' and 'One-Eyed Men': Rape, Commodification, and the Domestic Slave Trade in the United States," in *The Chattel Principle: Internal Slave Trades in the Americas*, ed. Walter Johnson (New Haven, CT: Yale University Press, 2004), 165–202, at 188, 167.

32 Orlando Patterson defines the enslaver-enslaved relationship as one of parasitism: "To all members of the community the slave existed only through the parasite holder, who was called the master. . . . [T]he slaveholder fed on the slave to gain the very direct satisfactions of power over another, honor enhancement, and authority." See Orlando Patterson, *Slavery and Social Death: A Comparative Study* (Cambridge, MA: Harvard University Press, 1982), 337. In this vein, *Insatiable City* is also inspired by Kyla Wazana Tompkins, *Racial Indigestion: Eating Bodies in the 19th Century* (New York: New York University Press, 2012), esp. 89–122. Also relevant here are Vincent Woodard, *The Delectable Negro: Human Consumption and Homoeroticism within U.S. Slave Culture*, ed. Justin A. Joyce and Dwight A. McBride (New York: New York University Press, 2014); and bell hooks, "Eating the Other: Desire and Resistance," in hooks, *Black Looks: Race and Representation* (Boston, MA: South End Press, 1992), 21–39.

33 My translation. They also inspected the person's "chin hair" to judge whether he was older than he claimed. M. Chambon, *Le Commerce de l'Amérique par Marseille,*

ou Explication des lettres patentes, portant reglement pour le commerce qui se fait de Marseille aux isles Françoise de l'Amérique, données au mois de février 1719. Et des lettres patentes du roi pour la liberté du commerce à la Côte de Guinée, données à Paris au mois de janvier 1716. Avec les reglemens que ledit commerce a occasionnés, par un citadin . . . 2 vols. (Avignon, France: 1764, repr. 1782), 400–401. See also Lauren R. Clay, "'Cruel Necessity': Capitalism, the Discourse of Sympathy, and the Problem of the Slave Trade in the Age of Human Rights," *Slavery and Abolition* 37, no. 2 (2016): 256–83. Cannibalism served as a literary trope and inflammatory rhetorical device in depictions of the slave trade and American and European slavery. Alan Rice, "'Who's Eating Whom': The Discourse of Cannibalism in the Literature of the Black Atlantic from Equiano's *Travels* to Toni Morrison's *Beloved*," *Research in African Literatures* 29, no. 4 (Winter 1998), 107–21; Rafia Zafar, "The Proof of the Pudding: Of Haggis, Hasty Pudding, and Transatlantic Influence," *Early American Literature* 31, no. 2 (1996): 133–49; Homi K. Bhabha, *The Location of Culture* (New York: Routledge, 1994), 118; Johnson, *River of Dark Dreams*, 13; George Fitzhugh, *Cannibals All! Or, Slaves without Masters* (Richmond, VA: A. Morris, 1857); and Frederick Douglass, *Oration, Delivered in Corinthian Hall, Rochester, by Frederick Douglass, July 5th, 1852* (Rochester, NY: Lee, Mann, and Co., 1852). Cannibalism was not confined to the written page or orator's stand. For a historical account of European slave traders cannibalizing enslaved Africans, see Usner, "From African Captivity," 28.

34   Orlando Patterson writes, too, of the response given by an elderly enslaved man to his enslaver, when the latter offered to emancipate him in old age and poor health. "'Master,' the withered slave demurred, 'you eated me when I was meat, and now you must pick me when I am bone.'" The bondsman "understood perfectly the parasitic nature of their interaction," Patterson writes (*Slavery and Social Death*, 338). Henrietta Butler, interviewed in Ronnie W. Clayton, ed., *Mother Wit: The Ex-Slave Narratives of the Louisiana Writers' Project* (New York: Peter Lang, 1990), 38–39. The unequal social dynamics between WPA interviewers and interviewees, which may have prompted incomplete descriptions of enslavement, coupled with edits and deletions of transcripts by WPA editors, have deterred some scholars' use of these interviews. Other thinkers, though, offer compelling ways to interpret these unique sources taking their context into account. Stephanie E. Jones-Rogers, *They Were Her Property: White Women as Slave Owners in the American South* (New Haven, CT: Yale University Press, 2020), xviii–xx; Saidiya V. Hartman, *Scenes of Subjection: Terror, Slavery, and Self-Making in Nineteenth-Century America* (New York: Oxford University Press, 1997), 10–12; and John W. Blassingame, "Reading the Testimony of Slaves: Approaches and Problems," *Journal of Southern History* 41, no. 4 (November 1975): 473–92, at 486.

35   *The Picayune's Guide to New Orleans* (New Orleans, LA: Nicholson and Co., 1896), 34.

36   On the development of a twentieth-century tourism industry that commodified images of Black people on product packaging and souvenirs, see Rebecca Cawood McIntyre, *Souvenirs of the Old South: Northern Tourism and Southern Mythology* (Gainesville: University Press of Florida, 2011); Karen L. Cox, *Dreaming of Dixie: How the South Was Created in American Popular Culture* (Chapel Hill: University of North Carolina Press, 2011); and Maurice M. Manring, *Slave in a Box: The Strange Career of Aunt Jemima* (Charlottesville: University of Virginia Press, 1998).

37   Mrs. W. J. Wright, letter to the editor, *Times-Picayune*, October 11, 1959, 24.

38   On the dynamic of "desire and disaster" in portrayals of Black New Orleanians in the twentieth-century tourism industry, see Thomas, *Desire and Disaster*, 7.

39   When possible, people in this book are identified by their name, place of birth, or nation. Otherwise, people of African and Afro-Caribbean descent are identified as Black, African American, Creole, and people "of color." In chapter 4, the adjective "of color" also describes Choctaw women vendors at the French Market.

40   "Défendons à nos sujets blancs de l'un et l'autre sexe, de contracter mariage avec les Noirs." See Louis XV, *Code noir, ou Édit du Roi, servant de règlement pour le gouvernement et l'administration de la justice, police, discipline et le commerce des esclaves nègres dans la province et colonie de la Loüisianne* (1727), https://archive.org/details /Louisiane1724N8608605/page/n2/mode/2up. See also Judith Kelleher Schafer, *Slavery, the Civil Law, and the Supreme Court of Louisiana* (Baton Rouge: Louisiana State University Press, 1994), 1–2.

41   On race in early New Orleans, see Jennifer M. Spear, *Race, Sex, and Social Order in Early New Orleans* (Baltimore, MD: Johns Hopkins University Press, 2009); Vidal, *Caribbean New Orleans*; and Elizabeth Fussell, "Constructing New Orleans, Constructing Race: A Population History of New Orleans," *Journal of American History* 94, no. 3 (December 2007): 846–55.

42   Schafer, *Slavery, the Civil Law*, 6. Andrew N. Wegmann, *An American Color: Race and Identity in New Orleans and the Atlantic World* (Athens: University of Georgia Press, 2022); Kenneth R. Aslakson, *Making Race in the Courtroom: The Legal Construction of Three Races in Early New Orleans* (New York: New York University Press, 2014); Shirley Elizabeth Thompson, *Exiles at Home: The Struggle to Become American in Creole New Orleans* (Cambridge, MA: Harvard University Press, 2009); and Judith Kelleher Schafer, *Becoming Free, Remaining Free: Manumission and Enslavement in New Orleans* (Baton Rouge: Louisiana State University Press, 2003).

43   As quoted in Virginia R. Domínguez, *White by Definition: Social Classification in Creole Louisiana* (New Brunswick, NJ: Rutgers University Press, 1986), 291. *Le Carillon* was a satirical publication that protested the purported indignities of Reconstruction for white Louisianians. See Bobs M. Tusa, "*Le Carillon*: An English Translation of Selected Satires," *Louisiana History* 35, no. 1 (Winter 1994): 67–84. This directive reflected neither the lived realities of New Orleanians nor the federal government's perspective. Enumerators of the 1870 federal census categorized Americans as white, black, "mulatto," Chinese, or Indian. See *Compendium of the Ninth Census* (Washington, DC: Government Printing Office, 1872). On the challenges posed by Sicilian immigrants to the city's coalescing racial hierarchy, see chapter 4.

44   Henry Louis Gates Jr., *Stony the Road: Reconstruction, White Supremacy, and the Rise of Jim Crow* (New York: Penguin Books, 2019); Grace Elizabeth Hale, *Making Whiteness: The Culture of Segregation in the South, 1890–1940* (New York: Pantheon Books, 1998); Matthew Frye Jacobson, *Whiteness of a Different Color: European Immigrants and the Alchemy of Race* (Cambridge, MA: Harvard University Press, 1998); and David R. Roediger, *The Wages of Whiteness: Race and the Making of the American Working Class* (London: Verso, 1991).

45   Gwendolyn Midlo Hall, "The Formation of Afro-Creole Culture," in *Creole New Orleans: Race and Americanization*, ed. Arnold R. Hirsch and Joseph Logsdon (Baton Rouge: Louisiana State University Press, 1992), 58–87, at 60. See also Charles Stewart, ed., *Creolization: History, Ethnography, Theory* (Walnut Creek, CA: Left Coast Press, 2007); and Harris, *Beyond Gumbo*.

46 Shirley Elizabeth Thompson writes, "The term *Creole* displayed an impressive elasticity, taking on a variety of forms to fit a range of individual and communal needs" (*Exiles at Home*, 9). On the changing definitions of "Creole" throughout Louisiana history, see Carl A. Brasseaux, *French, Cajun, Creole, Houma: A Primer on Francophone Louisiana* (Baton Rouge: Louisiana State University Press, 2005); Sybil Kein, ed., *Creole: The History and Legacy of Louisiana's Free People of Color* (Baton Rouge: Louisiana State University Press, 2000); Hirsh and Logsdon, eds., *Creole New Orleans*; Hall, *Africans in Colonial Louisiana*; Domínguez, *White by Definition*; and Campanella, *Bienville's Dilemma*, 163–66.

47 For an example of this exclusionary rhetoric, see James S. Zacharie, *New Orleans Guide with Descriptions of the Routes to New Orleans, Sights of the City Arranged Alphabetically, and Other Information Useful to Travelers; also, Outlines of the History of Louisiana* (New Orleans: F. F. Hansell and Bro., Ltd., 1893). This history is explored in chapters 4 and 5.

48 "Hotel et Restaurant de Louisiane," *North and South*, January 1902, 7.

49 Enoc P. Waters, "Color Lines Blurred in Strange New Orleans, City of Contrasts," *Chicago Defender*, March 20, 1943.

50 Molly Moore, "Cooking to Beat the Band," *Washington Post*, November 27, 1978. Hundreds of Black and white counter-protestors outnumbered the roughly eighty-five KKK members. "New Orleans Klan Rallies Early, Missing Irate Blacks: National Director Present," *New York Times*, November 27, 1978, A16; "Klan Rally Gets Police Protection," *Chicago Tribune*, November 27, 1978, 3. Creole scholar Sybil Kein writes, "Creoles are the New World's people, and, given the known historical data, the term should not exclude anyone based on color, caste, or pigmentation." See Kein, "Introduction," in *Creole*, ed. Kein, xv. Similarly, geographer Richard Campanella writes, "New Orleans is the only American city that can reasonably claim to have rendered its own ethnicity. Creole is a place-based ethnicity" (*Bienville's Dilemma*, 161).

51 Jeffery U. Darensbourg, ed., *Bulbancha Is Still a Place: Indigenous Culture from New Orleans: The Language Issue* (Bulbancha, LA: POC Zine Project, 2019).

52 Tiya Miles argues for "the immeasurable value of material culture to the histories of the marginalized" in *All That She Carried: The Journey of Ashley's Sack, a Black Family Keepsake* (New York: Random House, 2021), 4.

53 Emphasis in original. Saidiya V. Hartman described her search for "the subaltern" in archival sources as archaeological: "The effort to 'brush history against the grain' requires excavations at the margins of monumental history in order that the ruins of the dismembered past be retrieved" (*Scenes of Subjection*, 10); Marisa J. Fuentes, *Dispossessed Lives: Enslaved Women, Violence, and the Archive* (Philadelphia: University of Pennsylvania Press, 2018), 7.

54 Saidiya V. Hartman, *Wayward Lives, Beautiful Experiments: Intimate Histories of Social Upheaval* (New York: W. W. Norton, 2019), 360–61. With similar methodological approaches, see Jessica Marie Johnson, *Wicked Flesh: Black Women, Intimacy, and Freedom in the Atlantic World* (Philadelphia: University of Pennsylvania Press, 2020); Fuentes, *Dispossessed Lives*; and Rashauna Johnson, *Slavery's Metropolis: Unfree Labor in New Orleans during the Age of Revolutions* (New York: Cambridge University Press, 2016).

55 Miles, *All That She Carried*, 36. Similarly, in his study of the visual culture of Atlantic slavery and emancipation, Marcus Wood writes, "I had no idea of the ingenuity, and frequently the poisonous beauty, with which the memory of slavery was lov-

ingly repainted by the dominant cultures of the slave diaspora. In the natural world venomous things frequently advertise their nature with a flamboyant beauty, and then nonvenomous things copy them." See Marcus Wood, *The Horrible Gift of Freedom: Atlantic Slavery and the Representation of Emancipation* (Athens: University of Georgia Press, 2010).

56 These are, in the words of Christina Sharpe, "the continuous and changing present of slavery's as yet unresolved unfolding" (*In the Wake*, 13–14). On uncomfortable histories of Southern food and calls to "correct the excesses of southern food fetishism," as Elizabeth S. Engelhardt writes, see Kim Severson, "A Powerful, and Provocative, Voice for Southern Food," *New York Times*, May 9, 2017; John T. Edge and Tunde Wey, "Who Owns Southern Food?," *Oxford American*, June 3, 2016, https://main.oxfordamerican.org/magazine/item/870-who-owns-southern-food; Elizabeth S. D. Engelhardt, "Beyond Grits and Gravy: Appalachian Chicken and Waffles: Countering Southern Food Fetishism," *Southern Cultures* 21, no. 1 (Spring 2015): 73–83; and Patricia Yaeger, "Edible Labor," *Southern Quarterly* 30, nos. 2–3, (Winter/Spring 1992): 150–59.

Chapter One

1 Newton, "What a 'Looker-On' Saw in New Orleans," *Platteville* (WI) *American*, repr. *Milwaukee Daily Sentinel*, February 16, 1855.

2 Federal population censuses counted 3,205,000 enslaved people in the United States in 1850 and 3,954,000 in 1860. Laurence J. Kotlikoff estimated that more than 135,000 enslaved people were sold in New Orleans between 1804 and 1862. The US census counted 244,809 enslaved people in Louisiana in 1850 and 331,726 in 1860. See Claudia Dale Goldin, *Urban Slavery in the American South, 1820–1860: A Quantitative History* (Chicago: University of Chicago Press, 1976), 67; Laurence J. Kotlikoff, "The Structure of Slave Sale Prices in New Orleans, 1804 to 1862," *Economic Inquiry* 17 (October 1979): 496–518, at 497, 512; *Seventh Census of the United States* (Washington, DC: Robert Armstrong, 1853), 473; *Eighth Census of the United States* (Washington, DC: Government Printing Office, 1864), 194.

3 Sampling the prices paid at New Orleans slave auctions between 1804 and 1862, Kotlikoff calculated the mean sale price for an enslaved male field hand in 1855 to be about $1,150. Enslaved women household laborers tended to sell at a 5 percent premium, placing the mean price for a cook such as Harriet around $1,200 ("Structure of Slave Sale Prices," 498, 504). Christine McKittrick writes, "This is where historic blackness comes from: the list, the breathless numbers, the absolutely economic, the mathematics of the unliving" ("Mathematics Black Life," *Black Scholar* 44, no. 2 [Summer 2014]: 16–28, at 17).

4 Emphasis in original. Newton, "What a 'Looker-On.'"

5 Histories of New Orleans's prominent, public slave trade include Walter Johnson, *Soul by Soul: Life inside the Antebellum Slave Market* (Cambridge, MA: Harvard University Press, 1999); Maurie D. McInnis, "Mapping the Slave Trade in Richmond and New Orleans," *Buildings and Landscapes* 20, no. 2 (Fall 2013): 102–24; Walter Johnson, *River of Dark Dreams: Slavery and Empire in the Cotton Kingdom* (Cambridge, MA: Belknap Press, 2013); THNOC, *Purchased Lives: New Orleans and the Domestic Slave Trade, 1898–1865,* online exhibition, accessed September 8, 2020, https://www.THNOC.org/virtual/purchased-lives; Richard Campanella, "On the Structural Basis of Social Memory: Cityscapes of the New Orleans Slave

Trade, Part I," *Preservation in Print* (March 2013): 16–17; Richard Campanella, "On the Structural Basis of Social Memory: Cityscapes of the New Orleans Slave Trade, Part II," *Preservation in Print* (April 2013): 18–19; Steven Deyle, *Carry Me Back: The Domestic Slave Trade in American Life* (Oxford: Oxford University Press, 2005); Richard Tansey, "Bernard Kendig and the New Orleans Slave Trade," *Louisiana History* 23, no. 2 (Spring 1982): 159–78; and Judith Kelleher Schafer, "New Orleans Slavery in 1850 as Seen in Advertisements," *Journal of Southern History* 47, no. 1 (February 1981): 33–56.

6 J. S. Buckingham, *The Slave States of America*, vol. 1 (London: Fisher, Son and Co., 1842), 340. Saidiya Hartman, too, finds the sensory pleasures and titillations of antebellum slave auctions as intrinsic to the business at hand, writing, "The stimulating effects of intoxicants, the simulation of good times, and the to-and-fro of half-naked bodies on display all acted to incite the flow of capital." See Saidiya V. Hartman, *Scenes of Subjection: Terror, Slavery, and Self-Making in Nineteenth-Century America* (New York: Oxford University Press, 1997), 38.

7 "An Account of Louisiana, Being an Abstract of Documents in the Offices of the Departments of State and of the Treasury," *National Intelligencer and Washington Advertiser*, November 16, 1803.

8 "An Account of Louisiana. (Continued.)," *National Intelligencer*, November 18, 1803.

9 A. Peace-Maker, "To the Senate of the United States," *National Intelligencer*, October 24, 1803. Disease and warfare had reduced the populations of Native nations in the region, but Americans would impose further harm and forced removal in the nineteenth century. See Daniel H. Usner Jr., *American Indians in Early New Orleans: From Calumet to Raquette* (Baton Rouge: Louisiana State University Press, 2018); and F. Todd Smith, *Louisiana and the Gulf South Frontier, 1500–1821* (Baton Rouge: Louisiana State University Press, 2014).

10 "The subscriber Has Received," *Louisiana Gazette*, June 23, 1807.

11 "Sheriff's Sale"; "For Sale"; "A Plantation for Sale"; "Negroes for Sale," *Louisiana Gazette*, June 23, 1807.

12 Gwendolyn Midlo Hall, *Africans in Colonial Louisiana: The Development of Afro-Creole Culture in the Eighteenth Century* (Baton Rouge: Louisiana State University Press, 1992), 11, 29–35, 41–43. For histories of slavery and freedom in New Orleans under colonial and early American governance, see Alejandro de la Fuente and Ariela J. Gross, *Becoming Free, Becoming Black: Race, Freedom, and Law in Cuba, Virginia, and Louisiana* (Cambridge: Cambridge University Press, 2020); Jessica Marie Johnson, *Wicked Flesh: Black Women, Intimacy, and Freedom in the Atlantic World* (Philadelphia: University of Pennsylvania Press, 2020); Cécile Vidal, *Caribbean New Orleans: Empire, Race, and the Making of a Slave Society* (Williamsburg, VA and Chapel Hill, NC: Omohundro Institute of Early American History and Culture and the University of North Carolina Press, 2019); Rashauna Johnson, *Slavery's Metropolis: Unfree Labor in New Orleans during the Age of Revolutions* (New York: Cambridge University Press, 2016); Jennifer M. Spear, *Race, Sex, and Social Order in Early New Orleans* (Baltimore, MD: Johns Hopkins University Press, 2009); Brett Rushforth, *Bonds of Alliance: Indigenous and Atlantic Slaveries in New France* (Chapel Hill: University of North Carolina Press, for the Omohundro Institute of Early American History and Culture, 2012); and Thomas N. Ingersoll, *Mammon and Manon in Early New Orleans: The First Slave Society in the Deep South, 1718–1819* (Knoxville: University of Tennessee Press, 1999).

13 During the first few decades of the eighteenth century, most enslaved Africans

brought to Louisiana were abducted from Senegambia and the Bight of Benin. Eltis and Richardson estimate the total number of captives taken from Africa and brought to the Gulf Coast between 1719 and 1866 to have been twenty-two thousand, with an additional four thousand dying en route. European and American traders brought eight and a half times as many African captives to Charleston, South Carolina, and six times as many to the Chesapeake. Even these terrible numbers were dwarfed by the nearly five million Africans abducted and brought to Brazil and more than one million brought to Jamaica, within a total number of nearly eleven million Africans abducted and brought to the Americas between 1501 and 1867. See Ingersoll, *Mammon and Manon*, 11; *Seventh Census of the United States* (1853), ix; David Eltis and David Richardson, *Atlas of the Transatlantic Slave Trade* (New Haven, CT: Yale University Press, 2010), 220, 216, 212, 257, 234, 204; Thomas N. Ingersoll, "The Slave Trade and the Ethnic Diversity of Louisiana's Slave Community," *Louisiana History* 37, no. 2 (Spring 1996): 133–61.

14 The 1811 New Orleans directory reported 24,552 people living in Orleans Parish, comprised of 10,824 enslaved people, 8,001 whites, and 5,727 free people of color. See Thomas H. Whitney, *Whitney's New-Orleans Directory, and Louisiana & Mississippi Almanac for the Year 1811* (New Orleans, LA: Thomas H. Whitney, 1810).

15 In the *Gazette* of July 11, 1809, Thomas advertised "60 Hhds. Country sugar of excellent quality, An excellent Negro Woman, And a Boy a good house servant tolerable Cook." Abolitionist Ebenezer Davies was horrified by the volume of runaway ads published in New Orleans newspapers, writing, "Runaway slaves seems to be constantly advertised. . . . Human chattels assuming their natural right to go where they please are advertised with a woodcut representing them as bending forward in the act of running . . . a pitiable figure!" Marcus Wood argues that runaway ads can be read as abbreviated, urgent biographies: "a grim, minimal, and deeply moving set of micro narratives articulating the price of freedom." See Ebenezer Davies, *American Scenes, and Christian Slavery: A Recent Tour of Four Thousand Miles in the United States* (London: John Snow, 1849), 11; Marcus Wood, *The Horrible Gift of Freedom: Atlantic Slavery and the Representation of Emancipation* (Athens: University of Georgia Press, 2010), 133–34. See also Viola Franziska Müller, *Escape to the City: Fugitive Slaves in the Antebellum Urban South* (Chapel Hill: University of North Carolina Press, 2022); and S. Charles Bolton, *Fugitivism: Escaping Slavery in the Lower Mississippi Valley* (Fayetteville: University of Arkansas Press, 2019).

16 On the rise of American sugar and cotton and territorial expansion of the United States, see Calvin Schermerhorn, *The Business of Slavery and the Rise of American Capitalism, 1815–1860* (New Haven, CT: Yale University Press, 2015); Edward E. Baptist, *The Half Has Never Been Told: Slavery and the Making of American Capitalism* (New York: Basic Books, 2014); Sven Beckert, *Empire of Cotton: A Global History* (New York: Alfred A. Knopf, 2014); Adam Rothman, *Slave Country: American Expansion and the Origins of the Deep South* (Cambridge, MA: Harvard University Press, 2005); and Johnson, *River of Dark Dreams*.

17 On the development of the map pictured in figure 1.2, see Laura Kilcer VanHuss, *Charting the Plantation Landscape from Natchez to New Orleans* (Baton Rouge: Louisiana State University Press, 2021).

18 The physically excruciating nature of sugarcane production in particular prompted extraordinary demand in Louisiana for enslaved men, such that the state's enslaved population developed unique demographics. See Michael Tadman, *Speculators and Slaves: Masters, Traders, and Slaves in the Old South* (Madison: University of Wis-

consin Press, 1989), 64–71. See also Richard Follett, *The Sugar Masters: Planters and Slaves in Louisiana's Cane World, 1820–1860* (Baton Rouge: Louisiana State University Press, 2005); Robert H. Gudmestad, *A Troublesome Commerce: The Transformation of the Interstate Slave Trade* (Baton Rouge: Louisiana State University Press, 2003); Deyle, *Carry Me Back*; and Walter Johnson, ed., *The Chattel Principle: Internal Slave Trades in the Americas* (New Haven, CT: Yale University Press, 2004). See also chapter 3.

19 In 1850, the nation's most valuable agricultural products were Indian corn (valued at almost $300 million), wheat ($100 million), and cotton ($98.6 million). See Tench Coxe, *A Statement of the Arts and Manufactures of the United States of America, for the Year 1810* (Philadelphia, PA: A. Cornman, 1814), 154–58; Superintendent of the Census, *Report of the Superintendent of the Census for December 1, 1852* (Washington, DC: Robert Armstrong, 1853), 67, 82, 96–97, 176.

20 Virginia, Maryland, Kentucky, Delaware, Missouri, and the District of Columbia constituted the Upper South; the Lower South consisted of North Carolina, South Carolina, Tennessee, Georgia, Florida, Alabama, Mississippi, Louisiana, Arkansas, and Texas (Deyle, *Carry Me Back*, fn. 2, 298). Previous generations of historians debated the scale of the domestic slave trade with quantitative and qualitative methods. Contemporary scholars agree that earlier assessments undercounted the number of bondspeople moved to the Lower South. See Joshua D. Rothman, *The Ledger and the Chain: How Domestic Slave Traders Shaped America* (New York: Basic Books, 2021); Schermerhorn, *Business of Slavery*; Deyle, *Carry Me Back*, esp. 283–96; Johnson, *Soul by Soul*; Johnson, *Chattel Principle*; Gudmestad, *Troublesome Commerce*; Tadman, *Speculators and Slaves*; and Frederic Bancroft, *Slave-Trading in the Old South* (Baltimore, MD: J. H. Furst, 1931).

21 Jacob Stroyer, *My Life in the South* (Salem, MA: Salem Observer Book and Job Print, 1885), 42–44.

22 Kotlikoff, "Structure of Slave Sale Prices," 497. In 1850, the New Orleans population was 116,375, and in 1860 it was 168,785. Richard C. Wade, *Slavery in the Cities: The South, 1820–1860* (New York: Oxford University Press, 1964), 326.

23 More than thirty thousand of these notices are accessible thanks to the free database "Freedom on the Move," which digitizes "runaway ads" printed in newspapers throughout the United States, making them text searchable for the researcher. See Freedom on the Move Project, accessed August 12, 2021, app.freedomonthemove .org.

24 On European colonization and the growth of early New Orleans, see Lawrence N. Powell, *The Accidental City: Improvising New Orleans* (Cambridge, MA: Harvard University Press, 2012); Richard Campanella, *Bienville's Dilemma: A Historical Geography of New Orleans* (Lafayette: Center for Louisiana Studies, University of Louisiana at Lafayette, 2008); Elizabeth Fussell, "Constructing New Orleans, Constructing Race: A Population History of New Orleans," *Journal of American History* 94, no. 3 (December 2007): 846–55; Spear, *Race, Sex, and Social Order*; and "Peoples & Places," Center for Louisiana Studies, University of Louisiana at Lafayette, accessed August 12, 2021, https://louisianastudies.louisiana.edu/programming -special-projects/louisiana-101/peoples-places.

25 In 1804, revolutionary Jean-Jacques Dessalines announced the nation of Haiti, discarding the French colonial name of Saint-Domingue. Rebecca J. Scott, "Paper Thin: Freedom and Re-Enslavement in the Diaspora of the Haitian Revolution," *Law and History Review* 29, no. 4 (November 2011): 1061–87; Nathalie Dessens, *From*

Saint-Domingue to New Orleans: Migration and Influences (Gainesville: University Press of Florida, 2007); Carl A. Brasseaux and Glenn R. Conrad, eds., *The Road to Louisiana: The Saint-Domingue Refugees, 1792–1809* (Lafayette: Center for Louisiana Studies, University of Louisiana at Lafayette, 1992); and Johnson, *River of Dark Dreams*, 24–54.

26   The Mississippi River's curves make cardinal directions less helpful in orienting oneself in New Orleans. Accordingly, residents have long relied on alternative descriptors, rooted in one's positional relation to the river. Instructions to proceed "upriver" or "downriver" assume an understanding of "the flow direction of the river," writes geographer Richard Campanella. Major avenues—Poydras Street, Canal Street, Esplanade Avenue—divide the city into wedges; destinations may be "above" or "below" these references. "Lakeside" and "riverside" offer additional means to characterize a destination's proximity to Lake Pontchartrain or the Mississippi (*Bienville's Dilemma*, 289–93).

27   Justin A. Nystrom, *Creole Italian: Sicilian Immigrants and the Shaping of New Orleans Food Culture* (Athens: University of Georgia Press, 2018); Laura D. Kelley, *The Irish in New Orleans* (Lafayette: University of Louisiana at Lafayette, 2014); Center for Louisiana Studies, "Peoples & Places"; and Brian M. McGowan, "The Second Battle of New Orleans: The Crescent City and the Anglo 'Invasion' of 1846," *Louisiana History* 51, no. 1 (Winter 2010): 27–40.

28   Advertisement, "Hotel of the Marine and of the Colonies," in *The New-Orleans Annual Advertiser for 1832, Annexed to the City Directory* (New Orleans, LA: Stephen E. Percy and Co., 1832).

29   *Eighth Census of the United States* (1864), 196; Goldin, *Urban Slavery*, 52.

30   Louis Hughes, *Thirty Years a Slave: From Bondage to Freedom: The Institution of Slavery as Seen on the Plantation and in the Home of the Planter* (Milwaukee, WI: South Side Printing Company, 1897), 68.

31   A. Oakey Hall, *The Manhattaner in New Orleans; or, Phases of "Crescent City" Life* (New York: J. S. Redfield, Clinton Hall, 1851), 16.

32   Emphasis in original. Mrs. [Matilda Charlotte] Houston, *Texas and the Gulf of Mexico: Or, Yachting in the New World*, vol. 1 (London: John Murray, Albemarle Street, 1844), 158–59.

33   "AVIS," *Le Moniteur*, September 26, 1807.

34   Whitney, *Whitney's New-Orleans Directory* (1811). The city's restaurant culture had yet to develop. The 1822 city directory listed one "Cook shop/Restaurateur," operated by Manuel Espinosa at 3 Condé (later, Chartres), below St. Ann, close to the Place d'Armes and St. Louis Cathedral. The 1832 directory listed one restaurant, a "French restaurant" operated by Cheri Bessy at 73 Chartres. By 1842, the directory listed 33 restaurants. See John Adems Paxton, *New-Orleans Directory and Register* (New Orleans, LA: John Adems Paxton, 1822); *New-Orleans Annual Advertiser* (1832); and *New Orleans Directory for 1842, Comprising the Names, Residences, and Occupations of the Merchants, Business Men, Professional Gentlemen and Citizens of New Orleans, Lafayette, Algiers and Gretna. Two Volumes in One* (New Orleans, LA: Pitts and Clarke, 1842).

35   Samuel Wilson Jr., "Maspero's Exchange: Its Predecessors and Successors," *Louisiana History* 30, no. 2 (Spring 1989): 191–220.

36   Henry C. Castellanos, *New Orleans as It Was: Episodes of Louisiana Life*, ed. George F. Reinecke (Baton Rouge: Louisiana State University Press, 1895, repr. 1978), 144.

37   For histories of the early New Orleans cityscape, see Dell Upton, *Another City: Ur-*

ban Life and Urban Spaces in the New American Republic (New Haven, CT: Yale University Press, 2008); Powell, *Accidental City*; Campanella, *Bienville's Dilemma*; Johnson, *Slavery's Metropolis*; and Liliane Crété, *Daily Life in Louisiana, 1815–1830*, trans. Patrick Gregory (Baton Rouge: Louisiana State University Press, 1981).

38 In New Orleans during this era, a person judged to be a "quarteroon" or "quadroon" was said to have one Black grandparent, that is, to be of one quarter African descent. A "mulatto" was judged to have one Black parent and be of one-half African descent. On the history of this racist mathematics, see Spear, *Race, Sex, and Social Order*, esp. 97–98; Benjamin Henry Boneval Latrobe, diary entry dated January 12, 1819, in Latrobe, *Impressions Respecting New Orleans: Diary and Sketches 1818–1820*, ed. Samuel Wilson Jr. (New York: Columbia University, 1951), 22. On the "racial-commercial-sexual-sublime" on display at the New Orleans levee, see Johnson, *River of Dark Dreams*, 80–81. See also chapter 3.

39 Bernhard, Duke of Saxe-Weimar Eisenach, *Travels through North America, during the Years 1825 and 1826*, vol. 2 (Philadelphia, PA: Carey, Lea and Carey, 1828), 55.

40 Mary Harris, interviewed in Ronnie W. Clayton, ed., *Mother Wit: The Ex-Slave Narratives of the Louisiana Writers' Project* (New York: Peter Lang, 1990), 94–95. Works Progress Administration (WPA) organizers instructed interviewers to attempt to replicate the dialect of interviewees when they transcribed their conversations. In the process, though, WPA interviewers flattened and erased regional distinctions. See Lauren Tilton, "Race and Place: Dialect and the Construction of Southern Identity in the Ex-Slave Narratives," *Current Research in Digital History* 2 (August 2019), https://doi.org/10.31835/crdh.2019.14.

41 Bernhard, *Travels through North America*, 64, 55, 70. Dining happened in less luxurious settings, too. For a description of a boardinghouse meal, see G. W. Featherstonhaugh, *Excursion through the Slave States, from Washington on the Potomac to the Frontier of Mexico; with Sketches of Popular Manners and Geological Notices*, vol. 1 (New York: Harper and Brothers, 1844), 140.

42 Eliza Ripley, *Social Life in Old New Orleans: Being Recollections of My Girlhood* (New York: Arno Press, 1912, repr. 1975), 43, 44, 212, 213.

43 Scholars have examined the gendered violence of the "fancy trade" in New Orleans, in which enslavers bought and sold women for sexual slavery. Given that women predominated among enslaved cooks and domestic service staff, violence in the kitchen was gendered, too. As explored in chapter 3, the torturous labor of Louisiana sugar production exacted its own gendered toll on the overwhelmingly male workforce of sugar. Thus, Louisiana's food system abused men and women alike, albeit in segregated, gendered settings. Such violence was not confined to antebellum decades. In 1930, a New Orleans police officer shot and killed Hattie McCray, a fourteen-year-old Black girl, in the kitchen of the restaurant where she was working, because McCray had refused his advances. The officer was convicted of her murder but avoided the death penalty when the judge declared him insane. See Frederick Douglass, "Love of God, Love of Man, Love of Country: An Address Delivered in Syracuse, New York, on September 24, 1847," *National Anti-Slavery Standard*, October 28, 1847, archived online at the Frederick Douglass Papers Project, https://frederickdouglasspapersproject.com/item/10276. On the fancy trade, see Edward Baptist, "'Cuffy,' 'Fancy Maids,' and 'One-Eyed Men': Rape, Commodification, and the Domestic Slave Trade in the United States," in *Chattel Principle*, ed. Johnson, 165–202. On the eroticization of "quadroon" women in literature and popular culture, see Emily Clark, *The Strange History of the American Quadroon: Free Women*

of Color in the Revolutionary Atlantic World (Chapel Hill: University of North Carolina Press, 2013). See also "White Policeman, Girl Killer, Declared Insane," *Chicago Defender*, June 28, 1930, 2.

44 Deborah Gray White, *Ar'n't I a Woman? Female Slaves in the Plantation South* (New York: W. W. Norton, 1985), 129. On the culinary work of enslaved Americans, see Kelley Fanto Deetz, *Bound to the Fire: How Virginia's Enslaved Cooks Helped Invent American Cuisine* (Lexington: University Press of Kentucky, 2017); Michael W. Twitty, *The Cooking Gene: A Journey through African American Culinary History in the Old South* (New York: Amistad, 2017); Jessica B. Harris, *High on the Hog: A Culinary Journey from Africa to America* (New York: Bloomsbury, 2011); Frederick Douglass Opie, *Hog and Hominy: Soul Food from Africa to America* (New York: Columbia University Press, 2008); and Rebecca Sharpless, *Cooking in Other Women's Kitchens: Domestic Workers in the South, 1865–1960* (Chapel Hill: University of North Carolina Press, 2010), 1–6.

45 Hite remembered her mother selling corn to their enslaver for fifty cents per barrel. She used the money to buy silk dresses. "Never did save money," Hite explained. "We used to play wid it" (Elizabeth Ross Hite, interviewed in Clayton, ed., *Mother Wit*, 102). Israel Campbell, who was enslaved on several Louisiana plantations, remembered enslavers using vegetable gardens as a means of manipulating bondspeople. He described the gardens as "an indulgence with which overseers sometimes stimulate[d] their best slaves" (*An Autobiography. Bond and Free: or, Yearnings for Freedom, from My Green Brier House. Being the Story of My Life in Bondage, and My Life in Freedom* [Philadelphia, PA: Israel Campbell, 1861], 317, 314). On African ingredients and cooking techniques among enslaved people, see Ibrahima Seck, *Bouki Fait Gombo: A History of the Slave Community of Habitation Haydel (Whitney Plantation) Louisiana, 1750–1860* (New Orleans: University of New Orleans Press, 2014), 119–29.

46 Campbell, *Autobiography*, 318–19.

47 References to hunger appear throughout the published narratives of formerly enslaved people, WPA interviews, and other texts. Some of the most devastating describe the mothers of newborns who were so exhausted by their work and undernourished by poor rations that they could not sustain their infants. For other descriptions of hunger among bondspeople, see Herbert C. Covey and Dwight Eisnach, eds., *What the Slaves Ate: Recollections of African American Foods and Foodways from the Slave Narratives* (Westport, CT: Greenwood, 2009); White, *Ar'n't I a Woman?*, 155; and John W. Blassingame, ed., *Slave Testimony: Two Centuries of Letters, Speeches, Interviews, and Autobiographies* (Baton Rouge: Louisiana State University Press, 1977).

48 Joseph Holt Ingraham, *The South-West, by a Yankee*, vol. 1 (New York: Harper and Brothers, 1835), 115.

49 Houston, *Texas and the Gulf of Mexico*, 151–52. Many antebellum visitors commented on the confusion of pleasure and profit in the city. "Although the commercial transactions of New Orleans since the increased cultivation of cotton had risen to a great amount," one local told a traveler during the winter of 1834–1835, "yet he believed that gambling was the principal branch of business carried on" (Featherstonhaugh, *Excursion through the Slave States*, 264). See also Frances Milton Trollope, *Domestic Manners of the Americans*, vol. 2, 4th ed. (London: Printed for Whittaker, Treacher, 1832), 136–37.

50 Hall, *Manhattaner*, 23–24, 33. As early as 1819, Benjamin Latrobe perceived that the

compressed nature of New Orleans's business season was responsible for the crazed speed of commerce there. "The Americans, coming [to New Orleans] to make money, & considering their residence as temporary, are doubly active in availing themselves of the enlarged opportunities of becoming wealthy which the place offers," he wrote on January 22, 1819. Travelers' frenzied behaviors at the table and the bar followed suit (*Impressions*, 32).

51 On the history of yellow fever in New Orleans, see Kathryn Olivarius, *Necropolis: Disease, Power, and Capitalism in the Cotton Kingdom* (Cambridge, MA: Harvard University Press, 2022); Benjamin H. Trask, *Fearful Ravages: Yellow Fever in New Orleans, 1796–1905* (Lafayette: Center for Louisiana Studies, University of Louisiana at Lafayette, 2005); Jo Ann Carrigan, *The Saffron Scourge: A History of Yellow Fever in Louisiana, 1796–1905* (Lafayette: University of Louisiana at Lafayette Press, 1994); and George Augustin, *History of Yellow Fever* (New Orleans, LA: Searcy and Pfaff, 1909).

52 Paxton, *New-Orleans Directory* (1822), 42. B. M. Norman described these part-year residents as "migratory citizens, who live at the hotels and boarding houses, [and] embrace nearly . . . one half the business men of the city" (*Norman's New Orleans and Environs: Containing a Brief Historical Sketch of the Territory and State of Louisiana, and the City of New Orleans, from the Earliest Period to the Present Time: Presenting a Complete Guide to All Subjects of General Interest in the Southern Metropolis; with a Correct and Improved Plan of the City, Pictorial Illustrations of Public Buildings, Etc.* [New Orleans, LA: B. M. Norman, 1845], 76). Buckingham divided these seasonal visitors into three groups: those seeking "health and pleasure," those conducting business, and those seeking to profit off the first two groups via "speculation, gambling, and fraud" (*Slave States*, 343, 347).

53 Lewis Webb, diary entry dated May 18, 1853, L. H. Webb diaries, 1853, record group 49 (hereafter Webb), Louisiana State Museum, New Orleans (hereafter LSM). On the 1853 epidemic, see New Orleans Sanitary Commission, *Report of the Sanitary Commission of New Orleans on the Epidemic Yellow Fever of 1853* (New Orleans: Picayune, 1854), and Erasmus Darwin Fenner, *History of the Epidemic Yellow Fever at New Orleans, La., in 1853* (New York: Hall, Clayton, 1854).

54 Brian William Cowan, *The Social Life of Coffee: The Emergence of the British Coffeehouse* (New Haven, CT: Yale University Press, 2005), 132–35, 126; Campanella, "On the Structural Basis . . . Part I"; "Exchange Coffee House," *Louisiana Gazette*, August 19, 1806. See also Christine Sismondo, *America Walks into a Bar: A Spirited History of Taverns and Saloons, Speakeasies and Grog Shops* (New York: Oxford University Press, 2011); and Wilson, "Maspero's Exchange."

55 J. Passmore Edwards, *Uncle Tom's Companions: Or, Facts Stranger Than Fiction. A Supplement to Uncle Tom's Cabin: Being Startling Incidents in the Lives of Celebrated Fugitive Slaves* (London: Edwards and Co., 1852), 99.

56 Cowan, *Social Life*; Markman Ellis, *The Coffee House: A Cultural History* (London: Weidenfeld and Nicolson, 2004), 180–84; and Brian William Cowan, "New Worlds, New Tastes: Food Fashions after the Renaissance," in *Food: The History of Taste*, ed. Paul Freedman (Berkeley: University of California Press, 2007), 196–231.

57 On February 19, 1808, the firm Hillen and Wederstrandt announced in the *Louisiana Gazette*, "Just landed & for sale, about 80,000 lbs. first quality Green COFFEE" ("COFFEE," *Louisiana Gazette*, February 19, 1808). On the history of coffee imports in New Orleans, see Thomas E. Redard, "The Port of New Orleans: An Economic History, 1821–1860" (PhD diss., Louisiana State University, 1985),

https://digitalcommons.lsu.edu/gradschool_disstheses/4151/; Ryen Stevens, "Caffeinating the Port of New Orleans," Loyola University New Orleans Documentary and Oral History Studio, December 19, 2019, https://docstudio.org/2019/12/19/caffeinating-the-port-of-new-orleans/. New Orleans continues to serve as a major site for importing, roasting, and grinding coffee beans for American consumers. Folgers, which claimed more than double the 2020 market share of ground coffee in the United States compared to Starbucks, its next highest competitor, roasts its coffee in New Orleans (Louisiana State Museum, "Coffee Trade and Port of New Orleans," online exhibit, accessed October 30, 2020, http://www.crt.state.la.us/louisiana-state-museum/online-exhibits/coffee-trade-and-port-of-new-orleans/index; "Where We Roast: New Orleans, LA," Folgers Coffee, accessed January 13, 2023, https://www.folgerscoffee.com/our-story/where-we-roast; "Market Share of Ground Coffee in the United States in 2020, by Leading Brands," Statista, accessed January 13, 2023, https://www.statista.com/statistics/451969/market-share-of-ground-coffee-in-the-us-by-leading-brand/).

58 Edward Russell, entry dated January 27, 1835, in travel journal and transcript, 1834–1835, MSS 424.2 (hereafter Russell travel journal), THNOC.

59 Judah P. Benjamin to Samuel L. M. Barlow, April 28, 1855, MSS 33.1, THNOC.

60 John Gibson, Gibson's Guide and Directory of the State of Louisiana, and the Cities of New Orleans and Lafayette (New Orleans, LA: John Gibson, 1838), 320–21.

61 New Orleans Directory for 1842 (1842).

62 Whitney, Whitney's New-Orleans Directory (1811); Paxton, New-Orleans Directory (1822); New-Orleans Annual Advertiser (1832); and New Orleans Directory for 1842 (1842). This count of coffeehouses is approximate. Conflicting spellings of a proprietor's name can cause a single establishment to appear twice in the same directory. Multiple proprietors for one business can prompt that business to be listed more than once. Furthermore, the publishers of the 1842 directory admitted, "The various languages spoken in the city . . . open many avenues to mistake and omission" (introduction, New Orleans Directory for 1842 [1842]).

63 For example, M. Clifford operated a coffeehouse at the corner of New Levee near the St. Mary Market in 1832. In 1842, Jean Bisa operated a coffeehouse situated at the Red Stores, "between the two markets," a reference to the French Market. New-Orleans Annual Advertiser (1832); New Orleans Directory for 1842 (1842).

64 New Orleans Directory for 1842 (1842).

65 Weekly Delta, May 29, 1852, as quoted in Robert C. Reinders, End of an Era: New Orleans: 1850–1860 (New Orleans, LA: Pelican Publishing Company, 1964); Ingraham, South-West, 113, 114. Here, too, New Orleans coffeehouses departed from their British counterparts, which had developed as venues that offered stimulation without intoxication (see Cowan, Social Life, 44–45, 159–61).

66 English writer Frances Milton Trollope characterized excessive drinking as a problem driven by American men and often divorced from dining. "By a strange contradiction, in the country where hard drinking is more prevalent than in any other, there is less wine taken at dinner," she observed of her American meals. "Ladies rarely exceed one glass, and the great majority of females never take any. In fact, the hard drinking, so universally acknowledged, does not take place at jovial dinners, but . . . in solitary dram-drinking" (Domestic Manners, vol. 2, 132). See also Buckingham, Slave States, 299; and Houston, Texas and the Gulf of Mexico, 144–45.

67 Editor, Natchez Daily Courier, "The City of New Orleans," printed in Boston Weekly Messenger, July 28, 1836, 4.

68   Houston, *Texas and the Gulf of Mexico*, 145.

69   In 1806, the Louisiana legislature prohibited enslaved people and "Indian[s]" from
      purchasing alcohol and punished anyone who gave or sold alcohol to them. See Sec-
      tions 3 and 4, "An Act to Regulate Inns and Other Houses of Entertainment," May 21,
      1806; and Section 24, "Black Code: An Act Prescribing the Rules and Conduct to Be
      Observed with Respect to Negroes and Other Slaves of This Territory," June 7, 1806,
      in *Acts Passed at the First Session of the First Legislature of the Territory of Orleans*
      (New Orleans, LA: Bradford and Anderson, 1807), 38, 40, 164, 166.

70   John Brown, *Slave Life in Georgia: A Narrative of the Life, Sufferings, and Escape
      of John Brown, a Fugitive Slave, Now in England*, ed. Louis Alexis Chamerovzow
      (London: W. M. Watts, 1855), 106–7, 124–25. For further analysis of Brown's skillful
      efforts to influence his sale inside the slave pen, see Johnson, *Soul by Soul*, 166, 178.
      Following his kidnapping in Washington, DC, in 1841, Solomon Northup was also
      sold in Freeman's slave pen in New Orleans. See Solomon Northup, *Twelve Years a
      Slave: Narrative of Solomon Northup, a Citizen of New-York, Kidnapped in Washing-
      ton City in 1841, and Rescued in 1853, from a Cotton Plantation near the Red River in
      Louisiana* (Auburn, NY: Derby and Miller, 1853), 75–88.

71   Brown later escaped to Canada and England (Brown, *Slave Life in Georgia*, 126,
      128–32).

72   Entries dated January 26, 1835, and January 31, 1835, Russell travel journal, THNOC.

73   Entry dated February 1, 1835, Russell travel journal, THNOC. Russell would not
      build the wealth he dreamed of; he died later that year.

74   *Thirteenth Census of the United States Taken in the Year 1910* (Washington, DC:
      Government Printing Office, 1913), 568–69.

75   Eugene Davis would fight for the Confederate Army and later serve as mayor of
      Charlottesville. His wife Patsy Morris Davis died in 1848, the year after these let-
      ters were sent. Eugene Davis to Ann C. Morris and Patsy Morris Davis, February 4
      and 6, 1847, in "Two Letters from New Orleans," unpublished booklet, May 6, 1947
      (hereafter Davis letter), vertical files: Descriptions, New Orleans, 1803–1859, in the
      Louisiana Research Collection, Tulane University Special Collections, New Orleans
      (hereafter TUSC).

76   Ingraham claimed to have invented the nickname "Crescent City" for New Orleans.
      See Ingraham, *South-West*, 182 and 91.

77   On the quantification of competition among American cities, see Eli Cook, *The Pric-
      ing of Progress: Economic Indicators and the Capitalization of American Life* (Cam-
      bridge, MA: Harvard University Press, 2017). On hotels, see A. K. Sandoval-Strausz,
      Hotel: An American History (New Haven, CT: Yale University Press, 2007).

78   Buckingham, *Slave States*, 331.

79   Busy barrooms were important revenue generators for hotels. A pair of lawsuits
      quantified the importance of the City Hotel's barroom and its earnings to the estab-
      lishment's overall operations, showing the barroom alone to earn multiple times the
      annual rent for the property. When Patsey and George Shall leased Bishop's Hotel
      in 1838, they changed its name to the City Hotel. See Patsey Shall v. Thomas Banks,
      Louisiana Supreme Court (June 1844); Patsey Shall wife of George Shall v. Thomas
      Banks, no. 18,216, First Judicial District Court of Louisiana (1839).

80   Gibson, *Gibson's Guide* (1838), 334, 331.

81   Geographer Peirce F. Lewis characterized the Creole and American rivalry as mak-
      ing the mid-nineteenth-century city "rather like a double-yolked egg." The Third
      Municipality, home primarily to immigrants and free and enslaved New Orleanians

of color, extended from Esplanade Avenue downriver (*New Orleans: The Making of an Urban Landscape*, 2nd ed. [Santa Fe, NM: Center for American Places, 2003], 46).

82　On the unique public prominence of slave auctions in New Orleans, see McInnis, "Mapping the Slave Trade"; as well as Richard Campanella, "The St. Louis and the St. Charles: New Orleans' Legacy of Showcase Exchange Hotels," *Preservation in Print* (April 2015): 16–17; and Martha Ann Peters, "The St. Charles Hotel: New Orleans Social Center, 1837–1860," *Louisiana History* 1, no. 3 (Summer 1960): 191–211. On the London Coffee House, see "Black Founders: The Free Black Community in the Early Republic," online exhibit, Library Company of Philadelphia, accessed January 23, 2023, https://www.librarycompany.org/blackfounders/section4.htm.

83　Hall, *Manhattaner*, 19.

84　Campanella notes similarities in design between the St. Charles Hotel and the US Capitol building ("St. Louis and the St. Charles," 17). Even if the St. Charles Hotel would serve as the pride of the Crescent City, many of its components originated far from there, signaling New Orleans's ties to national and global economies. "All the stone work, the greater part of the joiners' work and iron work, had . . . to be prepared at the north," recalled architect James Gallier. His foreman and bookkeeper, trained by a wine seller, hailed from England. Other pieces—"brickwork, stone work, plastering, painting, slating, and ironwork"—Gallier contracted to local artisans, many of them likely Creoles of color. With timber in short supply for this and other building projects, Gallier entered into shared ownership of a local sawmill that included "twenty-five negroes" but soon left the agreement. See James Gallier, *Autobiography of James Gallier, Architect*, facsimile with introduction by Sam Wilson Jr. (Paris: E. Briere, 1864; fac. New York: Da Capo Press, 1973), 22, 26–33. On Creole artisans in the building trades, see Tara A. Dudley, *Building Antebellum New Orleans: Free People of Color and Their Influence* (Austin: University of Texas Press, 2021); Margot Moscou, *New Orleans' Free-Men-of-Color Cabinet Makers in the New Orleans Furniture Trade 1800–1850* (New Orleans, LA: Xavier Review Press, 2008); Mary Gehman, "Visible Means of Support: Businesses, Professions, and Trades of Free People of Color," in *Creole: The History and Legacy of Louisiana's Free People of Color*, ed. Sybil Kein (Baton Rouge: Louisiana State University Press, 2000), 208–22; and Marcus Christian, *Negro Ironworkers in Louisiana, 1718–1900* (Gretna, LA: Pelican Publishing Company, 1972).

85　Buckingham, *Slave States*, 331–33.

86　Descriptions and specifications for the first iteration of the St. Charles Hotel appear in Gibson, *Gibson's Guide* (1838), 331–34, and Norman, *Norman's New Orleans*, 137–41. A second fire, which began in the hotel's kitchen, razed the St. Charles again in 1894. The hotel's third iteration opened in 1896. The hotel was demolished totally in 1974, though another hotel now stands on the same block (Campanella, "St. Louis and the St. Charles," 17).

87　Emphasis in original. Webb could not afford to keep his own fireplace burning in his boardinghouse room and so the hotel functioned as a surrogate office and drawing room. Of the activity around him, he wrote, "The rotunda of the St. Charles at night . . . is more like a stock and merchant exchange than the office of a hotel" (diary entry dated January 24, 1853, Webb, LSM). Famed landscape architect Frederick Law Olmsted offered a rare dissent on the visual appeal of the St. Charles Hotel, decreeing it to be "stupendous, tasteless, ill-contrived and inconvenient" (*A Journey in the Seaboard Slave States: With Remarks on Their Economy* [London: Sampson Low, Son, and Co., 1856], 581). Travelers paid dearly for their time in New Orleans's luxury hotels. When J. S. Buckingham checked out of the St. Charles in April 1839, he was stunned at the charges: $12 per day, for "three persons and a man-servant, having no private sitting-room . . . dining at the public table, and using no wine." Four years later, Matilda Houston was shocked, too, by a bill of $17 per day at the St. Charles "for three rooms, food, lights, in short every thing (except wine) included for my husband, myself and my maid." See Gibson, *Gibson's Guide* (1838), 334, 331; Buckingham, *Slave States*, 395; Houston, *Texas and the Gulf of Mexico*, 165.

88   On the "powerful contrast" between refined architecture and crude slave auctions at the St. Charles and St. Louis Hotels, see McInnis, "Mapping the Slave Trade," 113–14.

89   Gallier, *Autobiography*, 23, 22.

90   At street level, the St. Charles Hotel also offered a billiard room, more than a dozen private shops, a flagged passage leading to a private supper room, and hot and cold bathing rooms. These plans date to the hotel's reconstruction after its 1851 fire but reflect many aspects of Gallier's original design. See George Purves, "Basement Story Sketch for the Saint Charles Hotel," and "Sketch of Principle [*sic*] Story for St. Charles Hotel," 1851–1852, THNOC; Hall, *Manhattaner*, 9.

91   Gibson, *Gibson's Guide* (1838), 332.

92   Surrounding the barroom were the guts that enabled this massive organism to operate. Out of patrons' view were the furnace, boiler, scullery, "colored servants hall" and porter's room, ironing room and hot-air drying room, and the "Yard," which connected to interior and exterior passages through which enslaved people were conveyed to the barroom for auction. See Purves, "Basement Story Sketch"; Gallier, *Autobiography*, 23–24. I am grateful to Tara A. Dudley for her generous response to my inquiry about the Yards at the St. Charles and St. Louis Hotels (email message to author, April 15, 2023).

93   Hall, *Manhattaner*, 9–10.

94   A. D. K., "Studying Southern Institutions," *New York Daily Tribune*, April 28, 1861, 6. On women's attendance at public slave auctions, see Stephanie E. Jones-Rogers, *They Were Her Property: White Women as Slave Owners in the American South* (New Haven, CT: Yale University Press, 2020), 127–46.

95   Among the bondspeople being auctioned, the reporter noted "the almost universal infusion of white blood, which tells its own story about the morality of the institution." A. D. K., "Studying Southern," 6. On rape and other forms of sexual violence against enslaved people, see Baptist, "'Cuffy'"; and Vincent Woodard, *The Delectable Negro: Human Consumption and Homoeroticism within U.S. Slave Culture*, ed. Justin A. Joyce and Dwight A. McBride (New York: New York University Press, 2014).

96   Gallier, *Autobiography*, 24.

97   Buckingham, *Slave States*, 347–48. On the "Quadroon mistress" as a marker of purported moral decay, see Clark, *Strange History*.

98   Emphasis in original. "Sad State of Society," *Liberator*, citing reporting in the *New Orleans Picayune*, January 16, 1846, 12. Using historic annual average consumer price indexes, daily revenue of $600 to $800 in 1846 equated to approximately $20,000 to $27,000 in 2023. See "Consumer Price Index, 1800-," Federal Reserve Bank of Minneapolis, accessed August 4, 2023, https://www.minneapolisfed.org /about-us/monetary-policy/inflation-calculator/consumer-price-index-1800-. Two years earlier, in 1844, the *Milwaukee Sentinel* had reported, "The receipts for

wines and liquors at the St. Charles Hotel . . . for six months, amounted to $60,000," or nearly 2 million dollars in 2023 ("Salmagundi," *Milwaukee Sentinel*, March 9, 1844).

99 Hall, *Manhattaner*, 11–12, 10. On mid-nineteenth-century fine dining, see Robert F. Moss, *The Lost Southern Chefs: A History of Commercial Dining in the Nineteenth-Century South* (Athens: University of Georgia Press, 2022); David S. Shields, *The Culinarians: Lives and Careers from the First Age of American Fine Dining* (Chicago: University of Chicago Press, 2017); and Paul Freedman, "American Restaurants and Cuisine in the Mid-Nineteenth Century," *New England Quarterly* 84 (March 2011): 5–59. On white caterers, hoteliers, and restaurant owners and their patrons in nineteenth-century New Orleans, see David S. Shields, *Southern Provisions: The Creation and Revival of a Cuisine* (Chicago: University of Chicago Press, 2015), 61–91.

100 Lieutenant Colonel Arthur Cunyghame, *A Glimpse at the Great Western Republic* (London: Richard Bentley, 1851), 217.

101 St. Charles Hotel, "Bill of Fare" (hereafter Bill of Fare), June 14, 1848, New Orleans Hotel collection, MSS 411.2, THNOC. One reporter used the dearth of diners in the Gentlemen's Ordinary of the St. Charles to characterize the city's profound seasonal swing in businessmen. "At New Orleans, the number of deaths [from yellow fever], daily, have diminished, owing not to any diminution of virulence in the disease, but to a diminution of subjects on which to act, the city being so nearly deserted," he wrote in September 1847. "A gentleman writes from thence, that he sat down to dinner at the St. Charles hotel with but one other person at the table" ("Chronicle," *Baltimore Niles' National Register*, September 25, 1847, 64).

102 Davis letter, TUSC. Some hotels only accepted "bachelor," that is, male, travelers. See Ingraham, *South-West*, 184–85.

103 Ripley, *Social Life*, 62–63. On gendered spaces in nineteenth- and early twentieth-century US cities, see Emily Remus, *A Shoppers' Paradise: How the Ladies of Chicago Claimed Power and Pleasure in the New Downtown* (Cambridge, MA: Harvard University Press, 2019); Evan Friss, *The Cycling City: Bicycles and Urban America in the 1890s* (Chicago: University of Chicago Press, 2015); and Cindy R. Lobel, *Urban Appetites: Food and Culture in Nineteenth-Century New York* (Chicago: University of Chicago Press, 2014).

104 Houston specified that when she and her husband stayed at the St. Charles they dined in private, in their room, citing this choice as a "Yankee" habit (*Texas and the Gulf of Mexico*, 157–65); see also Teresa Griffin Vielé, *Following the Drum: A Glimpse of Frontier Life* (New York: Rudd and Carleton, 1858). For descriptions of white women's social lives in antebellum New Orleans, see Lillian Foster, *Way-Side Glimpses, North and South* (New York: Rudd and Carleton, 1859), 154; Ripley, *Social Life*, 63, 162; Houston, *Texas and the Gulf of Mexico*, 157–65; and Marise Bachand, "A Season in Town: Plantation Women and the Urban South, 1790–1877" (PhD diss., University of Western Ontario, 2011), https://ir.lib.uwo.ca/cgi/viewcontent.cgi?article=1383&context=etd.

105 After breakfast at the St. Charles, women lingered at table to "digest simultaneously scandal and scrambled eggs" wrote Foster in *Way-Side Glimpses*, 154. Ripley remembered, "In the season flocks of Nashville, Louisville and Cincinnati belles descended upon New Orleans, sat in gorgeous attire and much chatter of voices on the divans under the chandelier of the St. Charles parlor" (*Social Life*, 162). See also Marise Bachand, "Gendered Mobility and the Geography of Respectability in Charleston

and New Orleans, 1790–1861," *Journal of Southern History* 81, no.1 (February 2015): 41–78; and Peters, "St. Charles Hotel."

106   Gibson, *Gibson's Guide* (1838), 329–30.

107   A. Ducatel, 21: 231, 473–77, November 9, 1843, New Orleans Notarial Archives, New Orleans, Louisiana (hereafter NONA).

108   Families with children were less common guests during this era. The notary counted only twenty-four children's beds, in fustic, and one child's cane chair. A. Ducatel, 21: 231, 473–77, November 9, 1843, NONA.

109   Hock was a white wine imported from Germany and popular in England and the United States. Other glassware noted in the inventory included plates of varying sizes, carafes for guests' toilettes, etc. My translation. A. Ducatel, 21: 231, 473–77, November 9, 1843, NONA.

110   A. Ducatel, 21: 231, 473–77, November 9, 1843, NONA.

111   Throughout New Orleans, the writer scolded, "the habit of lounging and drinking in bar-rooms prevails to a fearful extent" (Vielé, *Following the Drum*, 72, 74).

112   Norman, *Norman's New Orleans*, 143. Nott & Co. v. Oakey et al., 19 La. 18, Louisiana Supreme Court (1841); Nott & Co. v. Bank of Orleans, 19 La. 22, Louisiana Supreme Court (1841); P. J. A. Deslix, ed., "Auction Sales," in *Digest of the Reported Decisions of the Supreme Court of the State of Louisiana from December 1838 to February 1843* (New Orleans, LA: J. L. Sollée, 1845), 61.

113   Davies, *American Scenes*, 57–58, 62, 61.

114   Ingraham, too, wrote about an enslaved person as an aesthetic object: "A statue of dazzling ebony, by name Antoine, to which the slightest look or word will give instant animation, stands in the centre of the room, contrasting beautifully in colour with the buff paper-hangings and crimson curtains. He is a slave" (*South-West*, 88). For additional descriptions of St. Louis Hotel auctions see Davies, *American Scenes*, 49–65; and Buckingham, *Slave States*, 333–35.

115   The Hotel Royal operated in the former space of the St. Louis Hotel until 1912. See Hughes, *Thirty Years a Slave*, 206–8; "Omni Royal Orleans Hotel History," Omni Hotels and Resorts, accessed January 27, 2023, https://www.omnihotels.com/hotels /new-orleans-royal-orleans/property-details/history.

116   Like the St. Charles Hotel, the St. Louis had at least one detractor among travelers of means. A. Oakey Hall judged the St. Louis rotunda a "gloomy looking place," even during its heyday (*Manhattaner*, 17); Campanella, "St. Louis and the St. Charles," 16.

117   Martha Griffith Browne, *Autobiography of a Female Slave* (New York: Redfield, 1857), 164–65. On Browne's embrace of abolitionism, see Joe Lockard, "'A Light Broke Out over My Mind': Mattie Griffith, Madge Vertner, and Kentucky Abolitionism," *Filson Club Quarterly* 76, no. 3 (Summer 2002): 245–85.

118   Kelly Birch, "Slavery and the Origins of Louisiana's Prison Industry, 1803–1861" (PhD diss., University of Adelaide, 2017), 153–64, https://digital.library.adelaide .edu.au/dspace/bitstream/2440/123239/1/Birch2017_PhD.pdf; Dudley, *Building Antebellum New Orleans*.

Chapter Two

1   As cited in George Wilson Pierson, *Tocqueville in America* (Baltimore, MD: Johns Hopkins University Press, 1996), 619–20.

2   Harry Smith, *Fifty Years of Slavery in the United States of America* (Grand Rapids: West Michigan Printing Company, 1891), 15.

3   William Cooper Nell, *The Colored Patriots of the American Revolution, with Sketches of Several Distinguished Colored Persons: To Which Is Added a Brief Survey of the Condition and Prospects of Colored Americans* (Boston, MA: Robert F. Wallcut, 1855), 273.

4   Lewis Garrard Clarke and Milton Clarke, *Narratives of the Sufferings of Lewis and Milton Clarke, Sons of a Soldier of the Revolution, during a Captivity of More Than Twenty Years among the Slaveholders of Kentucky, One of the So Called Christian States of North America, Dictated by Themselves* (Boston, MA: Bela Marsh, 1846), 125. Other accounts of bondspeople going to extreme lengths to avoid New Orleans appear in William H. Heard, *From Slavery to the Bishopric in the A.M.E. Church: An Autobiography* (Philadelphia, PA: A. M. E. Book Concern, 1928), 27; Rev. William Troy, *Hair-Breadth Escapes from Slavery to Freedom* (Manchester: Guardian Steam-Printing Offices, 1861), 100–102; and Smith, *Fifty Years*, 15.

5   Frederick Douglass, *Oration Delivered in Corinthian Hall, Rochester, by Frederick Douglass, July 5th, 1852* (Rochester, NY: Lee, Mann, and Co., 1852).

6   Recent scholarship has debated the insistence on "resistance" and "agency" among enslaved and oppressed historical actors. Reflexive assertions that histories of resistance, regardless of the specific context, provided an equal counterbalance to histories of oppression threaten to lighten the weight and blur the violence of the excruciating conditions of enslavement, discrimination, and other forms of suppression. In the time frame considered by this study, the ambient atmosphere of threat to New Orleanians of color never cleared; it only changed shape. Of a later era, Christina Sharpe writes, "The weather is the total climate; and that climate is antiblack. . . . it is the atmosphere: slave law transformed into lynch law, into Jim and Jane Crow, and other administrative logics that remember the brutal conditions of enslavement after the event of slavery has supposedly come to an end" (*In the Wake: On Blackness and Being* [Durham, NC: Duke University Press, 2016], 104, 106). See also Marisa J. Fuentes, *Dispossessed Lives: Enslaved Women, Violence, and the Archive* (Philadelphia: University of Pennsylvania Press, 2018), 9–10; Walter Johnson, "On Agency," *Journal of Social History* 37, no. 1 (Fall 2003): 113–24; and Saidiya V. Hartman, *Scenes of Subjection: Terror, Slavery, and Self-Making in Nineteenth-Century America* (New York: Oxford University Press, 1997), 52–59.

7   Bernhard, Duke of Saxe-Weimar Eisenach, *Travels through North America, during the Years 1825 and 1826*, vol. 2 (Philadelphia, PA: Carey, Lea and Carey, 1828), 57–58, 82; J. S. Buckingham, *The Slave States of America*, vol. 1 (London: Fisher, Son and Co., 1842), 377.

8   "Slave Trading Years Ago," *New York Times*, February 15, 1891, 16.

9   Elizabeth Ross Hite, interviewed in Ronnie W. Clayton, ed., *Mother Wit: The Ex-Slave Narratives of the Louisiana Writers' Project* (New York: Peter Lang, 1990), 103.

10   William Walker, *Buried Alive (behind Prison Walls) for a Quarter of a Century: Life of William Walker*, ed. Thomas S. Gaines (Saginaw, MI: Friedman and Hynan, 1892), 11.

11   Solomon Northup, *Twelve Years a Slave: Narrative of Solomon Northup, a Citizen of New-York, Kidnapped in Washington City in 1841, and Rescued in 1853, from a Cotton Plantation near the Red River in Louisiana* (Auburn, NY: Derby and Miller, 1853), 76–88. Other descriptions of New Orleans slave pens appear in John Brown, *Slave Life in Georgia A Narrative of the Life, Sufferings, and Escape of John Brown, a Fugitive Slave, Now in England*, ed. Louis Alexis Chamerovzow (London: W. M. Watts, 1855), 110–18; Octavia V. Rogers Albert, *The House of Bondage: Or Charlotte Brooks*

and Other Slaves Original and Life-Like, as They Appeared in Their Old Plantation and City Slave Life; Together with Pen-Pictures of the Peculiar Institution, with Sights and Insights into Their New Relations as Freedmen, Freemen, and Citizens (New York: Hunt and Eaton, 1890), 105; Clarke and Clarke, *Narratives of the Sufferings*, 127; and Walker, *Buried Alive*, 10–13. See also Walter Johnson, *Soul by Soul: Life inside the Antebellum Slave Market* (Cambridge, MA: Harvard University Press, 1999).

12 Walker also described his terror of his approaching enslaver in terms of another sense, writing, "It seemed to me as though I could hear his voice" (*Buried Alive*, 12).

13 Brown, *Slave Life in Georgia*, 112–13, 192. On feeding and supplying liquor to bondspeople in coffles and before auctions, see Hartman, *Scenes of Subjection*, 33, 37–39.

14 Hiram Mattison, *Louisa Picquet, the Octoroon: A Tale of Southern Slave Life* (New York: Hiram Mattison, 1861), 25. More often, this narrative is analyzed for the insight it sheds on sexual violence in slavery. See Andrea H. Livesey, "Race, Slavery, and the Expression of Sexual Violence in *Louisa Picquet, the Octoroon*," *American Nineteenth Century History* 19, no. 3 (2018): 267–88.

15 Manda Cooper, interviewed in Clayton, ed., *Mother Wit*, 143–44.

16 Hite, interviewed in Clayton, ed., *Mother Wit*, 106.

17 Johnson, *Soul by Soul*, 25. Louis XV, *Code noir, ou Édit du Roi, servant de règlement pour le gouvernement et l'administration de la justice, police, discipline et le commerce des esclaves nègres dans la province et colonie de la Loüisianne* (1727), https://archive.org/details/Louisiane1724N8608605/page/n2/mode/2up; record book of licenses, bakers' declarations, and statements of public works, 1812, and passports, 1818–1831, Office of the Mayor, records, Louisiana Division/City Archives, New Orleans Public Library (hereafter LDCA NOPL). On the cosmopolitan lives of enslaved people in the Atlantic World and analysis of this passport system, see Rashauna Johnson, *Slavery's Metropolis: Unfree Labor in New Orleans during the Age of Revolutions* (New York: Cambridge University Press, 2016). Food work enabled twentieth-century mobility, too. Rebecca Sharpless argues that domestic work created a "middle ground between slavery and an open economy" (*Cooking in Other Women's Kitchens: Domestic Workers in the South, 1865–1960* [Chapel Hill: University of North Carolina Press, 2010], xi).

18 Benjamin Henry Boneval Latrobe, diary entries dated January 12, 1819, and March 16, 1819, in Latrobe, *Impressions Respecting New Orleans: Diary and Sketches 1818–1820*, ed. Samuel Wilson Jr. (New York: Columbia University, 1951), 22, 101.

19 On food vendors and marketplaces as integral to nineteenth-century US cities, see Gergely Baics, *Feeding Gotham: The Political Economy and Geography of Food in New York, 1790–1860* (Princeton, NJ: Princeton University Press, 2016); Cindy R. Lobel, *Urban Appetites: Food and Culture in Nineteenth-Century New York* (Chicago: University of Chicago Press, 2014); and Sandra Margaret Frink, "Spectacles of the Street: Performance, Power, and Public Space in Antebellum New Orleans" (PhD diss., University of Texas at Austin, 2004), http://hdl.handle.net/2152/12771.

20 Studies of women food vendors in the Atlantic World include Shauna Sweeney, "Market Marronage: Fugitive Women and the Internal Marketing System in Jamaica, 1781–1834," *William and Mary Quarterly* 76, no. 2 (April 2019): 197–222; Jessica B. Harris, "'I'm Talkin' 'bout the Food I Sells': African American Street Vendors and the Sound of Food from Noise to Nostalgia," in *The Larder: Food Studies Methods from the American South*, ed. John T. Edge, Elizabeth S. D. Engelhardt, and Ted Ownby (Athens: University of Georgia Press, 2013), 333–41; Richard Graham,

Feeding the City: From Street Market to Liberal Reform in Salvador, Brazil, 1780–1860 (Austin: University of Texas Press, 2010); Sheryllynne Haggerty, "Miss Fan Can Tun Her Han! Female Traders in Eighteenth-Century British-American Atlantic Port Cities," *Atlantic Studies* 6, no. 1 (April 2009): 29–42; Robert Olwell, "'Loose, Idle and Disorderly': Slave Women in the Eighteenth-Century Charleston Marketplace," in *More than Chattel: Black Women and Slavery in the Americas*, ed. David Barry Gaspar and Darlene Clarke Hine (Bloomington: Indiana University Press, 1996), 97–110; Daniel H. Usner Jr., "Food Marketing and Interethnic Exchange in the Eighteenth Century Lower Mississippi Valley," *Food and Foodways* 1 (1986): 279–310; and Ashley Rose Young, "Nourishing Networks: The Public Culture of Food in Nineteenth-Century America" (PhD diss., Duke University, 2017), https://dukespace.lib.duke.edu/dspace/handle/10161/16358.

21   Eliza Ripley, *Social Life in Old New Orleans: Being Recollections of My Girlhood* (New York: Arno Press, 1912, repr. 1975), 41.

22   Marcus Christian, "Street-Vendors and Street-Cries," in *The Negro in Louisiana*, unpublished manuscript, ca. 1942–1976, Dillard (University) Project, 1–16, Marcus Christian collection, MSS 11, Louisiana and Special Collections, University of New Orleans, https://louisianadigitallibrary.org/islandora/object/uno-p15140coll42%3A28. On the history of pralines and praline vendors, see Chanda Nunez, "Just Like Ole' Mammy Used to Make: Reinterpreting New Orleans African-American Praline Vendors as Entrepreneurs" (Master's thesis, University of New Orleans, 2011), https://scholarworks.uno.edu/cgi/viewcontent.cgi?article=1127&context=td.

23   The blackberry seller announced her early-morning arrival in city neighborhoods with the "slap-slap of heelless old slippers on the banquette," the writer wrote. "The black goddess has been up betimes harvesting among the white-flowered briars 'back of town.'" Her description clarified that the *marchande* had worked through the night to pick berries from thorny bushes, then walked the city streets in meager shoes to sell her harvest. Doris Kent, "Merry, Carefree Life of our Street 'Merchants,'" *Times-Picayune*, March 21, 1920, 50.

24   Emancipation petition of Manuel Borges, no. 122B, 1817, Emancipation petitions, 1813–1843 (hereafter Emancipation petitions), Orleans Parish Court, records, LDCA NOPL. Borga's enslaver, Manuel Borges, appears in the 1822 and 1832 city directories as a grocer; see John Adems Paxton, *New-Orleans Directory and Register* (New Orleans, LA: John Adems Paxton, 1822); and *The New-Orleans Annual Advertiser for 1832, Annexed to the City Directory* (New Orleans, LA: Stephen E. Percy and Co., 1832). Borga registered with the mayor's office as a free person of color on August 9, 1841; see "Register of Free Colored Persons Entitled to Remain in the State," vol. 1, 1840–1856 (hereafter Register, vol. 1), 7, Office of the Mayor, records, LDCA NOPL. On the history of *calas* and *calas* vendors, see Christian, "Street-Vendors and Street-Cries," 3, 6; Nunez, "Just Like Ole' Mammy," 10–12; and Francis Lam, "Calas: The Rice Fritter That Freed the Slaves," *Salon*, February 26, 2010, https://www.salon.com/2010/02/26/calas_rice_fritter_that_freed_slaves/.

25   Fatima's initial enslaver in New Orleans was the widow of James Rice Fitzgerald. On Laclotte's flight to New Orleans, see Anne Ulentin, "Shades of Grey: Slaveholding Free Women of Color in Antebellum New Orleans, 1800–1840" (PhD diss., Louisiana State University, 2012), 145, https://digitalcommons.lsu.edu/gradschool_dissertations/3072/. See also Emancipation petition of Laurence Laclotte, no. 108A, 1821, Emancipation petitions, Orleans Parish Court, records, LDCA NOPL;

M. Lafitte, 20: 14–15, March 1, 1821, NONA; entry for August 9, 1841, Register, vol. 1, 25, LDCA NOPL.

26 Elizabeth Ross Hite disdained the notion that enslavers could keep bondspeople and their knowledge separated from each other. Hite recalled how quickly enslaved people shared news amongst themselves. "News? . . . Shucks, we knew everything de master talked about. De house girl would tell us and we would pass it around. Dats how we knew dat master was afraid of de Yankees" (interviewed in Clayton, ed., *Mother Wit*, 106).

27 Letter to the editor, *Louisiana Gazette*, November 29, 1808.

28 Louis Hughes remembered that the plantation's gardener, Uncle Gooden, sold excess cabbages, sweet potatoes, and corn in the Memphis market, earning eight to ten dollars with each trip, but "this the madam took for 'pin money'" (*Thirty Years a Slave: From Bondage to Freedom: The Institution of Slavery as Seen on the Plantation and in the Home of the Planter* [Milwaukee, WI: South Side Printing Company, 1897], 65–66). See also Israel Campbell, *An Autobiography. Bond and Free: or, Yearnings for Freedom, from My Green Brier House. Being the Story of My Life in Bondage, and My Life in Freedom* (Philadelphia, PA: Israel Campbell, 1861), 317.

29 Similarly, William Beckett, a free Black man born in Norfolk, Virginia, told the New Orleans mayor's office in 1840 that he had worked in the past as a cook and fireman on steamboats "and now sells chickens." Entry for Wm. Beckett, July 27, 1840; and entry for Joseph W. Prince, July 19, 1841, both in Register, vol. 1, LDCA NOPL, 6, 62. On steamboats as a means of escape from slavery, see Thomas C. Buchanan, "Levees of Hope: African American Steamboat Workers, Cities, and Slave Escapes on the Antebellum Mississippi," *Journal of Urban History* 30, no. 3 (March 2004): 360–77. While the flexible, mobile nature of food work could be helpful to job seekers, one Black writer cautioned against the lure of service jobs that were easily procured but of limited potential for most. Thomas Smallwood criticized, "The coloured men of the present generation are of no service to themselves . . . they are flying from city to city, seeking employment at the hotels, and steamboats; as waiters, cooks, and barbers. Their highest ambition is to be a good waiter, or barber, and then they are made" (*A Narrative of Thomas Smallwood (Coloured Man): Giving an Account of His Birth—the Period He Was Held in Slavery—His Release—and Removal to Canada, etc. Together with an Account of the Underground Railroad. Written by Himself* [Toronto: James Stephens, 1851], 55–56).

30 Ja. H. Leverich in New Orleans to Thomas Murdoch, Esq. in London, postmarked December 10, 1838, folder 3, MSS 439: Thomas Murdoch letters, 1830–1842, THNOC.

31 Louis C. Hunter with Beatrice Jones Hunter, *Steamboats on the Western Rivers: An Economic and Technological History* (New York: Dover Publications, 1993), 645.

32 For a fuller consideration of the New Orleans levees, see chapter 3. On steamboat traffic in New Orleans, see Walter Johnson, *River of Dark Dreams: Slavery and Empire in the Cotton Kingdom* (Cambridge, MA: Belknap Press, 2013); Calvin Schermerhorn, *The Business of Slavery and the Rise of American Capitalism, 1815–1860* (New Haven, CT: Yale University Press, 2015), 204–39; Robert H. Gudmestad, *Steamboats and the Rise of the Cotton Kingdom* (Baton Rouge: Louisiana State University Press, 2011); and Thomas C. Buchanan, *Black Life on the Mississippi: Slaves, Free Blacks, and the Western Steamboat World* (Chapel Hill: University of North Carolina Press, 2004).

33 Jacob D. Green, *Narrative of the Life of J. D. Green, a Runaway Slave, from*

Kentucky, Containing an Account of His Three Escapes, in 1839, 1846, and 1848 (Huddersfield: Henry Fielding, 1864), 37.

34 The day after Amolk's recapture, his enslaver, Lucius Duncan, sued the schooner's master for $1,000 in damages anyway. Duncan v. Hawks et al., 18 La. 548, Louisiana Supreme Court (1841). Another example of a New Orleanian who escaped via food work on the water surfaced in the Louisiana Supreme Court case Slatter v. Holton, no. 3894, 19 La. 39, Louisiana Supreme Court (1841).

35 Moses Grandy, *Narrative of the Life of Moses Grandy; Late a Slave in the United States of America* (London: C. Gilpin, 1843), 39–40, 46–49. For another example of a fugitive who used food work on a steamboat to reach freedom, see Troy, *Hair-Breadth Escapes*, 87–89.

36 E. A. Maccannon, *Commanders of the Dining Room: Biographic Sketches and Portraits of Successful Head Waiters* (New York: Gwendolyn Publishing Company, 1904), 11, 65, 151. At the time this book was published, the head waiter and assistant head waiter in the dining room of New Orleans's St. Charles Hotel were Black men: George A. Curry and George Goode. On Black waiters and hotelkeepers as "arbiter[s] of taste," see Rafia Zafar, *Recipes for Respect: African American Meals and Meaning* (Athens: University of Georgia Press, 2019), 12. On Black caterers in Philadelphia, see Danya Pilgrim, "Gastronomic Alchemy: How Black Philadelphia Caterers Transformed Taste into Capital, 1790 to 1925" (PhD diss., Yale University, 2019).

37 "A Sunday in New Orleans," *Portland Evening Advertiser*, repr. in *Daily National Intelligencer*, May 24, 1833.

38 Joseph Holt Ingraham, *The South-West, by a Yankee*, vol. 1 (New York: Harper and Brothers, 1835), 183. Most travelers ignored the culinary and service work of those who fed them, leaving them absent from their writings.

39 An ad for the National Hotel in the 1842 city directory specified, "The servants are all white, and have been carefully selected with reference to their capacity, honesty and civil deportment." When one English writer stayed at the St. Charles Hotel in late 1843, she recalled, "There are white helps of the male sex, (our attendant was English) and seven excellent Parisian cooks; I need not add that the *cuisine* was as good as possible." Similarly, an article in the *Chicago Press and Tribune* characterized the St. Charles as "one of the largest and best hotels in the country. . . . It is a significant commentary on Southern institutions that the servants, male and female, are all, or nearly all, white." See *New Orleans Directory for 1842: Comprising the Names, Residences, and Occupations of the Merchants, Business Men, Professional Gentlemen and Citizens of New Orleans, Lafayette, Algiers and Gretna. Two Volumes in One* (New Orleans, LA: Pitts and Clarke, 1842); Mrs. [Matilda Charlotte] Houston, *Texas and the Gulf of Mexico: Or, Yachting in the New World*, vol. 1 (London: John Murray, Albemarle Street, 1844), 163–64; "New Orleans and Homeward," *Chicago Press and Tribune*, March 29, 1860, 2. On the domestic workforce in antebellum Louisville, Kentucky, including that at the Galt House Hotel, and the shift from enslaved workers to foreign-born domestics as the antebellum period progressed, see Stephanie Cole, "Servants and Slaves in Louisville: Race, Ethnicity, and Household Labor in an Antebellum Border City," *Ohio Valley History* 11, no. 1 (Spring 2011): 3–25.

40 Drawing on 1850 and 1860 federal census reports and New Orleans newspapers, one historian finds only "minuscule" evidence of New Orleanians of color working in "eateries" of the day and concludes, "Restaurant cooking in antebellum New Orleans was Eurocentric and would remain so until the 1880s." This study disagrees with that assessment, for reasons discussed here. See David S. Shields, *Southern Provisions:*

The Creation and Revival of a Cuisine (Chicago: University of Chicago Press, 2015), 75, fn. 48, 361.

41 Robert C. Reinders details these circumstances, including the fact that "the census of 1850 was taken in the summer when free Negroes who worked in the city during the winter season were absent." Also critical: at the time when the 1860 census was enumerated, "out of state free Negroes were not then permitted in the city." An additional factor that limited or precluded the likelihood of discovering New Orleanians of color working in the food industry via censuses: the free schedules of the 1850 and 1860 censuses did not include enslaved workers, who were often "rented out" by their enslavers to work in places like hotels. Furthermore, census records did not identify many Creoles of color as such and left many names unlinked to occupations. See Robert C. Reinders, "The Free Negro in the New Orleans Economy, 1850–1860," *Louisiana History* 6, no. 3 (Summer 1965): 273–85, at 273–74, 283. Even in the early twentieth century, the US census did not offer accurate counts of the nation's domestic cooks (Sharpless, *Cooking in Other Women's Kitchens*, xiii).

42 Primary source repositories for such research include Register, vols. 1, 2 (1856–1859), and 3 (1859–1861), LDCA NOPL; also included are oaths and bonds for city licenses on taverns, coffee houses, hotels, boarding houses, and other establishments, 1828–1863; and oaths and bonds for city licenses on vehicles, 1834–1866; all housed in Office of the Mayor, records, LDCA NOPL, especially when cross-checked with city directories. Incidental newspaper references to cooks, waiters, and diners of color in New Orleans include "Multiple News Items," *Boston Daily Atlas*, January 5, 1843, A4; and "Distinctions of Color," *Boston Emancipator and Free American* 44, February 23, 1843, 167. The 1856 New Orleans court case *Gardère v. State* focused on an enslaved man whom a witness testified was "a waiter in the larger hotels of this city" (Gardère v. State, no. 10,957, First District Court of New Orleans, [1856], as cited in Judith Kelleher Schafer, *Becoming Free, Remaining Free: Manumission and Enslavement in New Orleans* [Baton Rouge: Louisiana State University Press, 2003], 77). In November 1856, Charles Barnabé Thevenot, a free man of color born in New Orleans, registered with the mayor's office and stated his place of employment as the St. Charles Hotel's Billiard Saloon (Register, vol. 2, 293, LDCA NOPL). On challenges and strategies related to researching African Americans in federal census records, see "African Americans in the Federal Census, 1790–1930: Using Federal Census Records to Find Information on African American Ancestors," presentation, National Archives and Records Administration (hereafter National Archives), Washington, DC, accessed July 14, 2021, https://www.archives.gov/files/research/census /african-american/african-american-census-research.ppt. Saidiya V. Hartman's description of her approach to WPA narratives is relevant to this research, too. She writes of "a combination of foraging and disfiguration—raiding for fragments upon which other narratives can be spun and misshaping and deforming the testimony through selective quotation and the amplification of issues germane to this study" (*Scenes of Subjection*, 12).

43 A. B. Chambers, ed., *Trials and Confessions of Madison Henderson, alias Blanchard, Alfred Amos Warrick, James W. Seward, and Charles Brown, Murderers of Jesse Baker and Jacob Weaver, as Given by Themselves; and a Likeness of Each, Taken in Jail Shortly after Their Arrest* (St. Louis, MO: Chambers and Knapp, 1841). On Mississippi River "rascal" culture see Thomas C. Buchanan, "Rascals on the Antebellum Mississippi: African American Steamboat Workers and the St. Louis Hanging of 1841," *Journal of Social History* 34, no. 4 (Summer 2001): 797–816.

44 Readers debated the veracity of these confessions when they were published. Later, scholars noted that these confessions were given "under extreme duress" and followed by a trial decided by an all-white jury. Recent researchers have interpreted the confessions as opportunities for the men to shape their biographies as their executions approached. Many elements of the confessions—the identities of the men's enslavers, the trajectories of their travels—have been confirmed. See Buchanan, *Black Life*, 126–28, 143–44.

45 Brown also engaged in petty theft and resold things "on the river," like silver spoons and jewelry, that enslaved people had stolen. Brown's reference to a stint working at New Orleans's "Richeson hotel" likely refers to a hotel run by John Richardson at 22 and 24 Conti Street listed in the 1832 city directory. See Chambers, ed., *Trials and Confessions*, 65, 68–72; Brown, ed. Chamerovzow, *Slave Life*, 106–9; and *New-Orleans Annual Advertiser* (1832). Other studies of these confessions include Mary Seematter, "Trials and Confessions: Race and Justice in Antebellum St. Louis," *Gateway Heritage* 12, no. 2 (Fall 1991): 36–46; and Walter Johnson, *The Broken Heart of America: St. Louis and the Violent History of the United States* (New York: Basic Books, 2020), 94–103.

46 The confession of Madison Henderson, the group's leader, likewise involved food, but less centrally. Henderson's focus was to help his enslaver, "the chief of a company of negro traders," with the work of "stealing negroes," as Henderson described. Henderson spun "false tales" to ensnare men and women so they could be trafficked by his enslaver. Once Henderson joined up with his three collaborators, their targets expanded to "Champaign [,] . . . bottles of cherries," cigars, "a box of catsup[,] and some demijohns of brandy"—the result of one sweep of a New Orleans grocery store at Poydras and Tchoupitoulas Streets (Chambers, ed., *Trials and Confessions*, 26).

47 Warrick was born free in New Bern, North Carolina. As a young man, he agreed to go to New Orleans with a "negro trader," where Warrick was sold into slavery (Chambers, ed., *Trials and Confessions*, 37–38, 41, 14). See also Timothy F. Reilly, "Slave Stealing in the Early Domestic Trade as Revealed by a Loyal Manservant," *Louisiana History* 55, no. 1 (Winter 2014): 5–39.

48 Chambers, ed., *Trials and Confessions*, 56.

49 Buchanan, *Black Life*, 144; Seematter, "Trials and Confessions," 46.

50 Warrick detested the sugarcane fields. "This I did not like, and my arms got sore," he recounted in his confession, "so they gave me an easier work, keeping crows out of the field." Still, Warrick suffered from hunger brought on by meager rations. He escaped by boat with the plantation's cook and one other bondsperson. Upon reaching New Orleans, Warrick found a job as a fireman on the steamboat *Maid of Orleans*, bound for St. Louis. See Chambers, ed., *Trials and Confessions*, 42–43.

51 Lucette Barberousse may have belonged to the group of about three thousand people who arrived in New Orleans in the wake of the Haitian Revolution and were designated as slaves, even if they had been born in freedom and later enslaved (or re-enslaved) on Cuban soil. See Rebecca J. Scott, "Paper Thin: Freedom and Re-Enslavement in the Diaspora of the Haitian Revolution," *Law and History Review* 29, no. 4 (November 2011): 1061–87, at 1061–63.

52 The inventory identified five adult enslaved women among Latoison's possessions and estimated their collective value as $1,950, more than one-third of the estate's value. The three children of Lucette Barberousse were not identified in the document. See C. Pollock, 49: 429–31, June 24, 1835, NONA.

53 Marie Agnès Latoison was the widow of Jean St. Laurent. They had one "legitimate"

son ("legitimate" inserted later in the estate file), Jean Jerome Henry St. Laurent, father of Marie Olive St. Laurent. By the time Latoison passed away in 1835, she had been predeceased by her husband, her son, and her only sister, Ursule Olive Latoison, also a free woman of color, who had named Latoison as her sole heir when she died in New Orleans in 1814. See Louisiana, Orleans Parish Estate Files, 1804–1846 (hereafter Orleans Estate Files), Laurent, St. Jean Marie Agnes Lafoison [sic] (1835), Provo, UT, USA: Ancestry.com Operations, Inc., 2014 (hereafter Ancestry); Boyer, Pierre (1843), Orleans Estate Files, Ancestry; Latoison, Ursule Olive (1814). Orleans Estate Files, Ancestry; C. Pollock, 49: 429–31, June 24, 1835, NONA. Notarial documents recording the inheritance of Lucette Barberousse and her family by St. Laurent up to Barberousse's manumission by Michel Grabiel are collated in C. Pollock, 58: 396–98, November 8, 1838, NONA. On the history of Boyer's trade, see Margot Moscou, *New Orleans' Free-Men-of-Color Cabinet Makers in the New Orleans Furniture Trade 1800–1850* (New Orleans, LA: Xavier Review Press, 2008).

54 These notarial acts used the French unit *piastres* rather than dollars. Grabiel's name is spelled in a variety of ways in different records. I use the spelling "Michel Grabiel" since he signed an 1865 letter with the signature "M. Grabiel" and his tomb in St. Louis Cemetery no. 2 reads "Michel Grabiel." Card Index to Naturalizations in Louisiana (P2087), microfilm serial P2087, roll 6, National Archives, Ancestry; Union Provost Marshals' File of Papers Relating to Individual Civilians, 1861–1867, microfilm publication M345, 300 rolls, NAID: 2133278, War Department Collection of Confederate Records, record group 109, National Archives, Ancestry (hereafter Union Provost); "Michel Grabiel," Find a Grave, database and images, accessed July 18, 2021, www.findagrave.com/memorial/145451505/michel-grabiel; Michel Grabiel gravestone at St. Louis Cemetery no. 2, New Orleans, Orleans Parish, LA.

55 Grabiel's quotes are my translation from French. Estimates of the age of the infant Lucette are inconsistent in notarial documents. In this and other sources, the spelling of individuals' names—including those of Barberousse and Jasie—is also inconsistent. See C. Pollock, 58: 396–98, November 8, 1838, NONA.

56 Barberousse's purchase of her daughters and their manumission are collated in J. Cuvillier, 29: 31, May 10, 1841, NONA. Barberousse's former enslaver, Marie [Olive Genevieve Antoinette] St. Laurent, died on July 14, 1842, at the age of twenty-eight. St. Laurent left no children. According to Orleans Parish estate files, her estate was "indebted to several creditors. . . . [T]he whole of the property of the deceased consists of a sum of twenty dollars and of only one young negress aged about 14." St. Laurent's widower, Pierre Boyer, petitioned to have "the said slave sold to meet the debts and charges of the succession." Debts outstanding at the time of his wife's death included charges for her "final illness," including a payment due to a pharmacist (Boyer, Orleans Estate Files).

57 The 1840 census counted seven of the women in Barberousse's household as free and two as enslaved, though it would not be until the following year—1841—that Barberousse would manumit her three daughters. Barberousse became a grandmother in mid-1840 when her oldest daughter, Annette, had a daughter named Marie-Agnès. See Department of State, *Compendium of the Enumeration of the Inhabitants and Statistics of the United States, as Obtained at the Department of State, from the Returns of the Sixth Census* (Washington: Thomas Allen, 1841); and Register, vol. 1, 5, LDCA NOPL.

58 About two years later, Grabiel married New Orleans-born Carmelite Castellanos. Twenty years in the future, when the Union Army occupied New Orleans during

the Civil War, Grabiel wrote to Union forces to declare his sympathies and request protection. For these opinions, neighbors vandalized his business and threatened him. Grabiel became a naturalized citizen of the United States in 1868. By this time, he was suffering from mental decline. He passed away from "senile marasmus" at the age of 58 in 1877. *New Orleans Directory for 1842* (1842); Chain of title, 530–32 St. Philip Street, Vieux Carré Digital Survey (hereafter VCDS), THNOC, accessed July 18, 2021, https://www.THNOC.org/vcs/property_info.php?lot=18350; *Compendium of the Seventh Census of the United States* (1854); Union Provost; *Compendium of the Ninth Census* (Washington, DC: Government Printing Office, 1872); "Miguel Grabiel, d. June 7, 1877," and "Camelite [*sic*] Castellanos Grabiel, d. January 1, 1913," Louisiana Death Records, Louisiana Secretary of State, accessed July 19, 2021, https://www.sos.la.gov/HistoricalResources/ResearchHistoricalRecords/LocateHistoricalRecords/Pages/LouisianaDeathRecords.aspx; "Carmelite *Castellanos* Grabiel (Gabriel) (Apr 1825–1 Jan 1913)," Find a Grave, database and images, accessed July 18, 2021, www.findagrave.com/memorial/160369354/carmelite -grabiel_(gabriel); Carmelite Castellanos Grabiel gravestone at St. Louis Cemetery no. 2, New Orleans, Orleans Parish, LA.

59 The 1842 city directory listed Miguel Grabielle living at 291 Dauphin[e] Street. In the early 1890s, the city changed its system for numbering properties. In 1909, the name of Hospital Street changed to Governor Nicholls Street. For a guide to converting between old and new numbered addresses, see "Alphabetical and Numerical Index of Changes in Street Names and Numbers, Old and New, 1852 to Current Date, 1938" [hereafter Street Names Index], LDCA NOPL, accessed December 21, 2021, http://nutrias.org/~nopl/info/louinfo/numberchanges/numberchanges.htm. On the history of street names in the French Quarter, see Charles Edwards O'Neill, "The French Regency and the Colonial Engineers: Street Names of Early New Orleans," *Louisiana History* 39, no. 2 (Spring 1998): 207–14.

60 Mandeville owned the property at 1241 Dauphine Street, at the intersection of Barrack St., between June 1810 and May 1847. For chain of title and description of the house, see "1241 Dauphine Street," VCDS, THNOC, accessed December 21, 2021, https://www.THNOC.org/vcs/property_info.php?lot=23047-01%2027. See also Janet Morrison, "'Big Businesswoman': Eulalie Mandeville and the World of Female Free Black Entrepreneurs in Antebellum New Orleans," *Louisiana History* 62, no. 1 (Winter 2021): 61–86.

61 The notarial act described the three women and baby as "all four quarteroons." This description, coupled with Lucette Barberousse's designation as "mulatresse" in the estate inventory and mayor's registry, indicates that the fathers of Lucette, her daughters, and her granddaughter were all likely white men. When Barberousse manumitted her daughters and granddaughter, she is identified in the notarial record as "Marie Agnès alias Lucette Barberousse" (J. Cuvillier, 29: 31, May 10, 1841, NONA).

62 See Schafer, *Becoming Free*; and Reinders, "Free Negro," 284. Other slaveholding states enacted similar measures, giving free people of color little place to turn. See Michael P. Johnson and James L. Roark, eds., *No Chariot Let Down: Charleston's Free People of Color on the Eve of the Civil War* (Chapel Hill: University of North Carolina Press, 2016).

63 In a related demographic development, the census of 1850 recorded an explosion of European immigrants to New Orleans. Tens of thousands of newcomers from Ireland and Germany made an astounding 49 percent of the city's 1850 population

foreign-born. These groups' social statuses, availability for unskilled and skilled work, and skin color further troubled the waters of the city's tenuous social order. The precise figures reported by federal censuses for free New Orleanians of color were 19,226 in 1840; 9,905 in 1850; and 10,689 in 1860. See Richard C. Wade, *Slavery in the Cities: The South, 1820–1860* (New York: Oxford University Press, 1964), 326; and Schafer, *Becoming Free*, xxi, 1–2, 9. On the racialization of Irish and other European immigrants in the United States, see Matthew Frye Jacobson, *Whiteness of a Different Color: European Immigrants and the Alchemy of Race* (Cambridge, MA: Harvard University Press, 1998).

64 Free people of color paid 50 cents to register, risking a fine of $50 and one month of imprisonment if they did not. Entries in the four volumes of the mayor's registry are not unique; as time passed, some people registered more than once. Thus, the researcher can occasionally see changes in occupation and details related to the conditions of manumission for a single person. The research potential for this registry is greatly enhanced not just by its digitization but by the transcription of its entries in the "Free Black Database," a project led and self-funded by Brian Mitchell of University of Arkansas Little Rock. The registry's transcription enables the researcher to search for people manumitted by the same enslaver, members of the same family, or individuals who registered with the mayor across successive years, among other possibilities. NB: The number of free people of color who registered does not reflect the total population of free New Orleanians of color during this era. See Brian K. Mitchell, "Free Black Database," *Slave Biographies: Atlantic Database Network*, accessed May 26, 2021, http://slavebiographies.org/databases.php. See also Brian K. Mitchell, "Free Blacks Database: New Orleans, 1840–1860," *Journal of Slavery and Data Preservation* 1, no. 1 (2020): 16–19; Schafer, *Becoming Free*, 131; Wade, *Slavery in the Cities*, 326.

65 Lucette Barbarousse [*sic*] and her daughters were added to the mayor's registry on August 11, 1841. Her daughters' names appear as "Annette Marie Anasthasie," aged eighteen; "(Marie de) Anastasie" [Louisa], aged fourteen; and "(Etienne) Anastasie, alias Nounnoune," aged twelve, all born in New Orleans. Barberousse's mother, Jasie, registered five days later, on August 16. Register, vol. 1, 5, 21, 305, LDCA NOPL.

66 Register, vol. 1, 275, LDCA NOPL. The registry also shows free New Orleanians of color working as cigar makers, shoemakers, bricklayers, barbers, carpenters, and planters, among other occupations.

67 The registry also exposed the reality that some free Louisianians of color—like Marie Agnès Latoison and Marie Olive St. Laurent—were enslavers themselves, manumitting, buying, and selling bondspeople. Analyzing data published by historian Carter G. Woodson in 1924 and 1925, Thomas J. Pressly calculated that 40 percent of free Black heads of families in Louisiana in 1830 were slaveholders, a percentage only exceeded by the 43 percent of free Black heads of families in South Carolina who were enslavers. In Louisiana in 1830, 964 free Black people enslaved 4,274 bondspeople, the largest total number of bondspeople held by enslavers of color in any state or territory included in the census. Some Louisianians of color may have been enslaving bondspeople in order to manumit them, as in the case of Lucette Barberousse's brief enslavement of her daughters. See Pressly, "'The Known World' of Free Black Slaveholders: A Research Note on the Scholarship of Carter G. Woodson," *Journal of African American History* 91, no. 1 (Winter 2006): 81–87, at 84. On free Louisianians of color as enslavers, see Morrison, "'Big Businesswoman,'" 70–72; Ulentin, "Shades of Grey"; Woodson, *Free Negro Heads of Families in the United States in 1830*

(Washington, DC: Association for the Study of Negro Life and History, Inc., 1925); and Woodson, "Free Negro Owners of Slaves in the United States in 1830," *Journal of Negro History* 9 (January 1924): 41–85.

68 Grabiel and Barberousse signed the notarial document with a mark rather than a signature (C. Pollock, 58: 396–98, November 8, 1838, NONA).

69 For histories of the city's prosperous Creoles of color, see Tara A. Dudley, *Building Antebellum New Orleans: Free People of Color and Their Influence* (Austin: University of Texas Press, 2021); Melissa Daggett, *Spiritualism in Nineteenth-Century New Orleans: The Life and Times of Henry Louis Rey* (Jackson: University Press of Mississippi, 2017); and Shirley Elizabeth Thompson, *Exiles at Home: The Struggle to Become American in Creole New Orleans* (Cambridge, MA: Harvard University Press, 2009).

70 The vast majority of people who registered with the mayor's office before 1842 cited an arrival date in Louisiana before 1825. Many were likely trying to evade an 1830 legislative act that required free people of color who had arrived in Louisiana after 1825 to leave within sixty days or be imprisoned. Any free person of color permitted to remain in the state needed to register with the mayor's office. In 1831, the legislature modified the act to allow manumitted people to remain in the state. In 1842, the legislature further amended the 1830 act to allow free people of color who had arrived in Louisiana before 1838, rather than 1825, to remain in the state. Schafer notes that these penalties were rarely enforced. However, pressure on free people of color increased in other ways, including a total ban on manumissions in 1857. See Schafer, *Becoming Free*, 6–9, 132, 89; Register, vol. 1, 289, LDCA NOPL.

71 *New-Orleans Annual Advertiser* (1832); *New-Orleans Directory: Revised and Corrected for 1835* (1835).

72 *New Orleans Directory for 1842* (1842); B. M. Norman, *Norman's New Orleans and Environs: Containing a Brief Historical Sketch of the Territory and State of Louisiana, and the City of New Orleans, from the Earliest Period to the Present Time: Presenting a Complete Guide to All Subjects of General Interest in the Southern Metropolis; with a Correct and Improved Plan of the City, Pictorial Illustrations of Public Buildings, Etc.* (New Orleans, LA: B. M. Norman, 1845), 67; John Gibson, *Gibson's Guide and Directory of the State of Louisiana, and the Cities of New Orleans and Lafayette* (New Orleans, LA: John Gibson, 1838), 166.

73 Register, vol. 1, 239, LDCA NOPL; "Dictionary of Louisiana Biography—W," Louisiana Historical Association, accessed July 11, 2021, https://www.lahistory.org /resources/dictionary-louisiana-biography/dictionary-of-louisiana-biography -w/. In 1840, William Scott appeared in the federal census as head of a household of eight people living in the First Ward of the First Municipality (bounded by the river and Canal, Basin, and St. Louis Streets), indicating that he lived in the same building as his shop, or nearby. See "New Orleans Ward Boundaries, 1805–1880," LDCA NOPL, accessed June 1, 2021, http://nutrias.org/facts/wards.htm; *Sixth Census of the United States* (1840), Ancestry.

74 Michel and Co., *New-Orleans Directory for 1841* (New Orleans, LA: J. L. Sollée, 1840); *New Orleans Directory for 1842* (1842); Michel and Co., *New-Orleans Directory for 1843* (New Orleans: J. L. Sollée, 1842); *New-Orleans Annual and Commercial Directory 1844* (New Orleans, LA: J. J. Calberthwaite and Co., 1844); *New Orleans Annual and Commercial Register for 1846* (New Orleans: E. A. Michel and Co., 1846).

75 In 1850, Scott still lived in the First Municipality's First Ward. Scott's neighbor, a German-born tailor, owned real estate valued at $2,000. Other immediate neigh-

bors worked as a cook, waiter, laborer, copper-plate printer, merchant, and dentist. In 1850, Scott was head of a household of eleven people, all classified as mulatto or white. These included Martha Scott (twenty-four), mulatto, born in Kentucky; and John Miller (thirty-one), a shoemaker, and Mary (twenty-six), his wife, both born in Germany. Their nine-month-old son Henry had been born in Louisiana. Irish-born Bridget Kelly (sixteen) also lived in the house. Scott's block was cosmopolitan; of the forty-two people listed on this census page, twenty-three were born outside the United States—most in Ireland and Germany, and others in France, England, Russia, Belgium, and Scotland. *Seventh Census of the United States* (1850), Ancestry.

76   Apollo Street would change its name to Carondelet Street that year (Street Names Index, LDCA NOPL). See also Bennet Dowler, *Cohen's New Orleans and Lafayette Directory: Including Carrollton, Algiers, Gretna, and McDonogh, for 1852* (New Orleans, LA: Office of the *Daily Delta*, 1852); H. Cohen and A. Cohen, *Cohen's New Orleans Directory for 1855: Including Jefferson City, Gretna, Carrollton, Algiers, and McDonogh* (New Orleans: Office of the *Picayune*: 1855); and Census of merchants, v. 1, First District, 1854, Office of the Treasurer, records (hereafter Census of merchants), LDCA NOPL.

77   "NEGROES FOR SALE," *Daily Crescent*, July 4, 1854, 4.

78   This municipal census noted the Miller and Ashbury dime bar operating at 161 Gravier Street in 1854; the address appears as Square 199 in the city's First District. The barroom either predated Scott's operation recorded at that address in the 1855 city directory or Scott may have operated within this business. See Census of merchants, LDCA NOPL; Cohen and Cohen, *Cohen's New Orleans Directory for 1855*. For a complementary effort using this census to reconstruct the location of slave dealers, see Maurie D. McInnis, "Mapping the Slave Trade in Richmond and New Orleans," *Buildings and Landscapes* 20, no. 2 (Fall 2013): 102–24, at 116–20.

79   Proceeding on Gravier Street away from the river, or left, in the upriver direction of Baronne, the walker would have found more slave dealers before encountering Freret's cotton press. See Census of merchants, LDCA NOPL.

80   The 1861 census of the town of Brantford in the Canadian province of Ontario noted a sixty-two-year-old American-born "mulatto" man named William Scott who was working as a grocer. It is uncertain whether this was the same William Scott who had lived in New Orleans. See William C. Scott, Brantford, Brant, Ontario, Canada, citing p. 109, line 7, Library and Archives Canada film number C-1108, Public Archives, Toronto, FHL microfilm 349, 249, "Canada, Ontario Census, 1861," database, FamilySearch, https://familysearch.org/ark:/61903/1:1:MQQD-PF4: 9 March 2018.

81   Reinders, "Free Negro," 283.

82   W. H. Rainey, *A. Mygatt & Co.'s New Orleans Business Directory, with a Map* (New Orleans, LA: A. Mygatt and Co., 1858), 205.

83   Register, vol. 1, 27, 343, LDCA NOPL.

84   When Louise Milon married Wollaston Hawley in August 1836, she was indebted to her eleven-year-old daughter, Emma Frederica Schreiner, in the amount of $5,000. Seven years later, when the widowed Hawley leased the St. Louis Hotel, her son-in-law, George A. Fosdick, served as her security. Hawley's daughter Emma was Fosdick's "minor spouse." Born in 1825, Emma may have been just shy of eighteen at the time. See "Bail par les commissaires liquidateurs de la compagnie & Banque des Améliorations à Mme. Veuve L. Hawley," A. Ducatel, 21: 231, 473–77, November 9, 1843, NONA.

85   Furthermore, even though Hawley told the notary that she had purchased Buck-

ner from John Henderson in 1839, no notarial record of the sale could be found. A notarial act documented Henderson's sale of an enslaved person in 1839, but not to Hawley. See A. Ducatel, 21: 231, 473–77, November 9, 1843, NONA; C. Pollock, 61: 515, 1839, NONA.

86 The history of the "intense pressure" sustained by free people of color is expertly investigated by Judith Kelleher Schafer in *Becoming Free*, xv.

87 "New Orleans, Louisiana, U.S., Birth Records Index, 1790–1915," Ancestry; Register, vol. 3, 47, LDCA NOPL. Blair's wife, Jane, and sister-in-law, Margaret, registered with the mayor on the same day in November 1841. Both were recommended by Antonio Juneau, a fellow grocer. See Register, vol. 1, 19, 23, LDCA NOPL; *New Orleans Directory for 1842* (1842).

88 See Jennifer M. Spear, *Race, Sex, and Social Order in Early New Orleans* (Baltimore, MD: Johns Hopkins University Press, 2009); and Louisiana State University Libraries, "Terminology" in "Free People of Color in Louisiana," online exhibit, accessed December 21, 2021, https://lib.lsu.edu/sites/all/files/sc/fpoc/terminology .html.

89 My translation. Register, vol. 1, 19, LDCA NOPL. On the history of South Asian peddlers who emigrated to New Orleans in the late 1800s and early 1900s, see Vivek Bald, *Bengali Harlem and the Lost Histories of South Asian America* (Cambridge, MA: Harvard University Press, 2013), 26–28, 32–36, 65–69. Blair arrived in New Orleans and built a life there several generations before this later wave of immigrants.

90 In multiple published narratives, free people of color described harassment by whites in antebellum New Orleans. "In New Orleans they might have settled comfortably, had not the unhappy prejudice which exists there against their colour caused them perpetual uneasiness," wrote Charles Stuart about Reuben Maddison, who had purchased his freedom in Kentucky, and his wife. "When they walked in the streets, they were cursed and pushed out of their way by white people passing along. Even when they assembled together . . . for religious worship, they could have no peace at all from the annoyances of the white men." See Stuart, *Reuben Maddison: A True Story* (Birmingham, England: B. Hudson, 1835), 16–17. See also J. Passmore Edwards, *Uncle Tom's Companions: Or, Facts Stranger Than Fiction. A Supplement to Uncle Tom's Cabin: Being Startling Incidents in the Lives of Celebrated Fugitive Slaves* (London: Edwards and Co., 1852), 137.

91 Michel and Co., *New-Orleans Directory for 1841* (1840); *New Orleans Directory for 1842* (1842); *New-Orleans Directory for 1843* (1842); *New-Orleans Annual and Commercial Directory 1844* (1844); *New Orleans Annual and Commercial Register for 1846* (1846); Cohen and Cohen, *Cohen's New Orleans Directory for 1855* (1855); B. W. Cohen and A. Michel, *Cohen's New Orleans and Southern Directory, for 1856* (New Orleans, LA: *Daily Delta* Print, 1855); Charles Gardner and Edward Clifton Wharton, *Gardner and Wharton's New Orleans Directory for the Year 1858: Embracing the City Record, a General Directory of the Citizens, and a Business and Firm Directory* (New Orleans, LA: E. C. Wharton, 1857); Charles Gardner, *Gardner's New Orleans Directory, for 1861: Including Jefferson City, Gretna, Carrollton, Algiers, and McDonogh* (New Orleans, LA: C. Gardner, 1861); and Charles Gardner, *Gardner's New Orleans Directory, for 1866: Including Jefferson City, Gretna, Carrollton, Algiers, and McDonogh* (New Orleans, LA: C. Gardner, 1866). On the ambiguous racial status of South Asian immigrants in turn-of-the-twentieth-century United States, see Bald, *Bengali Harlem*, 49–59.

92 The city's 1854 census of merchants showed a retail grocery, with J. W. Murphy as

proprietor, at the corner of Villere and Customhouse. Blair likely worked at this grocery. The businesses located on the four corners of the intersection of Customhouse
and Villere in 1854 are reflected in the census's Squares 12, 13, 24, and 25 of the city's
Second District. See Census of merchants, LDCA NOPL.

93   See Emily Epstein Landau, *Spectacular Wickedness: Sex, Race, and Memory in
Storyville, New Orleans* (Baton Rouge: Louisiana State University Press, 2018); and
Alecia P. Long, *The Great Southern Babylon: Sex, Race, and Respectability in New
Orleans, 1865–1920* (Baton Rouge: Louisiana State University Press, 2004).

94   Mary Jane Blair and Paul Stloi marriage record, June 30, 1848, Jefferson County,
Kentucky, US, County Marriage Records, 1783–1965, Ancestry.

95   Records of the demolished Girod Street Cemetery included a Prosper Blair who died
on August 13, 1858, at the height of one of the city's deadliest yellow fever epidemics.
Cemetery records stated his age as twenty-one, placing his year of birth at 1837. This
man could have been Prosper Blair's eldest son, Pierre Soude Prosper Blair, born in
1835. See Girod Street Cemetery records, 1817–1930, Louisiana, Orleans Parish, cemetery records, 1805–1944, LSM.

96   Register, vol. 3, 47, LDCA NOPL. In 1859, Prosper Blair's nineteen-year-old daughter, Victorine Julia Blair, registered with the mayor. She was described as a "mulatresse" and working as a housekeeper. The 1860 federal census classified her as
"black." She lived in a household of four young people in the city's Fourth Ward,
likely close to her parents. Her home was humble, valued by the enumerator at only
$100. Most of her immediate neighbors were white and many were German immi-
grants. *Eighth Census of the United States* (Washington, DC: GPO, 1864).

97   After Union forces arrived, some enslaved people escaped to fight for the Union
Army. Others resisted the waning authority of their defeated enslavers. Even if Louisiana abolished slavery in 1864, the same state constitution did not guarantee the
right to vote to Louisianians of color. See Adam Rothman, *Beyond Freedom's Reach:
A Kidnapping in the Twilight of Slavery* (Cambridge, MA: Harvard University Press,
2015); and Ira Berlin, Barbara J. Fields, Thavolia Glymph, Joseph P. Reidy, and Leslie S. Rowland, *Freedom: A Documentary History of Emancipation, 1861–1867: The
Destruction of Slavery*, series 1, vol. 1 (New York: Cambridge University Press, 1985),
187–245.

98   Blair appeared as "Prosper Blair" in *Bailey's Columbus Directory for 1871–1872* (Columbus, OH: Bailey, Publisher, 1871). The 1895 Columbus directory listed Elizabeth
Blair as "(wid Prosper)." R. L. Polk and Co., *Columbus City Directory 1895–6* (Columbus, OH: Franklin Printing Co., 1895). An Elizabeth Blair also appeared in the
1878 directory of Columbus, working as a laundress, and again in 1879, though she
was not identified with Prosper Blair. See *Wiggins & McKillop's Annual Columbus
Directory* (Columbus, OH: Wiggins and McKillop, 1878); *Columbus City Directory
for 1879* (Columbus, OH: G. J. Brand and Co., 1879).

99   "Dora [Blair] Bowles," Illinois, Illinois Death Certificates Database, 1916–1950,
https://apps.ilsos.gov/isavital/idphdeathsrch.jsp; and "Beatrice Bowles," Illinois
Statewide Death Index, Pre-1916, https://www.ilsos.gov/departments/archives
/databases/death.html, both online at the Illinois State Archives, accessed July 13,
2021.

100   Frederick Douglass, "The Color Line," *North American Review* 132, no. 295 (June
1881): 567–77, at 568; W. E. B. Du Bois, *The Souls of Black Folk*, in *The Norton Anthology of African American Literature*, 2nd ed., ed. Henry Louis Gates Jr. and Nellie Y. McKay (New York: W. W. Norton, 2004), 692.

101 The 1900 census described members of the Bowles family living in Chicago as "Black." Benny and Dora lived with their two young children as well as two of Benny's brothers, a niece, and a lodger. All four men in the house worked as Pullman porters. The 1910 census described the Bowles family as "Mulatto." In 1920, the census taker's scribble was transcribed as "W" for "white," though it was likely "M" for "mulatto." By 1920, children James (twenty-one), Arthur (nineteen), and Seetta (seventeen) worked as an operator at an elevator store, a railroad laborer, and a milliner, respectively. Many of the Bowles' younger neighbors in 1920 had been born in Illinois, like Arthur and Seetta. Neighbors who were of Benny and Dora's generation had been born in Mississippi, Louisiana, Missouri, Kentucky, and Georgia, reflecting the movements of the Great Migration. See Bureau of the Census, *Twelfth Census of the United States, Taken in the Year 1900*, 4 vols. (Washington, DC: US Census Office, 1902); *Thirteenth Census of the United States Taken in the Year 1910* (Washington, DC: Government Printing Office, 1913); Bureau of the Census, *Fourteenth Census of the United States Taken in the Year 1920* (Washington, DC: Government Printing Office, 1922).

102 "Mrs. Dora *Blair* Bowles, (1871–14 Jul 1924)," Find a Grave, accessed July 14, 2021, www.findagrave.com/memorial/186107923/dora-bowles; "Benjamin G. Bowles (1868–30 Dec 1921)," Find a Grave, accessed July 14, 2021, www.findagrave.com/memorial/177095727/benjamin-g-bowles. Thirteen victims of the 1919 Chicago Race Riot were buried in Lincoln Cemetery. Their bodies were not found until 2019. See Justin Dunnavant, Delande Justinvil, and Chip Colwell, "Craft an African American Graves Protection and Repatriation Act," *Nature*, May 19, 2021; "Lincoln Cemetery," Dignity Memorial, accessed December 21, 2021, https://www.dignitymemorial.com/funeral-homes/blue-island-il/lincoln-cemetery/6241.

103 My translation. "Une Scène dans un Café à la Nlle-Orléans," *L'Union*, July 7, 1864.

104 The writer transcribed the waiter's speech as an accented Louisiana Creole. When the proprietor scolded the waiter, he responded, "*Moi ne savais pas mousho*," rather than in the French spoken by the proprietor ("Une Scène dans un Café à la Nlle-Orléans").

105 *L'Union* began to publish in 1862, ceased production on July 19, 1864, and was succeeded by the *New Orleans Tribune*. See Mark Charles Roudané, "The *New Orleans Tribune*: An Introduction to America's First Black Daily Newspaper," accessed March 23, 2016, http://roudanez.com/the-new-orleans-tribune/.

106 New Orleanians stewed under Union occupation. Famously, the city's white women antagonized Union soldiers in the streets. See LeeAnn Whites and Alecia P. Long, eds., *Occupied Women: Gender, Military Occupation, and the American Civil War* (Baton Rouge: Louisiana State University Press, 2009).

107 "History of the Codes of Louisiana: Black Code," Law Library of Louisiana, accessed April 7, 2022, https://lasc.libguides.com/c.php?g=254608&p=1697981. See also Rothman, *Beyond Freedom's Reach*; and Steven Hahn, Steven F. Miller, Susan E. O'Donovan, John C. Rodrigue, and Leslie S. Rowland, eds., *Freedom: A Documentary History of Emancipation, 1861–1867: Land and Labor, 1865*, series 3, vol. 1 (Chapel Hill: University of North Carolina Press, 2008).

Chapter Three

1 The reporter also observed that Black freedmen seemed to have replaced Irish immigrant laborers on the levees. See "Local Intelligence," *New Orleans Times*, June 28, 1865.

2   For accounts of postbellum travels to New Orleans, see "New Orleans," *Chicago Daily Tribune*, December 26, 1872, 2; "The New Orleans of Today," *Boston Daily Globe*, November 28, 1876, 3; "New Orleans in Winter," *New York Times*, March 16, 1884, 5; Jules Dayot, "New Orleans Creoles," *Los Angeles Times*, September 7, 1890, 9; and "In the Train of Rex," *Boston Daily Globe*, February 7, 1894, 6.

3   On this era of thorough economic and social transformations, see Joshua Specht, *Red Meat Republic: A Hoof-to-Table History of How Beef Changed America* (Princeton, NJ: Princeton University Press, 2019); Richard White, *The Republic for Which It Stands: The United States during Reconstruction and the Gilded Age, 1865–1896* (New York: Oxford University Press, 2017); Matthew Frye Jacobson, *Barbarian Virtues: The United States Encounters Foreign Peoples at Home and Abroad, 1876–1917* (New York: Hill and Wang, 2000); and Gail Bederman, *Manliness and Civilization: A Cultural History of Gender and Race in the United States, 1880–1917* (Chicago: University of Chicago Press, 1995).

4   Bureau of Statistics, *Statistical Abstract of the United States, 1885* (Washington, DC: Government Printing Office, 1886), 165, 166.

5   On theories of monstrosity that take on new dimensions in the people, places, and machines of Louisiana sugar, during and after slavery, see Christina Sharpe, *Monstrous Intimacies: Making Post-Slavery Subjects* (Durham, NC: Duke University Press, 2010); Catherine Spooner, *Contemporary Gothic* (London: Reaktion Books, 2006); and Marie-Hélène Hunt, *Monstrous Imagination* (Cambridge, MA: Harvard University Press, 1993).

6   Lewis Webb, diary entry dated January 16, 1853, L. H. Webb diaries, 1853, record group 49 (hereafter Webb), LSM. Other written descriptions of the levee's goods, people, and animals show a similar construction to Webb's, in which the writing emulates the place's confusion. Sentences are litanies of words prevented from colliding by commas. "'Tis a busy, driving, dreadful place," wrote a reporter in 1857. "You, yourself—a man, a stranger—you are useless, and you are jostled . . . and are in danger of having your legs broken by machinery, your head mashed by swaying hardware, or of being rolled into the river by casks of whisky or sugar" ("Up the Mississippi," *Emerson's Magazine and Putnam's Monthly* 5, no. 41 [October 1857]: 436).

7   Webb, diary entry dated January 25, 1853, Webb, LSM.

8   Still, by 1884, Louisiana counted fewer miles of track than any Southern state and barely more than the New Mexico and Utah territories. See Bureau of Statistics, *Statistical Abstract of the United States, 1905* (Washington, DC: Government Printing Office, 1906), 551; *Statistical Abstract of the United States, 1885*, 196. On the reconstruction of postbellum New Orleans, see Justin A. Nystrom, *New Orleans after the Civil War: Race, Politics, and a New Birth of Freedom* (Baltimore, MD: Johns Hopkins University Press, 2015); Lawrence N. Powell, ed., *Reconstructing Louisiana*, vol. 6, Louisiana Purchase Bicentennial Series in Louisiana History (Lafayette: Center for Louisiana Studies, University of Louisiana Lafayette, 2001); and John W. Blassingame, *Black New Orleans, 1860–1880* (Chicago: University of Chicago Press, 1973).

9   For an overview of this promotional literature, see Gary A. Van Zante, *New Orleans 1867: Photographs by Theodore Lilienthal* (London: Merrell, 2008), 288–92.

10   Edwin L. Jewell, ed., *Jewell's Crescent City Illustrated: The Commercial, Social, Political and General History, Including Biographical Sketches of Its Distinguished Citizens* (New Orleans, LA: n.p., 1873), 19.

11   A. B. Griswold and Co., *Guide Book* (New Orleans: 1873), 10, 30.

12   *Souvenir of New Orleans and the Exposition* (New Orleans: L. Schwarz, 1885), Li-

brary of Congress (hereafter LOC). New Orleans's political leadership understood photography's potential to attract prospective investment and immigrants. In 1867, the city council commissioned a series of photographs to be displayed at the Paris Exposition. The photographs won a top prize, but they did not generate the desired waves of European immigrants to replace formerly enslaved laborers. See Van Zante, *New Orleans 1867*, 11–39. See also Peter B. Hales, *Silver Cities: Photographing American Urbanization, 1839–1939* (Albuquerque: University of New Mexico Press, 2005), 123–26.

13 "Loafs along the Levee," *Daily Picayune*, December 28, 1873.

14 *The Picayune's Guide to New Orleans* (New Orleans, LA: Nicholson and Co., 1896), 36–37.

15 On the American industrial sublime, see Walter Johnson, *River of Dark Dreams: Slavery and Empire in the Cotton Kingdom* (Cambridge, MA: Belknap Press, 2013), 73–84; Darcy Grimaldo Grigsby, *Colossal: Engineering the Suez Canal, Statue of Liberty, Eiffel Tower, and Panama Canal* (Pittsburgh, PA: Periscope, 2012); David E. Nye, *American Technological Sublime* (Cambridge, MA: MIT Press, 1994); and Thomas J. Schlereth, *Victorian America: Transformations in Everyday Life, 1876–1915* (New York: Harper Collins, 1991).

16 Joseph H. Beale, *Picturesque Sketches of Great American Cities* (New York: Empire Co-Operative Association, 1889), 76–77.

17 Daniel Rosenberg, *New Orleans Dockworkers: Race, Labor, and Unionism, 1892–1923* (Albany: State University of New York Press, 1988), 48. On roustabouts farther north, see Gregg Andrews, *Shantyboats and Roustabouts: The River Poor of St. Louis, 1875–1930* (Baton Rouge: Louisiana State University Press, 2022).

18 Julian Ralph, "The Old Way to Dixie," *Harper's New Monthly Magazine* 86, no. 512 (January 1893), 176, 175. Jazz musician "Jelly Roll" Morton, raised in turn-of-the-century New Orleans, also remembered the backbreaking nature of roustabouts' labor. Roustabouts "had a captain over them with a whip or lash in their hands," Morton remembered. "They were just like in slavery." As quoted in Rosenberg, *New Orleans Dockworkers*, 48.

19 Peter Barber, interviewed in Ronnie W. Clayton, ed., *Mother Wit: The Ex-Slave Narratives of the Louisiana Writers' Project* (New York: Peter Lang, 1990), 26. WPA interviews with former roustabouts and levee workers in New Orleans, Houston, and other cities noted the pay as an attraction to workers. "As a roustabout and common laborer, I used to make $1.50 a day," said Martin Dragney (interviewed in Clayton, ed., *Mother Wit*, 62). See also Frank Moss, interviewed in Clayton, ed., *Mother Wit*, 173–75; and Robert St. Ann, interviewed in Clayton, ed., *Mother Wit*, 191–92.

20 Ralph, "Old Way to Dixie," 166.

21 "The Great South: Old and New Louisiana – II," *Scribner's Monthly* 7, no. 2 (December 1873): 133–35; and Franklin, "Strolling About the Quaint Old City of New Orleans," *Leslie's Weekly*, December 11, 1902, 558. Turn-of-the-century American popular culture also emasculated Black men as thieves or dandies or vilified them as predatory sexual beasts, maternalized Black women as "mammies," and objectified Black girls as playful "pickaninnies." On the history of such stereotypes, see Henry Louis Gates Jr., *Stony the Road: Reconstruction, White Supremacy, and the Rise of Jim Crow* (New York: Penguin Books, 2019), 94–100, 126–57; David Brion Davis, *The Problem of Slavery in the Age of Emancipation* (New York: Alfred A. Knopf, 2014), 3–44; Karen L. Cox, *Dreaming of Dixie: How the South Was Created in American*

Popular Culture (Chapel Hill: University of North Carolina Press, 2011); and Psyche Williams-Forson, *Building Houses out of Chicken Legs: Black Women, Food, and Power* (Chapel Hill: University of North Carolina Press, 2006).

22 *Reports from the Consuls of the United States*, vol. 24 (Washington, DC: Government Printing Office, 1887), 266.

23 Rosenberg, *New Orleans Dockworkers*, 44; Eric Arnesen, *Waterfront Workers of New Orleans: Race, Class, and Politics, 1863–1923* (New York: Oxford University Press, 1991), viii.

24 For an overview of levee occupations, see Rosenberg, *New Orleans Dockworkers*, 47–55; and Arnesen, *Waterfront Workers*, 38–42. White observers of levee workers also drew associations between a worker's race, job, and clothing. One onlooker noted that the levee's cotton classers and sugar graders, all white men, wore paper aprons to keep their clothing uncontaminated by the substances they assessed: "Never a trace of lint appeared on them to betray his profession." Longshoremen and roustabouts, in contrast—"most of them negroes, a few, however, a muddy white"— wore "the most forlorn and ragged clothing," noted a journalist. "Clothing is nothing to them." These workers could not help but bear the marks of the commodities they moved. See Léon H. Grandjean, *Crayon Reproductions of Léon J. Frémaux's New Orleans Characters and Additional Sketches by Léon H. Grandjean* (New Orleans, LA: Alfred F. Bayhi, 1949); "Loafs along the Levee."

25 In the late 1800s, unionized Black dockworkers forged a powerful presence, negotiating pay increases and protecting their access to work. Nevertheless, the animosity, exclusion, and violence that white Louisianians leveled at their neighbors of color leaked onto the levee, too. White levee workers or mobs attacked Black levee workers in 1880, 1895, and 1900. On cooperation and conflict among New Orleans levee workers, see Rosenberg, *New Orleans Dockworkers*; Arnesen, *Waterfront Workers*; and Blassingame, *Black New Orleans*, 65. On white violence in New Orleans during this era, see Ida B. Wells-Barnett, *Mob Rule in New Orleans: Robert Charles and His Fight to Death, the Story of His Life, Burning Human Beings Alive, Other Lynching Statistics* (Chicago: n.p., 1900).

26 John Alexander Murray Wilson, "What One Sees in New Orleans," 1897, manuscript, MSS 362, THNOC; entry for February 8, 1903, box 5, folder 4: Untitled pocket ledger / From PA to New Orleans / unnamed Leather Worker Union member, 1903, Collection 65: Anthony Stanonis travel scrapbook and diary collection, collection no. 65 (hereafter Stanonis), Special Collections and Archives, J. Edgar and Louise S. Monroe Library, Loyola University New Orleans (hereafter Loyola).

27 In his shop at 902 Canal St., Greek immigrant John Scordillo hawked provocative postcards that prompted a visit from the police. One such card featured "the picture of a woman, with a cloth dress from the waist down," an officer recorded. "The dress is attached to the picture in such a manner that it can be raised up, showing the posterior of the woman, with don't worry, and other mottos printed on." March 12, 1910, box 1, series 2, folder: March 1910, New Orleans Police Department, Office of Inspector of Police, correspondence, 1899–1913, LDCA NOPL.

28 Postcards and stereographs were not always souvenirs of travel. Americans exchanged postcards for their aesthetic or humorous appeal or to convey a simple message. See Edward W. Earle, ed., *Points of View: The Stereograph in America—A Cultural History* (Rochester, NY: Visual Studies Workshop Press, 1979), 76; Brooke Baldwin, "On the Verso: Postcard Messages as a Key to Popular Prejudices," *Journal*

of Popular Culture 22, no. 3 (Winter 1988): 15–28, at 16; and Annette Pritchard and Nigel Morgan, "Mythic Geographies of Representation and Identity: Contemporary Postcards of Wales," *Journal of Tourism and Cultural Change* 1, no. 2 (2003): 111–30.

29 W. Y. Barnet, "New Orleans Entertains," *Banking and Mercantile World* 4, no. 6 (November–December 1902): 227–49, at 232, 246.

30 Barnet, "New Orleans Entertains," 247–48. On the popularization of "scientific racism" at this time, see Gates, *Stony the Road*, 67–77.

31 Barnet, "New Orleans Entertains," 248.

32 A woman named Melinda, who was born around 1854 and enslaved in Louisiana, likewise recalled postbellum pleasure visits from "city folks" to the sugar plantation during grinding season. "Dey all would come on dat big steamboat . . . 'De Belle of de Coast,'" she told a WPA interviewer. "Dem young people sho had a good time ridin' dem sugar carts" (interviewed in Clayton, ed., *Mother Wit*, 168). Her recollection of the steamboat's name dates these visits to between 1880 and 1897. See *Belle of the Coast (Packet, 1880–1897)*, photograph, University of Wisconsin–La Crosse Historic Steamboat Photographs, accessed March 15, 2022, https://digital.library.wisc .edu/1711.dl/HTJU44BXPEFE78A.

33 Frances Milton Trollope, *Domestic Manners of the Americans*, vol. 2, 4th ed. (London: Printed for Whittaker, Treacher, 1832), 131, 133.

34 John B. Rehder, *Delta Sugar: Louisiana's Vanishing Plantation Landscape* (Baltimore, MD: Johns Hopkins University Press, 1999), 127. For most years on record, the US imported more sugar than it produced. In 1830, Americans consumed 35,390 tons of imported sugar and 34,321 tons of domestic sugar. See Bureau of Statistics, *Statistical Abstract of the United States, 1905* (Washington, DC: Government Printing Office, 1906), 504.

35 Rehder, *Delta Sugar*, 55, 127.

36 Richard Follett, *The Sugar Masters: Planters and Slaves in Louisiana's Cane World, 1820–1860* (Baton Rouge: Louisiana State University Press, 2005), 24. In 1850, the US census counted nearly 250,000 enslaved people in Louisiana. See J. D. B. De Bow, *Compendium of the Seventh Census* (Washington, DC: Beverley Tucker, Senate Printer, 1854), 82.

37 Rehder, *Delta Sugar*, 127; Roy A. Ballinger, *A History of Sugar Marketing through 1974*, Agricultural Economic Report no. 382 (Washington, DC: US Department of Agriculture, March 1978), 6–7, https://www.ers.usda.gov/webdocs/publications /40532/aer-382.pdf?v=0; Bureau of Statistics, *Statistical Abstract of the United States, 1905*, 503. Most Louisiana sugar was not refined in the state; in 1840, the state counted five refineries. Department of State, *Compendium of the Enumeration of the Inhabitants and Statistics of the United States, as Obtained at the Department of State, from the Returns of the Sixth Census* (Washington, DC: Thomas Allen, 1841), 247.

38 Bureau of Foreign and Domestic Commerce, *Statistical Abstract of the United States, 1912* (Washington, DC: Government Printing Office. 1913), 253.

39 William O'Neal, *Life and History of William O'Neal, or, the Man Who Sold His Wife* (St. Louis, MO: A. R. Fleming and Co., 1896), 29–30.

40 In 1843, Norbert Rillieux, a free man of color born in New Orleans, transformed sugar production with his patent of a new technique for evaporating sugar under vacuum. This process eliminated the need to move boiling sugar from one kettle to another, reducing waste and producing a higher-quality sugar. Despite the importance of his innovation, planters did not permit Rillieux to sleep in their homes

when he visited to consult on the installation of his technology, because of his skin color. See Follett, *Sugar Masters*, 33–34; American Chemical Society National Historic Chemical Landmarks, "Norbert Rillieux and a Revolution in Sugar Processing," accessed March 14, 2022, http://www.acs.org/content/acs/en/education /whatischemistry/landmarks/norbertrillieux.html.

41   Albert Patterson, formerly enslaved on a sugar plantation in Plaquemines Parish, described one of these skilled workers to a WPA interviewer: "There was a colored man from Mississippi that knew when the sugar grain [granulated]" (interviewed in Clayton, ed., *Mother Wit*, 178).

42   For general descriptions of the sugar-making process in nineteenth-century Louisiana, see Rehder, *Delta Sugar*, 134–38; and Follett, *Sugar Masters*.

43   Mrs. [Matilda Charlotte] Houston, *Hesperos: Or, Travels in the West*, vol. 2 (London: John W. Parker, Albemarle Street, 1850), 156.

44   Lewis Garrard Clarke and Milton Clarke, *Narratives of the Sufferings of Lewis and Milton Clarke, Sons of a Soldier of the Revolution, during a Captivity of More Than Twenty Years among the Slaveholders of Kentucky, One of the So Called Christian States of North America, Dictated by Themselves* (Boston, MA: Bela Marsh, 1846), 127–28.

45   Ceceil George, interviewed in Clayton, ed., *Mother Wit*, 84–85. For additional first-hand accounts of the torture endured by enslaved people on sugarcane plantations, see Catherine Cornelius, Daffney Johnson, and Hunton Love, interviewed in Clayton, ed., *Mother Wit*, 45, 130, 161–62; Ottobah Cugoano, "Narrative of the Enslavement of Ottobah Cugoano, a Native of Africa; Published by Himself, in the Year 1787," in Thomas Fisher, *The Negro's Memorial, or, Abolitionist's Catechism by an Abolitionist*, by Thomas Fisher (London: Hatchard and Co., 1825), 125–26; Ashton Warner and Susanna Moodie, *Negro Slavery Described by a Negro: Being the Narrative of Ashton Warner, a Native of St. Vincent's. With an Appendix Containing the Testimony of Four Christian Ministers, Recently Returned from the Colonies, on the System of Slavery as It Now Exists* (London: Samuel Maunder, 1831), 25–28, 33–40, 129–35; Solomon Northup, *Twelve Years a Slave: Narrative of Solomon Northup, a Citizen of New-York, Kidnapped in Washington City in 1841, and Rescued in 1853, from a Cotton Plantation near the Red River in Louisiana* (Auburn, NY: Derby and Miller, 1853), 193–95, 208–13, 243–44; and C. L. R. James, *The Black Jacobins: Toussaint L'Ouverture and the San Domingo Revolution*, 2nd ed. (New York: Vintage Books, 1989), 12–13.

46   Beyond the sheer brutality of sugar production, the demographics of Louisiana's bondspeople were also shaped by the extraordinary demand for enslaved men for the cane fields and the effects of grueling labor on enslaved women's fertility. See Richard Follett, "'Lives of Living Death': The Reproductive Lives of Slave Women in the Cane World of Louisiana," *Slavery and Abolition* 26, no. 2 (August 2005): 289–304; and Michael Tadman, "The Demographic Cost of Sugar: Debates on Slave Societies and Natural Increase in the Americas," *American Historical Review* 105, no. 5 (December 2000): 1534–75.

47   Ellen Broomfield, interviewed in Clayton, ed., *Mother Wit*, 32.

48   I thank Reader 3 for pointing out the toxicity of jimsonweed. See Kit Chan, "Jimson Weed Poisoning—A Case Report," *Permanente Journal* 6, no. 4 (Fall 2002): 28–30.

49   Frederick Law Olmsted, *Journey in the Seaboard Slave States: With Remarks on Their Economy* (London: Sampson Low, Son, and Co., 1856), 660. On representations of enslaved people cohered with the products they made, see Michael O'Malley,

Face Value: The Entwined Histories of Money and Race in America (Chicago: University of Chicago Press, 2012).

50   Clarke and Clarke, *Narratives of the Sufferings*, 128, 127.

51   The chimes are the raised, beveled edge on either end of a wooden barrel. See William H. Robinson, *From Log Cabin to the Pulpit, or, Fifteen Years in Slavery* (Eau Claire, WI: James H. Tifft, 1913), 12. Lydia Lee, enslaved in Barataria Parish, recalled the work of sugar production as a process of purifying a filthy substance that initially seemed inedible. "De first juice you see is so black and dirty—just like de gutter water, you don't see how people goin' to eat it—den it keeps getting' clear" (interviewed in Clayton, ed., *Mother Wit*, 150).

52   Christina Sharpe acknowledged the violent contradictions inherent in sugar fused to slavery, writing, "Sugar as punishment; sugar as excess; sugar as pain; sugar as pleasure" (*In the Wake: On Blackness and Being* [Durham, NC: Duke University Press, 2016], 99).

53   Jessica Barbata Jackson, *Dixie's Italians: Sicilians, Race, and Citizenship in the Jim Crow Gulf South* (Baton Rouge: Louisiana State University Press, 2020); Justin A. Nystrom, *Creole Italian: Sicilian Immigrants and the Shaping of New Orleans Food Culture* (Athens: University of Georgia Press, 2018); Moon-Ho Jung, *Coolies and Cane: Race, Labor, and Sugar in the Age of Emancipation* (Baltimore, MD: Johns Hopkins University Press, 2006); and Walter Prichard, "The Effects of the Civil War on the Louisiana Sugar Industry," *Journal of Southern History* 5, no. 3 (August 1939): 315–32.

54   Annie Flowers, interviewed in Clayton, ed., *Mother Wit*, 71.

55   Octavia V. Rogers Albert, *The House of Bondage: Or Charlotte Brooks and Other Slaves Original and Life-Like, as They Appeared in Their Old Plantation and City Slave Life; Together with Pen-Pictures of the Peculiar Institution, with Sights and Insights into Their New Relations as Freedmen, Freemen, and Citizens* (New York: Hunt and Eaton, 1890), 51–52. Lizzie Chandler remembered that she earned only $1.20 in wages for a ten-hour day in Louisiana rice and cane fields after the Civil War. Chandler left agricultural work for a job as a chambermaid on a steamboat and found a greatly improved situation. There, she earned $3.00 in wages per trip, plus $6.00 to $7.00 in tips, plus extra to wash passengers' clothes. See Lizzie Chandler, interviewed in Clayton, ed., *Mother Wit*, 41.

56   See Rebecca J. Scott, *Degrees of Freedom: Louisiana and Cuba after Slavery* (Cambridge, MA: Belknap Press, 2008); John C. Rodrigue, *Reconstruction in the Cane Fields: From Slavery to Free Labor in Louisiana's Sugar Parishes, 1862–1880* (Baton Rouge: Louisiana State University Press, 2001); and John C. Rodrigue, "Labor Militancy and Black Grassroots Political Mobilization in the Louisiana Sugar Region, 1865–1868," *Journal of Social History* 67, no. 1 (February 2001): 115–42.

57   My translation. Prosper Jacotot, *Voyage d'un ouvrier dans la Vallée du Mississippi, du Saint-Louis à la Nouvelle-Orléans: Scènes de moeurs* (Dijon, France: 1888).

58   Khalil Gibran Muhammad, "The Sugar that Saturates the American Diet Has a Barbaric History as the 'White Gold' That Fueled Slavery," in Nikole Hannah-Jones et al., *The 1619 Project*, an ongoing initiative by the *New York Times Magazine*, August 14, 2019, https://www.nytimes.com/interactive/2019/08/14/magazine/sugar-slave-trade-slavery.html; Michael Hardy, "Blood and Sugar," *Texas Monthly*, January 2017, https://www.texasmonthly.com/articles/sugar-land-slave-convict-labor-history/; Thomas Beller, "Angola Prison and the Shadow of Slavery," *New Yorker*,

August 19, 2015, https://www.newyorker.com/culture/photo-booth/angola-prison
-louisiana-photos; Steve Hardy, "Angola Inmates Make Sugar Cane Syrup the Old-
Fashioned Way," *Advocate*, December 23, 2014, https://www.theadvocate.com
/baton_rouge/news/communities/west_feliciana/article_dbc913cb-9fc8-52ad
-9de8-8ac99fc9def5.html; Douglas A. Blackmon, *Slavery by Another Name: The
Re-Enslavement of Black Americans from the Civil War to World War II* (New York:
Anchor Books, 2008); and *Sugar House at Hope State Farm at the Louisiana State
Penitentiary at Mount Hope near Jeanerette Louisiana circa 1901*, ca. 1901, photo-
graph, taken from *Louisiana State Penitentiary 1901 Annual Report*, online at State
Library of Louisiana Historic Photograph Collection, State Library of Louisiana,
https://louisianadigitallibrary.org/islandora/object/state-lhp%3A9579. See also
Shane Mitchell, "Raising Cane," *Bitter Southerner*, November 24, 2020, https://
bittersoutherner.com/feature/2020/raising-cane-sapelo-island-shane-mitchell.

59   Bureau of Foreign and Domestic Commerce, *Statistical Abstract of the United States,
      1912*, 593. The percentage of domestically produced sugar increased after 1900 be-
      cause the United States claimed Hawaii and Puerto Rico as American territories.
      Ballinger, *History of Sugar Marketing*, 9, 11, 16.

60   Frederick Douglass, "Lecture on Pictures," delivered December 3, 1861, in Boston,
      MA, repr. in John Stauffer, Zoe Trodd, and Celeste-Marie Bernier, *Picturing Fred-
      erick Douglass: An Illustrated Biography of the Nineteenth Century's Most Photo-
      graphed American* (New York: Liveright, 2015), 127.

61   One writer observed in 1911, "Picture-Postcards are now like the poor—we have
      them always with us." See "Picture Postcards," *Photo Era* (April 1911), 192, as quoted
      in Edward W. Earle, "The Stereograph in America: Pictorial Antecedents and Cul-
      tural Perspectives," in *Points of View*, ed. Earle, 82. Scholars estimate that nearly one
      billion postcards were sold annually in the decade from 1905 and 1915. Although
      postcards and stereographs rose to prominence at the same time, only postcards
      persisted in popularity. Stereographs faded from use in the 1920s and 1930s due to
      the advent of radio, movies, and the automobile, which all promised new, multisen-
      sory diversions in the family parlor and far from it. See Baldwin, "On the Verso"; and
      Jessica B. Harris, *Vintage Postcards from the African World: In the Dignity of Their
      Work and the Joy of Their Play* (Jackson: University Press of Mississippi, 2020). On
      trade cards, see Kyla Wazana Tompkins, *Racial Indigestion: Eating Bodies in the
      19th Century* (New York: New York University Press, 2012), 145–81; Ricia Anne
      Chansky, "Time to Shop: Advertising Trade Card Rhetoric and the Construction of
      a Public Space for Women in the United States, 1880–1900," *Atenea* 29, no. 1 (June
      2009): 151–66; and Robert Jay, *The Trade Card in Nineteenth-Century America* (Co-
      lumbia: University of Missouri Press, 1987).

62   On the technical development of stereography and its popularity, see Earle, *Points
      of View*; Douglas Heil, *The Art of Stereography: Rediscovering Vintage Three-
      Dimensional Images* (Jefferson, NC: McFarland and Co., Inc., 2017); Paul Wing, *Ste-
      reoscopes: The First One Hundred Years* (Nashua, NH: Transition Publishing, 1996);
      Jib Fowles, "Stereography and the Standardization of Vision," *Journal of Ameri-
      can Culture* 17, no. 2 (June 1994): 89–93; Robert J. Silverman, "The Stereoscope
      and Photographic Depiction in the 19th Century," *Technology and Culture* 34, no. 4
      (1993): 729–56; William C. Darrah, *The World of Stereographs* (Gettysburg, PA: Dar-
      rah, 1977); and William C. Darrah, *Stereo Views: A History of Stereographs in Amer-
      ica and Their Collection* (Gettysburg, PA: Times and News Publishing Co., 1964).

63   *American Journal of Photography*, August 1, 1858, 82, as quoted in *Points of View*, ed. Earle, 32.

64   For analysis of various compositional strategies of stereography, see Heil, *Art of Stereography*. Scholars have interpreted the mode of looking at stereographs as "pre-cinematic," as the medium encouraged viewers to look around the image and look for a longer amount of time. See Van Zante, *New Orleans 1867*, fn. 7, 266.

65   Additional popular stereoviews included "London bridge, Ludgate hill, St. Mary's Church, Ireland; the Giant's causeway, the market place in Cologne and the interior of Westminster Abbey. Comic stereoscopic views are great favorites, representing such scenes as a husband with a bottle of whisky in the bedroom being lectured by his spouse, a Dutch courtship, a pillow fight, and so forth" ("Photographs by Whole-sale," *Washington Star*, repr. in *Daily Picayune*, August 30, 1890).

66   Fowles, "Stereography and the Standardization," 89; Darrah, *Stereo Views*, v, 109.

67   Fowles, "Stereography and the Standardization," 91.

68   The thematic variety of stereoviews is visible in the for sale/trade columns in *Stereo World*, published by the National Stereoscopic Association. See "Stereo Sale," *Stereo World* 5, no. 6 (January–February 1979): 32.

69   "Antituberculosis," *Times-Picayune*, February 10, 1911; "X-Ray in Surgery," *Times-Picayune*, August 20, 1916.

70   Edgar Maresmar, "Franklin School Pupils Like Stereoscope Views," *Times-Picayune*, April 30, 1922.

71   Sir David Brewster, *The Stereoscope: Its History, Theory, and Construction, with Its Application to the Fine and Useful Arts and to Education* (London: John Murray, 1856; Hastings-on-Hudson: Morgan and Morgan, 1971), 164.

72   A writer described the accuracy of a set of stereoviews of the Holy Land in rapturous detail: "We have only the plain unvarnished truth; the actual is absolutely before us, and we know it. There has been here no possibility of either adding or subtracting" (*Art Journal* [1858], 375, as quoted in *Points of View*, ed. Earle, 30). On stereography's power to help faraway viewers feel knowledgeable about a place, see Hoelscher, "The Photographic Construction of Tourist Space in Victorian America," *Geographical Review* 88, no. 4 (1998): 548–70.

73   Emphasis in original. Oliver Wendell Holmes, "The Stereoscope and Stereograph," *Atlantic Monthly* (June 1859), https://www.theatlantic.com/magazine/archive/1859/06/the-stereoscope-and-the-stereograph/303361/.

74   Holmes avowed the "impossibility of the stereograph's perjuring itself" (Oliver Wendell Holmes, *Soundings from the Atlantic* [Boston, MA: Ticknor and Fields, 1864], 174–75).

75   *Daily Picayune*, October 20, 1873.

76   *Daily Picayune*, January 15, 1874.

77   *Daily Picayune*, May 29, 1910. On the cross-class appeal of early twentieth-century popular media, see Lizabeth Cohen, *Making a New Deal: Industrial Workers in Chicago, 1919–1939* (Cambridge: Cambridge University Press, 1990), 99–158.

78   *Lagniappe* was a little something extra that a vendor included with a purchase, such as a bulb of garlic with a pound of potatoes. The author of the 1903 *Picayune's Guide* described locals' attachment to the practice, writing, "Some years ago an effort was made by certain progressive shopkeepers to abolish 'lagniappe.' There was a hue and cry and the old custom remained." Five years later, however, the 1908 *Picayune's Guide* reported mournfully that private markets had stopped giving lagniappe.

"Not more than a year ago the retail grocers of New Orleans decided not to give 'lagniappe' any longer. This was a death-blow to one of the most picturesque customs of the city. Lagniappe survives in many places, the street vendors, cake women and bakers generally continue to give it, but the practice is dying out." See *The Picayune's Guide to New Orleans: Revised and Enlarged*, 5th ed. (New Orleans, LA: Picayune, 1903), 71–72, and *The Picayune's Guide to New Orleans*, 8th ed. (New Orleans, LA: Picayune Job Print, 1908), 52.

79   Van Zante, *New Orleans 1867*, 261–67. See also Margaret Denton Smith, "Checklist of Photographers Working in New Orleans, 1840–1865," *Louisiana History* 20, no. 4 (Autumn 1979): 393–430.

80   Louisiana's sugar industry represents the largest single subject depicted in approximately two hundred stereographs of Louisiana scenes accessible via the Louisiana Digital Library, an amalgamation of objects held in libraries, museums, and archives throughout the state. Of 150 stereoscopic views of Louisiana scenes held by the New York Public Library, more than one-third are photographs of the levee. Similar trends may be found in the collection of stereograph cards preserved by the Library of Congress. See "Let's Discover Louisiana Together," Louisiana Digital Library, accessed March 20, 2023, https://louisianadigitallibrary.org/; "Louisiana," Robert N. Dennis collection of stereoscopic views, NYPL, accessed March 20, 2023, https://digitalcollections.nypl.org/collections/robert-n-dennis-collection-of-stereoscopic-views#/; and "Stereograph Cards," LOC, accessed March 20, 2023, https://www.loc.gov/pictures/collection/stereo/.

81   Charles Seaver, *The Mississippi River, New Orleans Series, A*, ca. 1880, stereograph, Rowles stereograph collection, LSM.

82   On the enormous tide of racist visual stereotypes of Black Americans at the turn of the twentieth century—the "everyday numbingly repeatable tropes of white supremacy"—see Gates, *Stony the Road*, 106–7, 136; and Stanley Lemons, "Black Stereotypes as Reflected in Popular Culture, 1880–1920," *American Quarterly* 29, no. 1 (Spring 1977): 102–16. Gates and others trace a progression from chromolithography to minstrel shows to moving pictures but omit stereography. On the persistent neglect of stereography by researchers, perhaps due to its lowbrow appeal and eclipse by other media, see Van Zante, *New Orleans 1867*, 7; and Fowles, "Stereography and the Standardization," 89.

83   On comedy that emanated from photographic depictions of race, see Tanya Sheehan, *Study in Black and White: Photography, Race, Humor* (University Park: Pennsylvania State Press, 2018). See also *Grinding Cane—A Branch Establishment*, ca. 1901, stereograph, Prints and Photographs Division (hereafter PPD), LOC; George François Mugnier, *Champion Sugar Mills*, ca. 1880, stereograph, Rowles stereograph collection, LSM; William H. Rau, *No Stop for Seeds or Rind*, ca. 1903, stereograph, PPD, LOC; and B. W. Kilburn, *Terrors of the Aligater* [sic] *Swamp, Fla., 1870–1880*, ca. 1870–1880, PPD, LOC. Stereoviews of Florida and Georgia scenes likewise emphasized the states' edible, agricultural products, including oranges, coconuts, date palms, and bananas. See Robert N. Dennis collection of stereoscopic views, NYPL.

84   On the relationship between looking and power, see Nicholas Mirzoeff, *The Right to Look: A Counterhistory of Visuality* (Durham, NC: Duke University Press, 2011); and bell hooks, "The Oppositional Gaze: Black Female Spectators," in hooks, *Black Looks: Race and Representation* (Boston, MA: South End Press, 1992), 115–31.

85   Gates, *Stony the Road*, 94–100, 126–57; Davis, *Problem of Slavery*, 3–44.

86 This pair of views demonstrated how stereography could empower the viewer with a sensation of "venturesomeness without risk" (Fowles, "Stereography and the Standardization," 91).

87 Nathaniel P. Weston, "'Frecher Versuch das Arbeitshaus zu zerstören': An Introduction to Vagrancy and Workhouses in New Orleans," *Louisiana History* 41, no. 4 (Autumn 2000): 467–81.

88 On the "compulsory visibility" of the Black body, see Harvey Young, *Embodying Black Experience: Stillness, Critical Memory, and the Black Body* (Ann Arbor: University of Michigan Press, 2010), 12.

89 For additional examples of this visual trope among New Orleans levee workers, see Edward L. Wilson, *Levee Loungers*, 1884, stereograph, Photographs and Prints Division, Schomburg Center for Research in Black Culture; NYPL, https://digitalcollections.nypl.org/items/510d47df-796c-a3d9-e040-e00a18064a99; Strohmeyer and Wyman, *Noon-Time Lunch o[n] the Levee, New Orleans, U.S.A.*, 1895, stereograph, LOC, https://www.loc.gov/pictures/item/2018649758/; J. F. Jarvis, *Levee Scene, New Orleans, U.S.A.*, 1891, stereograph, LOC, https://www.loc.gov/pictures/item/2018649349/; and Standard Scenic Company, *In the Midst of Levee, Life, and Cotton Traffic, New Orleans, La.*, 1907, stereograph, LOC, https://www.loc.gov/pictures/item/2015645058/.

90 In contrast to representations of roustabouts as unseeing or asleep, New Orleans newspapers and boosterish publications repeatedly used the adjective "wide-awake" to characterize entrepreneurs whom they claimed were laboring diligently for the city's modernization. See *Some Telling Facts of the Second District and the Famous French Market of the City of New Orleans, Issued as a Souvenir of All the Live, Up-to-Date Features of This Important Section. Within the Enclosed Pages Will Be Found Personal Sketches of Many of the Progressive and Enterprising Business Men and Leading Citizens* (New Orleans, LA: National Publishing Company, 1912), 24, 26. Louisiana newspapers also used this adjective to evoke cleverness, resourcefulness, and industrious energy, as in "Hygienic Home Treatment," *Daily Picayune*, February 11, 1912; *New Advocate*, April 29, 1912.

91 My translation. "Etablissements dans le Sud," *Abeille*, January 19, 1866.

92 "Labor-Vagrancy-Slavery," *Abeille*, January 25, 1866.

93 Weston, "'Frecher Versuch,'" 477–78. On vagrancy and idleness, see John K. Bardes, "Redefining Vagrancy: Policing Freedom and Disorder in Reconstruction New Orleans, 1862–1868," *Journal of Southern History* 84, no. 1 (February 2018): 69–112; Mary Farmer-Kaiser, "'Are They Not in Some Sorts Vagrants?': Gender and the Efforts of the Freedmen's Bureau to Combat Vagrancy in the Reconstruction South," *Georgia Historical Quarterly* 88, no. 1 (Spring 2004): 25–49; and Amy Dru Stanley, *From Bondage to Contract: Wage Labor, Marriage, and the Market in the Age of Slave Emancipation* (Cambridge: Cambridge University Press, 1998). On Black workers' slowdowns and other "daily acts of resistance," see Robin D. G. Kelley, *Race Rebels: Culture, Politics, and the Black Working Class* (New York: Free Press, 1994), esp. 17–34.

94 Reader letter, *Daily Picayune*, November 24, 1890. For additional allegations of laziness and sabotage among river workers, see *St. Louis Globe-Democrat*, repr. in *Daily Picayune*, April 28, 1884; *Mount Vernon* (IN) *Republican*, repr. in *Times-Picayune*, February 25, 1893; *Daily Picayune*, May 11, 1901.

95 "About This Collection," Wilson S. Howell photograph collection, LDCA NOPL, accessed March 21, 2022, https://cdm16880.contentdm.oclc.org/digital/collection/p16880coll4.

96 Sheila McNally, "Ariadne and Others: Image of Sleep in Greek and Early Roman Art," *Classical Antiquity* 4, no. 2 (October 1985): 152–92. See also Guy C. McElroy, *Facing History: The Black Image in American Art, 1710–1940* (Washington, DC: Corcoran Gallery of Art, 1990).

97 The most famous example of this pose was the late eighteenth-century abolitionist medallion created by the Wedgewood company. See Marcus Wood, *The Horrible Gift of Freedom: Atlantic Slavery and the Representation of Emancipation* (Athens: University of Georgia Press, 2010), 35–89. See also Kirk Savage, *Standing Soldiers, Kneeling Slaves: Race, War, and Monument in Nineteenth-Century America* (Princeton, NJ: Princeton University Press, 1997); Maurie McInnis, *Slaves Waiting for Sale: Abolitionist Art and the American Slave Trade* (Chicago: University of Chicago Press, 2011); Kay Kriz, *Slavery, Sugar, and the Culture of Refinement: Picturing the British West Indies, 1700–1840* (New Haven, CT: Yale University Press, 2008); Marcus Wood, *Blind Memory: Visual Representations of Slavery in England and America, 1780–1865* (London: Routledge, 1999); and Saidiya V. Hartman, *Scenes of Subjection: Terror, Slavery, and Self-Making in Nineteenth-Century America* (New York: Oxford University Press, 1997).

98 Cox, *Dreaming of Dixie*; Rebecca Cawood McIntyre, *Souvenirs of the Old South: Northern Tourism and Southern Mythology* (Gainesville: University Press of Florida, 2011); and Tara McPherson, *Reconstructing Dixie: Race, Gender, and Nostalgia in the Imagined South* (Durham, NC: Duke University Press, 2003).

99 On white perceptions of the indolent or "indifferent" other, see Klas Rönnbäck, "'The Men Seldom Suffer a Woman to Sit Down': The Historical Development of the Stereotype of the 'Lazy African,'" *African Studies* 73, no. 2 (August 2014): 211–27; Jennifer Roberts, "Landscapes of Indifference: Robert Smithson and John Lloyd Stephens in Yucatán," *Art Bulletin* 82, no. 3 (September 2000): 544–67; and David J. Langum, "Californios and the Image of Indolence," *Western Historical Quarterly* 9, no. 2 (April 1978): 181–96.

100 Americans who gazed at napping roustabouts may have felt they accomplished the double work of sophisticating themselves while ascertaining that the Black worker remained unsophisticated. On the relationship between "visual sophistication" and personal success in the Gilded Age, see Fowles, "Stereography and the Standardization," 91. The same stereotypes appeared in other media—music, theater, product packaging, children's toys, and film—such that Americans were fully embraced by racist messaging. For example, in the 1891 *Larry Dooley's Famous Mississippi Boat Song*, Philadelphia-based minstrel performer Frank Dumont rhymed, "Steamboat awhistling for a landing / Wake up de nigger's asleeping / Cotton bales come up de gangplank / Nigger's like ants acreeping / Mates keep a roaring and shouting / Lazy coon keeps on a shirking / I'll bet if a nigger's found dead / 'Twont be from over working." See *Larry Dooley's Famous Mississippi Boat Song* (New York: M. Witmark and Sons, 1891), Music Division, NYPL Digital Collections, https://digitalcollections.nypl.org/items/510d47dd-edbc-a3d9-e040-e00a18064a99.

101 Kirk Savage argues for the power of three dimensions in the context of monuments, writing, "The sculptural mold, like a photograph, was a mechanical impression of form. . . . Unlike the photograph, however, the mold was three-dimensional. . . . This gave the sculptural likeness a unique purchase on authenticity." Stereography bridged realms of photography and sculpture (Savage, *Standing Soldiers*, fn. 9, 217).

102 On photography of immigrants and Black Americans and the nature of their partic-

ipation in and compensation for photographic production, see Hales, *Silver Cities*, 354–70.

103   Arnesen explains that when steamboats docked in New Orleans, roustabouts sometimes had to step aside to allow unionized dockworkers to unload and load ships. Thus, photographers who captured idle roustabouts may have caught them during a brief, compulsory pause between punishing river trips (*Waterfront Workers*, 38).

104   Stereoscope, ca. 1895, wood and glass, 30 x 13.6 cm, Frederick Douglass National Historic Site, no. FRDO 2189, https://www.nps.gov/museum/exhibits/douglass/exb /visionary/FRDO2189_stereoscope.html; email from Mike Antonioni to author, April 1, 2022.

105   Douglass further declared, "This picture-making faculty. . . . is a mighty power, and the side to which it goes has achieved a wondrous conquest" ("Lecture on Pictures," 129–30, 133).

106   Stauffer, Trodd, and Bernier, *Picturing Frederick Douglass*, ix; Douglass, "Lecture on Pictures," 128.

107   Stauffer, Trodd, and Bernier, *Picturing Frederick Douglass*, ix–x, xxiii, xxv–xxvii.

108   bell hooks writes, "The history of black liberation movements in the United States could be characterized as a struggle over images as much as it has also been a struggle for rights. . . . The camera was the central instrument by which blacks could disprove representations of us created by white folks" ("In Our Glory: Photography and Black Life," in hooks, *Art on My Mind: Visual Politics* [New York: New Press, 1995], 57, 59). See also Gates, *Stony the Road*, 134.

109   Marilyn Creswell, "Sojourner Truth and the Power of Copyright Registration," LOC blog, December 8, 2020, https://blogs.loc.gov/copyright/2020/12/sojourner-truth -and-the-power-of-copyright-registration/; Darcy Grimaldo Grigsby, *Enduring Truths: Sojourner's Shadows and Substance* (Chicago: University of Chicago Press, 2015), and Augusta Rohrbach, "Shadow and Substance: Sojourner Truth in Black and White," in *Pictures and Progress: Early Photography and the Making of African American Identity*, ed. Maurice O. Wallace and Shawn Michelle Smith (Durham, NC: Duke University Press, 2012), 83–100.

110   Shawn Michelle Smith, "'Looking at One's Self through the Eyes of Others': W.E.B. Du Bois's Photographs for the 1900 Paris Exposition," *African American Review* 34, no. 4 (Winter 2000): 581–99. On visual representations of Black Americans, see also Jasmine Nichole Cobb, *Picture Freedom: Remaking Black Visuality in the Early Nineteenth Century* (New York: New York University Press, 2015); Gwendolyn DuBois Shaw, *Portraits of a People: Picturing African Americans in the Nineteenth Century* (Andover, MA: Addison Gallery of American Art in association with University of Washington Press, 2006); Wallace and Smith, eds., *Pictures and Progress*; Smith, *Photography on the Color Line: W.E.B. Du Bois, Race, and Visual Culture* (Durham, NC: Duke University Press, 2004); and Deborah Willis, *Reflections in Black: A History of Black Photographers, 1840 to the Present* (New York: Norton, 2000).

111   Photography could also furnish a means of earning money. In 1889, the *Weekly Pelican* published an advertisement calling for people to help sell 125,000 photograph albums "bound in royal crimson silk velvet plush." The ad promised, "Wherever shown, everyone wants to purchase" ("Shall We Start YOU in this Business," *Weekly Pelican*, October 12, 1889).

112   "Photographs of the Sun" and advertisements, *Weekly Pelican*, June 15, 1889.

113   On the lives and activism of Reconstruction-era New Orleanians of color, see Fatima Shaik, *Economy Hall: The Hidden History of a Free Black Brotherhood* (New Orleans, LA: Historic New Orleans Collection, 2021); Brian K. Mitchell, Barrington S. Edwards, and Nick Weldon, *Monumental: Oscar Dunn and His Radical Fight in Reconstruction Louisiana* (New Orleans, LA: Historic New Orleans Collection, 2021); Blassingame, *Black New Orleans*; and W. E. B. Du Bois, *Black Reconstruction: An Essay toward a History of the Part Which Black Folk Played in the Attempt to Reconstruct Democracy in America, 1860–1880* (New York: Harcourt, Brace and Co., 1935).

114   "What Has Democracy Done?," *Weekly Pelican*, June 15, 1889, 2.

115   Wells-Barnett, *Mob Rule in New Orleans*.

116   During this time frame, white mobs lynched 654 African Americans in Mississippi and 589 people in Georgia. However, violence was uniquely concentrated in Louisiana compared to many Southern states. Seven of the fifteen counties with the greatest number of lynchings in the South were Louisiana parishes. See Equal Justice Initiative, *Lynching in America: Confronting the Legacy of Racial Terror*, 3rd ed. (Montgomery, AL: Equal Justice Initiative, 2017), https://lynchinginamerica.eji.org /report/. See also James G. Hollandsworth, *An Absolute Massacre: The New Orleans Race Riot of July 30, 1866* (Baton Rouge, Louisiana State University Press, 2004), and Blassingame, *Black New Orleans*, 66–68.

117   Jules Lion, a French-born free man of color, brought professional photography to New Orleans. Trained as a lithographer and printer, Lion first exhibited his daguerreotypes in an exhibition hall across from the St. Charles Hotel in March 1840 to great public enthusiasm. See Willis, *Reflections in Black*, 4.

118   On Bedou's career, see Willis, *Reflections in Black*, 39–40; and Shawn Michelle Smith, "Snapshot 3: Unfixing the Frame(-Up): A.P. Bedou," in *Pictures and Progress*, ed. Wallace and Smith, 267–73.

119   Other important photographers of color who worked in New Orleans during and after Bedou's lifetime included Villard Paddio, Florestine Perrault Collins, and Harold Baquet. See Willis, *Reflections in Black*, 40, 44–45; Arthé A. Anthony, *Picturing Black New Orleans: A Creole Photographer's View of the Early Twentieth Century* (Gainesville: University Press of Florida, 2012); Arthé A. Anthony, "Florestine Perrault Collins and the Gendered Politics of Black Portraiture in 1920s New Orleans," *Louisiana History* 43, no. 2 (Spring 2002): 167–88; and photographic prints from the Harold F. Baquet Archive, 1975–2000, THNOC.

120   O. C. W. Taylor, *The Crescent City Pictorial: A Souvenir, Dedicated to the Progress of the Colored Citizens of New Orleans, Louisiana, "America's Most Interesting City"* (New Orleans, LA: O. C. W. Taylor, 1925).

121   These developments are detailed in Donald E. DeVore, *Defying Jim Crow: African American Community Development and the Struggle for Racial Equality in New Orleans, 1900–1960* (Baton Rouge: Louisiana State University Press, 2015), 104–6, 174. DeVore also explores the importance of the city's Black-owned businesses, especially insurance companies, funeral homes, and mom-and-pop stores (*Defying Jim Crow*, 153–67).

122   Amy Louise Wood, *Lynching and Spectacle: Witnessing Racial Violence in America, 1890–1940* (Chapel Hill: University of North Carolina Press, 2009); Dora Apel and Shawn Michelle Smith, *Lynching Photographs* (Berkeley: University of California Press, 2007); and Wood, *Horrible Gift*. On "visual slavery," see Williams-Forson,

Building Houses; and Gates, *Stony the Road*. By the early 1990s, bell hooks found "little change in the area of representation" of Black Americans in popular culture ("Introduction," in *Black Looks*, 1).

123   "Who Should Not Vote," *Daily Picayune*, January 4, 1898.

124   Repr. in *Daily Picayune*, February 7, 1898.

125   The *Abbeville* (LA) *Meridional* recognized the sticky nature of disfranchising illiterate Black citizens but maintaining the franchise for illiterate whites, writing, "There is wellnigh unanimous sentiment that the [outcome of the upcoming constitutional convention] must be so shaped as to eliminate the ignorant and corrupt negro vote, but in order to accomplish this it will be necessary to cut off the white man who stands in the same category. Right there is where the shoe pinches. We are in favor of saving every white man possible" (repr. in *Daily Picayune*, January 31, 1898).

126   As cited in Rosenberg, *New Orleans Dockworkers*, 20. See also DeVore, *Defying Jim Crow*; R. Volney Riser, *Defying Disfranchisement: Black Voting Rights Activism in the Jim Crow South, 1890–1908* (Baton Rouge: Louisiana State University Press, 2013); and Scott, *Degrees of Freedom*.

127   Rehder, *Delta Sugar*, 127. The author of the 1896 *Picayune's Guide* admitted that the city's famed levee was not as busy as in the city's antebellum days. "It is as nothing to what it was," he wrote, but he predicted that the "casual visitor from other parts" would still be entertained (*Picayune's Guide* [1896], 36).

128   By 1914, Americans ate eighty-nine pounds of sugar per capita. Only 5 percent of it was grown in Louisiana or Texas. Seventy-four percent was grown in Cuba, Hawaii, Puerto Rico, and the Philippines. See Ballinger, *History of Sugar Marketing*, 8–11, 16–18; Bureau of Foreign and Domestic Commerce, *Statistical Abstract of the United States, 1912*, 153; Department of Commerce, *The Cane Sugar Industry: Agricultural, Manufacturing, and Marketing Costs in Hawaii, Porto Rico, Louisiana, and Cuba* (Washington, DC: Government Printing Office, 1917), 20–21.

129   *The Picayune's Creole Cook Book*, 4th ed. (New Orleans, LA: Picayune Job Print, 1910), 312.

130   Tchoupitoulas Plantation Restaurant, dinner menu, n.d., menu 56-16, Job Prak menu collection, Culinary Institute of America menu collection (hereafter CIA menu), Conrad N. Hilton Library, Archives and Special Collections, Culinary Institute of America, Hyde Park, NY (hereafter CIA).

131   "Tchoupitoulas Plantation Restaurant," brochure, ca. 1968, Restaurants (Tchoupitoulas Plantation), vertical files, TUSC. See also Elmwood Plantation, dinner menu, menu 41-1464, Bruce P. Jeffer menu collection, CIA menu, CIA.

132   "Tchoupitoulas Plantation at Cedar Grove," accessed March 30, 2022, www .cgtplantation.com. This former plantation is located in the southern stretch of "Cancer Alley" or "Death Alley"—a stretch of eighty-five miles along the Mississippi River upriver from New Orleans. On land formerly dedicated to sugar production, refineries and plants that produce plastics and chemicals pollute the air with toxins. This small region counts some of the nation's highest rates of cancer and other diseases. See Lylla Younes, Al Shaw, and Claire Perlman, "In a Notoriously Polluted Area of the Country, Massive New Chemical Plants Are Still Moving In," *ProPublica*, October 30, 2019, https://projects.propublica.org/louisiana-toxic-air/. The bodies of thousands of enslaved people are buried underneath these plants, on the sites of former plantations. Forensic architects, archaeologists, and other scholars and community members are collaborating to locate burial places. See Alexandra Eaton, Christoph Koettl, Quincy G. Ledbetter, Victoria Simpson, and Aaron Byrd,

"Searching for the Lost Graves of Louisiana's Enslaved People," *New York Times*, June 27, 2021, video, 9:31, https://www.nytimes.com/video/us/100000007778616 /louisiana-cancer-alley-cemetery-african-americans-video.html.

Chapter Four

1   Pisatuntema was also known as "Emma." See David I. Bushnell Jr., "The Choctaw of Bayou Lacomb St. Tammany Parish Louisiana," *Bulletin* 48, Smithsonian Institution Bureau of American Ethnology (Washington, DC: Government Printing Office, 1909), 9, 29–30.

2   In the Old Testament story of Babel, strangers collaborated on a tower that could reach heaven. God perceived the powerful potential of their coordination, saying, "They have all one language . . . and now nothing will be restrained from them." He garbled their speech, the people scattered, and the job failed. See Gen. 11:1, 4–9 (AV).

3   Darensbourg, ed., *Bulbancha is Still a Place: Indigenous Culture from New Orleans: The Tricentennial Issue* (Bulbancha, LA: POC Zine Project, 2018); Sara Černe, "'It Carries My Feet to These Places': The Mississippi in Joy Harjo's and Heid E. Erdrich's Poetic Remappings," *Native American and Indigenous Studies* 10, no. 1 (Spring 2023): 1–27; Rachel Breunlin, "Decolonizing Ways of Knowing: Heritage, Living Communities, and Indigenous Understandings of Place," *Genealogy* 4, no. 3 (2020): 95; Paul Schmelzer, "Bulbancha Forever: From NOLA to Minneapolis, a Movement to Revitalize Indigenous Names Grows," *Ostracon*, January 4, 2021, https://theostracon.net/bulbancha-indigenous-naming-jeffery-darensbourg/; and "Bvlbancha Public Access," media channel, accessed April 6, 2023, https://www .bvlbanchapublicaccess.com/.

4   Richard Campanella, *Bienville's Dilemma: A Historical Geography of New Orleans* (Lafayette: Center for Louisiana Studies, University of Louisiana at Lafayette, 2008), 245. See also Daniel H. Usner Jr., *American Indians in Early New Orleans: From Calumet to Raquette* (Baton Rouge: Louisiana State University Press, 2018); and Daniel H. Usner Jr., *Indians, Settlers, and Slaves in a Frontier Exchange Economy: The Lower Mississippi Valley before 1783* (Chapel Hill: University of North Carolina Press, 1992).

5   By 1911, New Orleans counted thirty-four public markets, a greater number relative to the city's population than could be claimed by any other American metropolis. On the growth of New Orleans's public markets, see Campanella, *Bienville's Dilemma*, 243–48; Sally Reeves, "Making Groceries: Public Markets and Corner Stores in Old New Orleans," *Gulf South Historical Review* 16 (2000): 40–43; Robert A. Sauder, "Municipal Markets of New Orleans," *Journal of Cultural Geography* 2 (Fall/ Winter 1981): 82–95; Sauder, "The Origin and Spread of the Public Market System in New Orleans," *Louisiana History* 22, no. 3 (Summer 1981): 281–97; and Ashley Rose Young, "Nourishing Networks: The Public Culture of Food in Nineteenth-Century America" (PhD diss., Duke University, 2017), https://dukespace.lib.duke .edu/dspace/handle/10161/16358, 154–68. For histories of the development of public food markets in other cities, see Gergely Baics, *Feeding Gotham: The Political Economy and Geography of Food in New York, 1790–1860* (Princeton, NJ: Princeton University Press, 2016); Cindy R. Lobel, *Urban Appetites: Food and Culture in Nineteenth-Century New York* (Chicago: University of Chicago Press, 2014); Helen Tangires, *Public Markets and Civic Culture in Nineteenth-Century America* (Balti-

more, MD: Johns Hopkins University Press, 2003); and Roger Horowitz, Jeffrey M. Pilcher, and Sydney Watts, "Meat for the Multitudes: Market Culture in Paris, New York City, and Mexico City over the Long Nineteenth Century," *American Historical Review* 109, no. 4 (October 2004): 1055–83.

6   Choctaw people arrived in Louisiana beginning in the eighteenth century, having been pushed out of their homelands farther east, in present-day Mississippi. See Usner, *American Indians*; Usner, *Indians, Settlers, and Slaves*, 192–218; Daniel H. Usner Jr., "Food Marketing and Interethnic Exchange in the Eighteenth Century Lower Mississippi Valley," *Food and Foodways* 1 (1986): 279–310, at 287; John Magill, "French Market Celebrates 200th Anniversary," *Preservation in Print* 18, no. 4 (May 1991): 7–10; Sandra Margaret Frink, "Spectacles of the Street: Performance, Power, and Public Space in Antebellum New Orleans" (PhD diss., University of Texas at Austin, 2004), http://hdl.handle.net/2152/12771, 169–81; Tim Mueller, *Nations Within: The Four Sovereign Tribes of Louisiana* (Baton Rouge: Louisiana State University Press, 2003); and Fred B. Kniffen, Hiram F. Gregory, and George A. Stokes, *The Historic Indian Tribes of Louisiana: From 1542 to the Present* (Baton Rouge: Louisiana State University Press, 1994).

7   "Neutral ground" in New Orleans is the street median and, at the nineteenth-century French Market, the space between buildings. In designation and use, this area was far from neutral, though. See Magill, "French Market."

8   *Chahta Lekshikon*, an 1880 Choctaw-English dictionary, notes that the first vowel in these words is not equivalent to "U" in English. Rather, the printed letter takes more the form of a "V" and is pronounced "as u in tub." See Allen Wright, *Chahta Lekshikon: A Choctaw in English Definition for the Choctaw Academies and Schools* (St. Louis, MO: Presbyterian Publishing Company, 1880), 71, 5. I thank Jeffery Darensbourg's *Ostracon* interview for pointing me to this source. See also Schmelzer, "Bulbancha Forever."

9   "New French Market," *Times-Picayune*, September 13, 1932.

10   "Theo Grunewald," *New Orleans Item*, May 27, 1933.

11   Benjamin Henry Boneval Latrobe, diary entry dated January 9, 1819; and Mrs. B. H. B. Latrobe to Mrs. Catherine Smith, letter dated April 18, 1820, in Latrobe, *Impressions Respecting New Orleans: Diary and Sketches 1818–1820*, ed. Samuel Wilson Jr. (New York: Columbia University, 1951), 3, 18, 180.

12   Unlike most other visitors, Russell failed to find the French Market impressive as anything other than a shelter from the rain. He was annoyed by the "smell of the filthy streets" outdoors and the "smell of the French cookery" indoors. He acknowledged in his journal, however, that he may have been less vulnerable to the Crescent City's culinary charms due to his sufferings as a "dyspeptic"; he left New Orleans after less than a week. See Edward Russell, entries dated January 25, 28, and 27, 1835, travel journal and transcript, 1834–1835, MSS 424.2, THNOC.

13   A. Oakey Hall, *The Manhattaner in New Orleans; or, Phases of "Crescent City" Life* (New York: J. S. Redfield, Clinton Hall, 1851), 7.

14   "In the Old French Market, New Orleans—Drawn by John W. Alexander," *Harper's Weekly* 26, no. 1309 (January 21, 1881): 40. For additional descriptions of New Orleans as "Babel" or linguistically overwhelming, see "Up the Mississippi," *Emerson's Magazine and Putnam's Monthly* 5, no. 41 (October 1857): 436; "New Orleans," *Chicago Press and Tribune*, March 28, 1860; "The Old French Market in New Orleans," *Frank Leslie's Illustrated Newspaper* 1 no. 436 (March 31, 1883): 95; James S. Zacharie, *New Orleans Guide with Descriptions of the Routes to New Orleans, Sights of*

the City Arranged Alphabetically, and Other Information Useful to Travelers; also, Outlines of the History of Louisiana (New Orleans: F. F. Hansell and Bro., Ltd., 1893), 102; *The Picayune's Guide to New Orleans: Revised and Enlarged*, 5th ed. (New Orleans: Picayune, 1903), 34; etc. See also Nathalie Dessens, "The Sounds of Babel: Staging American Ethnic Diversity in Early Nineteenth-Century New Orleans," *Complutense Journal of English Studies* 23 (2015): 15–27.

15   Benjamin Henry Boneval Latrobe, diary entry dated January 12, 1819, in Latrobe, *Impressions*, 22.

16   Henry C. Castellanos, *New Orleans as it Was: Episodes of Louisiana Life*, ed. George F. Reinecke (Baton Rouge: Louisiana State University Press, 1895, repr. 1978), 64; Zacharie, *New Orleans Guide*, 216.

17   Carl E. Groenevelt, *New Orleans, Illustrated in Photo Etching from New and Original Plates, with Descriptive Text* (New Orleans: F. F. Hansell, 1892).

18   William H. Coleman, *Historical Sketch Book and Guide to New Orleans and Environs, with Map. Illustrated with Many Original Engravings; and Containing Exhaustive Accounts of the Traditions, Historical Legends, and Remarkable Localities of the Creole City* (New York: Will H. Coleman, 1885), 88.

19   Herbert W. Burdett, "Historic America: VI. New Orleans," *Illustrated American*, April 5, 1890, 153.

20   B. M. Norman, *Norman's New Orleans and Environs: Containing a Brief Historical Sketch of the Territory and State of Louisiana, and the City of New Orleans, from the Earliest Period to the Present Time: Presenting a Complete Guide to All Subjects of General Interest in the Southern Metropolis; with a Correct and Improved Plan of the City, Pictorial Illustrations of Public Buildings, Etc.* (New Orleans, LA: B. M. Norman, 1845), 135.

21   "In the Old French Market," *Harper's Weekly*, January 21, 1882, 39.

22   Zacharie, *New Orleans Guide*, 212.

23   Castellanos, *New Orleans as It Was*, 146.

24   In the eleventh chapter of the Bible's Book of Isaiah, the prophet predicted a harmonious new world in which "The wolf also shall dwell with the lamb, / and the leopard shall lie down with the kid" (Isa. 11:6 [AV]). See "The Old French Market," *Frank Leslie's Illustrated Newspaper* 1, no. 436 (March 31, 1883), 95.

25   Coleman, *Historical Sketch Book*, 258. Writing in the 1840s, Benjamin M. Norman had expressed a similarly exhilarated reaction to the market's sensations, where "all colors, nations, and tongues are commingled in one heterogeneous mass of delightful confusion" (*Norman's New Orleans*, 135).

26   Matthew Frye Jacobson, *Whiteness of a Different Color: European Immigrants and the Alchemy of Race* (Cambridge, MA: Harvard University Press, 1998), 32–38.

27   "Old French Market," *Frank Leslie's*.

28   *The Picayune's Guide to New Orleans: Revised and Enlarged*, 4th ed. (New Orleans, LA: Picayune, 1900), 46.

29   Castellanos, *New Orleans as It Was*, 146. Rose Nicaud, the best-documented coffee vendor at the nineteenth-century French Market, sold coffee there from the 1850s to 1870s. See Robyn Rene Andermann, "Brewed Awakening: Re-Imagining Education in Three Nineteenth-Century New Orleans Coffee Houses" (PhD diss., Louisiana State University, 2018), https://digitalcommons.lsu.edu/cgi/viewcontent.cgi?article=5575&context=gradschool_dissertations, 162–200.

30   "Up the Mississippi," 438. See also Louisiana Writers' Project, *Gumbo Ya-Ya: A Collection of Louisiana Folk Tales* (Boston, MA: Houghton Mifflin, 1945), 43–44.

31   On the history of the "exotic" quadroon, see Emily Clark, *The Strange History of the American Quadroon: Free Women of Color in the Revolutionary Atlantic World* (Chapel Hill: University of North Carolina Press, 2013). On the history of the mammy figure in connection with food, see Toni Tipton-Martin, *The Jemima Code: Two Centuries of African American Cookbooks* (Austin: University of Texas Press, 2015), 2–4; Kimberly Wallace-Sanders, *Mammy: A Century of Race, Gender, and Southern Memory* (Ann Arbor: University of Michigan Press, 2008); Psyche Williams-Forson, *Building Houses out of Chicken Legs: Black Women, Food, and Power* (Chapel Hill: University of North Carolina Press, 2006); Doris Witt, *Black Hunger: Soul Food and America* (Minneapolis: University of Minnesota Press, 2004); and Deborah Gray White, *Ar'n't I a Woman? Female Slaves in the Plantation South* (New York: W. W. Norton, 1985). See also chapter 5.

32   Greenleaf did not record purchases at the market on November 7, 1852, a Sunday. See Mary Longfellow Greenleaf diary, 1852 (hereafter Greenleaf), MSS 363, THNOC.

33   Diary entries dated January 5, February 5, February 6, and March 6, 1852, Greenleaf, THNOC.

34   Few published cookbooks were available in the United States in the first half of the nineteenth century. In her memoir, Eliza Moore Ripley described New Orleans kitchens of the 1840s where "the thrifty housewife made . . . cakes fit for the gods, with only Miss Leslie's cook book to refer to, and that was published in the twenties" (*Social Life in Old New Orleans: Being Recollections of My Girlhood* [New York: Arno Press, 1912, repr. 1975], 46). Ripley was referring to *Seventy-Five Receipts for Pastry, Cakes, and Sweetmeats*, by Eliza Leslie, published in 1828. In November 1852, Greenleaf also purchased dressmaking supplies, notepaper, candles, and a toothbrush. She donated to charity and purchased a six-month subscription to the *Daily Picayune* newspaper (Greenleaf, THNOC).

35   Records in Greenleaf's diary of payments to family servants—such as her note on November 6, 1852, "Paid Sarah 18.50"—indicate that the family likely employed servants rather than enslaved people. Greenleaf's brother, Henry Wadsworth Longfellow, was a noted abolitionist. Cataloguers at the Society for the Preservation of New England Antiquities note, "It is believed that Mary was anti-slavery but felt compassion for her New Orleans friends, saying they were misled by wicked leaders." See "Finding Aid: Henry Wadsworth Longfellow (1807–1882) Family Papers, 1768–1972, 35," Longfellow National Historic Site, Cambridge, MA, National Park Service, US Department of the Interior, accessed February 6, 2016, http://www.nps.gov/long/learn/historyculture/upload/HWLfamilyaidNMSCfinal.pdf.

36   Joseph Holt Ingraham, *The South-West, by a Yankee*, vol. 1 (New York: Harper and Brothers, 1835), 102.

37   Usner, "Food Marketing," 287; and Usner, *Indians, Settlers, and Slaves*, 201–18.

38   "Up the Mississippi," 438. Additional eyewitness descriptions of Black New Orleanians at the French Market include Latrobe, *Impressions*, 22; Hall, *Manhattaner*, 7; Zacharie, *New Orleans Guide*, 214; *Picayune's Guide* (1900), 46; and Catharine [also Catherine] Cole [Martha Reinhard Smallwood Field], *The Story of the Old French Market, New Orleans* (New Orleans, LA: New Orleans Coffee Company, 1916).

39   Ripley, *Social Life*, 4.

40   Coleman, *Historical Sketch Book*, 263.

41   "Up the Mississippi," 438.

42   Louisiana Creole formed from West African languages and French in early

eighteenth-century Louisiana. Following the Civil War, several Louisiana newspapers published phony letters to the editor and articles in Creole to ridicule and infantilize recently emancipated Black Louisianians and their speech. Historian Mark M. Smith argued that other publications, like *Emerson's*, did important work in recording perishable aural experiences before other technology existed to do so. Such mediation often crossed the line into exploitation, though. See Gwendolyn Midlo Hall, "The Formation of Afro-Creole Culture," in *Creole New Orleans: Race and Americanization*, ed. Arnold R. Hirsch and Joseph Logsdon (Baton Rouge: Louisiana State University Press, 1992), 58–87, at 59–60; Sybil Kein, "The Use of Louisiana Creole in Southern Literature," in *Creole: The History and Legacy of Louisiana's Free People of Color*, ed. Sybil Kein (Baton Rouge: Louisiana State University Press, 2000), 117–54, at 126–28; Mark M. Smith, *Listening to Nineteenth-Century America* (Chapel Hill: University of North Carolina Press, 2001).

43 The citizenship of Native people throughout the United States was not affirmed until the Indian Citizenship Act of 1924. Even then, the federal government allowed each state to decide whether or not to grant Native people living within the state the right to vote. See Indian Citizenship Act of 1924, H.R. 6355, 68th Cong. (1924), https://www.archives.gov/files/historical-docs/doc-content/images/indian-citizenship-act-1924.pdf; and Cathleen D. Cahill, *Recasting the Vote: How Women of Color Transformed the Suffrage Movement* (Chapel Hill: University of North Carolina Press, 2020).

44 Laurence H. Tribe, *American Constitutional Law*, 2nd ed. (Mineola, NY: Foundation Press, 1988), 550–59; and David A. J. Richards, *Conscience and the Constitution: History, Theory and Law of the Reconstruction Amendments* (Princeton, NJ: Princeton University Press, 1994), 204–32.

45 Homer Plessy, a New Orleans native, was an "octoroon," the state's designation for a person considered to be 7/8 white and 1/8 Black. He was arrested in New Orleans on June 7, 1892, after boarding an East Louisiana Railroad car reserved for white passengers. On the long fight to integrate New Orleans streetcars before and after *Plessy*, see Kendric Perkins, "Protests, Politics, and a Police Chase: The Fight to Integrate Streetcars in 1867," *First Draft* (THNOC blog), March 2, 2021, https://www.THNOC.org/publications/first-draft/symposium-2021/protests-politics-and-police-chase-fight-integrate-streetcars-1867; Blair L. M. Kelley, *Right to Ride: Streetcar Boycotts and African American Citizenship in the Era of Plessy v. Ferguson* (Chapel Hill: University of North Carolina Press, 2010); and Adam Fairclough, *Race and Democracy: The Civil Rights Struggle in Louisiana, 1915–1972* (Athens: University of Georgia Press, 1995).

46 Burdett, "Historic America," 153.

47 Groenevelt, *New Orleans*, n.p. On associations between the urban grid and neoclassical ideals of order and organization, see Dell Upton, *Another City: Urban Life and Urban Spaces in the New American Republic* (New Haven, CT: Yale University Press, 2008).

48 On "swarthy" Sicilian vendors, see Burdett, "Historic America," 153. Although William Coleman lauded the French Market's energy in his 1885 guidebook, he, too, could not help but notice its near-century's worth of accumulated grime, writing, "From the ceiling hang endless ropes of spider's webs, numberless flies, and incalculable dirt." Still, he reasoned, "this is the market, and the wilted cabbage leaves are a part of the place" (*Historical Sketch Book*, 258, 262).

49 On urban and suburban change and migration during this era, see Campanella,

Bienville's Dilemma, 40–44; 220–22; Peirce F. Lewis, *New Orleans: The Making of an Urban Landscape*, 2nd ed. (Santa Fe, NM: Center for American Places, 2003), 54–70; Alison Isenberg, *Downtown America: A History of the Place and the People Who Made It* (Chicago: Chicago University Press, 2004), 13–77; Kenneth T. Jackson, *Crabgrass Frontier: The Suburbanization of the United States* (New York: Oxford University Press, 1985); and Isabel Wilkerson, *The Warmth of Other Suns: The Epic Story of America's Great Migration* (New York: Random House, 2010). On turn-of-the-century New Orleans's allures, see Emily Epstein Landau, *Spectacular Wickedness: Sex, Race, and Memory in Storyville, New Orleans* (Baton Rouge: Louisiana State University Press, 2018); Rien Fertel, *Imagining the Creole City: The Rise of Literary Culture in Nineteenth-Century New Orleans* (Baton Rouge: Louisiana State University Press, 2014); and Bruce Boyd Raeburn, "Stars of David and Sons of Sicily: Constellations beyond the Canon in Early New Orleans Jazz," *Jazz Perspectives* 3, no. 2 (August 2009): 125–52.

50   Campanella, *Bienville's Dilemma*, 40.

51   Burdett, "Historic America," 154.

52   In 1914, the *Picayune* and *Times-Democrat* newspapers merged to form the *Times-Picayune*. The paper's travel guide was titled *The Picayune's Guide to New Orleans* up to and including its eleventh edition, published in 1913. Beginning with the twelfth edition, published in 1917, it was known as the *Times-Picayune's Guide to New Orleans*.

53   *Picayune's Guide* (1900), 46.

54   *Picayune's Guide*, 5th ed. (1903), 34, 35.

55   *The Picayune's Guide to New Orleans*, 10th ed. (New Orleans, LA: Picayune Job Print, 1910), 57.

56   *The Picayune's Guide to New Orleans* (New Orleans, LA: Nicholson and Co., 1896), 33.

57   *The Times-Picayune's Guide to New Orleans*, 14th ed. (New Orleans, LA: Times-Picayune, 1924), 17.

58   A. R. Waud, "Pictures of the South / The French Market, New Orleans," *Harper's Weekly* 10, no. 503 (August 18, 1866): 526; "The Old French Market in New Orleans," *Frank Leslie's Illustrated Newspaper* 1, no. 436 (March 31, 1883): 95; Coleman, *Historical Sketch Book*, 258, 263; Zacharie, *New Orleans Guide*, 214–15; *Picayune's Guide* (1900), 46; *The Picayune's Guide to New Orleans*, 8th ed. (New Orleans, LA: Picayune Job Print, 1908), 30; Bushnell, *Choctaw of Bayou Lacomb*, 13, 8; and Castellanos, *New Orleans as It Was*, 146–47.

59   Burdett, "Historic America," 154.

60   Zacharie, *New Orleans Guide*, 213. On racist stereotypes of Native people as silent and stoic, see Eddie Glenn, "A Heart Made of Knotty Pine: The Cigar Store Indian in American Cultural Imagery," *International Journal of the Image* 1, no. 3 (2011): 53–61; Carter Jones Meyer and Diana Royer, eds., *Selling the Indian: Commercializing and Appropriating American Indian Cultures* (Tucson: University of Arizona Press, 2001); and Philip J. Deloria, *Playing Indian* (New Haven, CT: Yale University Press, 1998).

61   Some travelers' accounts indicated that Choctaw vendors sought to capitalize on shoppers' interest in their appearance. In 1857, a reporter characterized a "party of Indian girls" at the market as "ready to sell their small wares and willing to be gazed upon." Black women in twentieth-century New Orleans showed a similarly savvy engagement with tourists when they dressed and played the part of the nineteenth-

century praline vendor. See "Up the Mississippi," 438; and Chanda Nunez, "Just Like Ole' Mammy Used to Make: Reinterpreting New Orleans African-American Praline Vendors as Entrepreneurs" (Master's thesis, University of New Orleans, 2011), https://scholarworks.uno.edu/cgi/viewcontent.cgi?article=1127&context=td.

62 "New-Orleans in Winter," March 16, 1884, 5; Coleman, *Historical Sketch Book*, 258; Burdett, "Historic America," *Illustrated American*, 154. Coleman also complained about Choctaw women's figures and dress, writing, "The Indian females are formless, and the bag that they wear has no pretensions to fitting. When in addition they have hung around them bundles, beads, babies, and other curiosities, they fail to arouse our poetic sentiments" (*Historical Sketch Book*, 258).

63 On white anxieties about interracial sex and mixed-race children during this era, see Henry Louis Gates Jr., *Stony the Road: Reconstruction, White Supremacy, and the Rise of Jim Crow* (New York: Penguin Books, 2019), 109–17, 136–41.

64 *Picayune's Guide* (1900), 46.

65 In 1910, anthropologist David I. Bushnell Jr., wrote, "In St. Tammany parish, Louisiana, are living at the present time some ten or twelve Choctaw, the last of the once numerous branch of the tribe that formerly occupied that section" ("Myths of the Louisiana Choctaw," *American Anthropologist* 12, no. 4 [October–December 1910]: 526–35, at 526). See also *The Picayune's Guide to New Orleans*, 8th ed. (New Orleans, LA: Picayune Job Print, 1908), 29. Native people living in Louisiana did not disappear, of course. In 2023, there were four federally recognized tribes and eleven state-recognized tribes in the state. Laine Kaplan-Levenson, "New Orleans: 300 // Bulbancha: 3000," December 20, 2018, in *TriPod*, produced by WWNO New Orleans Public Radio in collaboration with THNOC and the Midlo Center for New Orleans Studies at UNO, podcast, MP3 audio, 29:20, https://www.wwno.org/podcast /tripod-new-orleans-at-300/2018-12-20/new-orleans-300-bulbancha-3000; "Indian Affairs," Governor's Office of Indian Affairs, State of Louisiana, accessed May 27, 2023, https://gov.louisiana.gov/page/indian-affairs.

66 On Progressive women's varied activisms, see Sabine M. Meyer, *We Are What We Drink: The Temperance Battle in Minnesota* (Champaign: University of Illinois Press, 2015); Susan Rimby, *Mira Lloyd Dock and the Progressive Era Conservation Movement* (University Park: Pennsylvania State University Press, 2015); and Glenda Gilmore, *Gender and Jim Crow: Women and the Politics of White Supremacy in North Carolina, 1896–1920* (Chapel Hill: University of North Carolina Press, 1996). On the work of white women's groups and preservationists to convert the French Quarter into a segregated tourist attraction during the interwar years, see Anthony J. Stanonis, *Creating the Big Easy: New Orleans and the Emergence of Modern Tourism, 1918–1945* (Athens: University of Georgia Press, 2006).

67 Municipal regulations favored the city's public markets over private markets, setting up battles between vendors and customers. An 1893 ordinance set a boundary of 2,100 feet between private and public markets, attempting to protect public markets from competitors. The ordinance also ruled that a private market should be "not less than 10 by 15 ft in superficial area," seeking to prevent the proliferation of sidewalk food stands, many run by Sicilian immigrants. A 1900 ordinance expanded the protective sphere surrounding public markets to 3,200 feet. In response, private market owners commissioned maps hoping to demonstrate that their businesses lay outside public markets' restrictive areas, as measured by the footsteps of a person walking with an average gait. Public market vendors countered. In 1913, Dryades Market vendor John H. Hunsinger declared, "I think [private markets] are a disgrace to the

city. . . . [Y]ou will have every dago in the city getting a hole in the wall and starting
a place with a few vegetables and a little fruit and calling it a private market. They
will be dirty and nasty and a menace to the city." See "Report of the Market Committee," Housewives' League Division, March 24, 1914, folder 985-1-2, Market Committee records, 1913–1916, MS 985 (hereafter MS 985), TUSC; "Stallkeepers Have
an Inning," *Daily Picayune*, May 31, 1913; folder 985-1-9: Clippings, no date, MS 985,
TUSC.

68   Notes from the State Board of Health, 1912, folder 985-1-1, MS 985, TUSC.

69   "Dowling Steps In," unnamed newspaper, ca. June 1, 1913, folder 985-1-8: Clippings,
June 1913–1916, MS 985, TUSC. Still, the French Market's filth was nothing new. In
1821, John James Audubon had called the French Market "the Dirtiest place in all the
Cities of the United States" (as quoted in Magill, "French Market").

70   "Women Report on What They Found," *Daily Picayune*, May 21, 1913, 3.

71   A Resident, "Our City Markets," Letter from the People, *New Orleans Item*, May 19,
1913. On additional campaigns by the Housewives' League, including the establishment of cooperative curb markets in wealthy neighborhoods and resistance to
unionized Black domestic workers, see Anne Gessler, *Cooperatives in New Orleans:
Collective Action and Urban Development* (Oxford: University Press of Mississippi,
2020), ch. 2. On reforming women's enthusiasm for cleanliness, see Suellen Hoy,
Chasing Dirt: The American Pursuit of Cleanliness (New York: Oxford University
Press, 1996).

72   Mrs. Jacob Ambrose Storck, "Market Question in New Orleans," *Times-Democrat*,
May 25, 1913.

73   "Report of Investigating Committee," Housewives' League, March 19, 1915, folder
985-1-4, MS 985, TUSC.

74   "Climate and Marketing," *New Orleans Item*, May 18, 1913; "Women's Federation
Asks Change in Market System," *New Orleans Item*, 1913.

75   "Speech [at] Round Table Club," ca. December 1916, folder 985-1-5, MS 985, TUSC.
In many American cities, corporations and the federal government drove a top-
down eclipse of mom-and-pop grocery stores with chain supermarkets, beginning in
the 1910s and 1920s. In New Orleans, the process was more bottom-up, yet not without prejudice. Organized housewives lobbied for the specific amenities offered by
chain supermarkets and sought to abolish municipal regulations favoring the city's
historic public markets. See Tracy Deutsch, *Building a Housewife's Paradise: Gender,
Politics, and American Grocery Stores in the Twentieth Century* (Chapel Hill: University of North Carolina Press, 2010).

76   "Housewives Ask for Repeal of Market Statues," *New Orleans Item*, May 18, 1913.

77   "Lazy Housewives Blamed by Dealers," no source, ca. spring 1913; "City Markets
to Stay," *Times-Democrat*, May 31, 1913; and untitled clipping, *New Orleans Item*,
May 16, 1913, all in folder 985-1-7: Clippings, January-May 1913, MS 985, TUSC.

78   Judith Hyams Douglas, "The Market Problem," *Times-Democrat*, May 25, 1913.

79   Progressive pursuits of whiteness in all guises had direct implications in realms of
food. White tiles in kitchens and bathrooms and even white-colored foods, such as
Crisco cooking fat and béchamel sauce, were Progressive-era fads. Laura Shapiro,
Perfection Salad: Women and Cooking at the Turn of the Century (New York: Farrar,
Straus, and Giroux, 1986), 91–95, 214–15.

80   The Round Table Club commonly welcomed male intellectuals to address the club's
all-male membership. That a woman representing the Market Committee spoke to
the club indicated the topic's importance to the city's educated white citizens. See

Round Table Club v. Bond, 163 La. 175, 111 So. 667 (1927); John Smith Kendall, *History of New Orleans*, vol. 2 (Chicago: Lewis Publishing Company, 1922), 695.

81 "Speech [at] Round Table Club."

82 Bureau of the Census, *Twelfth Census of the United States, Taken in the Year 1900*, 4 vols. (Washington, DC: US Census Office, 1902). On Sicilian emigration to Louisiana and the group's work in the state's food industry, see Jessica Barbata Jackson, *Dixie's Italians: Sicilians, Race, and Citizenship in the Jim Crow Gulf South* (Baton Rouge: Louisiana State University Press, 2020); Justin A. Nystrom, *Creole Italian: Sicilian Immigrants and the Shaping of New Orleans Food Culture* (Athens: University of Georgia Press, 2018); Joseph Logsdon, "Immigration through the Port of New Orleans," in *Forgotten Doors: The Other Ports of Entry to the United States*, ed. M. Mark Stolarik (Philadelphia, PA: Balch Institute Press, 1988), 105–24; Frederick Spletstoser, "Back Door to the Land of Plenty: New Orleans as an Immigrant Port, 1820–1860" (PhD diss., Louisiana State University, 1978); Laura A. Guccione, "Sicilian Roots: How the Agricultural Pursuits of Immigrant Sicilians Shaped Modern New Orleans Cuisine" (Master's thesis, University of New Orleans, 2019), https://scholarworks.uno.edu/cgi/viewcontent.cgi?article=3835&context=td; and Jean Ann Scarpaci, *Italian Immigrants in Louisiana's Sugar Parishes: Recruitment, Labor Conditions, and Community Relations, 1880–1910* (New York: Arno Press, 1980). On local reactions to the influx of Sicilians, see Anthony V. Margavio, "The Reaction of the Press to the Italian American in New Orleans, 1880–1920," *Italian Americana* 4, no. 1 (Fall/Winter 1978): 72–83; and Arnold Shankman, "This Menacing Influx: Afro-Americans on Italian Immigration to the South, 1880–1915," *Mississippi Quarterly* 31, no. 1 (Winter 1977): 67–88.

83 Lafcadio Hearn, "Quaint New Orleans and its Inhabitants," *Harper's Weekly* 28, no. 1459 (December 6, 1884): 812; Coleman, *Historical Sketch Book*, 260.

84 In the 1930s, the razing of Gallatin Street, a short thoroughfare adjacent to the French Market, would exemplify the moralizing tone of the market's modernization. Gallatin had been "the most sinister street in New Orleans' history," claimed a local reporter, and a locale ruled by the Sicilian Mafia, where "half of the sailors [visiting the city] . . . were shanghaied." The market's renovation eliminated this stretch of street. See "Civic Progress Purges Sinister Gallatin St. Black Hand Den," *Item*, November 20, 1935. See also James Fentress, *Rebels and Mafiosi: Death in a Sicilian Landscape* (Ithaca, NY: Cornell University Press, 2000); Louis Andrew Vyhanek, *Unorganized Crime: New Orleans in the 1920s* (Lafayette: Center for Louisiana Studies, University of Southwestern Louisiana, 1998); and Nystrom, *Creole Italian*, 59–84.

85 Marco Rimanelli and Sheryl L. Postman, eds., *The 1891 New Orleans Lynchings and U.S.-Italian Relations: A Look Back* (New York: P. Lang, 1992).

86 Julia Truitt Bishop, "People Restive under Extortion, Must Bring About a Market Change," *Times-Democrat*, May 18, 1913.

87 Robert Bledsoe Mayfield, "Just 'Wops,'" *Times-Picayune*, January 4, 1916. Sapsago, or Schabziger, is a Swiss cheese made with skim milk and colored green with clover. See "Schabziger," Alan Davidson, *The Oxford Companion to Food* (Oxford: Oxford University Press, 1999), 704.

88 Throughout the world, Italian immigrants became "Italian" only as a diaspora community. US census takers counted Italian-born immigrants as "foreign-born white," yet the social history of New Orleans's Sicilians exemplified the trajectory described by Matthew Frye Jacobson as a "probationary white group" to one even-

tually "granted the scientific stamp of authenticity as [a member of] the unitary Caucasian race" (*Whiteness of a Different Color*, 7–8). See also Donna R. Gabaccia, *Italy's Many Diasporas* (Seattle: University of Washington Press, 2000); Peter G. Vellon, *A Great Conspiracy against Our Race: Italian Immigrant Newspapers and the Construction of Whiteness in the Early Twentieth Century* (New York: New York University Press, 2014); Jennifer Guglielmo and Salvatore Salerno, eds., *Are Italians White? How Race is Made in America* (New York: Routledge, 2003); and Thomas A. Guglielmo, *White on Arrival: Italians, Race, Color, and Power in Chicago, 1890–1945* (Oxford: Oxford University Press, 2003).

89   Storck, "Market Question."

90   "Stallkeepers Have an Inning." The 1910 census listed Frank Cleci [*sic*], twenty-six and born in Italy, working as a retail merchant of fruit with his older brother. Both had emigrated to the United States as children. See *Thirteenth Census of the United States Taken in the Year 1910* (Washington, DC: Government Printing Office, 1913).

91   "Women's Clubs Consider Market Management," unnamed newspaper, June 3, 1914, folder 985-1-8, MS 985, TUSC.

92   Donald E. DeVore, *Defying Jim Crow: African American Community Development and the Struggle for Racial Equality in New Orleans, 1900–1960* (Baton Rouge: Louisiana State University Press, 2015), 104–5.

93   Stereotypes linking people of color to disease and unhygienic practices were a racist trope in and beyond New Orleans. White Europeans and Americans blamed enslaved Africans for introducing yellow fever to New Orleans and then claimed falsely that they were immune to the disease. Nearly two centuries later, a New Orleans newspaper published a photograph with an arrow pinpointing the purported source of New Orleans's final yellow fever outbreak, in 1905. The photo's caption read, "The original point of infection . . . in 'Little Italy,'" adjacent to the French Market. An infected person had likely entered the city from a ship docked in port, but the photograph blamed the Sicilian neighborhood as ground zero for the outbreak that killed more than 450 people. See Norman, *Norman's New Orleans*, 62; Kathryn Olivarius, *Necropolis: Disease, Power, and Capitalism in the Cotton Kingdom* (Cambridge, MA: Harvard University Press, 2022); Nayan Shah, *Contagious Divides: Epidemics and Race in San Francisco's Chinatown* (Berkeley: University of California Press, 2001); Tera Hunter, *To 'Joy My Freedom: Southern Black Women's Lives and Labors after the Civil War* (Cambridge, MA: Harvard University Press, 1997); and M. B. Trezevant, "The Yellow-Fever Visitation in the 'Crescent City,'" unnamed newspaper, August 24, 1905, THNOC.

94   "Speech [at] Round Table Club."

95   J. B. Montgomery, "Race Women Prisoners Clean Streets of New Orleans; Ball and Chain About Ankles," *Chicago Defender*, November 4, 1916, 9.

96   Cole, *Story of the Old French Market*, 6, 9, 20, 12.

97   Cole, *Story of the Old French Market*, 21. Cole was New Orleans's first woman newspaper reporter and a champion of women's rights and animal rights, but much of her writing showed a racist perspective on Black Louisianians that she cloaked in saccharine nostalgia. See Catherine Cole papers, NA-118, Newcomb Archives and Vorhoff Collection at Tulane University, New Orleans, Louisiana (hereafter Newcomb and Vorhoff).

98   Cole, *Story of the Old French Market*, 8. The booklet's narrator was likewise harshly dismissive of market vendors, such as the "forlorn, toothless, grizzled negro, tremulous and foolish with age, [who] tries to sell some very bad pineapples" (*Story of the*

Old French Market, 8). On Lalaurie, see Tiya Miles, *Tales from the Haunted South: Dark Tourism and Memories of Slavery from the Civil War Era* (Chapel Hill: University of North Carolina Press, 2015), 48–79.

99   Society women's defamation of Black women in public markets was all the more hypocritical given their patronage of Nellie Murray. Formerly enslaved, Murray became the most prominent caterer for city elites from the mid-1880s until around 1906, designing and cooking lavish meals. In 1893, Murray traveled to the World's Columbian Exposition in Chicago in 1893 to oversee the food served at the Louisiana Mansion House. There, she served as the ambassador and authority of New Orleans's Creole cuisine to the world, even as Louisianians of color were suffering Jim Crow violence and discrimination at home. Wealthy white New Orleanians were eager to enjoy delicacies that Murray cooked for them but derided Black women's housekeeping practices and encouraged their expulsion from the city's public markets. See Zella Palmer, "Queen of Creole Cuisine," *64 Parishes*, accessed April 25, 2022, https://64parishes.org/queen-creole-cuisine; Zella Palmer, "Belle New Orleans: The History of Creole Cuisinières," *Africology* 11, no. 6 (April 2018): 186–91; and David S. Shields, *The Culinarians: Lives and Careers from the First Age of American Fine Dining* (Chicago: University of Chicago Press, 2017), 304–7.

100 [Lafcadio Hearn], *La Cuisine Creole: A Collection of Culinary Recipes from Leading Chefs and Noted Creole Housewives, Who Have Made New Orleans Famous for Its Cuisine* (New York: William H. Coleman, 1885). Also in 1885, the city's Christian Woman's Exchange published *The Creole Cookery Book* (New Orleans, LA: T. H. Thomason, 1885). See also Susan Tucker, M. A. Johnson, Wendy Bruton, and Sharon Stallworth Nossiter, eds., "New Orleans Cookbook Bibliography: Compiled by the New Orleans Culinary History Group," 3, 29, accessed April 29, 2022, http://www2.tulane.edu/~wclib/New%20Orleans%20Cookbook%20Bibliography%202011.pdf.

101 Zacharie, *New Orleans Guide*, 174, 176.

102 *Picayune's Guide* (1900), 93–94.

103 *Times-Picayune's Guide*, 14th ed. (1924), 17–18. This fiction, that "No Creole ever had colored blood. . . . Any trace of *café au lait* . . . was reason for complete ostracism," was repeated in Louisiana Writers' Project, *Gumbo Ya-Ya*, 139.

104 Alice Moore Dunbar-Nelson, "People of Color in Louisiana: Part I," *Journal of Negro History* (October 1916): 361–76, at 367.

105 "Concessions: Municipally Owned and Operated Enclosed Public Markets, June 1st, 1932"; "Rules and Regulations Governing the Municipally Owned and Operated Enclosed Public Markets, June 1st, 1932," both in KTA202 1937: Department of Public Markets, Report on Public Market System, French Market Corporation records (hereafter FMC records), LDCA NOPL.

106 "Theo Grunewald," *New Orleans Item*, April 25, 1933, and May 27, 1933.

107 "French Market Change Opposed: Council Members Not to Permit Removal from Location," *New Orleans States*, December 18, 1930.

108 Meigs O. Frost, "Aroused City Again Saves Old French Market," *New Orleans States*, January 1, 1931.

109 George N. Coad, "New Orleans Fears for French Market," *New York Times*, February 12, 1931.

110 "Rebuilt Markets Opened," *Times-Picayune*, June 25, 1932.

111 "Theo Grunewald," *New Orleans Item*, May 27, 1933.

112 "Electrical Icers Display Meats in Public Markets," *New Orleans States*, April 29, 1936.

113 "Green to Open Novel Grocery," *New Orleans Tribune*, January 29, 1933.

114 "New French Market," *Times-Picayune*, September 13, 1932.

115 Renovations to the French Market took place against the backdrop of the founding of the Vieux Carré Commission in 1936, a municipal body that continues to protect the "tout ensemble" of the French Quarter historic district. The Code of the City of New Orleans defines "tout ensemble" as "the historic character and ambience, characterized by quaint, historic or distinctive architectural styles; landscaped patios, courtyards, public alleys and squares . . . pleasing and proportionately scaled streetscapes." For example, VCC identifies a building's "Service Wing Balcony," the "outdoor corridor . . . connecting the rooms of the main house to the smaller service wing rooms" as an architectural element within its purview to protect. Put differently, these are the exterior galleries that linked the living quarters of enslaved people to the homes of their enslavers, still visible on many French Quarter buildings. See Vieux Carré Commission, "About Us," *Nola.gov*, accessed April 29, 2022, https://nola.gov/vcc/about-us/; and *Guidelines for Balconies, Galleries & Porches* (New Orleans, LA: Vieux Carré Commission, August 2015), https://nola.gov/nola/media/VCC/Documents/Design%20Guidelines/VCC-08_Porches-Galleries-Balconies_2015-08_FINAL.PDF; "New Orleans, Louisiana—Code of Ordinances, Chapter 166—Vieux Carré: Article V.—Bourbon Street Tourism Promotion Regulations, Sec. 166–151, Definitions (Code 1956, § 65-41)," New Orleans City Council, accessed May 22, 2023, https://library.municode.com/la/new_orleans/codes/code_of_ordinances?nodeId=PTIICO_CH166VICA.

116 "Old and New," *New Orleans Tribune*, June 11, 1936.

117 Margaret Dixon, "Today is French Market's Moving Day, Preparatory to Beginning Renovations," *Times-Picayune*, June 14, 1936.

118 "Instructions to Bidders, Specifications for the French Market, Buildings 'A' and 'B,' Public Market System, City of New Orleans, Project No. 9, Sam Stone Jr. and Co., Inc., Architects," section 2, 2. KT630 1934: Department of Public Markets, Specifications for the French Market, vols. 1 and 2, FMC records, LDCA NOPL.

119 "Instructions to Bidders," section 8, 1.

120 In fact, the New Orleans city council required that all contractors hired for municipal projects be city residents, which the council defined as "persons who have resided continuously in the City for at least six months previous to their employment on the public works" ("Instructions to Bidders," section 1, 5).

121 See "New Vegetable, Fruit, Poultry Stalls Entered," *Times-Picayune*, April 3, 1937.

122 "What a Difference!" *New Orleans Tribune*, October 18, 1937.

123 "Fish Market," *Times-Picayune*, November 2, 1937.

124 The city contracted with the French Market Corporation to manage daily market management, including finances, maintenance, and expansion. "French Mart Work Described to Club," unnamed newspaper, March 15, 1938, KT920n, Department of Public Markets, Scrapbook of news clippings on market-related matters, February 23, 1934–December 1938, FMC records, LDCA NOPL.

125 "New French Market," *New Orleans States*, March 17, 1938.

126 Emile V. Stier and James B. Keeling, *Glorified French Market: Progressing with Commerce, 1813–1938, a Treatise on the Famous French Market of New Orleans, Louisiana* (New Orleans, LA: French Market Corporation, 1938), 3, KTA910 1938, FMC records, LDCA NOPL.

127 Stier and Keeling, *Glorified French Market*, 4.

128   Stier and Keeling, *Glorified French Market*, 5, 16, 27.

129   Margaret Dixon, "Today is French Market's Moving Day, Preparatory to Beginning
       Renovations," *Times-Picayune*, June 14, 1936.

130   Unnamed article in unnamed newspaper, March 19, 1938, KT920n, FMC records,
       LDCA NOPL.

131   Caption to photograph titled *Prelude to Market Dedication*, unnamed newspaper,
       March 19, 1938, KT920n, FMC records, LDCA NOPL.

132   "A New Start," *New Orleans Tribune*, March 19, 1938.

133   Ralph Matthews, "Old Crescent City Taking On Change," *Baltimore Afro-
       American*, May 21, 1938, 13.

134   Harnett T. Kane, "New Orleans' Housewives Want 'One Stop' Stores," *New Orleans
       Item*, August 29, 1941.

135   The French Market underwent an additional major renovation in 1973 that
       prompted widespread dismay. One local resident said the renovated market re-
       minded her of a Florida shopping mall (Stella Pitts, "French Market Controversy
       is Nothing New," *Times-Picayune*, April 13, 1975). In an another, related vein, con-
       temporary scholars and activists are working to expand awareness and encourage
       greater use of the name "Bulbancha." In 2021, New Orleans's City Council Street Re-
       naming Commission received several anonymous suggestions to rename Lee Circle
       "Bulbancha Way." In 2022, though, the circle was renamed Tivoli Circle and the park
       inside was named Harmony Circle. See Darensbourg, ed., *Bulbancha Is Still a Place:
       . . . The Tricentennial Issue*; Schmelzer, "Bulbancha Forever"; "Street Renaming
       Form Submissions," City Council Street Renaming Commission, accessed May 26,
       2023, https://nolaccsrc.org/StreetRenamingPublicComments.pdf; Kenny Lopez,
       "Controversial Lee Circle Will Now Be Called Harmony Circle," *WGNO*, April 21,
       2022, https://wgno.com/news/local/controversial-lee-circle-will-now-be-called
       -harmony-circle/.

136   Frances Parkinson Keyes, *Dinner at Antoine's* (New York: Julian Messner, 1948), 73.

Chapter Five

1   Federal Writers' Project of the Works Progress Administration for the City of New
       Orleans, *New Orleans City Guide* (Boston, MA: Houghton Mifflin, 1938), xx. See Su-
       san Tucker, ed., *New Orleans Cuisine: Fourteen Signature Dishes and Their Histories*
       (Jackson: University of Press of Mississippi, 2009). Celebrity chef Paul Prudhomme
       brought Cajun cuisine to New Orleans in the late 1970s, ensuring everlasting con-
       fusion for tourists who would find restaurants and souvenir shops selling Cajun and
       Creole tastes and trinkets as a seemingly conjoined pair. Historically, residents of
       rural central and southwestern Louisiana, descendants of the Acadians expelled from
       Canada in the mid-eighteenth century, claimed a Cajun identity. Though French-
       speaking and Roman Catholic like the Creoles of New Orleans, they originated in
       a different strain of the French diaspora and had different ingredients at their fin-
       gertips. See Christopher Hodson, *The Acadian Diaspora: An Eighteenth-Century
       History* (New York: Oxford University Press, 2012); Carl A. Brasseaux, *French, Ca-
       jun, Creole, Houma: A Primer on Francophone Louisiana* (Baton Rouge: Louisiana
       State University Press, 2005); Paul Prudhomme, *Chef Paul Prudhomme's Louisiana
       Kitchen* (New York: Morrow, 1984); and C. Paige Gutierrez, *Cajun Foodways* (Jack-
       son: University Press of Mississippi, 1992). See also Visitor Services Department,

"What does it mean to be Cajun? 12 stories to understand this identity," THNOC, December 11, 2020, https://www.THNOC.org/publications/first-draft/what-does-it-mean-be-cajun-12-stories-understand-identity.

2 In addition, the Young Women's Christian Association maintained beds for thirty-six "transients" of color. The 1938 edition of The Negro Motorist Green Book listed an additional two hotels, bringing the total to four. See Federal Writers' Project, *New Orleans City Guide*, xxxiii–xxxiv; *The Negro Motorist Green Book* (Victor H. Green and Co., 1938), 3.

3 On the early twentieth-century growth of the city's tourism industry, see Kevin Fox Gotham, *Authentic New Orleans: Tourism, Culture, and Race in the Big Easy* (New York: New York University Press, 2007); Mark J. Souther, *New Orleans on Parade: Tourism and the Transformation of New Orleans* (Baton Rouge: Louisiana State University Press, 2006); and Anthony J. Stanonis, *Creating the Big Easy: New Orleans and the Emergence of Modern Tourism, 1918–1945* (Athens: University of Georgia Press, 2006).

4 Lena Richard, *Lena Richard's Cook Book* (New Orleans, LA: Rogers Printing Co., 1939), preface.

5 Jane Holt, "News of Food," *New York Times*, May 13, 1942, 16.

6 Ad for Sazarac [*sic*] Restaurant, *New York Times*, June 1, 1936, 3.

7 "To the Rescue of Savory Southern Cooking," *New York Times*, August 16, 1936, Sunday Magazine, 14.

8 Gene Slate, "Adventures in Food in the Creole Country," *New York Times*, October 9, 1938, 142; Kiley Taylor, "Victuals and Vitamins," *New York Times*, February 11, 1940, 114; Jane Holt, "News of Food," *New York Times*, June 2, 1941, 11.

9 Kimberly Wallace-Sanders, *Mammy: A Century of Race, Gender, and Southern Memory* (Ann Arbor: University of Michigan Press, 2008); Micki McElya, *Clinging to Mammy: The Faithful Slave in Twentieth-Century America* (Cambridge, MA: Harvard University Press, 2007); and Maurice M. Manring, *Slave in a Box: The Strange Career of Aunt Jemima* (Charlottesville: University of Virginia Press, 1998).

10 Catherine Mackenzie, "Fresh Food by Plane Delights the Gourmet," *New York Times*, February 13, 1938, 136.

11 Gourmet Society menu, New Orleans Restaurant, January 22, 1939, Buttolph collection of menus, Rare Book Division, NYPL.

12 "Godchaux Sugar Presents a New 'Sell-Idea' for the Grocers of America," Godchaux Sugar, vertical files, LDCA NOPL.

13 Umberto Eco chronicled his 1975 "journey into hyperreality, in search of instances where the American imagination demands the real thing and, to attain it, must fabricate the absolute fake." New Orleans was the optimum setting, Eco declared, in which to gauge the disappointment involved in encountering reality after enjoying a simulation. He explained, "When, in the space of twenty-four hours, you go . . . from the fake New Orleans of Disneyland to the real one, and from the wild river of Adventureland to a trip on the Mississippi, where the captain of the paddle-wheel steamer says it is possible to see alligators on the banks of the river, and then you don't see any, you risk feeling homesick for Disneyland, where the wild animals don't have to be coaxed." Mid-century New Orleans food producers, restaurant entrepreneurs, and writers were masters at fabricating an edited, enchanting culinary history that delighted tourists. See Eco, "Travels in Hyperreality," in *Travels in Hyperreality: Essays* (San Diego, CA: Harcourt Brace Jovanovich, 1986), 8, 44.

14 Kiley Taylor, "Victuals and Vitamins," *New York Times*, August 25, 1940, 98.

15 On consumer desire for a romanticized Old South, see Martyn Bone, Brian Ward, and William A. Link, eds., *Creating and Consuming the American South* (Gainesville: University Press of Florida, 2015); Karen L. Cox, *Dreaming of Dixie: How the South Was Created in American Popular Culture* (Chapel Hill: University of North Carolina Press, 2011); Rebecca Cawood McIntyre, *Souvenirs of the Old South: Northern Tourism and Southern Mythology* (Gainesville: University Press of Florida, 2011); and Tara McPherson, *Reconstructing Dixie: Race, Gender, and Nostalgia in the Imagined South* (Durham, NC: Duke University Press, 2003).

16 Scoop [Merlin Samuel] Kennedy, *Dining in New Orleans* (New Orleans, LA: Bormon House, 1945), 51. Patricia Yaeger argues that the material culture photographed for a Southern cookbook (as well as the décor experienced in Southern restaurants) "elaborately concealed" the people and labor required to produce Southern food. The result: "a dreamy acceptance of a terrifying social habitus" ("Edible Labor," *Southern Quarterly* 30, nos. 2–3 [Winter/Spring 1992]: 150–59, at 152).

17 Kennedy, *Dining in New Orleans*, 79, 86, 55. On the theatrical nature of tourist attractions that rely on a "front" and "back" of house, see Jennie Germann Molz, "Tasting an Imagined Thailand: Authenticity and Culinary Tourism in Thai Restaurants," in *Culinary Tourism*, ed. Lucy Long (Lexington: University Press of Kentucky, 2013), 53–75; and Dean MacCannell, *The Tourist: A New Theory of the Leisure Class* (Berkeley: University of California Press, 1999).

18 "Emphasis on Creole Cuisine is Example to Other Cities," *Times-Picayune*, March 20, 1950.

19 Harry Heintzen, "The Creole Cookbook Invades Sweden," *Times-Picayune* Sunday magazine, May 29, 1955, 6–7. See also "Our Cookery Goes Places," *Times-Picayune*, December 27, 1954.

20 When traveling salesman and food writer Duncan Hines visited New Orleans in 1954, he made a critical culinary misstep. "He doesn't like the pride of New Orleans—chicory coffee," an *Item* journalist divulged. Hines's disastrous breakfast order of one sweet roll and "pure coffee," as opposed to the city's chicory blend, made news in multiple publications. See Mary Crossley, "Gourmet's Order: Sweet Roll, Coffee," *New Orleans Item*, February 1, 1954.

21 Hermann B. Deutsch, "Gumbo SOUP!" *New Orleans Item*, August 13, 1951.

22 "A Tradition in Old New Orleans," *Saturday Evening Post*, August 11, 1951.

23 Deutsch, "Gumbo."

24 Deutsch kept about twenty submissions of readers' gumbo recipes. In 1950 and 1955, he sponsored similar recipe contests for crawfish bisque, potlikker, and gumbo z'herbes, which resulted in several dozen submissions. See box 6, folder 5: Recipes, gumbo; and folder 6: Recipes, bisque, Hermann Bacher Deutsch papers, 1827–1970, MS 130 (hereafter HBD), TUSC.

25 William H. Coleman, *Historical Sketch Book and Guide to New Orleans and Environs, with Map. Illustrated with Many Original Engravings; and Containing Exhaustive Accounts of the Traditions, Historical Legends, and Remarkable Localities of the Creole City* (New York: Will H. Coleman, 1885), 91.

26 *The Original Picayune Creole Cook Book*, 10th ed. (New Orleans, LA: Times-Picayune Publishing Company, 1945), 26. On the long history of gumbo in Louisiana, see Lolis Eric Elie, "The Origin Myth of New Orleans Cuisine," *Oxford American* 68 (March 2010).

27 Alice Moore Dunbar-Nelson, "People of Color in Louisiana: Part I," *Journal of Negro History* (October 1916): 361–76, at 367. See also Rian T. Fertel, "'Everybody Seemed

Willing to Help': *The Picayune Creole Cook Book* as Battleground, 1900–2008," in *The Larder: Food Studies Methods from the American South*, ed. John D. Edge, Elizabeth S. D. Engelhardt, and Ted Ownby (Athens: University of Georgia Press, 2013), 10–31.

28   Jeanne R. Franklin to Hermann B. Deutsch, n.d., box 6, folder 5: Recipes, gumbo, HBD, TUSC; Bureau of the Census, *1913–1/1/1972, Population Schedules for the 1950 Census, 1950–1950* (Washington, DC: National Archives at Washington, DC) (hereafter 1950 census).

29   Ida Honold to Hermann B. Deutsch, August 29, 1951, box 6, folder 5: Recipes, gumbo, HBD, TUSC; 1950 census.

30   During his spring 1950 recipe contest for crawfish bisque, Deutsch received an anonymous letter from "A Creole who loves her crayfish." The letter concluded, "This 'Cajun' loves her crawfish but is very seldom able to obtain any." Calling the crustacean a crayfish, versus a crawfish, also denoted geographic and cultural distinctions. See Anonymous to Hermann B. Deutsch, March 1, 1950, box 6, folder 6: Recipes, bisque, HBD, TUSC.

31   1950 census.

32   Mrs. E. A. Bourgeois to Hermann B. Deutsch, August 16, 1951, box 6, folder 5: Recipes, gumbo, HBD, TUSC; 1950 census.

33   *New Orleans, Louisiana, City Directory* (New Orleans, LA: R. L. Polk and Company, 1949); Bureau of the Census, *Sixteenth Census of the United States: 1940* (Washington, DC: Government Printing Office, 1942); 1950 census. See also Mrs. George T. Guedry to Hermann B. Deutsch, August 24, 1951; Mrs. H. James Boisseau to Deutsch, n.d.; and Irma Fasnacht to Deutsch, n.d., all in box 6, folder 5: Recipes, gumbo, HBD, TUSC.

34   Blanche Copping, sixty-nine and from Baton Rouge, won Deutsch's filé gumbo contest. New Orleans resident Mrs. [Lucille] Roberts won the okra gumbo contest. When Deutsch published Roberts's winning recipe, he described her as a "Creole-for-generations-back housewife," who was a "great-granddaughter of a New Orleans judge, whose father migrated to the Louisiana colony from France." Deutsch honored a narrow definition of "Creole" when he tapped a winner claiming French colonial ancestry. See Mrs. J. C. Copping to Hermann B. Deutsch, August 20, 1951, box 6, folder 5: Recipes, gumbo, HBD, TUSC; and Hermann B. Deutsch, "Gumbo Winners," *Item*, September 10, 1951.

35   Furthermore, all but one of the letter writers were women. The lone recipe submitted by a man came from Joseph Anderson of Baton Rouge, whose recipe called for crabs, shrimp, and okra. The 1950 census counted multiple men with this name, Black and white, living in Baton Rouge in 1950. See Joseph Anderson to Hermann B. Deutsch, n.d., box 6, folder 5: Recipes, gumbo, HBD, TUSC; 1950 census.

36   Box 6, folder 5: Recipes, gumbo, HBD, TUSC. On Black cooks in white-owned kitchens, see Rebecca Sharpless, *Cooking in Other Women's Kitchens: Domestic Workers in the South, 1865–1960* (Chapel Hill: University of North Carolina Press, 2010).

37   When Mrs. L. E. Bentley won a *Times-Picayune* recipe contest for "Creole Kidney Hash" in October 1931, she acknowledged the recipe's source in a similar way. "When a girl I was a guest in a New Orleans home and the nicest food I ever ate was prepared by 'Aunt Lizzie,' a dear fat old negro woman. . . . One of her chef d'oeuvres was Creole Kidney Hash and this is how she told me she made it." The article's headline read: "Prize-winning recipe: Creole Kidney Hash, Mrs. L. E. Bentley." Aunt

Lizzie existed as a shadow cook—the stereotypical mammy, even, given Bentley's description. This detail gave the recipe context and authenticity, while the prize and attribution for the dish went to Bentley. See "Creole Cookery Extolled as Dishes Are Described," *Times-Picayune*, October 3, 1931, 22.

38 "Fresh Food . . . and Old Bottles," *Times-Picayune New Orleans States Magazine*, October 12, 1947, 147.

39 "Thanks to Plentiful Food, City Has Educated Palate," *Times-Picayune New Orleans States*, January 25, 1953, 12. On mid-century transformations in American shopping and cooking, see Tracy Deutsch, *Building a Housewife's Paradise Gender, Politics, and American Grocery Stores in the Twentieth Century* (Chapel Hill: University of North Carolina Press, 2010), and Laura Shapiro, *Something from the Oven: Reinventing Dinner in 1950s America* (New York: Viking Press, 2004).

40 Advertisement for Pap's Food Store, *Item*, March 3, 1953, 6.

41 "New Orleans: Home of the Higgins Boats," National World War II Museum, New Orleans, LA, July 2017, https://www.nationalww2museum.org/sites/default/files/2017-07/higgins-in-new-orleans-fact.pdf; Enoc P. Waters, "Color Lines Blurred in Strange New Orleans, City of Contrasts," *Chicago Defender*, March 20, 1943, 5; Waters, "More Wartime Income in New Orleans Fails to Improve Living Conditions," *Chicago Defender*, March 27, 1943, 8; Waters, "New Orleans City of Slums with Pride in Architecture," *Chicago Defender*, April 3, 1943, 5.

42 On the community of Black New Orleanians that developed in Los Angeles, see Lynell George, "Who's Your People?," *LA Weekly*, November 13–19, 1992; "Color Bar is Felt in New Orleans," *Atlanta Daily World*, August 10, 1940, 1; Enoc P. Waters, "Louisiana War Boom Puts Strain on Race Relations," *Chicago Defender*, April 10, 1943, 13; "New Orleans Realtors Requested to Make No Sales to Group," *Atlanta Daily World*, April 7, 1950, 3.

43 Advertisement for Rosenberg's Furniture Store, *Item*, March 3, 1953, 11; "Homes Growing in Size in N.O.," *Item*, March 3, 1953, 18; "The History and Politics Behind Pontchartrain Park," Preservation Resource Center of New Orleans, accessed May 5, 2022, https://prcno.org/resources/pontchartrain-park/. Such moves would reach their apex in the 1960s, with court-ordered public school integration. See Richard Campanella, *Bienville's Dilemma: A Historical Geography of New Orleans* (Lafayette: Center for Louisiana Studies, University of Louisiana at Lafayette, 2008), 182–83. On the social and political implications of postwar consumer spending, see Lizabeth Cohen, *A Consumer's Republic: The Politics of Consumption in Postwar America* (New York: Knopf, 2003).

44 "YWCA for Inclusion in Association Life," *Times-Picayune*, March 6, 1946, 7; "Advisory Group for Integration," *Times-Picayune*, December 3, 1950, 28; "Negro Job Plan Given Approval," *Times-Picayune*, November 17, 1951, 16; "New Plea to End Segregation Set," *Times-Picayune*, November 28, 1951, 38; "HST Again Urges Action on Rights," *Times-Picayune*, June 14, 1952, 1; "U.S. Segregation in Service Falls," *Times-Picayune*, October 19, 1952, 18. See also Donald E. DeVore, *Defying Jim Crow: African American Community Development and the Struggle for Racial Equality in New Orleans, 1900–1960* (Baton Rouge: Louisiana State University Press, 2015), 200; Kim Lacy Rogers, *Righteous Lives: Narratives of the New Orleans Civil Rights Movement* (New York: New York University Press, 1993); Adam Fairclough, *Race and Democracy: The Civil Rights Struggle in Louisiana, 1915–1972* (Athens: University of Georgia Press, 1995); and Sharlene Sinegal DeCuir, "Attacking Jim Crow: Black Activism in New Orleans 1925–1941" (Ph.D. diss., Louisiana State University, 2009), https://

digitalcommons.lsu.edu/cgi/viewcontent.cgi?article=2868&context=gradschool
_dissertations.

45 *New Orleans, Louisiana, City Directory* (1949), 16.

46 Flora MacFarland, "Question Box," *Cleveland Plain Dealer*, April 7, 1951, 10. Definitions of "Creole" as a person of mixed racial heritage appeared in syndicated
question-and-answer columns of New Jersey and Oregon newspapers, too. See
"Questions and Answers . . . by Haskins," *Portland Oregonian*, June 25, 1952, 19;
Trenton Evening Times, July 2, 1952.

47 Ray M. Thompson, *New Orleans, from A to Z: Questions You'll Ask about This City
of Charm and its Famous French Quarter . . . Alphabetically Answered* (New Orleans, LA: House of the Artists, 1951), 25.

48 "High Court Defines an Ala. Creole," *Item*, March 27, 1953.

49 "Ruling Called Error of Fact," *Item*, March 27, 1953.

50 Such views did not go unchallenged. University of New Orleans history professor
Joseph G. Tregle Jr. fought for decades to counter assertions that the term "Creole"
was tied to a white racial identity. "There are few things clung to so tenaciously or
taught so vehemently in New Orleans as the doctrine of the Creole," he wrote in
1952. "It is abundantly clear that in the 1820s and 1830s 'Creole' was generally used in
Louisiana to designate any person native to the state, be he white, black, or colored."
Tregle's words failed to penetrate the majority of culinary texts and travel guides
that reached New Orleans residents and tourists. As late as 1981, Tregle wrote to the
editor of a New Orleans newspaper to insist that "Creole" did not mean "white." As
quoted in Jeanne Weill, "When is a Creole Not a Tomato?," *New Orleans Magazine*,
March 1984, 57–58; Joseph G. Tregle Jr., "'Creole' in Context," letter to the editor,
unnamed newspaper, September 13, 1981, vertical files: Creole, LDCA NOPL. More
recently, poet Mona Lisa Saloy stated succinctly, "Creole is not a color, it's a culture"
(as quoted in Judy Walker, "'Creole Is Not a Color, It's a Culture' and Other High-
lights from Dillard University Black Hand in the Pot Culinary Lecture," *Times-
Picayune*, April 17, 2015). See also Elie, "Origin Myth"; and Jessica B. Harris, *Beyond
Gumbo: Creole Fusion Food from the Atlantic Rim* (New York: Simon and Schuster,
2003).

51 Robert Kennon, as quoted in "What Nation's Press Said about Court's Historic
School Opinion," *Baltimore Afro-American*, May 29, 1954, 7; "La. Gov. Takes Stand
Against De-Segregation," *Atlanta Daily World*, March 16, 1954, 1.

52 Rogers, *Righteous Lives*, 35; DeVore, *Defying Jim Crow*, 205–13. The fight to integrate
public schools in New Orleans was especially ugly, public, and protracted. See Paul
Burton, "U.S. Orders Louisiana Schools Opened to All," *Chicago Daily Defender*,
February 16, 1956, 1; "Racist Vows New Orleans Won't Comply," *Chicago Daily De-
fender*, February 16, 1956, 8; "Court Upholds Integration: Court Rules against New
Orleans Racists, But Howling Mobs Heckle Cleric, Girl," *Chicago Daily Defender*,
December 1, 1960, 1; "Parents of New Orleans 4 Say: 'We Will Win,'" *Baltimore
Afro-American*, December 3, 1960, 1; "Slowly but Surely, Segregationists Are Losing
'Battle of New Orleans,'" *Baltimore Afro-American*, January 7, 1961, 9.

53 Even if Swift characterized Azalea as Creole, she indicated a sense of possession of
Azalea and her recipe, writing, "I have a Creole cook." Swift's letter conformed to
conventions in which people of color could be classified as Creole but only in the
service of whites. See Lottie Keife Swift to Hermann B. Deutsch, August 23, 1951,
box 6, folder 5: Recipes, gumbo, HBD, TUSC.

54 White denigration of Black intelligence and culture via allegations of illiteracy—

and Blacks' use of literary forms to resist such discrimination—began in the earliest days of the African slave trade. Henry Louis Gates Jr. explained, "The Anglo-African literary tradition was created . . . to demonstrate that persons of African descent possessed the requisite degrees of reason and wit to create literature, that they were, indeed, full and equal members of the community of rational, sentient beings, that they could, indeed, write." Gates dated the first anthology of African American literature to 1845, when *Les Cenelles, Choix de poésies indigènes* was published in New Orleans. See Henry Louis Gates Jr. and Nellie Y. McKay, "Introduction: Talking Books," in *The Norton Anthology of African American Literature*, ed. Gates Jr. and McKay (New York: W. W. Norton, 2004), xxxvii–xlvii, at xxxviii.

55   "I went five times in one day [to the polls]," 7th Ward/Tremé resident Hazel Bean said in an oral history. "They wouldn't tell me what my mistakes was. You had to figure it out. . . . [B]ut I wasn't intending to give up." See "If You Don't Vote, Don't Squawk," oral history with Hazel Bean, in Donna L. Davis, ed., *Quartee Red Beans, Quartee Rice: Stories of the Treme/7th Ward*, Ethnic Heritage Project (New Orleans, LA: St. Mark's Community Center, 1979), Amistad Research Center, New Orleans, LA. On Louisiana's literacy tests designed to exclude Black voters, see Law Review editors, "Voting Rights: A Case Study of Madison Parish, Louisiana," *University of Chicago Law Review* 38, no. 4 (Summer 1971): 726–87; and Anthony Lewis, "U.S. Sues to Upset Louisiana's Law on Voting Tests," *New York Times*, December 29, 1961, 1.

56   Introduction, *The Picayune's Creole Cook Book*, 1st ed. (New Orleans, LA: Picayune, 1900).

57   The authors of *The Creole Cookery Book*, published in 1885, had a similar perspective. "In this time . . . it is befitting that the occult science of the gumbo should cease to be the hereditary lore of our negro mammies, and should be allowed its proper place in the gastronomical world" (Christian Woman's Exchange, *Creole Cookery Book* [New Orleans, LA: T. H. Thomason, 1885], preface). Other kinds of publications evinced a similar conversion from oral tradition to textual history. "It is not so long ago . . . that New Orleans had no other guide book than the traditions narrated by Grandparents and 'black Mammies,'" wrote the author of a 1928 city guide. "But, *tout cela a changé*! the printed letter now represents . . . the old black 'Mammies' and 'Daddies' and we read what once we listened to; more accurate . . . but less charming." Such depictions infantilized men and women of color as quaint yet unreliable pieces of local scenery. See Grace King, introduction to G. William Nott, *A Tour of the Vieux Carré* (New Orleans, LA: Tropical Printing Company, 1928), 3.

58   Susan Tucker reported this subtle change in Susan Tucker, M. A. Johnson, Wendy Bruton, and Sharon Stallworth Nossiter, eds., "New Orleans Cookbook Bibliography: Compiled by the New Orleans Culinary History Group," 107, accessed April 29, 2022, http://www2.tulane.edu/~wclib/New%20Orleans%20Cookbook%20Bibliography%202011.pdf.

59   On variations among editions of the *Picayune's Creole Cook Book*, see Fertel, "'Everybody Seemed Willing to Help,'" 10–31; and Tucker et al., eds., "New Orleans Cookbook Bibliography," 103–12.

60   Natalie V. Scott, *Mirations and Miracles of Mandy* (New Orleans, LA: R. H. True, 1929), introduction.

61   Scott, *Mirations and Miracles*.

62   Natalie V. Scott, *200 Years of New Orleans Cooking* (New York: Jonathan Cape and Harrison Smith, 1931), 122.

63 Federal Writers' Project, *New Orleans City Guide*, 165. A similar cookbook in this genre, which parrots the words of an invented cook, Mammy Lou, is Betty Benton Patterson, *Mammy Lou's Cookbook* (New York: Robert M. McBride, 1931). See Sharpless, *Cooking in Other Women's Kitchens*, 47–48.

64 Paul Freedman, *Ten Restaurants That Changed America* (New York: Liveright, 2016), ch. 2.

65 Kennedy, *Dining in New Orleans*, 27.

66 Roy L. Alciatore, *Centennial Souvenir du Restaurant Antoine* (New Orleans, LA: Antoine's, 1940), 19.

67 Meigs O. Frost, "Gourmets' Shrine," *Times-Picayune*, April 4, 1940.

68 Antoine's menu, 1943, menu collection and restaurant memorabilia (hereafter Menus), LDCA NOPL.

69 Arnaud's menu, ca. 1950s, Louisiana menu and restaurant collection, TUSC; La Louisiane, "A Dictionary of Delectable Dishes," ca. 1930s, Menus, LDCA NOPL.

70 "Trip to Coconut Grove, Florida and New Orleans, LA, Jan. 10 to Jan. 25, J.R. Abbot and H.M. Abbot," box 23, folder 2, Stanonis, Loyola.

71 Karen Trahan Leathem, "Two Women and Their Cookbooks: Lena Richard and Mary Land," exhibition guide, November 2–December 21, 2001, Newcomb College, at Newcomb and Vorhoff, http://www.slideshare.net/cookingwithdenay/lena -richard; Toni Tipton-Martin, *The Jemima Code: Two Centuries of African American Cookbooks* (Austin: University of Texas Press, 2015), 52–53; Jessica B. Harris, *High on the Hog: A Culinary Journey from Africa to America* (New York: Bloomsbury, 2011), 193–95.

72 Richard, *Lena Richard's Cook Book*, 90–91. Unlike restaurant menus, cookbooks offer no guarantee that the recipes they contained were prepared, and if so, how often. Scholars of English, Women's Studies, and American Studies have argued that cookbooks, especially community cookbooks, are best read not as accurate reflections of historical eating habits, but for subtler clues to the social ideals of a group, the gendered and racialized nature of labor, and the facets of ethnic and regional identities. These stained pages of Richard's cookbook do offer proof of meringues or custards enjoyed, however. See Jessamyn Neuhaus, *Manly Meals and Mom's Home Cooking: Cookbooks and Gender in Modern America* (Baltimore, MD: Johns Hopkins University, 2003); Janet Floyd and Laurel Forster, eds., *The Recipe Reader: Narratives—Contexts—Traditions* (Aldershot, England: Ashgate, 2003); and Anne L. Bower, ed., *Recipes for Reading: Community Cookbooks, Stories, Histories* (Amherst: University of Massachusetts Press, 1997).

73 Paddleford, "Cook from New Orleans Shows Northerners 'Tricks of the Trade,'" *New York Herald Tribune*, July 8, 1939, 7.

74 Paddleford, "Cook from New Orleans."

75 Tipton-Martin notes these alterations in *Jemima Code*, 52. With this change, this Northern publisher made a decision not unlike that of the *Picayune's Creole Cookbook* authors in 1922, when they edited "Creole negro cooks" to "Creole cooks," removing Black chefs from a position of authorial prominence.

76 *The Negro Motorist Green-Book* (New York: Victor H. Green, 1941), 15, Manuscripts, Archives and Rare Books Division, Schomburg Center for Research in Black Culture (hereafter Schomburg Manuscripts), NYPL; *Polk's New Orleans Classified Business Directory* (New Orleans: R. L. Polk and Co., 1942); and *The Negro Motorist Green Book: An International Travel Guide* (New York: Victor H. Green, 1949), 33, Schomburg Manuscripts, NYPL.

77 Kenneth Chorley to Lena Richard, April 30, 1943, Colonial Williamsburg Notebook 1943, Lena Richard papers, collection NAA-071 (hereafter LR papers), Newcomb and Vorhoff.

78 Colonial Williamsburg notebook 1943, LR papers, Newcomb and Vorhoff.

79 Leathem, "Two Women"; Clementine Paddleford, "Caterer, Back in New Orleans, Has Cabbage and Shrimp Trick," *New York Herald Tribune*, December 1, 1947; Christina Watkins, "Celebrating Black History Month: The Life of Chef Lena Richard, a Culinary Giant Who Broke Barriers," *WDSU*, February 17, 2022, https://www.wdsu.com/article/celebrating-black-history-month-the-life-of-chef-lena-richard-a-culinary-giant-who-broke-barriers/38964824#; Ashley Rose Young, "Chef Lena Richard: Culinary Icon and Activist," *O Say Can You See?* (National Museum of American History blog), June 10, 2020, https://americanhistory.si.edu/blog/lena-richard.

80 "Cook Who is Known for 'Dream Melon' to Teach Creole Cuisine," *Times-Picayune*, May 15, 1938, 7; "Norge Cooking School Attracts Huge Throngs," unnamed newspaper, possibly *Louisiana Weekly*, ca. 1949, Colonial Williamsburg Notebook 1943, LR papers, Newcomb and Vorhoff. The *Times-Picayune*'s 1938 Christmas gift guide recommended Lena Richard's cooking classes—a twelve-part series, "Art of Southern Cookery"—as a gift idea "For Her," alongside "Genuine Oriental Rugs, Furs of Quality, Blooming Pot Plants, Pomeranian Puppies," *Times-Picayune*, December 13, 1938, 28.

81 "Orleans Cateress Attracts Haute Monde," *Pittsburgh Courier*, May 28, 1938, 5.

82 "Notes on Books and Authors," *Times-Picayune*, September 1, 1940, 19.

83 Eva Beard, "Gulf Coast Has Flavor: In Food on Its Shores, Tourists Find Tang of the Sea," *New York Times*, November 14, 1937, 198.

84 Even if Black workers did most of the cooking in nineteenth- and twentieth-century New Orleans kitchens, Black-authored cookbooks did not figure in the city's culinary culture until well into the twentieth century. In part, cookbooks were not necessary, as kitchen staff relied on cooking knowledge that had been conveyed orally. Furthermore, white employers denied workers the time, funding, or support required to publish cookbooks. Just as whites' defense of authentic Creole food—and the notion of a white Creole identity—betrayed insecurity, so did the proliferation of Creole cookbooks in the twentieth century communicate a lack of knowledge among whites in the kitchen. Arjun Appadurai observes, "Authenticity is typically not the concern of the native participants in a culinary tradition . . . The concern with authenticity indicates some sort of doubt. . . . It is the problem of the outsider" ("On Culinary Authenticity," letters, *Anthropology Today* 2, no. 4 [August 1986]: 25). Nationally, Black-authored cookbooks increased during the era of civil rights activism, especially as soul food became popular. For a bibliography of the Black-authored culinary canon, see Tipton-Martin, *Jemima Code*. See also Neuhaus, *Manly Meals*, 313–14; and Doris Witt, *Black Hunger: Soul Food and America* (Minneapolis: University of Minnesota Press, 2004), 217–28. On the power residing in Black cooks' unwritten recipes, see Sharpless, *Cooking in Other Women's Kitchens*, xxi–xxiv.

85 Eugénie Lavedan Maylié to Hermann B. Deutsch, August 15, 1951, box 6, folder 5, Recipes, gumbo, HBD, TUSC.

86 Mayhaw trees produce a small, tart fruit, similar to a cranberry. See Eugénie Lavedan Maylié, *Maylié's Table d'Hote Recipes: And the History and Some Facts Concerning "La Maison Maylié et Esparbé"* (New Orleans, LA: Maylié's, 1941).

87 "Up and Down the Street," *Times-Picayune*, May 22, 1939, 18. On racist stereotypes

connecting Black Americans to watermelon, see William R. Black, "How Watermelons Became a Racist Trope," *Atlantic*, December 8, 2014; and Jacqueline Woodson, "The Pain of the Watermelon Joke," *New York Times*, November 28, 2014.

88   Paddleford, "Cook from New Orleans"; "Cook Who Is Known," *Times-Picayune*, May 15, 1938.

89   "'Cook Book' Author, Restaurateur Dies," *Times-Picayune*, November 28, 1950, 3.

90   "Around the Country," *Cleveland Call and Post*, December 9, 1950, 6D.

91   "Lena Richard, Restaurateur, Author, Dies," *Chicago Defender*, December 9, 1950, 20.

92   Lena Richard's daughter, Marie Richard, worked as an assistant on WDSU's show featuring Ruth Prevost as Amanda Lee. See "Cooking Show is Local Favorite," *Times-Picayune*, June 8, 1952, 18; Blake Pontchartrain, "Meet Chef Mandy Lee, Lena Richard's WDSU Cooking Show Successor," *Gambit*, March 19, 2023, https://www .nola.com/gambit/news/blake_pontchartrain/blake-pontchartrain-meet-chef -mandy-lee-lena-richards-wdsu-cooking-show-successor/article_18b355cc-c33c -11ed-87d7-539af56a8b2a.html; 1950 census.

93   On fried chicken as yet another stereotype binding food and race, see Psyche Williams-Forson, *Building Houses out of Chicken Legs: Black Women, Food, and Power* (Chapel Hill: University of North Carolina Press, 2006).

94   Ruth Prevost and Harnett T. Kane, *Mandy Lee's Recipes for Good New Orleans Dishes* (New Orleans, LA: WDSU-TV Channel 6 New Orleans, 1950); "The Week's Census," *JET* 5, no. 20 (March 25, 1954): 19; "Prevost," *Times-Picayune*, March 10, 1954, 2; "Ruth 'Amanda Lee' Porter Prevost," Find a Grave, database and images, accessed May 12, 2023, https://www.findagrave.com/memorial/110245174/ruth -prevost; Ruth Porter Brookter-Prevost gravestone, Harrison Jackson Square Cemetery, Slidell, St. Tammany Parish, LA.

95   Nathaniel Burton and Rudy Lombard, *Creole Feast: 15 Master Chefs of New Orleans Reveal Their Secrets* (New York: Random House, 1978); Sara Wood, "Remembering Rudy Lombard," blog, December 15, 2014, Southern Foodways Alliance, Center for the Study of Southern Culture, University of Mississippi, Oxford, Mississippi (hereafter SFA); Kennedy, *Dining in New Orleans*, 76. *Creole Feast* was a landmark work that continues to inspire scholars and artists. See Lolis Eric Elie, "The Afterlives of 'Creole Feast,'" *Bitter Southerner*, June 24, 2021; Todd A. Price, "Black Chefs Stirred the Pots for New Orleans' Cuisine. But Today, They Are Hard to Find," *Nashville Tennessean*, February 25, 2021; and Zella Palmer, dir., *The Story of New Orleans Creole Cooking* (New Orleans, LA: Dillard University Ray Charles Program in African American Material Culture and Louisiana Endowment for Humanities, 2020), https://www.youtube.com/watch?v=NgWCoZcCRvI. The Creole Feast food festival referenced in the introduction was organized by Lombard to celebrate the publication of this book. See p. 12.

96   During this era, many light-skinned people of color in New Orleans maintained Afro hairstyles to assert their Black identity. See Virginia R. Domínguez, *White by Definition: Social Classification in Creole Louisiana* (New Brunswick, NJ: Rutgers University Press, 1986), 161–81.

97   "The Issue of Color is a False Issue," oral history with Ronald Nabonne, in *Quartee Red Beans*, ed. Davis, Amistad. Additional oral histories that showed skepticism among New Orleanians of color in the 1970s about a Creole identity included "Creole and Non-Creole Conflict," oral history with Emilo "Monk" Dupre, and "Africa in New Orleans," oral history with Gerald Emelle, both in *Quartee Red Beans*. This was not the first era in which New Orleanians of color attempted to smooth internal

divisions rooted in skin color. In the 1930s, a Baltimore journalist reported on dynamics of colorism that he witnessed splitting New Orleanians of color. See Ralph Matthews, "Old Crescent City Taking On Change," *Baltimore Afro-American*, May 21, 1938, 13; Ralph Matthews, "Way Down Yonder in New Orleans," *Baltimore Afro-American*, March 17, 1934, 5; and Ralph Matthews, "Way Down Yonder in New Orleans," *Baltimore Afro-American*, March 3, 1934, 5.

98 Burton and Lombard, *Creole Feast*, xv, 53. See also Tipton-Martin, *Jemima Code*, 142–43.

99 Arnaud's restaurant à la carte menu, n.d., Restaurants (Arnaud's), vertical files, TUSC.

100 Burton and Lombard, *Creole Feast*, 5; Broussard Restaurant and Napoleon Patio menu, n.d., Restaurants (Broussard's), vertical files, TUSC.

101 Similarly, Corinne Dunbar restaurant on St. Charles Avenue ran for generations on a kitchen staffed exclusively by Black women, including Leona Victor, Clara Mathus, and Rosa Barganier. Kennedy recognized the proficient cooking of Black chefs in a variety of cuisines. "As in many a New Orleans 'French, Italian or German restaurant,' the cook at Segreto's is a colored man," Kennedy wrote. "His rich tomato sauce or succulent ravioli wouldn't be better if his name were Tessitore" (*Dining in New Orleans*, 46, 96); see also Burton and Lombard, *Creole Feast*, 61, 43.

102 Kennedy, *Dining in New Orleans*, 29. Adjusted for inflation, such profits would total more than $17 million in 2023. "Consumer Price Index Inflation Calculator," US Bureau of Labor Statistics, accessed May 17, 2023, https://www.bls.gov/data/inflation _calculator.htm.

103 Burton and Lombard, *Creole Feast*, 61.

104 Kennedy, *Dining in New Orleans*, 48. Kennedy reviewed one Black-owned restaurant, Delatour's. There, he wrote, "You may take down your hair and loft your chicken. In other words, this is a place for eating, not white ties. . . . Chances are you'll order fried chicken" (53).

105 Burton and Lombard, *Creole Feast*, 18, 20.

106 Prudence was executive chef at Galatoire's from the late 1980s until 2003, although Galatoire's did not publicly recognize Prudence in that role until 1997. In 2003, Galatoire's received its first nomination for a James Beard Award, for Outstanding Restaurant. Two restaurant managers attended the awards ceremony, but Prudence did not. Later that year, Prudence left the restaurant. The departure was not amicable. Prudence remembered, "Mentally I was sort of burned." In 2005, Galatoire's won the James Beard Award for Outstanding Restaurant. Prudence's decades-long career there had surely played a significant role in the win. See Milton Prudence, oral history transcript, July 19, 2006, in "New Orleans Eats," oral history project, SFA, https://www.southernfoodways.org/interview/tommys-cuisine/.

107 Leah Chase, *The Dooky Chase Cookbook* (Gretna, LA: Pelican Publishing Company, 1990), 12, 13. See also Nancy Harmon Jenkins, "A Lover of Food Who Nurtured a New Orleans Institution," *New York Times*, June 27, 1990.

108 University of Richmond Digital Scholarship Lab, "Mapping Inequality: Redlining in New Deal America," area no. D-8, New Orleans, LA, January 31, 1939, https://dsl .richmond.edu/panorama/redlining/#loc=15/29.968/-90.087&city=new-orleans -la&area=D8&adview=full. The 1940 census returns of the blocks surrounding the corner where Dooky Chase restaurant would stand painted a different picture. They showed a neighborhood of working families, the overwhelming majority of whom had been born in Louisiana and had been living at the same address for at least five

years. The Chases' neighbors worked as storekeepers, porters, a laundress, a seam-stress, a cigarmaker, and a delivery man. See ward 5, blocks 26–27, Bureau of the Census, *Sixteenth Census of the United States* (1940).

109 Also in 1957, Willie Mae Seaton purchased a property one block away from Dooky Chase, at the intersection of St. Ann and North Tonti Streets. A single mother of four children, Seaton had worked at a dry cleaner, driven a taxi, and earned a beauti-cian license. Seaton opened a bar, Willie Mae's Scotch House, and initially served food from Dooky Chase. "They brang us food. . . . And sometimes they have them white tablecloths," remembered Seaton in an oral history. Eventually, Seaton began serving her own food. Her renown rivaled that of Leah Chase; Seaton became fa-mous for her expertly fried chicken and red beans and rice. Of New Orleans food, Seaton said, "That's what carries our city. They say we have the best food in the nation. . . . This is called the Creole City, and they say Creole cooking—it means all of that good seasoning that you put into it." See Willie Mae Seaton (with Hazel Mae White), oral history transcript, July 1, 2006, New Orleans Eats, SFA, https://www.southernfoodways.org/interview/willie-maes-scotch-house/; Todd A. Price, "Willie Mae Seaton of Willie Mae's Scotch House Dies at 99," *Times-Picayune*, September 22, 2015. The eponymous Buster Holmes restaurant and Chez Hélène, helmed by Austin Leslie, were two other well-known Black-owned restaurants in twentieth-century New Orleans. See Buster Holmes, *The Buster Holmes Restau-rant Cookbook: New Orleans Handmade Cookin'* (Gretna, LA: Pelican Publishing Co., 1980); Todd A. Price, "Do You Remember Chez Helene?," *NOLA.com / Times-Picayune*, June 21, 2017; Chez Hélène menu, New Orleans, LA, 1983, menu 17-1046, Vinnie Oakes menu collection, CIA menu, CIA.

110 Chase, *Dooky Chase Cookbook*, 14.

111 Raphael Cassimere Jr., oral history, 2013, in "'A Haven for All of Us': Documenting the World of Dooky Chase Restaurant in the Era before Desegregation" (hereaf-ter Haven), Loyola Documentary and Oral History Studio (hereafter LDOHS), accessed May 5, 2022, http://cas.loyno.edu/history/haven-all-us-documenting-world-dooky-chase-restaurant-era-desegregation; interview clip available at https://vimeo.com/79107798.

112 Dooky Chase's menu, New Orleans, LA, 1986, menu 32-631, Patty O'Neill menu collection, CIA menu, CIA; Chase, *Dooky Chase Cookbook*, 52–53; David Grunfeld, "Photos: Gumbo z'herbes Served on Holy Thursday at Dooky Chase's Satisfies Our Souls," *NOLA.com / Times-Picayune*, April 6, 2023.

113 Mary Foster, "Dooky Chase Gumbo Fueled Civil Rights Movement," *Associated Press*, March 3, 2012.

114 "Segregation End Near, Group Told," *Times-Picayune*, February 15, 1957, 3.

115 "Nigeria Leader is Visitor Here," *Times-Picayune*, August 22, 1959, 47.

116 Cassimere Jr., oral history; Monisha Jackson, "Knights of Peter Claver," *New Orleans Historical*, April 5, 2017, https://neworleanshistorical.org/items/show/1356.

117 As quoted in Rogers, *Righteous Lives*, 69. On the singular role of food establishments in strategies of segregation and desegregation, see Angela Jill Cooley, *To Live and Dine in Dixie: The Evolution of Urban Food Culture in the Jim Crow South* (Athens: University of Georgia, 2015). Following the *Brown* decision, Louisiana and other states attempted to keep restaurants, among other spaces, segregated. See "New Bills Seek Curb on 'Mixing,'" *Times-Picayune*, June 1, 1956, 23; and "Café Racial Bill Passed in House," *Times-Picayune*, February 22, 1959, 93.

118 Louis Lautier, "Capital Spotlight," *Baltimore Afro-American*, October 8, 1960, 4;

"Lautier, Louis R., d. 1962," *Portraits of a City: The Scurlock Photographic Studio's Legacy to Washington, D.C.*, online exhibit, National Museum of American History, accessed May 18, 2023, https://amhistory.si.edu/archives/scurlock/about_the _scurlocks/notables/Lautier.htm.

119   Doratha Smith-Simmons, oral history transcript, August 21, 2017, MSS 936.4, NOLA Resistance Oral History Project (hereafter NROHP), THNOC. On CORE training and organization, see also Robert Heller, oral history transcript, September 4, 2019, MSS 936.29, NROHP, THNOC; and DeVore, *Defying Jim Crow*, 214–25.

120   Betty Daniels Rosemond, oral history transcript, August 7, 2019, MSS 936.26, NROHP, THNOC.

121   Katy Reckdahl, "Sit-Ins at Canal Street Lunch Counters 50 Years Ago Sparked a Civil Rights Case That Went All the Way to the Supreme Court," *Times-Picayune*, September 17, 2010. See also David J. Dennis, oral history transcript, September 27, 2017, MSS 936.10, NROHP, THNOC.

122   Lombard v. Louisiana, 373 U.S. 267 (1963). In fall 1962, a group of sixty New Orleans restaurants and lunch counters "quietly desegregated without incident"—the result of a two-year campaign by the Student Nonviolent Coordinating Committee, the NAACP, and CORE activists, like Lombard. See "Sit-In Roundup: New Orleans Seggies Napping as 60 Cafés Drop Color Bars," *Baltimore Afro-American*, September 22, 1962, 17.

123   Leah Chase, *And Still I Cook* (Gretna, LA: Pelican Publishing Company, 2003), 22. See also Carol Allen, *Leah Chase: Listen, I Say Like This* (Gretna, LA: Pelican Publishing Company, 2002).

124   Cassimere Jr., oral history.

125   Carmen Morial, oral history, 2013, Haven, LDOHS, interview clip available at https://vimeo.com/79107792.

126   Chase, *Dooky Chase Cookbook*, 14. Chase cooked in the Dooky Chase kitchen until shortly before her death at ninety-six. See Kim Severson, "Leah Chase, 96, Creole Chef Who Fed Presidents and Freedom Riders, Dies," *New York Times*, June 2, 2019.

127   Henry M. Stevens to Hermann B. Deutsch, August 27, 1951, box 9, folder 60: Correspondence, 1951 August-September, HBD, TUSC.

Epilogue

1   "St. Roch Market Improvements—New Orleans, LA," *Living New Deal*, accessed May 24, 2022, https://livingnewdeal.org/projects/st-roch-market-improvement -new-orleans-la/; Todd A. Price, "St. Roch Market: 144 Years of History in 27 Photos," *NOLA.com / Times-Picayune*, February 12, 2019; Adele Foster, "Lama Family Parlays St. Roch Market Seafood Fame to Old Mandeville," *Times-Picayune*, January 6, 2017; "City Celebrates Reopening Of Historic St. Roch Market," *Biz New Orleans*, April 10, 2015, https://www.bizneworleans.com/city-celebrates-reopening-of -historic-st-roch-market/.

2   At the time of the market's opening, two of the thirteen stalls were owned by the market operator. See "City Celebrates Reopening," *Biz New Orleans*; Todd A. Price, "St. Roch Market Loses Tunde Wey of Lagos and Ali Mills of The Mayhaw Bar," *NOLA.com / Times-Picayune*, August 5, 2015.

3   Todd A. Price, "What to Eat, Drink, and Buy at St. Roch Market," *NOLA.com / Times-Picayune*, April 9, 2015. The original website of St. Roch Market claimed, "Est. 1875," yet the structure's history was less continuous than this date suggested. The

website offered details about market vendors, special events, and renting the space, but no discussion of the public market's history. See http://www.strochmarket .com/, accessed March 22, 2016.

4   Jonathan Bullington, "Vandals Hit St. Roch Market," *NOLA.com / Times-Picayune*, May 1, 2015.

5   Todd A. Price, "St. Roch Market Operators Answer Critics, Share Their Vision," *Times-Picayune*, July 7, 2015.

6   On gentrification and demographic change, see Tara Bahrampour, Marissa J. Lang, and Ted Mellnik, "White People Have Flocked Back to City Centers—And Transformed Them," *Washington Post*, February 6, 2023; CC Campbell-Rock, "Gentrification is Changing New Orleans before Our Eyes," *Black Source Media*, March 13, 2022, https://blacksourcemedia.com/gentrification-is-changing-new-orleans -before-our-eyes/; Emmanuel Felton, John D. Harden, and Kevin Schaul, "Still Looking for a 'Black Mecca,' the New Great Migration," *Washington Post,* January 14, 2022; Lolis Elie, "Gentrification Might Kill New Orleans before Climate Change Does," *New York Times*, August 27, 2019; Rob Walker, "Airbnb Pits Neighbor against Neighbor in Tourist-Friendly New Orleans," *New York Times*, March 5, 2016; and Richard Campanella, "Gentrification and its Discontents: Notes from New Orleans," *NewGeography*, February 28, 2013, https://www.newgeography.com /content/003526-gentrification-and-its-discontents-notes-new-orleans.

7   Richard Campanella, *Bienville's Dilemma: A Historical Geography of New Orleans* (Lafayette: Center for Louisiana Studies, University of Louisiana at Lafayette, 2008), 53–58; Raymond A. Mohl, "Stop the Road: Freeway Revolts in American Cities," *Journal of Urban History* 30, no. 5 (July 2004): 674–706; Anna Livia Brand, "Black Mecca Futures: Re-Membering New Orleans's Claiborne Avenue," *Journal of Urban Affairs* 44, no. 6 (2022): 808–21; Ian McNulty, "The History of Morning Call Coffee Stand in Photos, from French Market to Canal Boulevard," *NOLA.com*, March 28, 2021; Justin Nystrom, "The Vanished World of the New Orleans Longshoreman," *Southern Spaces*, March 5, 2014, http://southernspaces.org/2014/vanished-world -new-orleans-longshoreman; Christopher A. Airriess and David L. Clawson, "Versailles: A Vietnamese Enclave in New Orleans, Louisiana," *Journal of Cultural Geography* 12, no. 1 (1991): 1–13; Theresa McCulla, "Fava Beans and Bánh Mì: Ethnic Revival and the New Orleans Gumbo," *Quaderni Storici* 51, no. 1 (2016): 71–102; Stella Pitts, "French Market Controversy Is Nothing New," *Times-Picayune*, April 13, 1975.

8   Alan Berube and Natalie Holmes, "Concentrated Poverty in New Orleans 10 Years after Katrina," Brookings Institution, August 27, 2015, https://www.brookings.edu /articles/concentrated-poverty-in-new-orleans-10-years-after-katrina/; Leonard N. Moore, *Black Rage in New Orleans: Police Brutality and African American Activism from World War II to Hurricane Katrina* (Baton Rouge: Louisiana State University Press, 2010); Kent B. Germany, *New Orleans after the Promises: Poverty, Citizenship, and the Search for the Great Society* (Athens: University of Georgia Press, 2007); Alan Berube and Bruce Katz, "Katrina's Window: Confronting Concentrated Poverty across America," Brookings Institution, October 1, 2005, https:// www.brookings.edu/research/katrinas-window-confronting-concentrated -poverty-across-america/; Campanella, *Bienville's Dilemma*, 59–64.

9   Joan Brunkard, Gonza Namulanda, and Raoult Ratard, "Hurricane Katrina Deaths, Louisiana, 2005," *Disaster Medicine and Public Health Preparedness* 2, no. 4 (2008): 215–23; Patrick Sharkey, "Survival and Death in New Orleans: An Empirical Look at the Human Impact of Katrina," *Journal of Black Studies* 37, no. 4 (March 2007):

482–501; Kevin U. Stephens Sr., David Grew, Karen Chin, Paul Kadetz, P. Gregg Greenough, Frederick M. Burkle Jr., Sandra L. Robinson, and Evangeline R. Franklin, "Excess Mortality in the Aftermath of Hurricane Katrina: A Preliminary Report," *Disaster Medicine* 1, no. 1 (2007): 15–20.

10   Antoine's restaurant also lost its cellar of sixteen thousand bottles of wine. See Brenda Maitland, "Heat Exhaustion: Wine Cellars Suffer Their Own Losses from Katrina," *Gambit*, May 23, 2006; Kim Severson, "In New Orleans, Cooks Are Stirring," *New York Times*, September 21, 2005.

11   Of these hundreds of thousands of "Katrina Refrigerators," anthropologist David Beriss wrote, "The mostly white exteriors proved to be an irresistible canvas for commentary about everything from FEMA and President Bush, to Saints owner Tom Benson (who had threatened to take the team from the city permanently), the mayor, and, of course, the general funkiness (not the good kind) of the fridges themselves" ("Katrina Fridges, 10 Years After," *Society for the Anthropology of Food and Nutrition*, August 28, 2015, https://foodanthro.com/2015/08/28/katrina-fridges-10 -years-after/).

12   Severson, "In New Orleans"; "One Million Meals and Counting in New Orleans," World Central Kitchen, August 22, 2020, https://wck.org/news/new-orleans; Lolis Eric Elie, *Tremé: Stories and Recipes from the Heart of New Orleans* (San Francisco, CA: Chronicle Books, 2013); Todd-Michael St. Pierre, *Taste of Tremé: Creole, Cajun, and Soul Food from New Orleans's Famous Neighborhood of Jazz* (Berkeley, CA: Ulysses Press, 2012); Lynnell L. Thomas, "'People Want to See What Happened': Treme, Televisual Tourism, and the Racial Remapping of Post-Katrina New Orleans," *Television and New Media* 13, no. 3 (2012): 213–24; Marcelle Bienvenu and Judy Walker, *Cooking Up a Storm: Recipes Lost and Found from the Times-Picayune of New Orleans* (San Francisco, CA: Chronicle Books, 2008); "Mission and History," Southern Food and Beverage Museum, accessed May 25, 2022, https://southernfood .org/mission-history.

13   "Mayor Landrieu Touts New Orleans 2015 Success in Tourism, Cultural Economy and Film," *Biz New Orleans*, December 30, 2015; "Culture & Tourism," *Katrina 10*, accessed March 22, 2016; Brett Anderson, "How Katrina Changed Eating in New Orleans," *New Yorker*, August 28, 2015; Kim Severson, "The New Orleans Restaurant Bounce, after Katrina," *New York Times*, August 4, 2015; "Mayor Landrieu Touts 2014 Success in Tourism, Special Events, Film," *Biz New Orleans*, December 30, 2014, https://www.bizneworleans.com/mayor-landrieu-touts-2014-success-in -tourism-special-events-film/; "Mayor Landrieu Touts New Orleans 2016 Successes and Unveils New Year Holiday Public Safety Plan," *Biz New Orleans*, December 27, 2016, https://www.bizneworleans.com/mayor-landrieu-touts-new-orleans-2016 -successes-unveils-new-year-holiday-public-safety-plan/.

14   Forty percent of adults who remained displaced one year after the storm lived in Texas, especially Houston and Dallas. See Narayan Sastry and Jesse Gregory, "The Location of Displaced New Orleans Residents in the Year After Hurricane Katrina," *Demography* 51, no. 3 (June 2014): 753–75; Kevin Fox Gotham and Richard Campanella, "Constructions of Resilience: Ethnoracial Diversity, Inequality, and Post-Katrina Recovery, the Case of New Orleans," *Social Sciences* 2, no. 4 (2013): 298–317; Alexis A. Merdjanoff, "There's No Place Like Home: Examining the Emotional Consequences of Hurricane Katrina on the Displaced Residents of New Orleans," *Social Science Research* 42, no. 5 (September 2013): 1222–35; Lynn Weber and Lori Peek, eds., *Displaced: Life in the Katrina Diaspora* (Austin: University of Texas

Press, 2012); Michelle Krupa, "Baton Rouge, Texas Trade Transplants with New Orleans Region, Census Data Show," *Times-Picayune*, April 12, 2012; Elizabeth Fussell,
Narayan Sastry, and Mark VanLandingham, "Race, Socioeconomic Status, and Return Migration to New Orleans after Hurricane Katrina," *Population and Environment* 31, no. 1 (2010): 20–42; and Wei Li, Christopher A. Airriess, Angela Chia-Chen
Chen, Karen J. Leong, and Verna Keith, "Katrina and Migration: Evacuation and Return by African Americans and Vietnamese Americans in an Eastern New Orleans
Suburb," *Professional Geographer* 62, no. 1 (2010): 103–18.

15   Nathan Babb, "'Baby Won't You Please Come Home': Studying Ethnoracial Segregation Trends in New Orleans Pre and Post Hurricane Katrina," *Journal of Public
and International Affairs*, Princeton University, May 5, 2021, https://jpia.princeton
.edu/news/baby-wont-you-please-come-home-studying-ethnoracial-segregation
-trends-new-orleans-pre-and-post; "An Unequal Recovery in New Orleans: Racial
Disparities Grow in City 10 Years After Katrina," *Democracy Now!*, transcript, August 28, 2015, https://www.democracynow.org/2015/8/28/an_unequal_recovery
_in_new_orleans. See also Sarah M. Broom, "The Yellow House," *New Yorker*,
August 24, 2015; and Gary Rivlin, *Katrina: After the Flood* (New York: Simon and
Schuster, 2015).

16   Andy Horowitz, *Katrina: A History, 1915–2015* (Cambridge, MA: Harvard University Press, 2020); Zhen Jiao, Socrates V. Kakoulides, John Moscona, Jabar Whittier,
Sudesh Srivastav, Patrice Delafontaine, and Anand Irimpen, "Effect of Hurricane
Katrina on Incidence of Acute Myocardial Infarction in New Orleans Three Years
after the Storm," *American Journal of Cardiology* 109, no. 4 (February 15, 2012): 502–
5; Jeremy I. Levitt and Matthew C. Whitaker, eds., *Hurricane Katrina: America's
Unnatural Disaster* (Lincoln: University of Nebraska Press, 2009); Robert D. Bullard and Beverly Wright, eds., *Race, Place, and Environmental Justice after Hurri-
cane Katrina: Struggles to Reclaim, Rebuild, and Revitalize New Orleans and the
Gulf Coast* (Boulder, CO: Westview Press, 2009); Michael Eric Dyson, *Come Hell or
High Water: Hurricane Katrina and the Color of Disaster* (New York: Basic Civitas,
2006); and Jed Horne, *Breach of Faith: Hurricane Katrina and the Near Death of a
Great American City* (New York: Random House, 2006).

17   Kim North Shine, "Revolver Restaurant in Hamtramck Thrives on Revolving Chef
Concept," *Detroit Metromode*, March 6, 2014, https://www.secondwavemedia.com
/metromode/devnews/0306revolver0336.aspx; Price, "What to Eat, Drink, and
Buy"; Brett Anderson, "8 Great Dishes to Try at the St. Roch Market," *NOLA.com /
Times-Picayune*, July 7, 2015; Price, "St. Roch Market Loses"; Maura Judkis, "Discomfort Food: Using Dinners to Talk about Race, Violence and America," *Washington Post*, August 23, 2016.

18   Brett Martin, "The Provocations of Chef Tunde Wey," *GQ*, March 6, 2019, https://
www.gq.com/story/chef-tunde-wey-profile; Tom Philpott, "This Hot Chef's
Pop-Up Dinners May Change How You Think about Race," *Mother Jones*, July
15, 2016, https://www.motherjones.com/environment/2016/07/tunde-wey-chef
-exploring-blackness-america/.

19   Tunde Wey, "Dining in the Era of Kaepernick," *Civil Eats*, October 26, 2016, https://
civileats.com/2016/10/26/bringing-race-to-the-table/.

20   Other projects included "Hot Chicken Shit," based in Nashville, Tennessee, described by Wey as "a project to sell hot chicken at extortionist prices to fund a community land trust in black neighborhoods," as well as "Love Will Trump: a dinner
series to spark romantic connections between US citizens and immigrants." See

"Food," *Fromlagos.com*, accessed May 26, 2022, http://www.fromlagos.com/food; Judkis, "Discomfort Food"; Deonna Anderson, "This Chef Is Fighting Gentrification with Hot Chicken," *Yes!*, September 1, 2018, https://www.yesmagazine.org /democracy/2018/09/01/this-chef-is-fighting-gentrification-with-hot-chicken; and Allie Wist, "Can a Blind Dinner Date Help Bring Down Border Walls?," *Saveur*, February 14, 2019, https://www.saveur.com/tunde-wey-dinner-series-marriage -trumps-all/.

21 The name "Saartj" referred to Sara Baartman, a Black woman born in 1789 in present-day South Africa. Dutch enslavers brought Baartman to Europe, where English and French entertainers displayed her for public crowds and enabled her sexual abuse. After Baartman's death, a French museum exhibited severed pieces of Baartman's body. See Sadiah Qureshi, "Displaying Sara Baartman, the 'Hottentot Venus,'" *History of Science* 42, no. 2 (2004): 233–57.

22 Black diners were also given the option of collecting the difference of $18 paid by a white diner who had come before them. It is unclear how Saartj functioned for diners who did not identify as white or Black. See Korsha Wilson, "The New Orleans Pop-Up Confronting White Diners with Their Privilege," *Eater*, March 1, 2018, https://www.eater.com/2018/3/1/17067350/tunde-wey-saartj-new-orleans; Saartj menu, March 7, 2018, *Wayback Marchine* internet archive, https://web.archive.org /web/20180307211504/https://www.saartj.com/menu/; Ann Maloney, "Could a Single Lunch Change Your Views on Race and Wealth?," *NOLA.com / Times-Picayune*, February 28, 2018.

23 Chelsea Ritschel, "Chef in New Orleans Charges Black Customers $12 and White Customers up to $30 in Social Experiment," *Independent*, March 2, 2018; Jessica Brodie, "Discomfort Food: Where You Pay More if You're White," *Sunday Times*, May 16, 2018; Maria Godoy, "Food Stall Serves Up a Social Experiment: White Customers Asked to Pay More," *Salt*, March 2, 2018, https://www.npr.org/sections /thesalt/2018/03/02/590053856/food-stall-serves-up-a-social-experiment -charge-white-customers-more-than-minori; Tunde Wey (@from_lagos), "You Can End Wealth Inequality in 15 Mins," Instagram, February 16, 2018, https://www .instagram.com/p/BfQqzXol3_a/?hl=en&taken-by=from_lagos.

24 On rice and other plants with African roots, see Judith A. Carney and Richard Nicholas Rosomoff, *In the Shadow of Slavery: Africa's Botanical Legacy in the Atlantic World* (Berkeley: University of California Press, 2011); Judith A. Carney, *Black Rice: The African Origins of Rice Cultivation in the Americas* (Cambridge, MA: Harvard University Press, 2001); Karen Hess, *The Carolina Rice Kitchen* (Columbia: University of South Carolina Press, 1992); and Kim Severson, "Finding a Lost Strain of Rice, and Clues to Slave Cooking," *New York Times*, February 13, 2018.

25 As cited in Martin, "Provocations." In February 2023, a *New York Times* profile of a new generation of Black chefs in New Orleans excited some readers and angered others, showing that the "discomfort" Wey observed was alive and well. "Who on earth would want foods that have been enjoyed by millions to be served with a side of racial guilt? No thanks," commented one reader. "Waiter, there's 500 years of oppression and racial horror in my soup," another wrote sarcastically. See Brett Anderson, "In Majority-Black New Orleans, Chefs Are Rewriting 'Whitewashed' History," *New York Times*, February 14, 2023.

SELECTED BIBLIOGRAPHY

This selected bibliography does not include unpublished sources, online sources, government documents including census returns, or city directories. Those sources are documented in the notes.

Manuscript Collections

Amistad Research Center, New Orleans, Louisiana
  Connie Harse papers, MSS 573

Conrad N. Hilton Library, Archives and Special Collections, Culinary Institute of America, Hyde Park, New York (CIA)
  Culinary Institute of America menu collection (CIA Menu)
    Bruce P. Jeffer menu collection
    Job Prak menu collection
    Patty O'Neill menu collection
    Vinnie Oakes menu collection

The Historic New Orleans Collection, New Orleans, Louisiana (THNOC)
  Edward Russell, travel journal and transcript, 1834–1835, MSS 424.2
  George Purves, "Basement Story Sketch for the Saint Charles Hotel," 1851–1852, MSS 1959.26.5
  George Purves, "Sketch of Principle [sic] Story for St. Charles Hotel," 1851–1852, MSS 1959.26.5
  Judah P. Benjamin to Samuel L. M. Barlow, April 28, 1855, MSS 33.1

Mary Longfellow Greenleaf diary, 1852, MSS 363
New Orleans Hotel collection, MSS 411.2
NOLA Resistance Oral History Project, MSS 936 (NROHP)
Photographic prints from the Harold F. Baquet Archive, 1975–2000
Thomas Murdoch letters, 1830–1842, MSS 439
Vieux Carré Digital Survey (VCDS)

Louisiana and Special Collections, University of New Orleans, New Orleans,
Louisiana
Marcus Christian collection, MSS 11

Louisiana Division/City Archives, New Orleans Public Library, New Orleans,
Louisiana (LDCA NOPL)
"Alphabetical and Numerical Index of Changes in Street Names and Numbers,
Old and New, 1852 to Current Date, 1938" (Street Names Index)
French Market Corporation records, 1936–1979 (FMC records)
George François Mugnier photograph collection
Menu collection and restaurant memorabilia (Menus)
New Orleans Police Department, Office of Inspector of Police, correspondence,
1899–1913
"New Orleans Ward Boundaries, 1805–1880"
Office of the Mayor, records
Oaths and bonds for city licenses on taverns, coffee houses, hotels, board-
ing houses, and other establishments, 1828–1863
Oaths and bonds for city licenses on vehicles, 1834–1866
Register of free colored persons entitled to remain in the state, vol. 1,
1840–1856; vol. 2, 1856–1859; vol. 3, 1859–1861 (Register, vols. 1, 2,
and 3)
Office of the Treasurer, records
Census of merchants, v. 1 First District, 1854 (Census of merchants)
Orleans Parish Court, records
Emancipation petitions, 1813–1843 (Emancipation petitions)
Vertical files
Wilson S. Howell photograph collection

Louisiana Research Collection, Tulane University Special Collections, New Or-
leans, Louisiana (TUSC)
Hermann Bacher Deutsch papers, 1827–1970, MS 130 (HBD)
Market Committee records, 1913–1916, MS 985 (MS 985)
Louisiana menu and restaurant collection
Vertical files

Louisiana State Museum, New Orleans, Louisiana (LSM)
    Cemetery records, 1805–1944
    L. H. Webb diaries, 1853, record group 49 (Webb)
    Rowles stereograph collection

Loyola Documentary and Oral History Studio, Loyola University New Orleans,
    New Orleans, Louisiana (LDOHS)
    "A Haven for All of Us': Documenting the World of Dooky Chase Restaurant
    in the Era before Desegregation." Oral history project, 2013 (Haven)

National Archives and Records Administration, Washington, DC
    Card Index to Naturalizations in Louisiana (P2087), microfilm serial P2087,
    roll 6
    Union Provost Marshals' File of Papers Relating to Individual Civilians, 1861–
    1867, microfilm publication M345, 300 rolls, NAID: 2133278, War Depart-
    ment Collection of Confederate Records, record group 109 (Union Provost)

New Orleans Notarial Archives, New Orleans, Louisiana (NONA)
    A. Ducatel, 21: 231, 473–77, November 9, 1843
    C. Pollock, 49: 429–31, June 24, 1835
    C. Pollock, 58: 396–98, November 8, 1838
    C. Pollock, 61: 515, 1839
    F. Grima, 7: 504, September 28, 1835
    J. Cuvillier, 29: 31, May 10, 1841
    M. Lafitte, 20: 14–15, March 1, 1821

New York Public Library, New York, New York (NYPL)
    Buttolph collection of menus, Rare Book Division
    Manuscripts, Archives and Rare Books Division, Schomburg Center for Re-
    search in Black Culture (Schomburg Manuscripts)
    Music Division, NYPL Digital Collections
    Photographs and Prints Division, Schomburg Center for Research in Black Cul-
    ture
    Robert N. Dennis collection of stereoscopic views

Newcomb Archives and Vorhoff Collection at Tulane University, New Orleans,
    Louisiana (Newcomb and Vorhoff)
    Catherine Cole papers, collection NA-118
    Lena Richard papers, collection NAA-071 (LR papers)

Southern Foodways Alliance, Center for the Study of Southern Culture, Univer-
    sity of Mississippi, Oxford, Mississippi (SFA)
    "New Orleans Eats," oral history project, 2006 (New Orleans Eats)

Special Collections and Archives, J. Edgar and Louise S. Monroe Library, Loyola University New Orleans, New Orleans, Louisiana (Loyola)
  Anthony Stanonis travel scrapbook and diary collection, collection no. 65 (Stanonis)

University Library, Xavier University of Louisiana, New Orleans, Louisiana Media Collection
  St. Mark's Community Center, Treme/7th Ward Griots: A Video Documentary: An Oral History of New Orleans' Oldest and Most Diverse Black Community, *1977*

Xavier University of Louisiana Archives and Special Collections, New Orleans, Louisiana
  Arthur P. Bedou photographs collection

Periodicals

Abbeville (LA) *Meridional*
Abeille (New Orleans)
Atlanta Daily World
Associated Press
Baltimore Niles' National Register
Boston Daily Atlas
Boston Daily Globe
Boston Emancipator and Free American
Boston Liberator
Boston Weekly Messenger
Le Carillon (New Orleans)
Chicago Daily Tribune
Chicago Defender
Chicago Press and Tribune
Chicago Tribune
Cleveland Call and Post
Cleveland Plain Dealer
Emerson's Magazine and Putnam's Monthly
Frank Leslie's Illustrated Newspaper
Harper's New Monthly Magazine
Harper's Weekly
The Illustrated American
The Independent (UK, online)
Lafayette (LA) *Advocate*

Leslie's Weekly
Los Angeles Times
Louisiana Gazette
Milwaukee Daily Sentinel
Milwaukee Sentinel
Le Moniteur (New Orleans)
Mount Vernon (IN) *Republican*
Nashville Tennessean
Natchez (MS) *Daily Courier*
Washington National Intelligencer and Washington Advertiser
New Orleans Daily Crescent
New Orleans Daily Picayune
New Orleans Delta
New Orleans Gambit
New Orleans Item
New Orleans Picayune
New Orleans States
New Orleans Times
New Orleans Times-Democrat
New Orleans Times-Picayune
New Orleans Times-Picayune New Orleans States
New Orleans Tribune
New Orleans Weekly Delta
New Orleans Weekly Pelican
New York Daily Tribune
New York Herald Tribune
New York Times
New Yorker
NOLA.com / Times-Picayune
North and South
Pittsburgh Courier
Platteville (WI) *American*
Portland (ME) *Evening Advertiser*
Portland (OR) *Oregonian*
Saturday Evening Post
Scribner's Monthly
St. Louis Globe-Democrat
Sunday Magazine
The Sunday Times (UK)
Trenton Evening Times

L'Union (New Orleans)
Washington Constitution
Washington Post
Washington Star

Court Decisions

Duncan v. Hawks et al., 18 La. 548, Louisiana Supreme Court (1841)

Gardère v. State, no. 10,957, First District Court of New Orleans (1856)

Lombard v. Louisiana, 373 U.S. 267 (1963)

Patsey Shall v. Thomas Banks, Louisiana Supreme Court (1844)

Patsey Shall wife of George Shall v. Thomas Banks, no. 18,216, First Judicial District Court of Louisiana (1839)

Nott & Co. v. Oakey et al., 19 La. 18, Louisiana Supreme Court (1841)

Nott & Co. v. Bank of Orleans, 19 La. 22, Louisiana Supreme Court (1841)

Round Table Club v. Bond, 163 La. 175, 111 So. 667 (1927)

Slatter v. Holton, no. 3894, 19 La. 39, Louisiana Supreme Court (1841)

Primary and Secondary Sources

Adams, Thomas Jessen, and Matt Sakakeeny, eds. *Remaking New Orleans: Beyond Exceptionalism and Authenticity*. Durham, NC: Duke University Press, 2019.

Airriess, Christopher A., and David L. Clawson. "Versailles: A Vietnamese Enclave in New Orleans, Louisiana." *Journal of Cultural Geography* 12, no. 1 (1991): 1–13.

Albert, Octavia V. Rogers. *The House of Bondage: Or Charlotte Brooks and Other Slaves Original and Life-Like, as They Appeared in Their Old Plantation and City Slave Life; Together with Pen-Pictures of the Peculiar Institution, with Sights and Insights into Their New Relations as Freedmen, Freemen, and Citizens*. New York: Hunt and Eaton, 1890.

Alciatore, Roy L. *Centennial Souvenir du Restaurant Antoine*. New Orleans, LA: Antoine's, 1940.

Allen, Carol. *Leah Chase: Listen, I Say Like This*. Gretna, LA: Pelican Publishing Company, 2002.

Andrews, Gregg. *Shantyboats and Roustabouts: The River Poor of St. Louis, 1875–1930*. Baton Rouge: Louisiana State University Press, 2022.

Anthony, Arthé A. "Florestine Perrault Collins and the Gendered Politics of Black Portraiture in 1920s New Orleans." *Louisiana History* 43, no. 2 (Spring 2002): 167–88.

———. *Picturing Black New Orleans: A Creole Photographer's View of the Early Twentieth Century*. Gainesville: University Press of Florida, 2012.

Apel, Dora, and Shawn Michelle Smith. *Lynching Photographs*. Berkeley: University of California Press, 2007.

Appadurai, Arjun. "On Culinary Authenticity." Letters. *Anthropology Today* 2, no. 4 (August 1986): 25.

Arnesen, Eric. *Waterfront Workers of New Orleans: Race, Class, and Politics, 1863–1923*. New York: Oxford University Press, 1991.

Aslakson, Kenneth R. *Making Race in the Courtroom: The Legal Construction of Three Races in Early New Orleans*. New York: New York University Press, 2014.

Augustin, George. *History of Yellow Fever*. New Orleans: Searcy and Pfaff, 1909.

Bachand, Marise. "Gendered Mobility and the Geography of Respectability in Charleston and New Orleans, 1790–1861." *Journal of Southern History* 81, no.1 (February 2015): 41–78.

Baics, Gergely. *Feeding Gotham: The Political Economy and Geography of Food in New York, 1790–1860*. Princeton, NJ: Princeton University Press, 2016.

Bald, Vivek. *Bengali Harlem and the Lost Histories of South Asian America*. Cambridge, MA: Harvard University Press, 2013.

Baldwin, Brooke. "On the Verso: Postcard Messages as a Key to Popular Prejudices." *Journal of Popular Culture* 22, no. 3 (Winter 1988): 15–28.

Ballinger, Roy A. *A History of Sugar Marketing through 1974*. Agricultural Economic Report no. 382. Washington, DC: US Department of Agriculture, March 1978. https://www.ers.usda.gov/webdocs/publications/40532/aer-382.pdf?v=0.

Bancroft, Frederic. *Slave-Trading in the Old South*. Baltimore, MD: J. H. Furst, 1931.

Baptist, Edward E. "'Cuffy,' 'Fancy Maids,' and 'One-Eyed Men': Rape, Commodification, and the Domestic Slave Trade in the United States." In *The Chattel Principle: Internal Slave Trades in the Americas*, edited by Walter Johnson, 165–202. New Haven, CT: Yale University Press, 2004.

———. *The Half Has Never Been Told: Slavery and the Making of American Capitalism*. New York: Basic Books, 2014.

Bardes, John K. "Redefining Vagrancy: Policing Freedom and Disorder in Reconstruction New Orleans, 1862–1868." *Journal of Southern History* 84, no. 1 (February 2018): 69–112.

Barnet, W. Y. "New Orleans Entertains." *Banking and Mercantile World* 4, no. 6 (November–December 1902): 227–49.

Beale, Joseph H. *Picturesque Sketches of Great American Cities*. New York: Empire Co-Operative Association, 1889.

Beckert, Sven. *Empire of Cotton: A Global History*. New York: Alfred A. Knopf, 2014.

Bederman, Gail. *Manliness and Civilization: A Cultural History of Gender and Race in the United States, 1880–1917*. Chicago: University of Chicago Press, 1995.

Berlin, Ira, Barbara J. Fields, Thavolia Glymph, Joseph P. Reidy, and Leslie S. Rowland. *Freedom: A Documentary History of Emancipation, 1861–1867: The Destruction of Slavery*. Series 1, vol. 1. New York: Cambridge University Press, 1985.

Bernhard, Duke of Saxe-Weimar Eisenach. *Travels through North America, during the Years 1825 and 1826*. Vol. 2. Philadelphia, PA: Carey, Lea and Carey, 1828.

Berry, Daina Ramey. *The Price for Their Pound in Flesh: The Value of the Enslaved, from Womb to Grave, in the Building of a Nation*. Boston, MA: Beacon Press, 2017.

Bhabha, Homi K. *The Location of Culture*. New York: Routledge, 1994.

Bienvenu, Marcelle, and Judy Walker. *Cooking Up a Storm: Recipes Lost and Found from the Times-Picayune of New Orleans*. San Francisco, CA: Chronicle Books, 2008.

Blackmon, Douglas A. *Slavery by Another Name: The Re-Enslavement of Black Americans from the Civil War to World War II*. New York: Anchor Books, 2008.

Blassingame, John W. *Black New Orleans, 1860–1880*. Chicago: University of Chicago Press, 1973.

———. "Reading the Testimony of Slaves: Approaches and Problems." *Journal of Southern History* 41, no. 4 (November 1975): 473–92.

———., ed. *Slave Testimony: Two Centuries of Letters, Speeches, Interviews, and Autobiographies*. Baton Rouge: Louisiana State University Press, 1977.

Bolton, S. Charles. *Fugitivism: Escaping Slavery in the Lower Mississippi Valley*. Fayetteville: University of Arkansas Press, 2019.

Bone, Martyn, Brian Ward, and William A. Link, eds. *Creating and Consuming the American South*. Gainesville: University Press of Florida, 2015.

Bower, Anne L., ed. *Recipes for Reading: Community Cookbooks, Stories, Histories*. Amherst: University of Massachusetts Press, 1997.

Brand, Anna Livia. "Black Mecca Futures: Re-Membering New Orleans's Claiborne Avenue." *Journal of Urban Affairs* 44, no. 6 (2022): 808–21.

Brasseaux, Carl A. *French, Cajun, Creole, Houma: A Primer on Francophone Louisiana*. Baton Rouge: Louisiana State University Press, 2005.

Brasseaux, Carl A., and Glenn R. Conrad, eds. *The Road to Louisiana: The Saint-*

Domingue Refugees, 1792–1809. Lafayette: Center for Louisiana Studies, University of Louisiana at Lafayette, 1992.

Breunlin, Rachel. "Decolonizing Ways of Knowing: Heritage, Living Communities, and Indigenous Understandings of Place." *Genealogy* 4, no. 3 (2020): 95.

Brewster, Sir David. *The Stereoscope: Its History, Theory, and Construction, with Its Application to the Fine and Useful Arts and to Education*. 1856. Reprint. London: John Murray, 1856; Hastings-on-Hudson: Morgan and Morgan, 1971.

Brown, John. *Slave Life in Georgia: A Narrative of the Life, Sufferings, and Escape of John Brown, a Fugitive Slave, Now in England*. Edited by Louis Alexis Chamerovzow. London: W. M. Watts, 1855.

Browne, Martha Griffith. *Autobiography of a Female Slave*. New York: Redfield, 1857.

Brunkard, Joan, Gonza Namulanda, and Raoult Ratard. "Hurricane Katrina Deaths, Louisiana, 2005." *Disaster Medicine and Public Health Preparedness* 2, no. 4 (2008): 215–23.

Buchanan, Thomas C. *Black Life on the Mississippi: Slaves, Free Blacks, and the Western Steamboat World*. Chapel Hill: University of North Carolina Press, 2004.

———. "Levees of Hope: African American Steamboat Workers, Cities, and Slave Escapes on the Antebellum Mississippi." *Journal of Urban History* 30, no. 3 (March 2004): 360–77.

———. "Rascals on the Antebellum Mississippi: African American Steamboat Workers and the St. Louis Hanging of 1841." *Journal of Social History* 34, no. 4 (Summer 2001): 797–816.

Buckingham, J. S. *The Slave States of America*. Vol. 1. London: Fisher, Son and Co., 1842.

Bullard, Robert D., and Beverly Wright, eds. *Race, Place, and Environmental Justice after Hurricane Katrina: Struggles to Reclaim, Rebuild, and Revitalize New Orleans and the Gulf Coast*. Boulder, CO: Westview Press, 2009.

Burton, Nathaniel, and Rudy Lombard. *Creole Feast: 15 Master Chefs of New Orleans Reveal Their Secrets*. New York: Random House, 1978.

Bushnell, David I., Jr. "The Choctaw of Bayou Lacomb, St. Tammany Parish, Louisiana." *Bulletin* 48, Smithsonian Institution Bureau of American Ethnology, 1–37. Washington, DC: Government Printing Office, 1909.

———. "Myths of the Louisiana Choctaw." *American Anthropologist* 12, no. 4 (October–December 1910): 526–35.

Cahill, Cathleen D. *Recasting the Vote: How Women of Color Transformed the Suffrage Movement*. Chapel Hill: University of North Carolina Press, 2020.

Campanella, Richard. *Bienville's Dilemma: A Historical Geography of New Orleans*. Lafayette: Center for Louisiana Studies, University of Louisiana at Lafayette, 2008.

———. "On the Structural Basis of Social Memory: Cityscapes of the New Orleans Slave Trade, Part I." *Preservation in Print* (March 2013): 16–17.

———. "On the Structural Basis of Social Memory: Cityscapes of the New Orleans Slave Trade, Part II." *Preservation in Print* (April 2013): 18–19.

———. "The Seduction of Exceptionalism." *Louisiana Cultural Vistas* (Summer 2014): 24–25.

———. "The St. Louis and the St. Charles: New Orleans' Legacy of Showcase Exchange Hotels." *Preservation in Print* (April 2015): 16–17.

Campbell, Israel. *An Autobiography. Bond and Free: or, Yearnings for Freedom, from My Green Brier House. Being the Story of My Life in Bondage, and My Life in Freedom*. Philadelphia, PA: Israel Campbell, 1861.

Carico, Aaron. *Black Market: The Slave's Value in National Culture After 1865*. Chapel Hill: University of North Carolina Press, 2020.

Carney, Judith A. *Black Rice: The African Origins of Rice Cultivation in the Americas*. Cambridge, MA: Harvard University Press, 2001.

Carney, Judith A., and Richard Nicholas Rosomoff. *In the Shadow of Slavery: Africa's Botanical Legacy in the Atlantic World*. Berkeley: University of California Press, 2011.

Carrigan, Jo Ann. *The Saffron Scourge: A History of Yellow Fever in Louisiana, 1796–1905*. Lafayette: University of Louisiana at Lafayette Press, 1994.

Castellanos, Henry C. *New Orleans as It Was: Episodes of Louisiana Life*. 1895. Reprint. Edited by George F. Reinecke. Baton Rouge: Louisiana State University Press, 1978.

Černe, Sara. "'It Carries My Feet to These Places': The Mississippi in Joy Harjo's and Heid E. Erdrich's Poetic Remappings." *Native American and Indigenous Studies* 10, no. 1 (Spring 2023): 1–27.

Chambers, A. B., ed. *Trials and Confessions of Madison Henderson, alias Blanchard, Alfred Amos Warrick, James W. Seward, and Charles Brown, Murderers of Jesse Baker and Jacob Weaver, as Given by Themselves; and a Likeness of Each, Taken in Jail Shortly after Their Arrest*. St. Louis, MO: Chambers and Knapp, 1841.

Chambon, M. *Le Commerce de l'Amérique par Marseille, ou Explication des lettres patentes, portant reglement pour le commerce qui se fait de Marseille aux isles Françoise de l'Amérique, données au mois de février 1719. Et des lettres patentes du roi pour la liberté du commerce à la Côte de Guinée, données à Paris au mois de janvier 1716. Avec les reglemens que ledit commerce a occasionnés, par un citadin* . . . 2 vols. Avignon, France: 1764. Reprint. 1782.

Chan, Kit. "Jimson Weed Poisoning—A Case Report." *Permanente Journal* 6, no. 4 (Fall 2002): 28–30.

Chansky, Ricia Anne. "Time to Shop: Advertising Trade Card Rhetoric and the Construction of a Public Space for Women in the United States, 1880–1900." *Atenea* 29, no. 1 (June 2009): 151–66.

Chase, Leah. *And Still I Cook*. Gretna, LA: Pelican Publishing Company, 2003.

———. *The Dooky Chase Cookbook*. Gretna, LA: Pelican Publishing Company, 1990.

Christian, Marcus. *Negro Ironworkers in Louisiana, 1718–1900*. Gretna, LA: Pelican Publishing Company, 1972.

Christian Woman's Exchange. *The Creole Cookery Book*. New Orleans, LA: T. H. Thomason, 1885.

Clark, Emily. *The Strange History of the American Quadroon: Free Women of Color in the Revolutionary Atlantic World*. Chapel Hill: University of North Carolina Press, 2013.

Clark, Emily, Ibrahima Thioub, and Cécile Vidal, eds. *New Orleans, Louisiana and Saint-Louis, Senegal: Mirror Cities in the Atlantic World, 1659–2005*. Baton Rouge: Louisiana State University Press, 2019.

Clarke, Lewis Garrard, and Milton Clarke. *Narratives of the Sufferings of Lewis and Milton Clarke, Sons of a Soldier of the Revolution, during a Captivity of More Than Twenty Years among the Slaveholders of Kentucky, One of the So Called Christian States of North America, Dictated by Themselves*. Boston, MA: Bela Marsh, 1846.

Clay, Lauren R. "'Cruel Necessity': Capitalism, the Discourse of Sympathy, and the Problem of the Slave Trade in the Age of Human Rights." *Slavery and Abolition* 37, no. 2 (2016): 256–83.

Clayton, Ronnie W., ed. *Mother Wit: The Ex-Slave Narratives of the Louisiana Writers' Project*. New York: Peter Lang, 1990.

Cobb, Jasmine Nichole. *Picture Freedom: Remaking Black Visuality in the Early Nineteenth Century*. New York: New York University Press, 2015.

Cohen, Lizabeth. *A Consumer's Republic: The Politics of Consumption in Postwar America*. New York: Knopf, 2003.

———. *Making a New Deal: Industrial Workers in Chicago, 1919–1939*. Cambridge: Cambridge University Press, 1990.

Cole, Catharine [also Catherine] [Martha Reinhard Smallwood Field]. *The Story of the Old French Market, New Orleans*. New Orleans, LA: New Orleans Coffee Company, 1916.

Cole, Stephanie. "Servants and Slaves in Louisville: Race, Ethnicity, and Household Labor in an Antebellum Border City." *Ohio Valley History* 11, no. 1 (Spring 2011): 3–25.

Coleman, William H. *Historical Sketch Book and Guide to New Orleans and Environs, with Map. Illustrated with Many Original Engravings; and Containing Exhaustive Accounts of the Traditions, Historical Legends, and Remarkable Localities of the Creole City.* New York: Will H. Coleman, 1885.

Cook, Eli. *The Pricing of Progress: Economic Indicators and the Capitalization of American Life.* Cambridge, MA: Harvard University Press, 2017.

Cooley, Angela Jill. *To Live and Dine in Dixie: The Evolution of Urban Food Culture in the Jim Crow South.* Athens: University of Georgia, 2015.

Covey, Herbert C., and Dwight Eisnach, eds. *What the Slaves Ate: Recollections of African American Foods and Foodways from the Slave Narratives.* Westport, CT: Greenwood, 2009.

Cowan, Brian William. "New Worlds, New Tastes: Food Fashions after the Renaissance." In *Food: The History of Taste,* edited by Paul Freedman, 196–231. Berkeley: University of California Press, 2007.

———. *The Social Life of Coffee: The Emergence of the British Coffeehouse.* New Haven, CT: Yale University Press, 2005.

Cox, Karen L. *Dreaming of Dixie: How the South Was Created in American Popular Culture.* Chapel Hill: University of North Carolina Press, 2011.

Coxe, Tench. *A Statement of the Arts and Manufactures of the United States of America, for the Year 1810.* Philadelphia, PA: A. Cornman, 1814.

Crété, Liliane. *Daily Life in Louisiana, 1815–1830.* Translated by Patrick Gregory. Baton Rouge: Louisiana State University Press, 1981.

Cugoano, Ottobah. "Narrative of the Enslavement of Ottobah Cugoano, a Native of Africa; Published by Himself, in the Year 1787." In Thomas Fisher, *The Negro's Memorial, or, Abolitionist's Catechism by an Abolitionist,* 120–27. London: Hatchard and Co., 1825.

Cunyghame, Lieutenant Colonel Arthur. *A Glimpse at the Great Western Republic.* London: Richard Bentley, 1851.

Daggett, Melissa. *Spiritualism in Nineteenth-Century New Orleans: The Life and Times of Henry Louis Rey.* Jackson: University Press of Mississippi, 2017.

Darensbourg, Jeffery U., ed. *Bulbancha Is Still a Place: Indigenous Culture from New Orleans: The Language Issue.* Bulbancha, LA: POC Zine Project, 2019.

———., ed. *Bulbancha Is Still a Place: Indigenous Culture from New Orleans: The Tricentennial Issue.* Bulbancha, LA: POC Zine Project, 2018.

Darrah, William C. *Stereo Views: A History of Stereographs in America and Their Collection.* Gettysburg, PA: Times and News Publishing Co., 1964.

———. *The World of Stereographs.* Gettysburg, PA: Darrah, 1977.

Davidson, Alan. *The Oxford Companion to Food.* Oxford: Oxford University Press, 1999.

Davies, Ebenezer. *American Scenes, and Christian Slavery: A Recent Tour of Four Thousand Miles in the United States*. London: John Snow, 1849.

Davis, David Brion. *The Problem of Slavery in the Age of Emancipation*. New York: Alfred A. Knopf, 2014.

Davis, Donna, ed. *Quartee Red Beans, Quartee Rice: Stories of the Treme/7th Ward*. Ethnic Heritage Project. New Orleans, LA: St. Mark's Community Center, January 1979.

Dawdy, Shannon Lee. *Building the Devil's Empire: French Colonial New Orleans*. Chicago: University of Chicago Press, 2008.

Deetz, Kelley Fanto. *Bound to the Fire: How Virginia's Enslaved Cooks Helped Invent American Cuisine*. Lexington: University Press of Kentucky, 2017.

Deloria, Philip J. *Playing Indian*. New Haven, CT: Yale University Press, 1998.

Deslix, P. J. A., ed. "Auction Sales." In *Digest of the Reported Decisions of the Supreme Court of the State of Louisiana from December 1838 to February 1843*. New Orleans: J. L. Sollée, 1845.

Dessens, Nathalie. *From Saint-Domingue to New Orleans: Migration and Influences*. Gainesville: University Press of Florida, 2007.

Dessens, Nathalie. "The Sounds of Babel: Staging American Ethnic Diversity in Early Nineteenth-Century New Orleans." *Complutense Journal of English Studies* 23 (2015): 15–27.

Deutsch, Tracy. *Building a Housewife's Paradise: Gender, Politics, and American Grocery Stores in the Twentieth Century*. Chapel Hill: University of North Carolina Press, 2010.

DeVore, Donald E. *Defying Jim Crow: African American Community Development and the Struggle for Racial Equality in New Orleans, 1900–1960*. Baton Rouge: Louisiana State University Press, 2015.

Deyle, Steven. *Carry Me Back: The Domestic Slave Trade in American Life*. Oxford: Oxford University Press, 2005.

Diner, Hasia. *Hungering for America: Italian, Irish, and Jewish Foodways in the Age of Migration*. Cambridge, MA: Harvard University Press, 2001.

Domínguez, Virginia R. *White by Definition: Social Classification in Creole Louisiana*. New Brunswick, NJ: Rutgers University Press, 1986.

Douglass, Frederick. "The Color Line." *North American Review* 132, no. 295 (June 1881): 567–77.

———. "Lecture on Pictures." Delivered December 3, 1861, in Boston, MA. Reprinted in John Stauffer, Zoe Trodd, and Celeste-Marie Bernier, *Picturing Frederick Douglass: An Illustrated Biography of the Nineteenth Century's Most Photographed American*, 126–41. New York: Liveright, 2015.

———. "Love of God, Love of Man, Love of Country: An Address Delivered in

Syracuse, New York, on September 24, 1847." *National Anti-Slavery Standard*, October 28, 1847. Archived online at the Frederick Douglass Papers Project. https://frederickdouglasspapersproject.com/item/10276.

——. *Oration, Delivered in Corinthian Hall, Rochester, by Frederick Douglass, July 5th, 1852*. Rochester, NY: Lee, Mann, and Co., 1852.

Du Bois, W. E. B. *Black Reconstruction: An Essay toward a History of the Part Which Black Folk Played in the Attempt to Reconstruct Democracy in America, 1860–1880*. New York: Harcourt, Brace and Co., 1935.

——. *The Souls of Black Folk*. In *The Norton Anthology of African American Literature*, 2nd ed., edited by Henry Louis Gates Jr. and Nellie Y. McKay, 692–766. New York: W. W. Norton, 2004.

Dudley, Tara A. *Building Antebellum New Orleans: Free People of Color and Their Influence*. Austin: University of Texas Press, 2021.

Dunbar-Nelson, Alice Moore. "People of Color in Louisiana: Part I." *Journal of Negro History* (October 1916): 361–76.

Dyson, Michael Eric. *Come Hell or High Water: Hurricane Katrina and the Color of Disaster*. New York: Basic Civitas, 2006.

Earle, Edward W., ed. *Points of View: The Stereograph in America—A Cultural History*. Rochester, NY: Visual Studies Workshop Press, 1979.

——. "The Stereograph in America: Pictorial Antecedents and Cultural Perspectives." In *Points of View: The Stereograph in America—A Cultural History*, edited by Edward W. Earle, 9–23. Rochester, New York: Visual Studies Workshop Press, 1979.

Eco, Umberto. *Travels in Hyperreality: Essays*. San Diego, CA: Harcourt Brace Jovanovich, 1986.

Edge, John T., Elizabeth S. D. Engelhardt, and Ted Ownby, eds. *The Larder: Food Studies Methods from the American South*. Athens: University of Georgia Press, 2013.

Edwards, J. Passmore. *Uncle Tom's Companions: Or, Facts Stranger Than Fiction. A Supplement to Uncle Tom's Cabin: Being Startling Incidents in the Lives of Celebrated Fugitive Slaves*. London: Edwards and Co., 1852.

Egerton, John. *Southern Food: At Home, on the Road, in History*. Chapel Hill: UNC Press, 1993.

Elie, Lolis Eric. *Tremé: Stories and Recipes from the Heart of New Orleans*. San Francisco, CA: Chronicle Books, 2013.

Ellis, Elizabeth N. *The Great Power of Small Nations: Indigenous Diplomacy in the Gulf South*. Philadelphia: University of Pennsylvania Press, 2022.

——. "The Natchez War Revisited: Violence, Multinational Settlements, and Indigenous Diplomacy in the Lower Mississippi Valley." *William and Mary Quarterly* 77, no. 3 (July 2020): 441–72.

Ellis, Markman. *The Coffee House: A Cultural History*. London: Weidenfeld and Nicolson, 2004.

Eltis, David, and David Richardson. *Atlas of the Transatlantic Slave Trade*. New Haven, CT: Yale University Press, 2010.

Engelhardt, Elizabeth S. D. "Beyond Grits and Gravy: Appalachian Chicken and Waffles: Countering Southern Food Fetishism." *Southern Cultures* 21, no. 1 (Spring 2015): 73–83.

———. *A Mess of Greens: Southern Gender and Southern Food*. Athens: University of Georgia Press, 2011.

Ethridge, Robbie. *From Chicaza to Chickasaw: The European Invasion and the Transformation of the Mississippian World, 1540–1715*. Chapel Hill: University of North Carolina Press, 2010.

Fairclough, Adam. *Race and Democracy: The Civil Rights Struggle in Louisiana, 1915–1972*. Athens: University of Georgia Press, 1995.

Farmer-Kaiser, Mary. "'Are They Not in Some Sorts Vagrants?': Gender and the Efforts of the Freedmen's Bureau to Combat Vagrancy in the Reconstruction South." *Georgia Historical Quarterly* 88, no. 1 (Spring 2004): 25–49.

Featherstonhaugh, G. W. *Excursion through the Slave States, from Washington on the Potomac to the Frontier of Mexico; with Sketches of Popular Manners and Geological Notices*. Vol. 1. New York: Harper and Brothers, 1844.

Federal Writers' Project of the Works Progress Administration for the City of New Orleans. *New Orleans City Guide*. Boston, MA: Houghton Mifflin, 1938.

Fenner, Erasmus Darwin. *History of the Epidemic Yellow Fever at New Orleans, La., in 1853*. New York: Hall, Clayton, 1854.

Fentress, James. *Rebels and Mafiosi: Death in a Sicilian Landscape*. Ithaca, NY: Cornell University Press, 2000.

Ferris, Marcie Cohen. *The Edible South: The Power of Food and the Making of an American Region*. Chapel Hill: University of North Carolina Press, 2014.

———. *Matzoh Ball Gumbo: Culinary Tales of the Jewish South*. Chapel Hill: University of North Carolina Press, 2005.

Fertel, Rien T. "'Everybody Seemed Willing to Help': *The Picayune Creole Cook Book* as Battleground, 1900–2008." In *The Larder: Food Studies Methods from the American South*, edited by John T. Edge, Elizabeth S. D. Engelhardt, and Ted Ownby, 10–31. Athens: University of Georgia Press, 2013.

———. *Imagining the Creole City: The Rise of Literary Culture in Nineteenth-Century New Orleans*. Baton Rouge: Louisiana State University Press, 2014.

Fitzhugh, George. *Cannibals All! Or, Slaves without Masters*. Richmond, VA: A. Morris, 1857.

Floyd, Janet, and Laurel Forster, eds. *The Recipe Reader: Narratives—Contexts—Traditions*. Aldershot, England: Ashgate, 2003.

Follett, Richard. "'Lives of Living Death': The Reproductive Lives of Slave Women in the Cane World of Louisiana." *Slavery and Abolition* 26, no. 2 (August 2005): 289–304.

———. *The Sugar Masters: Planters and Slaves in Louisiana's Cane World, 1820–1860*. Baton Rouge: Louisiana State University Press, 2005.

Forret, Jeff, and Christine E. Sears, eds. *New Directions in Slavery Studies: Commodification, Community, and Comparison*. Baton Rouge: Louisiana State University Press, 2015.

Foster, Lillian. *Way-Side Glimpses, North and South*. New York: Rudd and Carleton, 1859.

Fowles, Jib. "Stereography and the Standardization of Vision." *Journal of American Culture* 17, no. 2 (June 1994): 89–93.

Freedman, Paul. "American Restaurants and Cuisine in the Mid-Nineteenth Century." *New England Quarterly* 84 (March 2011): 5–59.

———. *Ten Restaurants That Changed America*. New York: Liveright, 2016.

Friss, Evan. *The Cycling City: Bicycles and Urban America in the 1890s*. Chicago: University of Chicago Press, 2015.

Fuente, Alejandro de la, and Ariela J. Gross. *Becoming Free, Becoming Black: Race, Freedom, and Law in Cuba, Virginia, and Louisiana*. Cambridge: Cambridge University Press, 2020.

Fuentes, Marisa J. *Dispossessed Lives: Enslaved Women, Violence, and the Archive*. Philadelphia: University of Pennsylvania Press, 2018.

Fussell, Elizabeth. "Constructing New Orleans, Constructing Race: A Population History of New Orleans." *Journal of American History* 94, no. 3. (December 2007): 846–55.

Fussell, Elizabeth, Narayan Sastry, and Mark VanLandingham. "Race, Socioeconomic Status, and Return Migration to New Orleans After Hurricane Katrina." *Population and Environment* 31, no. 1 (2010): 20–42.

Gabaccia, Donna R. *Italy's Many Diasporas*. Seattle: University of Washington Press, 2000.

———. *We Are What We Eat: Ethnic Food and the Making of Americans*. Cambridge, MA: Harvard University Press, 1998.

Gallier, James. *Autobiography of James Gallier, Architect*. Facsimile with introduction by Sam Wilson Jr. Paris: E. Briere, 1864; fac. New York: Da Capo Press, 1973.

Gates, Henry Louis, Jr. *Stony the Road: Reconstruction, White Supremacy, and the Rise of Jim Crow*. New York: Penguin Books, 2019.

Gates, Henry Louis, Jr., and Nellie Y. McKay. "Introduction: Talking Books." In *The Norton Anthology of African American Literature*, edited by Gates Jr. and McKay, xxxvii–xlvii. New York: W. W. Norton, 2004.

Gehman, Mary. "Visible Means of Support: Businesses, Professions, and Trades of Free People of Color." In *Creole: The History and Legacy of Louisiana's Free People of Color*, edited by Sybil Kein, 208–22. Baton Rouge: Louisiana State University Press, 2000.

Germany, Kent B. *New Orleans after the Promises: Poverty, Citizenship, and the Search for the Great Society*. Athens: University of Georgia Press, 2007.

Gessler, Anne. *Cooperatives in New Orleans: Collective Action and Urban Development*. Oxford: University Press of Mississippi, 2020.

Gilmore, Glenda. *Gender and Jim Crow: Women and the Politics of White Supremacy in North Carolina, 1896–1920*. Chapel Hill: University of North Carolina Press, 1996.

Glenn, Eddie. "A Heart Made of Knotty Pine: The Cigar Store Indian in American Cultural Imagery." *International Journal of the Image* 1, no. 3 (2011): 53–61.

Goldin, Claudia Dale. *Urban Slavery in the American South, 1820–1860: A Quantitative History*. Chicago: University of Chicago Press, 1976.

Gotham, Kevin Fox. *Authentic New Orleans: Tourism, Culture, and Race in the Big Easy*. New York: New York University Press, 2007.

Gotham, Kevin Fox, and Richard Campanella. "Constructions of Resilience: Ethnoracial Diversity, Inequality, and Post-Katrina Recovery, the Case of New Orleans." *Social Sciences* 2, no. 4 (2013): 298–317.

Graham, Richard. *Feeding the City: From Street Market to Liberal Reform in Salvador, Brazil, 1780–1860*. Austin: University of Texas Press, 2010.

Grandjean, Léon H. *Crayon Reproductions of Léon J. Frémaux's New Orleans Characters and Additional Sketches by Léon H. Grandjean*. New Orleans, LA: Alfred F. Bayhi, 1949.

Grandy, Moses. *Narrative of the Life of Moses Grandy; Late a Slave in the United States of America*. London: C. Gilpin, 1843.

Green, Jacob D. *Narrative of the Life of J. D. Green, a Runaway Slave, from Kentucky, Containing an Account of His Three Escapes, in 1839, 1846, and 1848*. Huddersfield: Henry Fielding, 1864.

Grigsby, Darcy Grimaldo. *Colossal: Engineering the Suez Canal, Statue of Liberty, Eiffel Tower, and Panama Canal*. Pittsburgh, PA: Periscope, 2012.

———. *Enduring Truths: Sojourner's Shadows and Substance*. Chicago: University of Chicago Press, 2015.

Groenevelt, Carl E. *New Orleans, Illustrated in Photo Etching from New and Original Plates, with Descriptive Text*. New Orleans: F. F. Hansell, 1892.

Gudmestad, Robert H. *Steamboats and the Rise of the Cotton Kingdom*. Baton Rouge: Louisiana State University Press, 2011.

———. *A Troublesome Commerce: The Transformation of the Interstate Slave Trade*. Baton Rouge: Louisiana State University Press, 2003.

Guglielmo, Jennifer, and Salvatore Salerno, eds. *Are Italians White? How Race is Made in America*. New York: Routledge, 2003.

Guglielmo, Thomas A. *White on Arrival: Italians, Race, Color, and Power in Chicago, 1890–1945*. Oxford: Oxford University Press, 2003.

Gutierrez, C. Paige. *Cajun Foodways*. Jackson: University Press of Mississippi, 1992.

Haggerty, Sheryllynne. "Miss Fan Can Tun Her Han! Female Traders in Eighteenth-Century British-American Atlantic Port Cities." *Atlantic Studies* 6, no. 1 (April 2009): 29–42.

Hahn, Steven, Steven F. Miller, Susan E. O'Donovan, John C. Rodrigue, and Leslie S. Rowland, eds. *Freedom: A Documentary History of Emancipation, 1861–1867: Land and Labor, 1865*. Series 3, vol. 1. Chapel Hill: University of North Carolina Press, 2008.

Hale, Grace Elizabeth. *Making Whiteness: The Culture of Segregation in the South, 1890–1940*. New York: Pantheon Books, 1998.

Hales, Peter B. *Silver Cities: Photographing American Urbanization, 1839–1939*. Albuquerque: University of New Mexico Press, 2005.

Haley, Andrew. *Turning the Tables: Restaurants and the Rise of the American Middle Class, 1880–1920*. Chapel Hill: University of North Carolina Press, 2011.

Hall, A. Oakey. *The Manhattaner in New Orleans; or, Phases of "Crescent City" Life*. New York: J. S. Redfield, Clinton Hall, 1851.

Hall, Gwendolyn Midlo. *Africans in Colonial Louisiana: The Development of Afro-Creole Culture in the Eighteenth Century*. Baton Rouge: Louisiana State University Press, 1992.

———. "The Formation of Afro-Creole Culture." In *Creole New Orleans: Race and Americanization*, edited by Arnold R. Hirsch and Joseph Logsdon, 58–87. Baton Rouge: Louisiana State University Press, 1992.

Harris, Jessica B. *Beyond Gumbo: Creole Fusion Food from the Atlantic Rim*. New York: Simon and Schuster, 2003.

———. *High on the Hog: A Culinary Journey from Africa to America*. New York: Bloomsbury, 2011.

———. "'I'm Talkin' 'bout the Food I Sells': African American Street Vendors and the Sound of Food from Noise to Nostalgia." In *The Larder: Food Studies Methods from the American South*, edited by John T. Edge, Elizabeth S. D. Engelhardt, and Ted Ownby, 333–42. Athens: University of Georgia Press, 2013.

———. *Iron Pots and Wooden Spoons: Africa's Gifts to New World Cooking*. New York: Simon and Schuster, 1989.

——. *Vintage Postcards from the African World: In the Dignity of Their Work and the Joy of Their Play*. Jackson: University Press of Mississippi, 2020.

Hartman, Saidiya V. *Scenes of Subjection: Terror, Slavery, and Self-Making in Nineteenth-Century America*. New York: Oxford University Press, 1997.

——. *Wayward Lives, Beautiful Experiments: Intimate Histories of Social Upheaval*. New York: W. W. Norton, 2019.

Heard, William H. *From Slavery to the Bishopric in the A.M.E. Church: An Autobiography*. Philadelphia: A. M. E. Book Concern, 1928.

[Hearn, Lafcadio]. *La Cuisine Creole: A Collection of Culinary Recipes from Leading Chefs and Noted Creole Housewives, Who Have Made New Orleans Famous for Its Cuisine*. New York: William H. Coleman, 1885.

Heil, Douglas. *The Art of Stereography: Rediscovering Vintage Three-Dimensional Images*. Jefferson, NC: McFarland and Co., Inc., 2017.

Hess, Karen. *The Carolina Rice Kitchen*. Columbia: University of South Carolina Press, 1992.

Hodson, Christopher. *The Acadian Diaspora: An Eighteenth-Century History*. New York: Oxford University Press, 2012.

Hoelscher, Steven. "The Photographic Construction of Tourist Space in Victorian America." *Geographical Review* 88, no. 4 (1998): 548–70.

Hollandsworth, James G. *An Absolute Massacre: The New Orleans Race Riot of July 30, 1866*. Baton Rouge, Louisiana State University Press, 2004.

Holmes, Buster. *The Buster Holmes Restaurant Cookbook: New Orleans Handmade Cookin'*. Gretna, LA: Pelican Publishing Co., 1980.

Holmes, Oliver Wendell. *Soundings from the Atlantic*. Boston, MA: Ticknor and Fields, 1864.

——. "The Stereoscope and Stereograph." *Atlantic Monthly* (June 1859): 738–48.

hooks, bell. "Eating the Other: Desire and Resistance," in hooks, *Black Looks: Race and Representation*, 21–39. Boston, MA: South End Press, 1992.

——. "In Our Glory: Photography and Black Life." In hooks, *Art on My Mind: Visual Politics* (New York: New Press, 1995).

——. "The Oppositional Gaze: Black Female Spectators," in hooks, *Black Looks: Race and Representation*, 115–31. Boston, MA: South End Press, 1992.

Horne, Jed. *Breach of Faith: Hurricane Katrina and the Near Death of a Great American City*. New York: Random House, 2006.

Horowitz, Andy. *Katrina: A History, 1915–2015*. Cambridge, MA: Harvard University Press, 2020.

Horowitz, Roger, Jeffrey M. Pilcher, and Sydney Watts. "Meat for the Multitudes: Market Culture in Paris, New York City, and Mexico City over the Long

Nineteenth Century." *American Historical Review* 109, no. 4 (October 2004): 1055–83.

Houston, Mrs. [Matilda Charlotte]. *Texas and the Gulf of Mexico: Or, Yachting in the New World.* Vol. 1. London: John Murray, Albemarle Street, 1844.

———. *Hesperos: Or, Travels in the West.* Vol. 2. London: John W. Parker, Albemarle Street, 1850.

Hoy, Suellen. *Chasing Dirt: The American Pursuit of Cleanliness.* New York: Oxford University Press, 1996.

Hughes, Louis. *Thirty Years a Slave: From Bondage to Freedom: The Institution of Slavery as Seen on the Plantation and in the Home of the Planter.* Milwaukee, WI: South Side Printing Company, 1897.

Hunt, Marie-Hélène. *Monstrous Imagination.* Cambridge, MA: Harvard University Press, 1993.

Hunter, Louis C., with Beatrice Jones Hunter. *Steamboats on the Western Rivers: An Economic and Technological History.* New York: Dover Publications, 1993.

Hunter, Tera. *To 'Joy My Freedom: Southern Black Women's Lives and Labors after the Civil War.* Cambridge, MA: Harvard University Press, 1997.

Ingersoll, Thomas N. *Mammon and Manon in Early New Orleans: The First Slave Society in the Deep South, 1718–1819.* Knoxville: University of Tennessee Press, 1999.

———. "The Slave Trade and the Ethnic Diversity of Louisiana's Slave Community." *Louisiana History* 37, no. 2 (Spring 1996): 133–61.

Ingraham, Joseph Holt. *The South-West, by a Yankee.* Vol. 1. New York: Harper and Brothers, 1835.

Isenberg, Alison. *Downtown America: A History of the Place and the People Who Made It.* Chicago: Chicago University Press, 2004.

Jackson, Jessica Barbata. *Dixie's Italians: Sicilians, Race, and Citizenship in the Jim Crow Gulf South.* Baton Rouge: Louisiana State University Press, 2020.

Jackson, Kenneth T. *Crabgrass Frontier: The Suburbanization of the United States.* New York: Oxford University Press, 1985.

Jacobson, Matthew Frye. *Barbarian Virtues: The United States Encounters Foreign Peoples at Home and Abroad, 1876–1917.* New York: Hill and Wang, 2000.

———. *Whiteness of a Different Color: European Immigrants and the Alchemy of Race.* Cambridge, MA: Harvard University Press, 1998.

Jacotot, Prosper. *Voyage d'un ouvrier dans la Vallée du Mississippi, du Saint-Louis à la Nouvelle-Orléans: Scènes de moeurs.* Dijon, France: 1888.

James, C. L. R. *The Black Jacobins: Toussaint L'Ouverture and the San Domingo Revolution.* 2nd ed. New York: Vintage Books, 1989.

Jay, Robert. *The Trade Card in Nineteenth-Century America*. Columbia: University of Missouri Press, 1987.

Jewell, Edwin L., ed. *Jewell's Crescent City Illustrated: The Commercial, Social, Political and General History, Including Biographical Sketches of Its Distinguished Citizens*. New Orleans, LA: n.p., 1873.

Jiao, Zhen, Socrates V. Kakoulides, John Moscona, Jabar Whittier, Sudesh Srivastav, Patrice Delafontaine, and Anand Irimpen. "Effect of Hurricane Katrina on Incidence of Acute Myocardial Infarction in New Orleans Three Years after the Storm." *American Journal of Cardiology* 109, no. 4 (February 15, 2012): 502–5.

Johnson, Jessica Marie. *Wicked Flesh: Black Women, Intimacy, and Freedom in the Atlantic World*. Philadelphia: University of Pennsylvania Press, 2020.

Johnson, Michael P., and James L. Roark, eds. *No Chariot Let Down: Charleston's Free People of Color on the Eve of the Civil War*. Chapel Hill: University of North Carolina Press, 2016.

Johnson, Rashauna. *Slavery's Metropolis: Unfree Labor in New Orleans during the Age of Revolutions*. New York: Cambridge University Press, 2016.

Johnson, Walter. *The Broken Heart of America: St. Louis and the Violent History of the United States*. New York: Basic Books, 2020.

———, ed. *The Chattel Principle: Internal Slave Trades in the Americas*. New Haven, CT: Yale University Press, 2004.

———. "On Agency." *Journal of Social History* 37, no. 1 (Fall 2003): 113–24.

———. *River of Dark Dreams: Slavery and Empire in the Cotton Kingdom*. Cambridge, MA: Belknap Press, 2013.

———. *Soul by Soul: Life inside the Antebellum Slave Market*. Cambridge, MA: Harvard University Press, 1999.

Jones-Rogers, Stephanie E. *They Were Her Property: White Women as Slave Owners in the American South*. New Haven, CT: Yale University Press, 2020.

Jung, Moon-Ho. *Coolies and Cane: Race, Labor, and Sugar in the Age of Emancipation*. Baltimore, MD: Johns Hopkins University Press, 2006.

Kein, Sybil, ed. *Creole: The History and Legacy of Louisiana's Free People of Color*. Baton Rouge: Louisiana State University Press, 2000.

———. "The Use of Louisiana Creole in Southern Literature." In *Creole: The History and Legacy of Louisiana's Free People of Color*, edited by Sybil Kein, 117–54. Baton Rouge: Louisiana State University Press, 2000.

Kelley, Blair L. M. *Right to Ride: Streetcar Boycotts and African American Citizenship in the Era of Plessy v. Ferguson*. Chapel Hill: University of North Carolina Press, 2010.

Kelley, Laura D. *The Irish in New Orleans*. Lafayette: University of Louisiana at Lafayette, 2014.

Kelley, Robin D. G. *Race Rebels: Culture, Politics, and the Black Working Class.* New York: Free Press, 1994.

Kendall, John Smith. *History of New Orleans.* Vol. 2. Chicago: Lewis Publishing Company, 1922.

Kennedy, Scoop [Merlin Samuel]. *Dining in New Orleans.* New Orleans, LA: Bormon House, 1945.

Keyes, Frances Parkinson. *Dinner at Antoine's.* New York: Julian Messner, 1948.

Kniffen, Fred B., Hiram F. Gregory, and George A. Stokes. *The Historic Indian Tribes of Louisiana: From 1542 to the Present.* Baton Rouge: Louisiana State University Press, 1994.

Kotlikoff, Laurence J. "The Structure of Slave Sale Prices in New Orleans, 1804 to 1862." *Economic Inquiry* 17 (October 1979): 496–518.

Kriz, Kay. *Slavery, Sugar, and the Culture of Refinement: Picturing the British West Indies, 1700–1840.* New Haven, CT: Yale University Press, 2008.

Landau, Emily Epstein. *Spectacular Wickedness: Sex, Race, and Memory in Storyville, New Orleans.* Baton Rouge: Louisiana State University Press, 2018.

Langum, David J. "Californios and the Image of Indolence." *Western Historical Quarterly* 9, no. 2 (April 1978): 181–96.

Latrobe, Benjamin Henry Boneval. *Impressions Respecting New Orleans: Diary and Sketches 1818–1820.* Edited by Samuel Wilson Jr. New York: Columbia University Press, 1951.

Law Review editors. "Voting Rights: A Case Study of Madison Parish, Louisiana." *University of Chicago Law Review* 38, no. 4 (Summer 1971): 726–87.

Lemons, Stanley. "Black Stereotypes as Reflected in Popular Culture, 1880–1920." *American Quarterly* 29, no. 1 (Spring 1977): 102–16.

Leonhardt, Olive, and Hilda Phelps Hammon. *Shaking Up Prohibition in New Orleans: Authentic Vintage Cocktails from A to Z.* Edited by Gay Leonhardt. Baton Rouge: Louisiana State University Press, 2015.

Leslie, Eliza. *Seventy-Five Receipts for Pastry, Cakes, and Sweetmeats.* Boston, MA: Munroe and Francis, 1828.

Levitt, Jeremy I., and Matthew C. Whitaker, eds. *Hurricane Katrina: America's Unnatural Disaster.* Lincoln: University of Nebraska Press, 2009.

Lewis, Peirce F. *New Orleans: The Making of an Urban Landscape.* 2nd ed. Santa Fe, NM: Center for American Places, 2003.

Li, Wei, Christopher A. Airriess, Angela Chia-Chen Chen, Karen J. Leong, and Verna Keith. "Katrina and Migration: Evacuation and Return by African Americans and Vietnamese Americans in an Eastern New Orleans Suburb." *Professional Geographer* 62, no. 1 (2010): 103–18.

Livesey, Andrea H. "Race, Slavery, and the Expression of Sexual Violence in *Lou-*

isa Picquet, the Octoroon." *American Nineteenth Century History* 19, no. 3 (2018): 267–88.

Lobel, Cindy R. *Urban Appetites: Food and Culture in Nineteenth-Century New York*. Chicago: University of Chicago Press, 2014.

Lockard, Joe. "'A Light Broke Out over My Mind': Mattie Griffith, Madge Vertner, and Kentucky Abolitionism." *Filson Club Quarterly* 76, no. 3 (Summer 2002): 245–85.

Logsdon, Joseph. "Immigration through the Port of New Orleans." In *Forgotten Doors: The Other Ports of Entry to the United States*, edited by M. Mark Stolarik, 105–24. Philadelphia, PA: Balch Institute Press, 1988.

Long, Alecia P. *The Great Southern Babylon: Sex, Race, and Respectability in New Orleans, 1865–1920*. Baton Rouge: Louisiana State University Press, 2004.

Louisiana Writers' Project. *Gumbo Ya-Ya: A Collection of Louisiana Folk Tales*. Boston, MA: Houghton Mifflin, 1945.

Lowe, Lisa. *The Intimacies of Four Continents*. Durham, NC: Duke University Press, 2015.

MacCannell, Dean. *The Tourist: A New Theory of the Leisure Class*. Berkeley: University of California Press, 1999.

Maccannon, E. A. *Commanders of the Dining Room: Biographic Sketches and Portraits of Successful Head Waiters*. New York: Gwendolyn Publishing Company, 1904.

Magill, John. "French Market Celebrates 200th Anniversary." *Preservation in Print* 18, no. 4 (May 1991): 7–10.

Manring, Maurice M. *Slave in a Box: The Strange Career of Aunt Jemima*. Charlottesville: University of Virginia Press, 1998.

Margavio, Anthony V. "The Reaction of the Press to the Italian American in New Orleans, 1880–1920." *Italian Americana* 4, no. 1 (Fall/Winter 1978): 72–83.

Marler, Scott P. *The Merchants' Capital: New Orleans and the Political Economy of the Nineteenth-Century South*. Cambridge: Cambridge University Press, 2013.

Mattison, Hiram. *Louisa Picquet, the Octoroon: A Tale of Southern Slave Life*. New York: Hiram Mattison, 1861.

Maylié, Eugénie Lavedan. *Maylié's Table d'Hote Recipes: And the History and Some Facts Concerning "La Maison Maylié et Esparbé."* New Orleans, LA: Maylié's, 1941.

McCulla, Theresa. "Fava Beans and Báhn Mì: Ethnic Revival and the New Orleans Gumbo." *Quaderni Storici* 51, no. 1 (2016): 71–102.

McElroy, Guy C. *Facing History: The Black Image in American Art, 1710–1940.* Washington, DC: Corcoran Gallery of Art, 1990.

McElya, Micki. *Clinging to Mammy: The Faithful Slave in Twentieth-Century America.* Cambridge, MA: Harvard University Press, 2007.

McGowan, Brian M. "The Second Battle of New Orleans: The Crescent City and the Anglo 'Invasion' of 1846." *Louisiana History* 51, no. 1 (Winter 2010): 27–40.

McInnis, Maurie D. "Mapping the Slave Trade in Richmond and New Orleans." *Buildings and Landscapes* 20, no. 2 (Fall 2013): 102–24.

———. *Slaves Waiting for Sale: Abolitionist Art and the American Slave Trade.* Chicago: University of Chicago Press, 2011.

McIntyre, Rebecca Cawood. *Souvenirs of the Old South: Northern Tourism and Southern Mythology.* Gainesville: University Press of Florida, 2011.

McKittrick, Christine. "Mathematics Black Life." *Black Scholar* 44, no. 2 (Summer 2014): 16–28.

McNally, Sheila. "Ariadne and Others: Image of Sleep in Greek and Early Roman Art." *Classical Antiquity* 4, no. 2 (October 1985): 152–92.

McNally, Tim. *The Sazerac.* Baton Rouge: Louisiana State University Press, 2020.

McPherson, Tara. *Reconstructing Dixie: Race, Gender, and Nostalgia in the Imagined South.* Durham, NC: Duke University Press, 2003.

Merdjanoff, Alexis A. "There's No Place Like Home: Examining the Emotional Consequences of Hurricane Katrina on the Displaced Residents of New Orleans." *Social Science Research* 42, no. 5 (September 2013): 1222–35.

Meyer, Carter Jones, and Diana Royer, eds. *Selling the Indian: Commercializing and Appropriating American Indian Cultures.* Tucson: University of Arizona Press, 2001.

Meyer, Sabine M. *We Are What We Drink: The Temperance Battle in Minnesota.* Champaign: University of Illinois Press, 2015.

Miles, Tiya. *All That She Carried: The Journey of Ashley's Sack, a Black Family Keepsake.* New York: Random House, 2021.

———. *Tales from the Haunted South: Dark Tourism and Memories of Slavery from the Civil War Era.* Chapel Hill: University of North Carolina Press, 2015.

Mirzoeff, Nicholas. *The Right to Look: A Counterhistory of Visuality.* Durham, NC: Duke University Press, 2011.

Mitchell, Brian K. "Free Blacks Database: New Orleans, 1840–1860." *Journal of Slavery and Data Preservation* 1, no. 1 (2020): 16–19.

Mitchell, Brian K., Barrington S. Edwards, and Nick Weldon. *Monumental: Oscar Dunn and His Radical Fight in Reconstruction Louisiana.* New Orleans, LA: Historic New Orleans Collection, 2021.

Mohl, Raymond A. "Stop the Road: Freeway Revolts in American Cities." *Journal of Urban History* 30, no. 5 (July 2004): 674–706.

Molz, Jennie Germann. "Tasting an Imagined Thailand: Authenticity and Culinary Tourism in Thai Restaurants." In *Culinary Tourism*, edited by Lucy Long, 53–75. Lexington: University Press of Kentucky, 2013.

Moore, Leonard N. *Black Rage in New Orleans: Police Brutality and African American Activism from World War II to Hurricane Katrina*. Baton Rouge: Louisiana State University Press, 2010.

Morrison, Janet. "'Big Businesswoman': Eulalie Mandeville and the World of Female Free Black Entrepreneurs in Antebellum New Orleans." *Louisiana History* 62, no. 1 (Winter 2021): 61–86.

Moscou, Margot. *New Orleans' Free-Men-of-Color Cabinet Makers in the New Orleans Furniture Trade 1800–1850*. New Orleans, LA: Xavier Review Press, 2008.

Moss, Robert F. *The Lost Southern Chefs: A History of Commercial Dining in the Nineteenth-Century South*. Athens: University of Georgia Press, 2022.

Mueller, Tim. *Nations Within: The Four Sovereign Tribes of Louisiana*. Baton Rouge: Louisiana State University Press, 2003.

Müller, Viola Franziska. *Escape to the City: Fugitive Slaves in the Antebellum Urban South*. Chapel Hill: University of North Carolina Press, 2022.

The Negro Motorist Green Book. New York: Victor H. Green and Co., 1938.

The Negro Motorist Green-Book. New York: Victor H. Green, 1941.

The Negro Motorist Green Book: An International Travel Guide. New York: Victor H. Green, 1949.

Nell, William Cooper. *The Colored Patriots of the American Revolution, with Sketches of Several Distinguished Colored Persons: To Which Is Added a Brief Survey of the Condition and Prospects of Colored Americans*. Boston, MA: Robert F. Wallcut, 1855.

Neuhaus, Jessamyn. *Manly Meals and Mom's Home Cooking: Cookbooks and Gender in Modern America*. Baltimore, MD: Johns Hopkins University, 2003.

New Orleans Sanitary Commission. *Report of the Sanitary Commission of New Orleans on the Epidemic Yellow Fever of 1853*. New Orleans: Picayune, 1854.

Norman, B[enjamin]. M[oore]. *Norman's New Orleans and Environs: Containing a Brief Historical Sketch of the Territory and State of Louisiana, and the City of New Orleans, from the Earliest Period to the Present Time: Presenting a Complete Guide to All Subjects of General Interest in the Southern Metropolis; with a Correct and Improved Plan of the City, Pictorial Illustrations of Public Buildings, Etc.* New Orleans, LA: B. M. Norman, 1845.

Northup, Solomon. *Twelve Years a Slave: Narrative of Solomon Northup, a Citizen of New-York, Kidnapped in Washington City in 1841, and Rescued in 1853, from a Cotton Plantation near the Red River in Louisiana.* Auburn, NY: Derby and Miller, 1853.

Nott, G. William. *A Tour of the Vieux Carré.* Introduction by Grace King. New Orleans, LA: Tropical Printing Company, 1928.

Nye, David E. *American Technological Sublime.* Cambridge, MA: MIT Press, 1994.

Nystrom, Justin A. *Creole Italian: Sicilian Immigrants and the Shaping of New Orleans Food Culture.* Athens: University of Georgia Press, 2018.

———. *New Orleans after the Civil War: Race, Politics, and a New Birth of Freedom.* Baltimore, MD: Johns Hopkins University Press, 2015.

O'Malley, Michael. *Face Value: The Entwined Histories of Money and Race in America.* Chicago: University of Chicago Press, 2012.

O'Neal, William. *Life and History of William O'Neal, or, the Man Who Sold His Wife.* St. Louis, MO: A. R. Fleming and Co., 1896.

O'Neill, Charles Edwards. "The French Regency and the Colonial Engineers: Street Names of Early New Orleans." *Louisiana History* 39, no. 2 (Spring 1998): 207–14.

Olivarius, Kathryn. *Necropolis: Disease, Power, and Capitalism in the Cotton Kingdom.* Cambridge, MA: Harvard University Press, 2022.

Olmsted, Frederick Law. *A Journey in the Seaboard Slave States: With Remarks on Their Economy.* London: Sampson Low, Son, and Co., 1856.

Olwell, Robert. "'Loose, Idle and Disorderly': Slave Women in the Eighteenth-Century Charleston Marketplace." In *More than Chattel: Black Women and Slavery in the Americas,* edited by David Barry Gaspar and Darlene Clarke Hine, 97–110. Bloomington: Indiana University Press, 1996.

Opie, Frederick Douglass. *Hog and Hominy: Soul Food from Africa to America.* New York: Columbia University Press, 2008.

The Original Picayune Creole Cook Book. 10th ed. New Orleans, LA: Times-Picayune Publishing Company, 1945.

Palmer, Zella. "Belle New Orleans: The History of Creole Cuisinières." *Africology* 11, no. 6 (April 2018): 186–91.

———, dir. *The Story of New Orleans Creole Cooking.* New Orleans, LA: Dillard University Ray Charles Program in African American Material Culture and Louisiana Endowment for Humanities, 2020. https://www.youtube.com /watch?v=NgWCoZcCRvI.

Paton, Diana. "Witchcraft, Poison, Law, and Atlantic Slavery." *William and Mary Quarterly* 69, no. 2 (April 2012): 235–64.

Patterson, Betty Benton. *Mammy Lou's Cookbook.* New York: Robert M. McBride, 1931.

Patterson, Orlando. *Slavery and Social Death: A Comparative Study*. Cambridge, MA: Harvard University Press, 1982.

Pesantubbee, Michelene. *Choctaw Women in a Chaotic World: The Clash of Cultures in the Colonial Southeast*. Albuquerque: University of New Mexico Press, 2005.

Peters, Martha Ann. "The St. Charles Hotel: New Orleans Social Center, 1837–1860." *Louisiana History* 1, no. 3 (Summer 1960): 191–211.

The Picayune's Creole Cook Book. 1st ed. New Orleans, LA: Picayune, 1900.

The Picayune's Creole Cook Book. 4th ed. New Orleans, LA: Picayune Job Print, 1910.

The Picayune's Guide to New Orleans. New Orleans, LA: Nicholson and Co., 1896.

The Picayune's Guide to New Orleans: Revised and Enlarged. 4th ed. New Orleans, LA: Picayune, 1900.

The Picayune's Guide to New Orleans: Revised and Enlarged. 5th ed. New Orleans, LA: Picayune, 1903.

The Picayune's Guide to New Orleans. 8th ed. New Orleans, LA: Picayune Job Print, 1908.

The Picayune's Guide to New Orleans. 10th ed. New Orleans, LA: Picayune Job Print, 1910.

Pierson, George Wilson. *Tocqueville in America*. Baltimore, MD: Johns Hopkins University Press, 1996.

Powell, Lawrence N. *The Accidental City: Improvising New Orleans*. Cambridge, MA: Harvard University Press, 2012.

———, ed. *Reconstructing Louisiana*. Vol. 6, Louisiana Purchase Bicentennial Series in Louisiana History. Lafayette: Center for Louisiana Studies, University of Louisiana Lafayette, 2001.

Pressly, Thomas J. "'The Known World' of Free Black Slaveholders: A Research Note on the Scholarship of Carter G. Woodson." *Journal of African American History* 91, no. 1 (Winter 2006): 81–87.

Prevost, Ruth, and Harnett T. Kane. *Mandy Lee's Recipes for Good New Orleans Dishes*. New Orleans, LA: WDSU-TV Channel 6 New Orleans, 1950.

Prichard, Walter. "The Effects of the Civil War on the Louisiana Sugar Industry." *Journal of Southern History* 5, no. 3 (August 1939): 315–32.

Pritchard, Annette, and Nigel Morgan. "Mythic Geographies of Representation and Identity: Contemporary Postcards of Wales." *Journal of Tourism and Cultural Change* 1, no. 2 (2003): 111–30.

Prudhomme, Paul. *Chef Paul Prudhomme's Louisiana Kitchen*. New York: Morrow, 1984.

Qureshi, Sadiah. "Displaying Sara Baartman, the 'Hottentot Venus.'" *History of Science* 42, no. 2 (2004): 233–57.

Raeburn, Bruce Boyd. "Stars of David and Sons of Sicily: Constellations beyond the Canon in Early New Orleans Jazz." *Jazz Perspectives* 3, no. 2 (August 2009): 125–52.

Ray, Krishnendu. *The Ethnic Restaurateur*. New York: Bloomsbury, 2016.

Reeves, Sally. "Making Groceries: Public Markets and Corner Stores in Old New Orleans." *Gulf South Historical Review* 16 (2000): 40–43.

Rehder, John B. *Delta Sugar: Louisiana's Vanishing Plantation Landscape*. Baltimore, MD: Johns Hopkins University Press, 1999.

Reilly, Timothy F. "Slave Stealing in the Early Domestic Trade as Revealed by a Loyal Manservant." *Louisiana History* 55, no. 1 (Winter 2014): 5–39.

Reinders, Robert C. *End of an Era: New Orleans: 1850–1860*. New Orleans, LA: Pelican Publishing Company, 1964.

Reinders, Robert C. "The Free Negro in the New Orleans Economy, 1850–1860." *Louisiana History* 6, no. 3 (Summer 1965): 273–85.

Remus, Emily. *A Shoppers' Paradise: How the Ladies of Chicago Claimed Power and Pleasure in the New Downtown*. Cambridge, MA: Harvard University Press, 2019.

Rice, Alan. "'Who's Eating Whom': The Discourse of Cannibalism in the Literature of the Black Atlantic from Equiano's *Travels* to Toni Morrison's *Beloved*." *Research in African Literatures* 29 no. 4 (Winter 1998), 107–21.

Richard, Lena. *Lena Richard's Cook Book*. New Orleans, LA: Rogers Printing Co., 1939.

Richards, David A. J. *Conscience and the Constitution: History, Theory and Law of the Reconstruction Amendments*. Princeton, NJ: Princeton University Press, 1994.

Richardson, Maggie Heyn. *Hungry for Louisiana: An Omnivore's Journey*. Baton Rouge: Louisiana State University Press, 2015.

Rimanelli, Marco, and Sheryl L. Postman, eds. *The 1891 New Orleans Lynchings and U.S.-Italian Relations: A Look Back*. New York: P. Lang, 1992.

Rimby, Susan. *Mira Lloyd Dock and the Progressive Era Conservation Movement*. University Park: Pennsylvania State University Press, 2015.

Ripley, Eliza. *Social Life in Old New Orleans: Being Recollections of My Girlhood*. 1912. Reprint. New York: Arno Press, 1975.

Riser, R. Volney. *Defying Disfranchisement: Black Voting Rights Activism in the Jim Crow South, 1890–1908*. Baton Rouge: Louisiana State University Press, 2013.

Rivlin, Gary. *Katrina: After the Flood*. New York: Simon and Schuster, 2015.

Roberts, Jennifer. "Landscapes of Indifference: Robert Smithson and John Lloyd Stephens in Yucatán." *Art Bulletin* 82, no. 3 (September 2000): 544–67.

Robinson, William H. *From Log Cabin to the Pulpit, or, Fifteen Years in Slavery.* Eau Claire, WI: James H. Tifft, 1913.

Rodrigue, John C. "Labor Militancy and Black Grassroots Political Mobilization in the Louisiana Sugar Region, 1865–1868." *Journal of Social History* 67, no. 1 (February 2001): 115–42.

———. *Reconstruction in the Cane Fields: From Slavery to Free Labor in Louisiana's Sugar Parishes, 1862–1880.* Baton Rouge: Louisiana State University Press, 2001.

Roediger, David R. *Wages of Whiteness: Race and the Making of the American Working Class.* London: Verso, 1991.

Rogers, Kim Lacy. *Righteous Lives: Narratives of the New Orleans Civil Rights Movement.* New York: New York University Press, 1993.

Rohrbach, Augusta. "Shadow and Substance: Sojourner Truth in Black and White." In *Pictures and Progress: Early Photography and the Making of African American Identity*, edited by Maurice O. Wallace and Shawn Michelle Smith, 83–100. Durham, NC: Duke University Press, 2012.

Rönnbäck, Klas. "'The Men Seldom Suffer a Woman to Sit Down': The Historical Development of the Stereotype of the 'Lazy African.'" *African Studies* 73, no. 2 (August 2014): 211–27.

Rosenberg, Daniel. *New Orleans Dockworkers: Race, Labor, and Unionism, 1892–1923.* Albany: State University of New York Press, 1988.

Rothman, Adam. *Beyond Freedom's Reach: A Kidnapping in the Twilight of Slavery.* Cambridge, MA: Harvard University Press, 2015.

———. *Slave Country: American Expansion and the Origins of the Deep South.* Cambridge, MA: Harvard University Press, 2005.

Rothman, Joshua D. *The Ledger and the Chain: How Domestic Slave Traders Shaped America.* New York: Basic Books, 2021.

Rushforth, Brett. *Bonds of Alliance: Indigenous and Atlantic Slaveries in New France.* Chapel Hill: University of North Carolina Press, for the Omohundro Institute of Early American History and Culture, 2012.

Sandoval-Strausz, A. K. *Hotel: An American History.* New Haven, CT: Yale University Press, 2007.

Sastry, Narayan, and Jesse Gregory. "The Location of Displaced New Orleans Residents in the Year after Hurricane Katrina." *Demography* 51, no. 3 (June 2014): 753–75.

Sauder, Robert A. "Municipal Markets of New Orleans." *Journal of Cultural Geography* 2 (Fall/Winter 1981): 82–95.

———. "The Origin and Spread of the Public Market System in New Orleans." *Louisiana History* 22, no. 3 (Summer 1981): 281–97.

Savage, John. "'Black Magic' and White Terror: Slave Poisoning and Colonial Society in Early 19th Century Martinique." *Journal of Social History* 40, no. 3 (Spring 2007): 635–62.

Savage, Kirk. *Standing Soldiers, Kneeling Slaves: Race, War, and Monument in Nineteenth-Century America*. Princeton, NJ: Princeton University Press, 1997.

Scarpaci, Jean Ann. *Italian Immigrants in Louisiana's Sugar Parishes: Recruitment, Labor Conditions, and Community Relations, 1880–1910*. New York: Arno Press, 1980.

Schafer, Judith Kelleher. *Becoming Free, Remaining Free: Manumission and Enslavement in New Orleans*. Baton Rouge: Louisiana State University Press, 2003.

———. "New Orleans Slavery in 1850 as Seen in Advertisements." *Journal of Southern History* 47, no. 1 (February 1981): 33–56.

———. *Slavery, the Civil Law, and the Supreme Court of Louisiana*. Baton Rouge: Louisiana State University Press, 1994.

Schermerhorn, Calvin. *The Business of Slavery and the Rise of American Capitalism, 1815–1860*. New Haven, CT: Yale University Press, 2015.

Schlereth, Thomas J. *Victorian America: Transformations in Everyday Life, 1876–1915*. New York: Harper Collins, 1991.

Scott, Natalie V. *200 Years of New Orleans Cooking*. New York: Jonathan Cape and Harrison Smith, 1931.

———. *Mirations and Miracles of Mandy*. New Orleans, LA: R. H. True, 1929.

Scott, Rebecca J. *Degrees of Freedom: Louisiana and Cuba after Slavery*. Cambridge, MA: Belknap Press, 2008.

———. "Paper Thin: Freedom and Re-Enslavement in the Diaspora of the Haitian Revolution." *Law and History Review* 29, no. 4 (November 2011): 1061–87.

Seck, Ibrahima. *Bouki Fait Gombo: A History of the Slave Community of Habitation Haydel (Whitney Plantation) Louisiana, 1750–1860*. New Orleans, LA: University of New Orleans Press, 2014.

Seematter, Mary. "Trials and Confessions: Race and Justice in Antebellum St. Louis." *Gateway Heritage* 12, no. 2 (Fall 1991): 36–46.

Shah, Nayan. *Contagious Divides: Epidemics and Race in San Francisco's Chinatown*. Berkeley: University of California Press, 2001.

Shaik, Fatima. *Economy Hall: The Hidden History of a Free Black Brotherhood*. New Orleans, LA: Historic New Orleans Collection, 2021.

Shankman, Arnold. "This Menacing Influx: Afro-Americans on Italian Immigration to the South, 1880–1915." *Mississippi Quarterly* 31, no. 1 (Winter 1977): 67–88.

Shapiro, Laura. *Perfection Salad: Women and Cooking at the Turn of the Century*. New York: Farrar, Straus, and Giroux, 1986.

———. *Something from the Oven: Reinventing Dinner in 1950s America*. New York: Viking Press, 2004.

Sharkey, Patrick. "Survival and Death in New Orleans: An Empirical Look at the Human Impact of Katrina." *Journal of Black Studies* 37, no. 4 (March 2007): 482–501.

Sharpe, Christina. *In the Wake: On Blackness and Being*. Durham, NC: Duke University Press, 2016.

———. *Monstrous Intimacies: Making Post-Slavery Subjects*. Durham, NC: Duke University Press, 2010.

Sharpless, Rebecca. *Cooking in Other Women's Kitchens: Domestic Workers in the South, 1865–1960*. Chapel Hill: University of North Carolina Press, 2010.

Shaw, Gwendolyn DuBois. *Portraits of a People: Picturing African Americans in the Nineteenth Century*. Andover, MA: Addison Gallery of American Art in association with University of Washington Press, 2006.

Sheehan, Tanya. *Study in Black and White: Photography, Race, Humor*. University Park: Pennsylvania State Press, 2018.

Shields, David S. *The Culinarians: Lives and Careers from the First Age of American Fine Dining*. Chicago: University of Chicago Press, 2017.

———. *Southern Provisions: The Creation and Revival of a Cuisine*. Chicago: University of Chicago Press, 2015.

Silverman, Robert J. "The Stereoscope and Photographic Depiction in the 19th Century." *Technology and Culture* 34, no. 4 (1993): 729–56.

Sismondo, Christine. *America Walks into a Bar: A Spirited History of Taverns and Saloons, Speakeasies and Grog Shops*. New York: Oxford University Press, 2011.

Smallwood, Thomas. *A Narrative of Thomas Smallwood (Coloured Man): Giving an Account of His Birth—the Period He Was Held in Slavery—His Release—and Removal to Canada, etc. Together with an Account of the Underground Railroad. Written by Himself*. Toronto: James Stephens, 1851.

Smith, F. Todd. *Louisiana and the Gulf South Frontier, 1500–1821*. Baton Rouge: Louisiana State University Press, 2014.

Smith, Harry. *Fifty Years of Slavery in the United States of America*. Grand Rapids: West Michigan Printing Company, 1891.

Smith, Margaret Denton. "Checklist of Photographers Working in New Orleans, 1840–1865." *Louisiana History* 20, no. 4 (Autumn 1979): 393–430.

Smith, Mark M. *Listening to Nineteenth-Century America*. Chapel Hill: University of North Carolina Press, 2001.

Smith, Shawn Michelle. "'Looking at One's Self through the Eyes of Others':

W.E.B. Du Bois's Photographs for the 1900 Paris Exposition." *African American Review* 34, no. 4 (Winter 2000): 581–99.

———. "Snapshot 3: Unfixing the Frame(-Up): A.P. Bedou." In *Pictures and Progress: Early Photography and the Making of African American Identity*, edited by Maurice O. Wallace and Shawn Michelle Smith, 267–73. Durham, NC: Duke University Press, 2012.

Some Telling Facts of the Second District and the Famous French Market of the City of New Orleans, Issued as a Souvenir of All the Live, Up-to-Date Features of This Important Section. Within the Enclosed Pages Will Be Found Personal Sketches of Many of the Progressive and Enterprising Business Men and Leading Citizens. New Orleans, LA: National Publishing Company, 1912.

Souther, Mark J. *New Orleans on Parade: Tourism and the Transformation of New Orleans*. Baton Rouge: Louisiana State University Press, 2006.

Spear, Jennifer M. *Race, Sex, and Social Order in Early New Orleans*. Baltimore, MD: Johns Hopkins University Press, 2009.

Specht, Joshua. *Red Meat Republic: A Hoof-to-Table History of How Beef Changed America*. Princeton, NJ: Princeton University Press, 2019.

Spillers, Hortense J. *Black, White, and in Color: Essays on American Literature and Culture*. Chicago: University of Chicago Press, 2003.

Spooner, Catherine. *Contemporary Gothic*. London: Reaktion Books, 2006.

Stanley, Amy Dru. *From Bondage to Contract: Wage Labor, Marriage, and the Market in the Age of Slave Emancipation*. Cambridge: Cambridge University Press, 1998.

Stanonis, Anthony J. *Creating the Big Easy: New Orleans and the Emergence of Modern Tourism, 1918–1945*. Athens: University of Georgia Press, 2006.

———. "The Triumph of Epicure: A Global History of New Orleans Culinary Tourism." *Southern Quarterly* 46, no. 3 (Spring 2009): 145–61.

Stephens, Kevin U., Sr., David Grew, Karen Chin, Paul Kadetz, P. Gregg Greenough, Frederick M. Burkle Jr., Sandra L. Robinson, and Evangeline R. Franklin. "Excess Mortality in the Aftermath of Hurricane Katrina: A Preliminary Report." *Disaster Medicine* 1, no. 1 (2007): 15–20.

Stewart, Charles, ed. *Creolization: History, Ethnography, Theory*. Walnut Creek, CA: Left Coast Press, 2007.

St. Pierre, Todd-Michael. *Taste of Tremé: Creole, Cajun, and Soul Food from New Orleans's Famous Neighborhood of Jazz*. Berkeley, CA: Ulysses Press, 2012.

Stier, Emile V., and James B. Keeling. *Glorified French Market: Progressing with Commerce, 1813–1938, a Treatise on the Famous French Market of New Orleans, Louisiana*. New Orleans, LA: French Market Corporation, 1938.

Strachan, Sue. *The Café Brûlot*. Baton Rouge: Louisiana State University Press, 2021.

Stroyer, Jacob. *My Life in the South*. Salem, MA: Salem Observer Book and Job Print, 1885.

Stuart, Charles. *Reuben Maddison: A True Story*. Birmingham, England: B. Hudson, 1835.

Sweeney, Shauna. "Market Marronage: Fugitive Women and the Internal Marketing System in Jamaica, 1781–1834." *William and Mary Quarterly* 76, no. 2 (April 2019): 197–222.

Tadman, Michael. "The Demographic Cost of Sugar: Debates on Slave Societies and Natural Increase in the Americas." *American Historical Review* 105, no. 5 (December 2000): 1534–75.

———. *Speculators and Slaves: Masters, Traders, and Slaves in the Old South*. Madison: University of Wisconsin Press, 1989.

Tangires, Helen. *Public Markets and Civic Culture in Nineteenth-Century America*. Baltimore, MD: Johns Hopkins University Press, 2003.

Tansey, Richard. "Bernard Kendig and the New Orleans Slave Trade." *Louisiana History* 23, no. 2 (Spring 1982): 159–78.

Taylor, O. C. W. *The Crescent City Pictorial: A Souvenir, Dedicated to the Progress of the Colored Citizens of New Orleans, Louisiana, "America's Most Interesting City."* New Orleans, LA: O. C. W. Taylor, 1925.

Thomas, Lynnell L. *Desire and Disaster in New Orleans: Tourism, Race, and Historical Memory*. Durham, NC: Duke University Press, 2014.

———. "'People Want to See What Happened': Treme, Televisual Tourism, and the Racial Remapping of Post-Katrina New Orleans." *Television and New Media* 13, no. 3 (2012): 213–24.

Thompson, Ray M. *New Orleans, from A to Z: Questions You'll Ask about This City of Charm and its Famous French Quarter . . . Alphabetically Answered*. New Orleans, LA: House of the Artists, 1951.

Thompson, Shirley Elizabeth. *Exiles at Home: The Struggle to Become American in Creole New Orleans*. Cambridge, MA: Harvard University Press, 2009.

Tilton, Lauren. "Race and Place: Dialect and the Construction of Southern Identity in the Ex-Slave Narratives." *Current Research in Digital History* 2 (August 2019). https://doi.org/10.31835/crdh.2019.14.

The Times-Picayune's Guide to New Orleans. 14th ed. New Orleans: Times-Picayune, 1924.

Tipton-Martin, Toni. *The Jemima Code: Two Centuries of African American Cookbooks*. Austin: University of Texas Press, 2015.

Titus, Mary. "The Dining Room Door Swings Both Ways: Food, Race, and Domestic Space in the Nineteenth-Century South." In *Haunted Bodies: Gender and Southern Texts*, edited by Anne Goodwyn Jones and Susan V. Donaldson, 243–56. Charlottesville: University of Virginia Press, 1997.

Tompkins, Kyla Wazana. *Racial Indigestion: Eating Bodies in the 19th Century*. New York: New York University Press, 2012.

Trask, Benjamin H. *Fearful Ravages: Yellow Fever in New Orleans, 1796–1905*. Lafayette: Center for Louisiana Studies, University of Louisiana at Lafayette, 2005.

Tregle, Joseph G., Jr. "Foreword." In Henry C. Castellanos, *New Orleans as It Was: Episodes of Louisiana Life*, edited by George F. Reinecke. Baton Rouge: Louisiana State University Press, 1895, repr. 1978.

Tribe, Laurence H. *American Constitutional Law*. 2nd ed. Mineola, NY: Foundation Press, 1988.

Trollope, Frances Milton. *Domestic Manners of the Americans*. Vol. 1. 2nd ed. London: Printed for Whittaker, Treacher, 1832.

———. *Domestic Manners of the Americans*. Vol. 2. 4th ed. London: Printed for Whittaker, Treacher, 1832.

Troy, Rev. William. *Hair-Breadth Escapes from Slavery to Freedom*. Manchester: Guardian Steam-Printing Offices, 1861.

Tucker, Susan, ed., *New Orleans Cuisine: Fourteen Signature Dishes and Their Histories*. Jackson: University of Press of Mississippi, 2009.

Tusa, Bobs M. "*Le Carillon*: An English Translation of Selected Satires." *Louisiana History* 35, no. 1 (Winter 1994): 67–84.

Twitty, Michael W. *The Cooking Gene: A Journey through African American Culinary History in the Old South*. New York: Amistad, 2017.

Upton, Dell. *Another City: Urban Life and Urban Spaces in the New American Republic*. New Haven, CT: Yale University Press, 2008.

Usner, Daniel H., Jr. *American Indians in Early New Orleans: From Calumet to Raquette*. Baton Rouge: Louisiana State University Press, 2018.

———. "Food Marketing and Interethnic Exchange in the Eighteenth Century Lower Mississippi Valley." *Food and Foodways* 1 (1986): 279–310.

———. "From African Captivity to American Slavery: The Introduction of Black Laborers to Colonial Louisiana." *Louisiana History* 20, no. 1 (Winter 1979): 25–48.

———. *Indians, Settlers, and Slaves in a Frontier Exchange Economy: The Lower Mississippi Valley before 1783*. Chapel Hill: University of North Carolina Press, 1992.

Van Zante, Gary A. *New Orleans 1867: Photographs by Theodore Lilienthal*. London: Merrell, 2008.

VanHuss, Laura Kilcer. *Charting the Plantation Landscape from Natchez to New Orleans*. Baton Rouge: Louisiana State University Press, 2021.

Vellon, Peter G. *A Great Conspiracy against Our Race: Italian Immigrant News-*

papers and the Construction of Whiteness in the Early Twentieth Century. New York: New York University Press, 2014.

Vester, Katharina. *A Taste of Power: Food and American Identities*. Oakland: University of California Press, 2015

Vidal, Cécile. *Caribbean New Orleans: Empire, Race, and the Making of a Slave Society*. Williamsburg, VA, and Chapel Hill: Omohundro Institute of Early American History and Culture and University of North Carolina Press, 2019.

Vielé, Teresa Griffin. *Following the Drum: A Glimpse of Frontier Life*. New York: Rudd and Carleton, 1858.

Vyhanek, Louis Andrew. *Unorganized Crime: New Orleans in the 1920s*. Lafayette: Center for Louisiana Studies, University of Southwestern Louisiana, 1998.

Wade, Richard C. *Slavery in the Cities: The South, 1820–1860*. New York: Oxford University Press, 1964.

Walker, William. *Buried Alive (behind Prison Walls) for a Quarter of a Century: Life of William Walker*. Edited by Thomas S. Gaines. Saginaw, MI: Friedman and Hynan, 1892.

Wallace, Maurice O., and Shawn Michelle Smith, eds. *Pictures and Progress: Early Photographs and the Making of African-American Identity*. Durham, NC: Duke University Press, 2012.

Wallace-Sanders, Kimberly. *Mammy: A Century of Race, Gender, and Southern Memory*. Ann Arbor: University of Michigan Press, 2008.

Warner, Ashton, and Susanna Moodie. *Negro Slavery Described by a Negro: Being the Narrative of Ashton Warner, a Native of St. Vincent's. With an Appendix Containing the Testimony of Four Christian Ministers, Recently Returned from the Colonies, on the System of Slavery as It Now Exists*. London: Samuel Maunder, 1831.

Weber, Lynn, and Lori Peek, eds. *Displaced: Life in the Katrina Diaspora*. Austin: University of Texas Press, 2012.

Wegmann, Andrew N. *An American Color: Race and Identity in New Orleans and the Atlantic World*. Athens: University of Georgia Press, 2022.

Wells-Barnett, Ida B. *Mob Rule in New Orleans: Robert Charles and His Fight to the Death, the Story of His Life, Burning Human Beings Alive, Other Lynching Statistics*. Chicago: n.p., 1900.

Weston, Nathaniel P. "'Frecher Versuch das Arbeitshaus zu zerstören': An Introduction to Vagrancy and Workhouses in New Orleans." *Louisiana History* 41, no. 4 (Autumn 2000): 467–81.

White, Deborah Gray. *Ar'n't I a Woman? Female Slaves in the Plantation South*. New York: W. W. Norton, 1985.

White, Richard. *The Republic for Which It Stands: The United States during Reconstruction and the Gilded Age, 1865–1896*. New York: Oxford University Press, 2017.

Whites, LeeAnn, and Alecia P. Long, eds. *Occupied Women: Gender, Military Occupation, and the American Civil War*. Baton Rouge: Louisiana State University Press, 2009.

Wilkerson, Isabel. *The Warmth of Other Suns: The Epic Story of America's Great Migration*. New York: Random House, 2010.

Williams-Forson, Psyche. *Building Houses out of Chicken Legs: Black Women, Food, and Power*. Chapel Hill: University of North Carolina Press, 2006.

Willis, Deborah. *Reflections in Black: A History of Black Photographers, 1840 to the Present*. New York: Norton, 2000.

Wilson, Samuel, Jr. "Maspero's Exchange: Its Predecessors and Successors." *Louisiana History* 30, no. 2 (Spring 1989): 191–220.

Wing, Paul. *Stereoscopes: The First One Hundred Years*. Nashua, NH: Transition Publishing, 1996.

Witt, Doris. *Black Hunger: Soul Food and America*. Minneapolis: University of Minnesota Press, 2004.

Wood, Amy Louise. *Lynching and Spectacle: Witnessing Racial Violence in America, 1890–1940*. Chapel Hill: University of North Carolina Press, 2009.

Wood, Marcus. *Black Milk: Imagining Slavery in the Visual Cultures of Brazil and America*. Oxford: Oxford University Press, 2013.

———. *Blind Memory: Visual Representations of Slavery in England and America, 1780–1865*. London: Routledge, 1999.

———. *The Horrible Gift of Freedom: Atlantic Slavery and the Representation of Emancipation*. Athens: University of Georgia Press, 2010.

Woodard, Vincent. *The Delectable Negro: Human Consumption and Homoeroticism within U.S. Slave Culture*. Edited by Justin A. Joyce and Dwight A. McBride. New York: New York University Press, 2014.

Woodson, Carter G. *Free Negro Heads of Families in the United States in 1830*. Washington, DC: Association for the Study of Negro Life and History, Inc., 1925.

———. "Free Negro Owners of Slaves in the United States in 1830." *Journal of Negro History* 9 (January 1924): 41–85.

Wright, Allen. *Chahta Lekshikon: A Choctaw in English Definition for the Choctaw Academies and Schools*. St. Louis, MO: Presbyterian Publishing Company, 1880.

Yaeger, Patricia. "Edible Labor." *Southern Quarterly* 30, nos. 2–3 (Winter/Spring 1992): 150–59.

Young, Harvey. *Embodying Black Experience: Stillness, Critical Memory, and the Black Body*. Ann Arbor: University of Michigan Press, 2010.

Zacharie, James S. *New Orleans Guide with Descriptions of the Routes to New Orleans, Sights of the City Arranged Alphabetically, and Other Information Useful to Travelers; also, Outlines of the History of Louisiana*. New Orleans: F. F. Hansell and Bro., Ltd., 1893.

Zafar, Rafia. "The Proof of the Pudding: Of Haggis, Hasty Pudding, and Transatlantic Influence." *Early American Literature* 31, no. 2 (1996): 133–49.

———. *Recipes for Respect: African American Meals and Meaning*. Athens: University of Georgia Press, 2019.

INDEX

Page numbers in italics refer to figures.